D1733060

WITHDRAWN

The Critical Reception of Beethoven's Compositions
by His German Contemporaries, VOLUME 2

*Number 3 in the series North American Beethoven Studies
Edited by William Meredith*

The Critical Reception of *Beethoven's Compositions*

by His German Contemporaries, VOLUME 2

Wayne M. Senner, GENERAL EDITOR AND COMPILER

Robin Wallace, TRANSLATOR AND MUSICOLOGICAL EDITOR

William Meredith, MUSICOLOGICAL EDITOR

*Published by the University of Nebraska Press, Lincoln and London,
in association with the American Beethoven Society and the
Ira F. Brilliant Center for Beethoven Studies, San José State University*

♾

Library of Congress Cataloging-in-Publication Data
The critical reception of Beethoven's compositions by his German
contemporaries / Wayne M. Senner, general editor and compiler; Robin
Wallace, translator and musicological editor; William Meredith,
musicological editor.
    p.   cm. — (North American Beethoven Studies; no. 3)
Includes bibliographical references and indexes.
ISBN 0-8032-1250-X (cl. : alk paper, v. 1); 0-8032-1251-8 (cl. : alk paper, v. 2)
    1. Beethoven, Ludwig van, 1770–1827—Criticism and interpretation.
I. Senner, Wayne M.   II. Wallace, Robin.   III. Meredith, William
Rhea.   IV. Series: North American Beethoven studies; v. 3.
ML410.B42C75   1999
780'.92—dc21   98-55462
                                                                    CIP
                                                                     MN

Contents

Acknowledgments

Again, Wayne Senner would like to express his gratitude for the kind support and help rendered by the following libraries and archives during the compilation of the documents published in this volume: Bayerische Staatsbibliothek Munich, Beethoven Haus Bonn (in particular, Sieghard Brandenburg), Gesellschaft der Musikfreunde Vienna, Hessische Landes- und Hochschulbibliothek Darmstadt, Kreisarchiv und Wissenschaftliche Bibliothek Bonn, Österreichische Nationalbibliothek Vienna, Stadtarchiv Aachen, Stadtarchiv Trier, Stadtarchiv und Wissenschaftliche Stadtbibliothek Bonn, Stadtbibliothek Nürnberg, Stadt- und Universitätsbibliothek Frankfurt, Theaterbibliothek Porzheim, Universitätsbibliothek Bonn, Universitäts- und Stadtbibliothek Cologne, Universitätsbibliothek Freiburg, Universitätsbibliothek, Hamburg, Universitätsbibliothek Heidelberg, Universitätsbibliothek Regensburg, and the University of California (Berkeley) Library. He would also like to thank the German Academic Exchange Service and the Ira F. Brilliant Center for Beethoven Studies (in particular, Ira F. Brilliant and the late Charles Burdick) for their financial support of this project. Special thanks to Arizona State University for the sabbatical leave to undertake the research and compiling in Germany and Austria.

William Meredith and the Beethoven Center would like to thank Ira F. Brilliant and Charles Burdick (former dean of the College of Social Sciences, San José State University) for their financial and moral support of this project. Patricia Stroh, the center's curator, has lent her expertise and research skills to the project on many occasions. Special thanks are due to Ray White, Library of Congress, for his assistance with the *Berliner allgemeine musikalische Zeitung,* and to James Sealey for his fastidious work on the music examples. Finally, many musicologists assisted with answers to queries; special thanks are due to Bartlett Butler, Clemens Brenneis, Susan Jackson, Dorothea Link, Michael Lorenz, Sandra Rosenblum, Rita Steblin, Larry Synder, and James Webster.

Robin Wallace would like to thank the staff of the Mickel Library at Converse College for their assistance: Darlene Fawver, Miriam Cody, Wendi Arms, Patsy Copeland, Trudy Cox, Becky Poole, Becky Dalton, Camille McCutcheon, and Wade Woodward. A faculty research grant from Converse in 1996 also helped speed the progress of this edition. Mark Evan Bonds, University of North Carolina at Chapel Hill, provided valuable comments on a draft of the introductory essay. He would also like to thank the staff of the music library at Chapel Hill, who have been quite helpful during his research trips there.

Preface

The project of compiling documents for *The Critical Reception of Beethoven's Compositions by His Contemporaries* began in 1985 under the auspices of the Ira F. Brilliant Center for Beethoven Studies (San José State University) and at the urging of Ira Brilliant, the founder of the center. The focus of my search was based on the names of Beethoven's contemporaries provided in MacArdle, Thayer, and Solomon sources and in Kirchner, *Die Zeitschriften des deutschen Sprachgebietes von den Anfängen bis 1830* (Stuttgart, 1969) as well as Imogen Fellinger, *Verzeichnis der Musikzeitschriften des 19. Jahrhunderts* (Regensburg, 1968). For the next several years I visited archives, state, city, and university libraries; and newspaper collections in Aachen; Berkeley, California; Berlin; Bonn; Cologne; Darmstadt; Frankfurt; Munich; Nürnberg; Regensburg; and Vienna, searching through many hundreds of periodicals and monographic sources. All materials were collected on microfilm, transferred to xerox copies, and then retyped. During the final stage of my search I checked the documents I had gathered against another German collection, which, unknown to me, a team of German musicologists had been undertaking at the same time and which appeared in 1987 under the title *Ludwig van Beethoven: Die Werke im Spiegel seiner Zeit*, ed. Stefan Kunze (Laaber). The Kunze collection was useful in double-checking my own results. A few documents were also provided by William Meredith (director, Ira F. Brilliant Center for Beethoven Studies) and Robin Wallace (associate professor of music history, Converse College), the musicological editors of this project.

My original intention had been to provide as comprehensive a spectrum of early-nineteenth-century perceptions of Beethoven's works as possible by including letters, memoirs, notes, essays, sections of larger critical and biographical works, in addition to concert reports and reviews in periodical literature (including a large number of newspapers). By proceeding from a broader base, I hoped to provide a collection that would be useful to literary historians and scholars in reception aesthetics as well as musicologists. Nevertheless, the materials collected soon became overwhelming, and it was obvious that the principle of selection had to be narrowed. Without footnotes, commentary, and annotations, the introductory essays, the name and work indexes, the final German-language manuscript still amounted to more than 1,000 single-spaced pages and contained 520 documents. It was then decided to limit the collection to periodical documents, including newspaper sources. It was also decided that because of the large number of sources of biographical materials (*Thayer's Life of Beethoven,* H. C. Robbins Landon, *Beethoven: A Documentary Study,* Maynard Solomon, *Beethoven,* etc.) biographical accounts and anecdotes should be limited as much as the texts allowed.

The focus was to be on contemporary perceptions of Beethoven's music, including matters such as audience, setting, facilities, orchestra, instruments, and performers as well as the relationship of Beethoven's music to theoretical and critical ideas of the eighteenth and nineteenth centuries. This principle of selection was not always easy to carry out, given the frequent preoccupation with Beethoven the man *and* composer, and in some passages the biographical information is so closely intertwined with musical analysis that excision would have distorted the document. Even with the more restrictive selection process, the collection will appear in no less than four volumes of approximately 250 pages each.

The translation procedure for volume 2 was as follows. After the translation and the musicological annotations were completed by Professor Wallace, the manuscript was given to Professor Senner, the general editor, who edited the translations and added historical and literary annotations. Then the manuscript was sent to Professor Meredith, who added musicological annotations and offered some useful suggestions for improving the translations.

The format of all four volumes is the same, with slight exceptions: the first three volumes have an introductory essay. Each volume will have indexes of names, subjects, Beethoven's works, and periodicals; volume 4 will have complete indexes for all four volumes. Volume 1 begins with a general section, which includes documents that deal either with some general aspect of Beethoven's music or with so many different works that assigning the document to a specific opus number seemed fruitless. The general section is followed by documents on specific opus numbers up to op. 54.

Volume 2 begins with op. 55, the *Eroica,* and ends with op. 72, *Fidelio.* Each document has an entry number, and all documents are numbered consecutively throughout all four volumes. The text of each document is preceded by bibliographic information: author (sometimes unknown, often indicated only by initials or code words, some of which defied identification); title of article, note, and so on (or the type of information needed from a title) in quotation marks; title of the periodical (in italics); date; and page or column number, if available. Information within quotation marks often indicates the part of the journal the document was taken from (e.g., "News. Leipzig. Winter Concerts"). Such information was considered to be of importance, for the very position a review, notice, report, or article is given in a publication may reveal something about the writer's or the editor's unexpressed attitude toward Beethoven's works. If the date is part of the document, it is within the quotation marks; if not, it remains outside the quotation marks.

Footnoting from the original document is distinguished from our annotations by quotation marks. The only intrusions into the text are note numbers and measure numbers, the latter indicated with brackets. The orthography of names in the originals was also retained. Because of the frequency of some rather unusual spellings, the reader will occasionally be reminded of this principle. Cross-references are included at the beginning of each document and at the beginning of each opus number. More precisely, if a document deals with more than one opus number, the additional number is indicated at the beginning of the document. When documents deal with more than one opus number, the documents are placed according to the lowest opus number unless another, higher opus number overwhelmingly dominates the discussion. Documents that deal with a large number of works were placed in the general section in volume 1.

In the notes stemming from the reviews, we sought to identify individuals, terms, compositions, locations, and other details that would assist the reader. When formulating factual details for the short biographical notes, we have drawn (without further citation) from many standard reference works and tools: such works as the Kinsky-Halm thematic catalog, Kurt Dorfmüller, *Beiträge;* various editions of Thayer's biography; Johnson-Tyson-Winter, *Beethoven Sketchbooks; The New Grove Dictionary of Music and Musicians; Die Musik in Geschichte und Gegenwart; Beethoven-Handbuch;* Fétis, *Biographie universelle des musiciens et bibliographie generale de la musique;* Robert Eitner, *Biographisch-bibliographisches Quellen-Lexikon der Musiker und Musikgelehrten;* Emily Anderson, *The Letters of Beethoven;* Sieghard Brandenburg, *Ludwig van Beethoven: Briefwechsel Gesamtausgabe;* Barry Cooper, *The Beethoven Compendium; The Dictionary of Literary Biography;* Karl Goeeke, *Grundriß zur Geschichte der deutschen Dichtung aus den Quellen;* Joachim Kirchner, *Die Zeitschriften des deutschen Sprachgebiets von den Anfängen bis 1830; Neue deutsche Biographie, Deutsches biographisches Archiv;* and Wilhelm Kosch, *Deutsches Literatur-Lexikon.*

We intended to reproduce the music examples from the original periodicals. Because the music examples in BAMZ were not printed originally in a clear enough fashion to be directly reproduced, they have been reset in modern typography following the originals as closely as possible (including distinctions between staccato dots and strokes). In those cases where the original examples contained mistakes, corrections have been made and indicated with brackets.

The indexes were prepared by William Meredith and Patricia Stroh with assistance from Bonnie Elizabeth Fleming.

Although the original goal was to try to provide as complete a collection as possible, it is obvious that such a goal cannot be achieved. Nevertheless, these documents, most of which appear in English for the first time, should present readers with new insights into the perceptions that Beethoven's contemporaries had of his monumental music.

Robin Wallace would like to close with a few words on the translations in volumes 2–4. The language of most of these reviews is in many ways startlingly close to modern German. The most widely read journals, in fact, were printed in Roman type; it was perhaps something of an affectation for Schumann to adopt the Gothic *Fraktur* when he founded his highly successful *Neue Zeitschrift für Musik* in 1834. The reviews are thus readable and compelling, despite the almost universal tendency of German writers to string subordinate clauses together into sentences of daunting length. That immediacy in the translations has been captured by following the texts closely while transforming them into idiomatic English, and many of the lengthy sentences have been preserved intact, since in some cases they cannot be broken up without mangling the ideas they contain. In view of the large number of authors and writing styles represented here, however, it would have been futile and counterproductive to try to standardize the vocabulary completely.

While many terms can be translated with precision, others are necessarily vague; a few simple examples will suffice to demonstrate this. "Satz" can mean a phrase, a section of a piece, or a movement, or it can refer to the manner in which a composer writes. "Ton" can mean either "note" or "sound," but in some contexts it is conventional to translate it as "tone." "Ausführung" means "performance," but it is also used to describe the working-out of a musical idea or composition (the word "development" has been avoided because it has anachronistic connotations) as is its synonym "Durchführung." The words "eigenthümlich" and "sonderbar" can mean either "characteristic" or "unusual" in a positive sense, or "strange" or "peculiar" in a negative sense. "Beifall" can mean "applause" at a performance, but can also refer to more general forms of approval. "Verfasser," "Tonsetzer," and "Komponist" are used synonymously and are all translated as "composer," since English has no similar wealth of terms. A word as simple as "steigern," however, can be rendered in English as "raise," "increase," or "heighten" to reflect subtle elements of the context. "Phantasie" is usually translated here as "imagination" and "Gesang" as melody. In some places, however—most notably in Amadeus Wendt's lengthy essay on *Fidelio* (entry no. 240 in this volume)—they have been translated according to their context as "fantasy" and "song," respectively. The first consideration has always been to translate terms so that they make sense in context and read well. We hope the results, while they can of course never entirely substitute for an examination of the original texts, will be useful to those with neither the resources nor the patience to wade through those texts.

W. M. Senner

Abbreviations

A	*Abendzeitung nebst Intelligenzblatt für Literatur und Kunst,* Dresden, 1805–06 and 1817–27.
AMA (F)	*Allgemeiner musikalischer Anzeiger nebst einem kritischen Beiblatt Minerva,* Frankfurt, 1826–27.
AMA (V)	*Allgemeiner musikalischer Anzeiger,* Vienna, 1829–40.
AMBT	*Allgemeine Musikzeitung zur Beförderung der theoretischen und praktischen Tonkunst für Musiker und für Freunde der Musik überhaupt,* Frankfurt, 1827–28.
AMZ	*Allgemeine musikalische Zeitung,* Leipzig, 1798–1840.
AMZÖK	*Allgemeine musikalische Zeitung mit besonderer Rücksicht auf den österreichischen Kaiserstaat,* Vienna, 1817–24.
BAMZ	*Berliner allgemeine musikalische Zeitung,* 1824–30.
BMZ	*Berlinische musikalische Zeitung,* 1805–06.
BNS	*Berlinische Nachrichten von Staats- und gelehrten Sachen,* 1740–1872
C	*Cäcilia, eine Zeitschrift für die musikalische Welt herausgegeben von einem Vereine von Gelehrten, Kunstverständigen und Künstlern,* Mainz, 1824–48.
F	*Der Freymüthige oder Berlinische Zeitung für gebildete und unbefangene Leser,* Berlin, 1803–30.
HT	*Historisches Taschenbuch: Mit besonder Rücksicht auf die Österreichischen Staaten,* Vienna, 1802, 1807.
I	*Iris,* Berlin, 1830–41.
JLM	*Journal des Luxus und der Moden,* Weimar, 1785–1814. Continued as *Journal für Literatur, Kunst, Luxus und Mode,* Weimar, 1814–26.
JR	*Journal de la Roer,* 1811–14.
JT	*Jahrbuch der Tonkunst von Wien und Prag,* 1796.
KZ	*Kölnische Zeitung,* 1801–08.
L	*Libussa, Jahrbuch für 1845,* Prague.
LKK	*Leipziger Kunstblatt für gebildete Kunstfreunde,* 1817–18.
MM	*Magazin der Musik,* Hamburg, 1783–86.
MAM	*Münchener allgemeine Musikzeitung,* 1827–29.
MGS	*Morgenblatt für gebildete Stände,* Stuttgart, 1807–37.
ME	*Musikalische Eilpost,* Weimar, 1826.

MT	*Musikalisches Taschenbuch*, Penig, 1803–05.
MZ	*Musikalische Zeitung für die österreichischen Staaten*, Linz, 1812–13.
T	*Thalia: Ein Abendblatt, den Freunden der dramatischen Muse geweiht*, Vienna and Triest, 1810–11.
WAMZ	*Wiener allgemeine musikalische Zeitung*, Vienna, 1813.
WJ	*Wiener Journal für Theater, Musik und Mode*, Vienna, 1813.
WT	*Wiener allgemeine Theaterzeitung*, (1817–23)
WZ	*Wiener Zeitung*, Vienna, 1780–.
WZK	*Wiener Zeitschrift für Kunst, Literatur, Theater und Mode*, 1816–46
ZEW	*Zeitung für die elegante Welt*, Leipzig, 1801–30.
ZTM	*Zeitung für Theater und Musik zur Unterhaltung gebildeter, unbefangener Leser: Eine Begleiterin des Freymüthigen*, Berlin, 1821–27 (after 1822 *Zeitung für Theater, Musik und bildende Künste, Beilage zum Freymüthigen*).

Viennese and European Currencies, 1792–1827

AUSTRIAN CURRENCY

Because of changes in types of money used, the introduction of paper money, inflationary pressures, and the 1811 devaluation of Austrian currency, it is not possible to present a simple, single chart illustrating the values of currency from 1792 to 1827. The following discussion is heavily indebted to the work of Julia Moore.

1792–1811

When Beethoven arrived in Vienna in 1792, the standard currency was the Conventionsmünze (CM) florin, which was issued as a silver coin also called a silver gulden. One CM florin was divided into 60 kreuzer. The gold coin in circulation was called the ducat and was worth 4.5 CM florins:

$$1 \text{ ducat} = 4.5 \text{ CM florins}$$
$$1 \text{ CM florin} = 60 \text{ kreuzer}$$

In 1795 the Austrian government issued its first paper currency, Bankozettel (BZ) florins. Initially, one BZ florin equaled one CM florin. However, due to inflationary pressures arising from the requirement to finance the wars against Napoleon, the BZ florin constantly lost value from 1796 through 1811. The following chart lists these values:

Value of CM florin compared to BZ florin, 1795–1811

Year	CM florins (silver guldens)	BZ florins (annual average)
1795	100	100.00
1796	100	100.13
1797	100	101.61

Year	CM florins (silver guldens)	BZ florins (annual average)
1798	100	101.06
1799	100	107.83
1800	100	114.91
1801	100	115.75
1802	100	121.67
1803	100	130.75
1804	100	134.24
1805	100	135.25
1806	100	173.01
1807	100	209.43
1808	100	228.15
1809	100	296.03
1810	100	492.12
1811	100	500.00

Source: Moore, *Beethoven and Musical Economics*, p. 123.

1811–19

In July 1810 Emperor Franz II appointed Count Joseph Wallis as his finance minister. The BZ florin suffered continuing devaluation until February 1811. The devaluation continued because (1) the Austrian government focused almost exclusively on the problem of the declining value of the BZ florin and failed to take into account the relation of consumer prices to the amount of paper money in circulation and because (2) Count Wallis had "no recorded expertise in finance." In February 1811 a state bankruptcy was declared. The terms of the bankruptcy were laid out in a *Finanzpatent* with the following terms:

1. All currency, including BZ florins, were called in and replaced with a new paper florin, the Wiener Währung (WW).
2. The exchange rate was 1 WW florin for 5 BZ florins.
3. BZ florins remained legal tender until 1 January 1812.
4. All prices were to be divided by five.

During the next few years, inflation and currency devaluation wreaked havoc on those who held cash assets and on salaried employees, since they effectively lost four-fifths of the value of their income's purchasing power. The new WW florin failed to maintain a stable value against a theoretical silver gulden (which had last been produced in 1809). Another state bankruptcy was narrowly averted in 1816. Instead of prosperity, the conclusion of the Napoleonic Wars brought a recession to the Austrian economy.

Value of CM florin compared to WW florin, 1811–19

Year	CM florins	WW florins (annual average)
1811	100	218.75
1812	100	201.83
1813	100	159.16
1814	100	228.79
1815	100	351.06
1816	100	327.04
1817	100	332.82
1818	100	255.39
1819	100	249.19

Source: Moore, *Beethoven and Musical Economics*, p. 124.

1817–27

In 1817 Count Stadion founded the Privileged Austrian National Bank, an institution funded in part with private capital but serving as the government banker. The CM silver gulden was gradually reintroduced through the new bank and its value stabilized by May 1818 at 2.5 WW florins. Thereafter during Beethoven's lifetime, CM and WW florins remained in circulation at the relatively stable value of 1 CM florin for 2.5 WW florins. (See Moore, *Beethoven and Musical Economics*, pp. 128–30).

Viennese Currency Abbreviations

fl	gulden (florin)
BZ	Bankozettel
WW	Wiener Währung
CM	Conventionsmünze
d	ducat
k	kreuzer

Paper gulden: BZ (in circulation until 1811)
WW (in circulation from 1811)
Silver gulden: CM (out of circulation 1809–18)

OTHER EUROPEAN CURRENCIES (1800–18)

To calculate exchange rates during Beethoven's lifetime, it is necessary to adjust for inflation as outlined above.

1. English pound (before 1800 and after 1818)
1 pound equals 11 CM florins, 2.4 ducats, or 20 shillings.
2. German Reichsthaler (before 1800 and after 1818)
3 Reichsthaler equals 1 ducat or 4.5 florins.
3. French Louis d'or
1 Louis d'or equals 2 ducats or 9 florins.
4. Italian zecchinos
1 zecchino equals 1.2 ducats or 5.5 florins.

BIBLIOGRAPHY ON CURRENCY RATES
DURING BEETHOVEN'S LIFETIME

Cooper, Barry. "Economics and Logistics," in *Beethoven's Folksong Settings*. Oxford: Clarendon Press, 1994.

Hanson, Alice M. "Incomes and Outgoings in the Vienna of Beethoven and Schubert." *Music and Letters* 64 (1983): 173–83.

———. *Musical Life in Biedermeier Vienna*. Cambridge: Cambridge University Press, 1985.

Moore, Julia. "Beethoven and Inflation." *Beethoven Forum*, vol. 1. Lincoln: University of Nebraska Press, 1992.

———. *Beethoven and Musical Economics*. Ph.D. diss., University of Illinois, Urbana-Champaign, 1987.

Morrow, Mary Sue. *Concert Life in Haydn's Vienna: Aspects of a Developing Musical and Social Institution*. Stuyvesant NY: Pendragon Press, 1989.

Pribram, Alfred Frances. *Materialen zur Geschichte der Preise und Löhne in Österreich*. Vienna: Carl Ueberreuter, 1938.

The Critical Reception of Beethoven's Compositions
by His German Contemporaries, VOLUME 2

Beethoven's Critics

An Appreciation

Robin Wallace

—When you get the feeling that whatever note succeeds the last is the only possible note that can rightly happen at that instant, in that context, then chances are you're listening to Beethoven. . . . Our boy has the real goods, the stuff from Heaven, the power to make you feel at the finish: Something is right in the world. There is something that checks throughout, that follows its own law consistently: something we can trust, that will never let us down.
—But that is almost a definition of God.
—I meant it to be.

Leonard Bernstein, The Joy of Music

In the world of what is still usually called "classical" music, there is no better-known name than Ludwig van Beethoven. The popularity of his works, the frequency of their performance, and the number of recordings of them sold each year are unrivaled within this admittedly tiny corner of the commercial music industry. Beethoven's status as a cultural icon, meanwhile, reaches far beyond the world of those who truly know his music; in popular mythology, his position as one of the great artists of Western civilization is all but unassailable.

In recent years, though, that position has been increasingly challenged by at least some members of a group who might reasonably be expected to have a vested interest in maintaining it. Parodying Chuck Berry's famous song, the *New York Times* ran an article a few years ago titled "Musicologists Roll Over Beethoven." Citing a number of prominent academics, including Susan McClary, Lawrence Kramer, and Richard Taruskin, *Times* writer Edward Rothstein served notice to the public at large that Beethoven, along with other composers of traditional "great texts," is increasingly being subjected to the kind of postmodern dissection long familiar to students of literary criticism. Far from being the divine revelation hailed by Leonard Bernstein, his music is heard by some of these professorial critics as laden with evocations of violence and sexual repression.[1] The traditional assumption that its beauties are transcendent and timeless is thus called into question and yoked to social and personal issues that had long been held to be irrelevant to the understanding of music.

Plus ça change, plus c'est la même chose. What readers of these volumes will discover is that Beethoven's present-day detractors have little to say about him that was not already said long ago, while the composer was still alive and able, if he chose, to respond.[2] Perhaps none of the writers represented here went as far as McClary, who, in an early version of her essay "Getting Down Off the Beanstalk," notoriously compared the emotional world of Beethoven's Ninth Symphony to that of a rapist.[3] Neither, though, did they have to approach the composer through the protective shield built up by two centuries of awestruck reverence. In many other ways as well, their writings reveal to us a musical world quite different from our own, which we may well admire, and perhaps even envy.

Imagine that a contemporary composer of art music could excite the same sort of eager, curious enthusiasm that Beethoven aroused in his own time, or that some musicians can still arouse in ours. Say, for example, that the latest work of Pauline Oliveros or of David del Tredici could routinely attract a larger audience than such current standbys as a Pavarotti recital, a Philharmonic performance of Tchaikovsky, or even an appearance by a popular music group. Suppose that there were a forum, a magazine, in which this music and its implications could be intelligently discussed for a nonacademic readership, and that the writers for that magazine—and four or five other competing ventures—eagerly awaited each new work by a living composer, anxious to submit their first impressions to public scrutiny.

Try to conceive of a "highbrow" musical world in which conductors, pianists, and other soloists are expected to play primarily their own music, while the operagoing public values novelty as much as today's audiences do at the movies. Imagine the written record of a world in which an ambitious music critic, expected to do more than compare this and that artist's "readings" of canonized repertory, might indeed be in a position to influence what repertory was heard and which composers were taken most seriously. This is the sort of record that these volumes contain.

Although at least thirty-three different journals are represented in this collection, the most important of them was the *Allgemeine musikalische Zeitung* (AMZ), which was founded in 1798 and ceased publication at the end of 1848. During the fifty years of its existence, the AMZ served to draw together the music-loving community throughout German-speaking lands, and it treated them to a combination of reviews, essays on an astonishingly wide variety of subjects, and correspondence from throughout Europe. Samples of all of these types of commentary can be found in this collection.

The topics of the essays are particularly fascinating, since in many ways they anticipate what later became the most pressing concerns of the academic discipline of musicology. Griesinger's *Biographische Notizen* on Haydn, still an important biographical source today, appeared shortly after that composer's death in 1809.[4] Aesthetic issues like the nature and foundation of harmony and meter, the relationship between music and poetry, the role of comic elements in music, and the differences between national styles were frequently raised and discussed. Issues of performance practice were addressed on a regular basis, and interdisciplinary studies abound. The theory and practice of music education were discussed almost obsessively.

The correspondence reports, excerpts from which generally appear under the heading "News" in this collection, also make fascinating reading. Unlike the formal reviews, which are usually based on printed scores, these reports record reactions, by writer and audience alike, to performances. A social historian interested in the details of concert programs throughout Europe (the correspondents ultimately extended as far afield as New York) during the early nineteenth century has no better resource. Personalities often loom as large as music in this section, which appeared in most of the weekly issues and was sometimes substantial enough to squeeze out everything else. Using the indexes to the AMZ, it is possible to follow the careers of even the most obscure performers in what sometimes amounts to considerable detail, and I have taken advantage of this opportunity in writing some of the annotations in this volume.

Many of the other journals excerpted here established similar sections. In our collection, though, reviews and comments on performances are not separated from those based on publications; instead, all reviews of each work are given in chronological order, so the reader can trace the way in which reaction to the work took shape. One fascinating observation, for example, is the extent to which E. T. A. Hoffmann's epochal review of the Fifth Symphony (entry no. 206 in this volume) was quoted or paraphrased, often at considerable length, by later writers on the work, and on other Beethoven works as well. It is clear that Hoffmann's description of the symphony, which has traditionally been read as an isolated, though highly significant, document, was actually more than just an intellectual and critical milestone. Because parts of it were incorporated verbatim into a famous essay in Hoffmann's *Fantasiestücke in Callots Manier*, aspects of his description of this work attained wide currency throughout the literary world of the early nineteenth century. In turn, it helped critics and audiences alike to come to terms with a work that must initially have defied understanding. As the lengthy narrative excerpt from the *Musikalische Eilpost* of 1826 (entry no. 214 in this volume) makes clear, however, not everyone was delighted to be browbeaten with these now familiar clichés.

I was enticed today most of all by Beethoven's Symphony in C Minor, which, according to the program, would be performed in its entirety, and I had prepared myself for this in an appropriate manner. All the cares and trivialities of everyday life, which swarm around people like flakes of snow, lay shaken off before the door. . . . But alas! Damned be every joy that must be waited for; the devil gets wind of it . . . and we are cheated! . . . Just as the conductor gave the signal to begin, my evil demon approached me in the form of the accursed R. . . .

We were going to hear today the most heavenly symphony of our divine Beethoven, he said to me. God! What a work! "It moves the lever controlling horror, fear, dread, pain. It opens up to us the kingdom of the gigantic and the immeasurable. Glowing beams shoot through this kingdom's deep night, and we become aware of gigantic shadows that surge up and down, enclosing us more and more narrowly." . . . And so it went on! the entire essay from Hoffmann's *Fantasiestücken;* everything that has ever been written or said about Beethoven's compositions he stuffed in front of me, without letting anything disturb him—not even the symphony, which meanwhile resounded through the hall with fresh, magical life.

Although the remainder of the story diverges from the subject of the symphony, it has been included here in its entirety because it provides fascinating insights into the way music was heard and understood in Beethoven's time.

The reviews themselves, meanwhile, can be both long and frighteningly detailed. It is important to remember that not only were their first readers generally unfamiliar with the works under review, but in many cases they had few opportunities to hear or study them. Performances of Beethoven's larger symphonic works were infrequent, as reviewers constantly pointed out, and even professional musicians were unlikely to be able to examine them thoroughly, since score publication was still a rarity. For many, therefore, reading these reviews was an important way to shape and formulate their own understanding of what was still very much "new music."

It will probably come as no surprise that critics who were granted this kind of license often found fault with Beethoven's music. For years, it has been a standard ploy of program annotators to quote unfavorable early reviews of acknowledged masterworks, presumably to show today's audiences how greatly our understanding of music has advanced in the interim. An amusing collection of such snipes at composers from Beethoven through Webern can be found in Nicolas Slonimsky's famous and highly entertaining *Lexicon of Musical Invective*.[5] As our edition should make clear, however, most of Beethoven's initial reviews were quite favorable. An anonymous critic, reviewing the difficult final three Piano Sonatas, ops. 109, 110, and 111, in the AMZ in 1824, summarized the real situation accurately enough:

Somewhat more than thirty years have passed since the magnificent appearance of Beethoven's genius first enchanted susceptible and educated people in the world of musical art. This genius created a new epoch. All the conditions of a musical artwork: invention, spirit and feeling in melody, harmony and rhythm were fulfilled by Mr. v. B. in a new manner characteristic of him. It is just as well known that an opposition soon spoke against this originality, as is customary in similar circumstances. The striving to find fault, however, had only a small, fleeting success. Beethoven the hero triumphed completely. Scarcely had any of his artistic productions entered into the world than their fame was forever established.[6]

Thus, there is no question of a "misunderstood genius" writing solely for the benefit of posterity. Even the most difficult of Beethoven's later works found immediate champions, while other critics attacked these same works for sullying what they regarded as Beethoven's enormous and well-deserved reputation—which by 1810, at the latest, was largely unquestioned. Gottfried Weber's 1825 essay on *Wellingtons Sieg bei Vittoria* (which will appear in vol. 3 of this series) is one of the most vicious attacks ever aimed at a Beethoven work, but in this case it was the very popularity of the work that bothered the author. "Hold up this sensational and passing phenomenon against other earlier products of the *Beethovenian* fire—for example, to his C-Minor Symphony. . . . *This* is greatness, *this* jubilation and triumph and transfiguration! and—how vulgar, in such a comparison, does the present battle- and show-piece appear!"[7]

This is an extreme example, as a careful reading of these volumes should make clear. The determination of these critics to explain Beethoven's works and make them comprehensible to their readers, however, was indeed often matched by the temerity with which they were willing to correct and give advice to the great composer, and even to link his work with extramusical ideas—a tendency that will become increasingly apparent in the later volumes of this series. Like some current academics, they sometimes suggested that Beethoven's music had a masculine quality, although at the time this was generally cited approvingly. They frequently heard aspects of violence in his more dynamic works, many of which were, after all, conceived within the cauldron of the Napoleonic Wars. The suggestion that Beethoven might ultimately influence music history in a negative or destructive way was always present, especially at the end of his life when his fame was firmly established. Readers of Slonimsky's *Lexicon* are familiar with the letter to the editor in the London *Quarterly Musical Magazine and Review* of 1827, which suggested that "the effect which the writings of Beethoven have had on the art must, I fear, be considered as injurious. Led away by the force of his genius and dazzled by its creations, a crowd of imitators has arisen, who have displayed as much harshness, as much extravagance, and as much obscurity, with little or none of his beauty and grandeur."[8] Even as sympathetic a writer as Amadeus Wendt, in his essay on *Fidelio*, which appeared in the AMZ in 1815 (entry no. 240 in this volume), wrote that "I have heard several people say . . . that the impression made by this music is all too shocking and oppressive. . . . We wish to concede, as well, that the music of this opera strains the nerves of many with a gentle nature."

Although Wendt defused this objection through a literary metaphor, comparing Beethoven to Shakespeare, who embraced similar extremes, he summarized his own reservations about the composer as follows: "We can by no means fail to recognize, in taking an unbiased look at the most recent musical art, that Beethoven's example . . . has caused great damage, and his powerful spirit has manifested a very detrimental influence upon the art. . . . Musical art, upon which Beethoven now exercises so powerful an influence, and which is as much indebted *to him* as *he to it,* would be even more grateful to him if he strove more *generally* for the honor of musical art more than for the honor of *his* art, and only sacrificed to it devoutly in hours of undisturbed consecration."

Thus, there is nothing particularly new in what some of our postmodern critics have been writing about Beethoven. Far from damaging the composer's reputation, though, the reviews collected here actually provide important keys to its success that we would be hard-put to discover elsewhere. This point can easily become lost in the highly ideological world of current scholarship: Beethoven's first critics regarded it as their mission to explain how his music worked, and we can still learn from what they had to say.

When I first started doing research on this criticism, I was struck by the realization that some of the most eloquent writers among Beethoven's contemporaries heard his music in a rather complicated way. To the same extent that they recognized a transcendent dimension in it, they heard seemingly old-fashioned representations of concrete, objective meanings as well, which they saw as raised to new heights of realism by Beethoven's musical language.

This latter realization surprised me because it upset what had by that time become a fairly standard, if simplistic, view of early Romantic aesthetics. Beethoven, in that view, exemplified the goals of the new Romantic aesthetic of music found in the writings of people like Ludwig Tieck and Wilhelm Wackenroder (neither of whom was a musician).[9] According to that aesthetic, music was a completely autonomous art; unburdened by the detritus of merely phenomenal experience, it could soar into the unbounded ether of abstract thought and impress its contents directly on the listener's inmost soul.

As I soon discovered, however, even for a writer as metaphysically oriented as E. T. A. Hoffmann, that was not the whole story. His reviews of the *Coriolan* Overture, the Fifth Symphony, and the Piano Trios, op. 70—all written between 1810 and 1813 and translated in this volume—demonstrate that Hoffmann went to considerable lengths to show how the musical nuts and bolts fit together with the more fanciful things he heard in these works. Describing the opening of the overture, for example, Hoffmann writes:

This beginning grips and fascinates our feelings irresistibly, an effect that results from the entire idea, but primarily from the original instrumentation. In spite of the *fortissimo* marking, the first two measures are given to strings alone, which strike low C heavily and decisively, and an F-minor chord of a quarter note's duration breaks shrilly from the full orchestra in the third measure. The deathly quiet that follows, the new beginning by the string instruments with the same heavy, terrifying C, once again the shrill $^6_3$ on F, the deathly quiet again, the C in the string instruments for the third time, the chord raised to the seventh, and now at last two chords by the entire orchestra, which lead into the theme of the Allegro: all of this heightens our expectations; indeed it constricts the breast of the listener; it is the frightful, menacing murmur of the approaching storm.

Even more typical of some of the lengthier reviews contained in these volumes is the following passage from Ludwig Rellstab's description of the Fourth Symphony, which originally appeared in the BAMZ.

> Let us consider first the Adagio, in which the sweetest and most painful of melodies delightfully nestles against the one motive made, as it were, from bronze, which stands like a pillar around which tender green shoots are growing. This simple motive is used to produce the most stunning transition, mounting from the softest *piano* to *fortissimo*, from frightening pizzicatos in the string instruments to the mighty rhythmic thunder of the timpani. It almost sounds like the last thunderclaps of the retreating storm, resounding through the mountains, which faintly continue to threaten, while lovely blue skies and sunlight break through the clouds and the freshened earth smiles in the trembling brightness of the silver droplets. . . . I only want to mention further the entrance of the motive after the cadence, where it truly resembles faraway thunder, which resounds through the mountains with awesome beauty.

Many of Beethoven's contemporaries, particularly in the latter part of his life, tended to hear his music as descriptive and evocative—in short, as what would later be known as "program music." Far from being a mere survival of the eighteenth-century Doctrine of the Affections, this way of listening to music represented the leading edge of musical Romanticism. Of course, it never entirely died out; aspects of it permeate the musical *Zeitgeist* even of the present day, and the later nineteenth century was hardly lacking in music that was avowedly programmatic and autobiographical.

Nineteenth-century aesthetic writings, however, were also characterized by numerous attempts to define music as a self-sufficient art form, and these writings for many years largely defined the "official" view of Beethoven. One of the most familiar of these was Eduard Hanslick's treatise *Vom musikalisch-Schönen*, which proposed that "definite feelings and emotions are unsusceptible of being embodied in music."[10] Hanslick reacted both against the earlier tendency to trace the aesthetic value of music to its evocation of emotions and of nature and against the efforts of many of his contemporaries to draw connections between music and other art forms, and he has thus earned a reputation as one of the first musical autonomists.

Like many others in the nineteenth century, Hanslick perceived and recognized the subjective nature of musical expression, but dismissed it as the basis for true aesthetic understanding. Others sought to transcend this problem, however, and the musical writings of the German idealists abound in evocations of a "spirit," "will," or "subject," which is uniquely expressed through music. While Beethoven was still alive, Schopenhauer called music "as direct an objectification and copy of the whole will as the world itself,"[11] and his philosophy and outlook greatly influenced many later Romantic musicians, especially Wagner. The resulting mystification of music has certainly created a host of problems in our own time; its cultural fallout was aptly described by Henry Pleasants in his controversial book *The Agony of Modern Music:* "The layman is confronted with a mystery. He may be aware that the mystery is insoluble even to the professionals. But he modestly assumes that they are closer to enlightenment than he, and thus honors them with the respect due the initiated. Among the latter the composer, being closest to the mystery, the chosen instrument for the propagation of its enigmas, emerges as a sort of high priest, a man supernaturally ordained to communicate with the Infinite."[12]

Those words were written over forty years ago, but the attitude they describe survives unabated to the present day, and probably no composer has suffered more from it than Beethoven. His symphonies and concertos are still the staple fare of orchestras throughout the world, and they are played year in and year out by ensembles large and small, on instruments old and new, inside concert halls in the winter and under festival shells in the summer. Although this is undeniably due to the power and enduring appeal of Beethoven's music, people also come back, at least in part, because, like Bernstein, they believe that the music contains something of ultimate value that will enrich their lives. Of course, the majority would be hard pressed to say exactly what that content is, or how their lives are enriched by it more than they would be by hearing, say, one of the hundred or so Haydn symphonies that have not been similarly canonized. But such is the strength of the mythology of musical greatness that these sorts of questions simply do not matter. Beethoven is great because he is Beethoven. His music, as we all seem to know, is immortal, and nothing quite like it has been written since.

And thus Beethoven suffers from a kind of glib idolatry. His personality and his music have been raised to a symbolic level that makes it difficult to *listen* to him the way that Hoffmann and his contemporaries did. Few people, these days, will admit to leaving a Beethoven performance feeling, as did Hoffmann, "the pain of that interminable longing, in which every pleasure that had quickly arisen with sounds of rejoicing sinks away and founders, and we live on, rapturously beholding the spirits themselves, only in this pain, which, consuming love, hope, and joy within itself, seeks to burst our breast asunder with a full-voiced consonance of all the passions."

Hoffmann, we are forced to realize, was not simply hearing music; he was undergoing a profound experience that transformed his life, and he was eloquently expressing it in words. He had actually had the experience that modern concertgoers are conditioned to expect they will get from Beethoven, and it was obviously pretty unsettling.[13]

What Hoffmann had discovered was a whole new way of experiencing emotions, which corresponded to the nature of Beethoven's musical expression. They were revealed to him not as the packaged and perhaps predictable *Affekten* of the eighteenth century, but as things grand and terrible, opening, as Hoffmann himself had written, "the door of the underworld."[14] He had been introduced to that shadow realm of the human personality to which Faust had already descended, and into which Weber would shortly lead his unsuspecting Max. In the Romantic worldview, such descents tended to be followed by redemption, not because of anything music had to offer, but because it was simply in the nature of things for this to happen.

Thus it is that the best of Beethoven's contemporary critics effortlessly created what seems to us to be a synthesis between two very different ways of understanding music. On the one hand, they wanted to make it clear that the experience of listening to music could be a truly transcendent one. On the other hand, it was crucial to them that the content of a piece of music should be explicable in terms of the everyday world. Enlightenment did not only mean walking around with one's head in the clouds, but also with one's feet on the ground.

Even a sympathetic reader of twentieth-century criticism can easily be struck by the difficulty that modern writers seem to face in bridging this same epistemological fault line. The problem was made abundantly clear by a published tiff between two well-known scholars in the early 1990s over the work of Susan McClary, the Beethoven iconoclast mentioned above. Representing the ranks of traditional music theorists, Pieter van den Toorn mounted a withering critique of McClary's work up to 1991. Van den Toorn argued in favor of understanding music primarily in terms of its aesthetic immediacy and implied that McClary's sexual interpretations reflect a strong and irrational antimale bias. This was answered by the musicologist Ruth Solie in a way that made it clear she sought to represent the broad-based community of feminist scholarship, which van den Toorn had tarred with this rather broad brush.[15] The exchange still makes fascinating reading. Van den Toorn's frustration at McClary's "atheism" (Solie's term for McClary's refusal to consider the immediate, transcendental aspect of musical experience to be important) is mirrored by his own lack of sympathy for McClary's attempts to explain music as a social and ideological construct. As I have suggested, the "either, or" choice that this debate implies is a construction of modern aesthetics, which the Romantics would have found utterly baffling.[16]

Of course, not every writer collected here was as philosophically sophisticated as Wendt and Hoffmann. It would be a mistake to pretend that these critics spoke with a monolithic voice, for their approaches are often unique. More often, they are merely functional, aimed at bringing the most important details of the music to the attention of as broad an audience as possible. The significance of these early reviews, however, is not limited to questions of epistemology and aesthetics. In their very diversity, they will also serve to fill an important gap in our understanding of the history of Beethoven's reception.

Recent years have seen an extraordinary resurgence of interest in that history, understood in the broadest terms. It is usually defined so as to include a wide variety of writings (and even pictures, as is demonstrated in Alessandra Comini's fascinating study of the Beethoven myth)[17] from the nineteenth century and our own, and to be reflected in the way Beethoven's achievement has served as a model for other composers as seemingly hostile to each other's agendas as Wagner and Brahms. It even encompasses the way in which public taste has been shaped by the influence of Beethoven's works and by their canonization as standard repertory, which in turn has transformed the world of "serious" music forever.

I do not mean in any way to question the value of the extremely broad definition of Beethoven's reception mentioned above, which is implicit in most of what has been written about the subject. It has had the effect, however, of directing attention away from the writings of his immediate contemporaries, who served as the wellspring for all that was to follow. Apart from Hoffmann, Adolf Bernhard Marx is the earliest writer on Beethoven to be widely cited in the reception literature, and he lived until 1866, by which time the parameters of the critical tradition dealing with Beethoven's music had been well established. It is my fervent hope that these volumes, which consist entirely of writings from before 1831, will at least serve to refocus the attention of the scholarly world on the origins of that tradition rather than on its results.

For it is those very results that are increasingly being seen as the problem, not the solution. No writer has made this point more successfully than Scott Burnham in his examination of the "hero" myth surrounding the composer.[18] Paradigms from the initial programmatic reception of Beethoven have, Burnham suggests, become so definitive of the way that his music—and indeed all music—is now understood, that the initial programmatic content is no longer necessary for them to be invoked. What is worse, "the feeling of glorious consummation so singularly afforded by Beethoven's heroic style can lead to a collective self impermeable to any other musical impulse."[19]

The advantage of refocusing our view of Beethoven's reception on the years before 1830 is that we can see that the "covert" and dangerous assumptions about this music engendered by the later tradition do not necessarily follow from these earliest writings, aesthetically compelling as they are in their own right. Certainly, Beethoven's contemporaries were already interested in what Burnham calls the "processual" dimension of that music—their growing, though still tentative, awareness of its formal dynamics is one of the distinguishing features of their writings.[20] Never, though, did they treat those dynamics as anything more than a framework, making the music accessible to a public whose members were being invited to understand it for themselves. When their analyses did eventually become more sophisticated, in the writings of Hoffmann and others who followed him, mostly in the 1820s, the processual side of Beethoven's music was treated as only one side of an emphatically two-sided coin, and these writers would certainly have been reluctant to abandon either side of it. In light of their writings, therefore, it is certainly worth asking whether it is necessary for us to do so, or whether both sides can in fact be recontextualized so as to become once again meaningful in our own time.[21]

It is only natural that Beethoven's contemporaries sought to connect the experience of his music with what they considered to be most universal in the life of their own times. That the images thus evoked should have been largely military is hardly surprising for a century that was born listening to the footsteps of Napoleon. These images, however, are not the whole story; as Rellstab's commentary on the Fourth Symphony, quoted above, and countless other such commentaries make clear, Beethoven's contemporaries heard more than just struggle and heroism in his music. In fact, the idea of heroic self-definition was rarely applied to Beethoven before the very end of his life, and it arose largely in reaction to the Ninth Symphony, not the *Eroica*. Only occasionally did they hear Beethoven's works as autobiographical, despite the prominence of such readings in later reception history.[22] Nor did they hear formal perfection; in fact, they were as likely to comment on the apparent disunity of Beethoven's music as on its unity. What they did hear was a musical language in which, in Amadeus Wendt's words, "great powers are able to develop, [and] great contrasts are also at hand," and they recognized that Beethoven's importance as a composer lay in his ability to reconcile those contrasts, however they are conceived and understood. A willingness to see Beethoven's music as more than the sum of its parts seems to be the most fundamental, ineradicable element of his critical reception. If we in the late twentieth century find it hard to recover this attitude, the problem may be that we have paid too little attention to what his earliest critics had to say.

NOTES

1. Edward Rothstein, "Musicologists Roll Over Beethoven," *New York Times,* 26 November 1995, E 1: 5. Rothstein also discusses the contributions of more traditional writers like Joseph Kerman and Charles Rosen.

2. In a well-known comment on Gottfried Weber's scathing review of *Wellingtons Sieg bei Vittoria,* op. 91, Beethoven wrote "O du elender Schuft! Was ich *scheisse* ist besser als du je gedacht!" (quoted in Nicolas Slonimsky, *Lexicon of Musical Invective: Critical Assaults on Composers Since Beethoven's Time* [Seattle: University of Washington Press, 1965], 45), a pithy comment indeed, which should perhaps best remain untranslated. See also n. 7.

3. The comparison was originally made in McClary's essay "Getting Down Off the Beanstalk / The Presence of a Woman's Voice in Janika Vandervelde's 'Genesis II,' " *Minnesota Composers Forum* (January 1987), and was modified for the version of her essay that appeared in her book *Feminine Endings: Music, Gender, and Sexuality* (Minneapolis: University of Minnesota Press, 1991).

4. AMZ 11 (1809): 641–49, 657–68, 673–81, 689–99, 705–13, 721–33, 737–47, 776–81.

5. The work was originally published by Coleman-Ross in New York in 1953 and has been widely read and quoted. At the beginning of my book *Beethoven's Critics,* I was forced to take the late and much-lamented Slonimsky to task for contributing to a widespread misunderstanding in this regard. See my *Beethoven's Critics: Aesthetic Dilemmas and Resolutions during the Composer's Lifetime* (Cambridge: Cambridge University Press, 1986), 1.

6. AMZ 26 (1 April 1824): 213–25. The full text of this review will appear in vol. 3.

7. This passage immediately precedes the more familiar one quoted in Slonimsky, which provoked the response of Beethoven quoted in n. 2.

8. Slonimsky, *Lexicon,* 46.

9. See Ludwig Tieck and Wilhelm Wackenroder, *Herzensergießungen eines kunstlieben-den Klosterbruders* (Berlin: Unger, 1797), and *Phantasien über die Kunst* (Hamburg: Perthes, 1799). Typical of the current view of these works is Donald Crosby's statement, in his article on Tieck in the *Dictionary of Literary Biography,* that the *Phantasien* "forms the foundation of musical aesthetics for the Romantic movement" (*German Writers in the Age of Goethe, 1789–1832,* ed. James Hardin and Christopher E. Schweizer [Detroit: Gale Research, 1989] [*Dictionary of Literary Biography,* 90], 317). As recently as 1997, the musicologist Mary Sue Morrow, describing what she calls a paradigm shift between the musical worldviews of the late eighteenth and early nineteenth centuries, writes that this shift "was heralded not by an established writer on musical aesthetics, but by two young figures from the literary world, Ludwig Tieck (1773–1853) and Wilhelm Wackenroder (1773–98), in essays published in 1799" (Mary Sue Morrow, *German Music Criticism in the Late Eighteenth Century: Aesthetic Issues in Instrumental Music* [Cambridge: Cambridge University Press, 1997], 13).

10. Eduard Hanslick, *The Beautiful in Music,* trans. Gustav Cohen, ed. Morris Weitz (Indianapolis: Liberal Arts Press, 1957), 21.

11. Arthur Schopenhauer, *The World as Will and Idea,* trans. R. B. Haldane and J. Kemp (London: Kegan Paul, Trench, Trübner, n.d.), 333.

12. Henry Pleasants, *The Agony of Modern Music* (New York: Simon and Schuster, 1955), 13.

13. In this regard, it is worth noting Peter Kivy's comment in his recent book *Authenticities* (Ithaca NY: Cornell University Press, 1995), that it would surely "be folly to recapture, as I think some in the musicological community are indeed recommending, an understanding of Beethoven like that of E. T. A. Hoffmann's" (p. 211). Since I am the principal musicologist to whom Kivy attributes this point of view, along with the idea that "with regard to works of music . . . human understanding is not susceptible of improvement" (p. 214), I feel compelled to point out that it has never been my intent to suggest either of these things. Can human understanding of particular works of music change and advance with time? Of course it can. Would it be a good idea, in the late twentieth century, to return to Hoffmann's purple prose and "overblown poetic or

programmatic interpretations"? (p. 211). Kivy misreads me if he thinks I would find this desirable. At the same time, though, I am hardly alone in thinking that our understanding and appreciation of Beethoven's music has been declining rather than advancing during the last half century, and that studying what earlier writers have written may help to set it back in the right direction.

14. In his review of the Fifth Symphony, Hoffmann wrote that "Orpheus Lyra öffnete die Thore des Orcus." Orcus, a Latin term for the underworld, is translated here accordingly.

15. See Pieter C. van den Toorn, "Politics, Feminism, and Contemporary Music Theory," *Journal of Musicology* 9 (Summer 1991): 275–99. See also Ruth Solie, "What Do Feminists Want? A Reply to Pieter van den Toorn," *Journal of Musicology* 9 (Fall 1991): 399–410.

16. While van den Toorn does not deny that reflective understanding plays an important role in musical understanding, he sees it as subservient to the experience of immediacy, not as a defining feature of that experience.

17. Alessandra Comini, *The Changing Image of Beethoven: A Study in Mythmaking* (New York: Rizzoli, 1987).

18. Scott Burnham, *Beethoven Hero* (Princeton: Princeton University Press, 1995).

19. Burnham, *Beethoven Hero,* 159.

20. Burnham argues throughout his book that our present understanding of Beethoven is based largely on a sense, encouraged by his music and its reception, that music can be heard as an unfolding process, centering on the development of thematic material. "The story of thematic destiny," Burnham writes in his conclusion, "may well be the most convenient analogue for our feeling that there is an immanent presence, human and engaging, in Beethoven's music and, indeed, in all music. But have we simply talked ourselves into the idea that our engagement with music is due primarily to an unending fascination with its narrative flow? To ask this is to confront our most fundamental assumptions about the musical experience as we deal with it in academic music theory and criticism, assumptions about our epistemological interactions with music" (Burnham, *Beethoven Hero,* 163). The assumptions that Burnham is referring to had, of course, not yet been formulated when the material in these volumes was written, and it is intriguing to see the extent to which these critics, when they did resort to narrative descriptions, used them not as formal absolutes, but as a simple hermeneutic tool.

21. For two attempts to do just this, see my "Background and Expression in the First Movement of Beethoven's Op. 132," *Journal of Musicology* 7 (Winter 1989): 3–20, and "Myth, Gender, and Musical Meaning: *The Magic Flute,* Beethoven, and 19th-Century Sonata Form Revisited," *Journal of Musicological Research* 19 (1999): 1–25.

22. The very title of Burnham's *Beethoven Hero* refers to the fact, critiqued by Burnham throughout the book, that in our own time Beethoven himself tends to be seen as the autobiographical hero of his own works, at least those of the so-called heroic period.

OP. 55
SYMPHONY NO. IN E♭ MAJOR (*EROICA SYMPHONY*)

(See entry nos. 29, 33, 35, 90, 98, and 124, vol. 1; 172, 206, and 240, vol. 2; mentioned:
Septet, op. 20; Symphony No. 1, op. 21; String Quintet, op. 29; and Symphony No. 2, op. 36)

145.
"Vienna, 17 April 1805." *Der Freymüthige* 3 (17 April 1805): 332.

The management of the theater had granted the superb violin player Klement[1] the Sunday before Easter for a benefit concert. He played a violin concerto of his own composition with his customary artistry and charm, showing his power and assurance in the most difficult spots by means of a nice fermata.[2] Likewise a new symphony in E♭ by Beethoven was performed here, over which the musical connoisseurs and amateurs were divided into several parties.[3] One group, Beethoven's very special friends, maintains that precisely this symphony is a masterpiece, that it is in exactly the true style for more elevated music, and that if it does not please at present, it is because the public is not sufficiently educated in art to be able to grasp all of these elevated beauties. After a few thousand years, however, they will not fail to have their effect. The other group utterly denies this work any artistic value and feels that it manifests a completely unbounded striving for distinction and oddity, which, however, has produced neither beauty nor true sublimity and power. Through strange modulations and violent transitions, by placing together the most heterogeneous things, as when for example a pastorale is played through in the grandest style, with abundant scratchings in the bass, with three horns and so forth,[4] a true if not desirable originality can indeed be gained without much effort. However, genius does not proclaim itself by simply bringing forth the unusual and the fantastic, but rather by creating the beautiful and sublime. Beethoven himself has demonstrated the truth of this statement in his earlier works. The third, very small group stands in the middle; they admit that the symphony contains many beautiful qualities, but admit that the context often seems completely disjointed, and that the endless duration of this longest and perhaps also most difficult of all symphonies exhausts even connoisseurs, becoming unbearable to the mere amateur. They wish that Mr. v. B. would use his well-known great talent to give us works that resemble his first two Symphonies in C and D, his graceful Septet in E♭, the spirited Quintet in D Major,[5] and others of his earlier compositions, which will place B. forever in the ranks of the foremost instrumental composers. They fear, however, that if Beethoven continues on this path, both he and the public will come off badly. Music could quickly come to such a point, that everyone who is not precisely familiar with the rules and difficulties of the art would find absolutely no enjoyment in it, but, oppressed instead by a multitude of unrelated and overabundant ideas and a continuous tumult of the combined instruments, would leave the concert hall with only an unpleasant feeling of exhaustion. The public and Mr. v. Beethoven, who conducted the work himself, were not satisfied with each other this evening. To the public the symphony was too difficult, too long, and B. himself was too impolite, since he did not nod in acknowledgement of those who did applaud. Beethoven, on the other hand, did not find the applause to be sufficiently outstanding.

Since the symphony, as we have heard, will shortly appear in print, the musical world will soon be able to reach its own judgment upon it.[6]

NOTES

1. Franz Clement (1780–1842) was, at the time of this concert, a violin virtuoso at the height of his fame. In 1794 Beethoven first met Clement and praised him lavishly: "Nature and art vie with each other in making you a great artist." Beethoven's Violin Concerto (1806) was written specifically for Clement. The title page to the autograph reads "Concerto par Clemenza pour Clement primo Violino . . ." Clement's playing and reputation declined in the 1810s. By 1824 Beethoven, after rejecting him as a concertmaster for the Ninth's premiere, commented, "He has lost a great deal and seems too old to be entertaining with his capers on the fiddle!" For more on Clement, see Robert Haas, "The Viennese Violinist, Franz Clement," *Musical Quarterly* 34 (1948): 15–27; and Robin Stowell, *Beethoven: Violin Concerto* (Cambridge: Cambridge University Press, 1998), 20–29.

2. During the Classical period, the term *fermata* applied either to a pause on a note played without extempore elaborations (a simple fermata) or to a fermata that was embellished and elaborated. For a discussion of embellished fermatas with examples, see Daniel Gottlob Türk, *School of Clavier Playing,* trans. and ed. Raymond H. Haggh (Lincoln: University of Nebraska Press, 1982), 290, 293–96. The author of this review refers to the elaborated type of fermata here.

3. The first public performance of the *Eroica* Symphony took place on 7 April 1805 at the Theater-an-der-Wien. Three private performances preceded this concert. The first private performance was given in early August 1804 at Lobkowitz's Eisenberg Palace in Bohemia. See Walther Brauneis, " 'Composta per festeggiare il sovvenire di un gran uomo' Beethovens *Eroica* als Hommage des Fürsten Franz Joseph Maximilian von Lobkowitz für Louis Ferdinand von Preußer," *Oesterreichische Musikzeitschrift* 53 (1998): 4–24, and Jaroslav Macek, "Die Uraufführung von Beethovens 'Sinfonia eroica,'" *Ludwig van Beethoven in Herzen Europas* (forthcoming).

4. The author is perhaps referring to the trio of the scherzo, in which the three horns are featured prominently. A similar comment occurs in entry no. 148 below.

5. The first three works are the Symphony No. 1 in C, op. 21, the Symphony No. 2 in D, op. 36, and the Septet, op. 20. It is not clear which quintet is referred to, since the only Quintet in D Major is the Quintet Fugue, op. 137, published in the fall of 1827.

The quintets written by the date of this review are the String Quintet in E♭ Major, op. 4 (published 1796), the Quintet for Piano and Winds in E♭ Major, op. 16 (1801), and the String Quintet in C Major, op. 29 (1802). Because the first three works in the author's list were published between 1801–04 and because of its spirited finale, op. 29 may have been intended. Thayer suggested op. 29 (*Thayer's Life of Beethoven*, rev. and ed. Elliot Forbes, 2 vols. [Princeton: Princeton University Press, 1964] [henceforth Thayer-Forbes], 376).

6. The first edition of the parts for the symphony was published in October 1806 by the Bureau d'Arts et d'Industrie in Vienna. The first score edition was published in England by Cianchettini and Sperati in March–April 1809.

≈

146.
"Vienna, 9 April." *Allgemeine musikalische Zeitung* 7 (1 May 1805): 501–02.

(Mentioned: Symphony No. 1, op. 21; Symphony No. 2, op. 36)

At this concert I heard the new Beethoven symphony in E♭ (on the concert announcement, D♯ was mistakenly given),[1] conducted by the composer himself, and performed by a very well-comprised orchestra. But this time as well I found no reason at all to change the judgment that I had already formed about it. To be sure, this new work of B. has great and daring ideas, and, as one can expect from the genius of this composer, great power in the way it is worked out; but the symphony would improve immeasurably (it lasts an entire hour)[2] if B. could bring himself to shorten it, and to bring more light, clarity, and unity into the whole. These are qualities that in Mozart's Symphonies in G Minor and C Major, Beethoven's in C and D, and Eberl's in E♭ and D,[3] with all their wealth of ideas, all their interweaving of the instruments, and all their interchange of surprising modulations, are never lost at any point. Here, for example, in place of the Andante, there is a funeral march in C minor, which is subsequently developed fugally. But every fugal passage delights simply through a sense of order in apparent confusion. If, even after hearing it repeatedly, this very coherence now escapes even from our heightened powers of observation, then it must appear strange to every unbiased connoisseur of music. The symphony was also lacking a great deal else that would have enabled it to have pleased overall.

NOTES

1. Flat notes were commonly referred to by their enharmonic equivalents (e.g., D♯ for E♭) as late as the nineteenth century (Thayer-Forbes, 375, n. 9). In writings, the sharp and flat signs were also sometimes used to designate major and minor keys, respectively.

2. Beethoven apparently was aware of the complaints about the length of the symphony and according to a contemporary account replied, "If *I* write a symphony an hour long

it will be found short enough" (Thayer-Forbes, 376). A survey of ten recent recordings on modern and original instruments reveals a range of timings from forty-three to fifty minutes, with an average of approximately forty-seven minutes. These durations are in line with the 1811 Leipzig performance reviewed in entry no. 157. Beethoven took the unusual step of printing the following preface to the symphony on the first violin part of the first edition: "This symphony, which was purposefully written to be much longer than is usual, should be performed nearer the beginning rather than the end of a concert and shortly after an overture, an aria, and a concerto; if it is heard too late, it will lose its own proposed effect because the listener will already be tired out by the preceding performances." See Georg Kinsky, *Das Werk Beethovens: Thematisch-bibliographisches Verzeichnis seiner sämtlichen vollendeten Kompositionen,* ed. Hans Halm (Munich: G. Henle, 1955) (henceforth Kinsky-Halm), 129–30, for the original text.

3. The works mentioned by Mozart are K. 550 and K. 551; by Beethoven, ops. 21 and 36. The works by Eberl are probably op. 33 in E♭ major and op. 34 in D minor. See *The Symphony: 1720–1840,* ed. Barry Brook, reference volume (New York, 1986), 207.

The style of Austrian pianist, composer, and concertmaster Anton Eberl (1765 or 1766–1807) was close enough to Mozart's that several of his works were published under Mozart's name. A biographical sketch of Eberl appears in AMZ 9 (1806–07): 423–30.

≈

147.
"Miscellaneous News. Vienna, 2 May 1805."
Berlinische musikalische Zeitung 1 (1805): 174.

Klement, a very superior violin player, pleased in a grand concerto of his own composition and earned the applause that he received. A new Beethoven Symphony in E♭ is for the most part so shrill and complicated that only those who worship the failings and merits of this composer with equal fire, which at times borders on the ridiculous, could find pleasure in it. The young Mozart[1] was very encouragingly received at his concert by a full house and played his father's C-major keyboard concerto very nicely for his age. A cantata upon Haydn's seventy-third birthday also pleased.[2] We can expect much from Mozart's son, if too early and extensive praise does not spoil him.

NOTES

1. The reference is undoubtedly to Franz Xaver Wolfgang Mozart (1791–1844), known as Wolfgang Amadeus Mozart. The younger of Mozart's two surviving sons, he was not yet fourteen years old at the time of this performance. He later had a distinguished career as a pianist and composer, although he never rose to the degree of eminence that was predicted for him early in his life. This concert took place on 8 April 1805 (see Mary Sue Morrow, *Concert Life in Haydn's Vienna: Aspects of a Developing Musical and Social Institution* (Stuyvesant NY: Pendragon, 1989), 330).

2. Haydn was born on 31 March 1732 and baptized on 1 April. The cantata was composed by Franz Mozart. According to *The New Grove Dictionary of Music and Musicians* (ed. Stanley Sadie [London: Macmillan, 1980]), the manuscript is lost.

148.

"News. Mannheim." *Allgemeine musikalische
Zeitung* 9 (28 January 1807): 285–86.

The ninth public gathering (3 January 1807) was noteworthy through the performance of the newest Beethoven Symphony (E♭ major). Trying to perform such a colossal work was a great gamble, and only through the support of several members of the court orchestra could it be brought about. This, as well as the consideration that this symphony might otherwise never, or God knows when, get to be performed, made the undertaking commendable.

The opinions of the listeners about the work were divided. Many admired it, all found it horribly long—the first violin part consists of seventeen closely printed folio pages![1] The first movement is impressive and full of power and sublimity. The working-out is true and comprehensible; the reinforcement of the bass lines with the wind instruments, particularly the horns, heightens the effect considerably. As often as the composer seems to digress from his main idea, he returns to it just as skillfully and naturally and maintains a comprehensible unity, which adds great value to the piece.

The funeral march is new and bears the character of noble melancholy. As *long* as it is, even in relation to the other movements, we are still glad to linger in the emotion it arouses. The blending of harmonies is extremely pure and correct. Exact observation of the *piano* and *forte* markings is particularly important here. The scherzo menuetto is a piece full of lively, restless motion, against which the sustained tones of the three horns in the trio contrast exceptionally well.

The finale has much value, which I am far from denying it; however, it cannot very well escape from the charge of great bizarrerie. At the very least, for example, no composer before Beethoven has dared to begin a piece in E♭ major in such a way that the instruments begin *al unisono* on the leading tone, and then continue with progressions that belong to the scale of G minor, until finally the fourth and following measures are merciful enough to extricate our ear from this predicament and remove us to the actual key! The theme that follows immediately afterward, repeated twice *pizzicato,* comes out, for the sake of novelty, a little *too* empty. Are all these peculiarities necessary: *per festeggiar il Souvenire d'un grand Uomo*[2]—as Mr. Beethoven describes the purpose of his work on the title page?

Performance of this work, on the whole as well as for the individual parts, is difficult in the highest degree. The engraving is attractive and readable, but has several errors. For example, in the first oboe, p. 1, line 13; in the second oboe, p. 1, line 9; in the second horn, p. 5, line 6 and 7, etc.

1. The first violin part of the first edition contains seventeen pages, as mentioned here. Only the Ninth Symphony's violin part is longer, at eighteen pages and a title page. The number of pages in the first violin parts, compared to the other symphonies, is nine pages (First); ten pages (Sixth, Eighth); eleven pages (Fifth); and fourteen pages (Second, Fourth, Seventh).

2. Italian: "To celebrate the memory of a great man."

~

149.

"Review." *Allgemeine musikalische Zeitung* 9 (18 February 1807): 321–33.

(Mentioned: *Prometheus* Variations, op. 35; Symphony No. 2, op. 36)

This noteworthy and colossal work, the most extensive and artistically rich among all those that Beethoven's original, wonderful spirit has created, has already been discussed in these pages a few times and from various points of view. First the readership received reports from Vienna of its existence and characteristics in general, as well as of the impression that it made on the public at various performances. Several other contributors, most recently the correspondent from Mannheim,[1] or sometime earlier the reviewer of the keyboard reduction of the second Beethoven symphony,[2] have then added to similar reports many more observations in deeper detail about its purpose, its character, and the basis of the impression that it makes. *Now* the uniqueness and the rich content of the work seem to demand that above all we seriously examine its technical aspects and in this regard, as well as in regard to its related mechanical aspects, follow the composer step by step. This is a procedure that the thorough working-out of this composition itself invites, and that would find its justification, if needed, in the usefulness that young artists draw from such analyses and in the heightened satisfaction that educated amateurs will hereafter be able to feel upon hearing the work itself. Perhaps then someone will bring all of this together and into focus. If this does not happen, however, then at least our feelings, which are no longer indefinite and doubtful, will automatically lead to a satisfactory judgment, which will then gradually become general opinion and thus determine the status of the work of art, its influence in general, and its fate.

Consequently, in this essay the aesthetic aspects will certainly not be completely passed over, but inquiry will be made primarily into the technical and mechanical ones. The fact that the author will in the process deliver a series of individual observations and analyses that offer little to those who read only for entertainment, and will even seem dry to them, cannot be changed and lies in the nature of the thing. One must not always wish only to be entertained!

The symphony begins with an Allegro con brio in three quarter time in E♭ major. After the tonic triad has been powerfully sounded two times by the entire orchestra, the violoncello states, softly, but noticeably enough, the following simple principal subject, which hereafter is to be set up, turned around, and worked out from all sides:

OP. 55
Allegro con brio, mm. 3–4

Already in m. 7, where the diminished-seventh appears over C♯ in the bass, and in m. 9, where the $^6_4$ chord appears over D, the composer prepares the listener to be often agreeably deceived in the succession of harmonies. And even this preparatory deviation, where one expects to be led predictably to G minor but in place of the resolution of the $^6_4$ chord finds the fourth led upward to a fifth, and so, by means of the $^6_5$ chord, finds oneself unexpectedly back at home in E♭ major—even this is interesting and pleasing. In mm. 25ff. B. gives the idea a more striking and piquant effect by emphasizing the so-called weak beats, thereby appearing to bring about a duple meter (two-four time, as one can think of it to simplify its performance). The sharpness of this and similar, frequently occurring passages is extraordinarily impressive, particularly as they are to be played with the full force of the orchestra, and at once contrast very effectively with the gentler passages with which they are juxtaposed, which through this entire movement are just as new as they are beautiful, and are given primarily to the wind instruments.

In the second half of this movement, B. has masterfully worked out the principal idea, only briefly touched upon in the first part, in a careful and systematic way. As easy as it is to follow the composer's confident progress, however, this cannot be made visible without page-long examples, and thus the reviewer must be content here as well with isolated observations. It is, for example, completely surprising, thoroughly new and beautiful when, in the course of the second half, where the working-out of the previous ideas begins to become almost too much, a completely new melody, not previously heard, is suddenly taken up by the wind instruments and treated episodically [mm. 284ff.].[3] Not only are the sum total and variety of pleasing qualities thereby increased, but the listener is also refreshed enough to follow the composer gladly once again when he returns to the forsaken homeland, and clothes and develops the principal idea with even richer art. Only one passage need be excerpted here as showing a particularly good effect: that in which the wind instruments perform the principal idea canonically, while the basses emphatically and splendidly move against it in short notes:

OP. 55
Allegro con brio, mm. 338–42

An agreeable harmonic deception has already been mentioned above; the reviewer cannot resist mentioning a similar and even more successful one at the return of the principal idea. B. likewise begins here with the diminished-seventh chord on C♯, but this time moves not upward but downward to C and thus, by means of the seventh chord, arrives home unexpectedly and yet simply and naturally in F major. The progression of harmonies at both passages may be cited here, placed one below the other:

OP. 55
Allegro con brio, harmonic
reduction of mm. 6–10

OP. 55
Allegro con brio, harmonic
reduction of mm. 401–07

After the cadence in F, one horn now takes up the principal idea; the composer proceeds quickly and invasively into F minor and D♭ major, where the oboe once again takes up the same idea and carries it forward agreeably. The modulation from F to D♭ is as follows:

OP. 55
Allegro con brio, harmonic reduction
of mm. 414–16

The reviewer would have inserted the $\frac{6}{4}$ chord in the second measure thus:

OP. 55
Allegro con brio, m. 415

Also beautiful and with a very special effect is the place toward the end of this movement, where B. goes from E♭ to D♭ and C major and then, while the second violin plays the theme *pianissimo,* gives the following figure to the first violin:

OP. 55
Allegro con brio, mm. 567–71

Even from this little information, one can deduce that this Allegro, despite its length, is put together with a careful attention to unity that requires admiration. One can, however, also deduce that the abundance of ideas, as well as the artistic skill and the originality in their application, bring about an effect that is extremely rare in works of this kind, and that is often enough declared impossible by those who know this style only from afar or not at all. In order to have this effect, however, this Allegro, as likewise the entire work, certainly presupposes an audience that does not prefer a string of conventional little variations to everything else, because they hurry by nicely and one is over every few moments, but rather an audience that at least pays serious attention and can maintain its serious attentiveness. This can be taken for granted not only for this work but for every extensive and richly composed work of poetry or art.

This Allegro closes powerfully and splendidly and now follows a grand funeral march, in C minor, in two-four time, which the reviewer would like to declare without hesitation to be B's triumph, at least in regard to invention and design. It can perhaps be imagined that composers with talent, much education, and inexhaustible diligence could bring forth something that could be placed alongside works like the first movement. Pieces like this second movement, however, cannot be conceived, born, and raised with such perfection by any person without true *genius,* and every imitation, even the most skillful, which will assuredly not be lacking, will certainly not be able to be heard without recalling this original and its superiority. The entire piece is solemn and deeply gripping: the minore nobly plaintive and gloomy, and the majore soothing and lovely, where flute, oboe, and bassoon—to speak with Luther—seem to be leading a heavenly dance of tones with sweet melodies.[4]

Where B. repeats the theme, he goes into F minor and works out the passage masterfully and with great strictness in the noblest contrapuntal style [mm. 114ff.]. The beginning of this passage may be quoted here for the benefit of those disciples of art who believe that with a little excitement of a lively mind and with knowledge of instrumentation one needs nothing more than pen and ink in order to be profound—that everything will then come by itself by a direct route from heaven without any need for wearing out one's breeches sitting in a boring school.

OP. 55
Marcia funebre, mm. 114–20

Let us just simply inform these people that this passage, the beautiful effect of which they hopefully will not deny, is actually a double fugue in which the countersubject is stated in half notes.

The theme of the march comes up frequently in the course of what follows, but always with a new accompaniment. At the close of this movement, where the composer goes into A♭ major and the second violin begins alone, the listener will be reminded, though only briefly, of the beginning of a Haydn Andante in G major.[5] The close of the march is, however, as completely original as the beginning; it dies away like a hero. Fewer details may be excerpted here, since everything is so closely intertwined in a way that cannot be clarified through isolated examples. There is not even anything that can easily be praised in isolation; one must be able to enter into the whole and stay with it, or else calmly acknowledge: I am not up to this!

One observation concerning performance, however, must not be suppressed! If the entire funeral music is to come off properly, then every voice in the orchestra must enter into the idea itself with skill and the best intentions, at least so that, for example, the short notes are performed ostentatiously and solemnly, the sustained ones are given their full value and make an impression, and the most carefully measured contrasts of *forte, piano,* crescendo, and decrescendo are played precisely and *uniformly,* with regard for the degree of strength, weakness, rising up or falling off. Even for the most practiced orchestra this will only be possible if the movement is played through several times and all players adjust precisely to one another. Furthermore, because of the length and difficulty of all movements of this symphony, it is practically (even physically) impossible for the orchestra to perform everything in succession with equal energy and precision, or for the listener to follow everything with equal attention without some sort of respite. Since the *scherzo* that follows this march contrasts with it almost too sharply, and since surely every listener will want to let that sweet, melancholic feeling into which he has been placed at the end of the march fade away only gradually and not be torn from it all too suddenly, the reviewer finds it highly advisable that this march be followed, not perhaps by something else that is perhaps easier to grasp (may heaven protect every theater director from such an idea), but rather by a completely silent, solemn pause of a few minutes.[6]

The scherzo in three-four time that follows is a sort of companion piece to the one in Beethoven's Second Symphony, only a great deal stranger, more piquant, loftier, and also much longer. The tempo of the alla breve time that enters toward the end of this movement must be taken, as will quickly be seen, so that each half note lasts as long as an entire measure of the preceding and following three-four time [mm. 381–84]. The point where, in place of the previously occurring E♭, B♭ is taken up as the bass of the theme, so that it is supported by a $^6_4$ chord instead of by the root position triad, is striking [mm. 73–85]. B. probably did not realize, however, what a compliment he was paying thereby to soundness of method. This movement, for all the artistic passages it contains, is nevertheless more *ad hominem* than anything else, and that is even better. The reviewer would gladly cite some of the thoroughly original details in which it abounds if he did not have to think about saving space and did not have to be somewhat more detailed about the finale.

The theme of the finale, Allegro molto, has already been arranged once by B. for the keyboard,[7] and apparently he has diligently taken it up again in order to develop it more richly and grandly. It deserved this distinction. Except for a few variation themes of Haydn, the reviewer can think of none that is so well laid out, and used afterwards with such economy. Here it is:

OP. 55
Theme of Finale

After B. has let it be heard in various and at times striking, wonderful twists and combinations, he sets up the first four measures as a fugue theme, and, to be more precise, in this way:

OP. 55
Finale, mm. 117–25

He continues in this manner in strict style for about fifty measures and then returns to chordal writing once again in a more unusual manner, which excites the listener, modulating to D major as follows, and in the process has the flute brightly perform an idea that had previously accompanied the theme as a countersubject:

OP. 55
Finale, mm. 169–82 (the first three measures are an approximate harmonic reduction of mm. 169–74)

It is unfortunate, however, that the flute, which plays everything an octave higher, becomes extremely difficult to play in such a quick tempo if the player does not wish to sacrifice good intonation and proper performance. Not only this episode, but several other similar ones that follow, seemed to Beethoven (and to the reviewer) to be necessary, but they absolutely never distance themselves completely from the principal subject. Rather, the composer was usually able to weave those four first measures of the first theme into them very successfully and artistically. Thus, through piquant and yet comprehensible modulations into foreign keys, and through an excellent division among the various instruments (particularly through exquisite choice of the wind instruments), they give great and continually new charm to the whole. If many of these passages seem to be tossed off lightly and unrelated to the principal subject, they only seem so at *first glance*. Upon closer examination, the great richness of B's imagination is revealed as it again and again finds ways to let the principal theme, then the secondary subjects, glimmer through, now as an accompanying voice, now

OP. 55
Finale, mm. 227–30

as an obligatory bass line and so forth. Of many examples, only these two can be given here:

OP. 55
Finale, mm. 219–22

or:

As B. is now returning from these agreeable byways back to the main street, to the principal theme, he lets it begin in the second violin, in inversion, however—and has the first violin join in with a new, more lively counter-subject:

OP. 55
Finale, mm. 277–79

OP. 55
Finale, mm. 280–81

As the principal theme is then taken up by the bass, Beethoven, in a truly masterful way, lets this melody, already heard earlier and also singled out in these examples:

OP. 55
Finale, mm. 76–80

be played by the flutes, and then continued by the horns in this syncopated rhythm:

OP. 55
Finale, mm. 292–94

which creates an uncommonly beautiful and pleasant effect. At the organ point [mm. 328–48], however, he brings the theme back simply and doubled, diminished and inverted, whereupon, after a cadence on the dominant, the wind instruments now take up the melody just mentioned in slower motion, accompanied by a new bass line, and hence by a new and exquisite progression of harmonies. This Poco andante of over eighty measures makes a gentle, pleasant interruption (but in the reviewer's opinion, too long), which was certainly needed here (but just not so long). In order to make this interruption all the more accessible, the wind instruments are used in a particularly beautiful way and are arranged so that they form for the most part a so-called wind band among themselves, while the string instruments are almost constantly placed in contrast with them. Particularly distinguished are the places where first of all the bass, the bassoon, the clarinets, and the first horn state the theme as powerfully as possible, and the violins play lightly against them in triplets; and then where this modulation leads, ever more powerfully, from A♭ major to G minor:

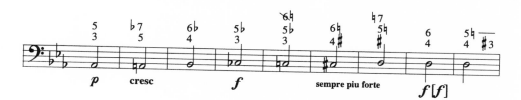

OP. 55
Finale, harmonic reduction of
mm. 409–19 (barlines indicate
changes of harmony, not
measures)

The entire finale concludes with a Presto, which begins with the final cadence of the Andante. At the beginning of this Presto, intentionally to be sure, a somewhat meager *unisonus* is taken up, and, in fact, in G minor, which admittedly sounds rather strange. However, after he is once again in the principal key, B. then remains in it until the conclusion of this short, brilliant, and very powerful final Presto. This conclusion itself once again combines all that a well-manned orchestra can give in terms of life, fullness, and energy. It is a true jubilation of all the instruments, which, as it does the listener, must grip, inspire, and carry away every member of the orchestra who is not as heavy as lead.

Incidentally, this finale is certainly once again long, very long; contrived, very contrived; indeed, several of its merits lie somewhat hidden. They presuppose a great deal if they are to be discovered and enjoyed, as they must be, in the very moment of their appearance, and not for the first time on paper afterwards. Much here is shrill and strange, but the reviewer is very far from criticizing this outright. Is this not also the case with any extremely rich painterly or poetic composition? Does it not also occur in music, for example in the greater works of the unceasingly (and, needless to say, most rightly) praised *Bachs?* To present such music *continually* to a mixed public would be unwise, indeed unfair; but to ignore it, or at least not to perform it publicly, would be even worse. As surely as the reproach of artificiality that is at times exaggerated, bizarrerie, affected difficulties of performance, etc. applies to Beethoven's *smaller* pieces, which either certainly say very little at all or at least say nothing that could not be said just as well or better in a simpler, more natural, more agreeable, lighter manner, so is it just for him to reject these reproaches here. In *such* a work the difficulties for the thoughtful listener or performing musician are almost always created by the thing itself. A conversation about commonplace things should not be obscure, difficult, and long; whoever demands, however, that the working-out of elevated, abstract subject matter be exhaustive and yet easy, graceful, and short, like that conversation, demands the impossible and does not himself, usually know exactly what he wants. This is not to say that there does not exist a *Nimium*[8] overall, and that Beethoven's genius does not, even in this work, show its peculiarity by at least touching on it so willingly. But the boundary *where* this Nimium (in *such* works, of course) begins can be determined, in regard to the mechanical and technical side, by nothing but the *impossibility* of proper performance, as this can be demonstrated by the nature of the instruments or of the hands. In regard to the artistic and aesthetic side, it can only be determined by the *genius himself,* who here as well is not limited by what is customary, but only (and may it happen here!) by the unalterable laws of mankind's aesthetic capability. And if he, the genius, is distinguished precisely by the willingness to expect more of this capability than is compatible with those laws, then he must bear that distinction in mind, so that he may be allowed to become a law unto himself and not simply scatter his creations out into the unknown.

Incidentally, as soon as this work is better known an abundance of reductions and arrangements will not fail to be made from it. The reviewer cannot prevent anyone from doing this, nor does he wish to do so; he simply wants to mention that, according to its nature, it cannot be reduced beyond the point where a full and *regular progression* of harmonies still remains possible. It has been reported to the editorship that Music Director Müller[9] has arranged it for two very accomplished players on one pianoforte with great care and precision, and in this form it was released several weeks ago by the Bureau de Musique in Leipzig.

The edition of the original version does honor to the publishers, for it will readily be grasped that financial gain could not have been their first priority. The engraving is clear and beautiful, but unfortunately not completely correct, which is all the more to be regretted with such a fully orchestrated, difficult, and learned work, since the mistakes are not always easy to discover and correct at the rehearsals, and the zeal of most directors will scarcely bring them to the point of consulting the handwritten score. For this reason, a catalog of at least the most significant printing errors may follow.

For the first violin, on p. 8 where the major key begins, there should be a repeat sign; also, on p. 10 a *forte* is missing at the next to last note of the March. Page 9, line 7, m. 1, the three sixteenth notes should not be F but G. Page 10, line 6, m. 3, a ♭ must appear before G. Page 12, line 2, m. 4, the second quarter note must be C and a *piano* must appear below it.

Violino II. Page 3, line 2, instead of a sharp, a flat must precede E. Page 5, line 1, a G and not an A flat must appear in the ninth and tenth measures. Page 5, line 2, m. 2, a sharp must appear before E instead of a flat. Page 6, line 13, m. 5, an F must appear in place of an A♭. Page 8, line 13, m. 7, a sharp must appear before the first note.

Viola. Page 5, line 7, m. 7, the next to the last eighth note must be F and not G.

Flauto I. Page 1, line 12, there must be five measures of rest instead of six. Page 6, line 10, the *forte* is missing at the conclusion of the repetition and at the end of the same line the last measure must be played twice.

Flauto II. Page 1, line. 9, five measures of rest must be played instead of six, and thus for all wind instruments with the exception of the second and third horns.

Clarinetto I. Page 4, line 4, m. 7, a sharp must appear before the first note. Page 6, line 4, the fermata is missing over the eighth note rest following the three measures of rest.

Fagotto I. Page 1, line 8, m. 2, a sharp must appear before A. Page 2, line 1, the first note must be G. Page 2, line 10, m. 1, a flat must not appear before C. Page 6, line 5, the third measure must be played twice.

Fagotto II. Page 2, line 2, m. 7, a flat must not appear before C. Page 4, line 2, m. 3, the first note must be E♭. Page 5, line 11, m. 3 must be *forte*.

Corno II. Page 1, line 9, these two measures must appear after the four measures of rest. Page 1, line 11, the eighth measure must be removed. Page 2, line 1, this measure must be inserted after the ninth measure. Page 2, line 14, this measure must be inserted after the ninth measure.

Page 4, the first thirty measures of the scherzo must not be repeated. Page 4, line 12, this measure must be inserted after the fifteenth measure.

Page 5, line 6, the number 1 must appear above the twelfth measure and the number 2 above the first measure of the following line and both numbers must indeed be bracketed 1 2. Page 6, line 2, in the sixth measure a dotted quarter note with a fermata must appear instead of the $\frac{3}{8}$.

NOTES

1. See entry no. 148 above.
2. See entry no. 120, vol. 1, p. 201.
3. As in vol. 1, the only editorial intrusions in the texts are the measure [mm.] notations. The "completely new melody" found at mm. 284ff. is a famous point of discussion about this symphony. It is actually closely related to the thematic material of the movement. See Robert Meikle, "Thematic Transformation in the First Movement of Beethoven's *Eroica* Symphony," *Music Review* 32 (1971): 205–18.
4. The Luther quotation may be a paraphrase of the following "tabletalk conversation" in which Luther praised the beauty of tenor *Lieder* compositions: "How strange and wonderful it is that one voice sings a simple unpretentious tune or tenor . . . while three, four, or five other voices are also sung: these voices play and sway in joyful exuberance around the tune and with every-varying art and tuneful sound wondrously adorn and beautify it, and in a celestial roundelay meet in friendly caress and lovely embrace" (*Luther and Music,* trans. and ed. Paul Nettl [Philadelphia: publisher, 1948], 15–16).
5. The reference is to the second movement of Haydn's Symphony No. 101, "Die Uhr" (The Clock), so-called because of the "tick-tock" accompaniment to the first subject of the second movement. The corresponding passage in Beethoven begins at m. 209.
6. The unprecedented length of the symphony and the contrasting affects of each movement presented new problems for audiences and concert organizers. Other suggestions or practices to alleviate these problems included performing only individual movements or breaking the symphony into parts (see entry no. 160).
7. The reviewer is referring to the Fifteen Variations in E♭, op. 35.
8. Latin: "a great deal."
9. August Eberhard Müller (1767–1817) was a well-known organist, pianist, and flutist, who lived in Leipzig from 1794 to 1810, holding the position of cantor of the Thomas Kirche from 1804. He was known for his four-hand arrangements. He published a number of pedagogical materials (including a 1796 guide to the correct performance of Mozart's piano concertos) and composed flute concertos and virtuosic piano works. See AMZ 19 (1817): 885–90.

Müller's four-hand piano arrangement of the *Eroica* was reprinted by Peters in Leipzig after 1814 and a new edition was prepared in 1835. See entry no. 152.

∽

150.

"News. Leipzig. Instrumental Music." *Allgemeine musikalische Zeitung* 9 (29 April 1807): 497–98.

Beethoven's grand *Eroica* Symphony (No. 3)—as he calls it himself—certainly makes up for a whole repository of new opera overtures and the like.

It has already been frequently discussed in these pages, recently in such an extensive review that practically nothing remains for us to add, apart from a few comments on the performance and on its reception by the local public. Such a work as this requires some special preparation on the part of the orchestra, as well as several precautions with regard to a mixed public, if it is to be given its due in terms of performance and reception, and in neither was it slighted in any way here. The audience had been made attentive and, as far as possible, prepared to expect exactly what it was offered, not only by means of a special announcement on the customary concert program, but also by a short characterization of each movement, particularly in regard to the composer's intended effect upon the feelings.[1] In both regards, the purpose was achieved completely. The most educated friends of art in the city were assembled in great numbers, a truly solemn attentiveness and deathlike silence reigned and was sustained not only throughout the whole (as is well-known, nearly hour-long) first performance, but also during the second and third, which, upon diverse requests, followed within a few weeks. Each movement unmistakably had the effect that it should have, and each time at the end of the entire piece loud demonstrations of applause gave vent to well-founded enthusiasm. The orchestra had voluntarily gathered for extra rehearsals without recompense, except for the honor and special enjoyment of the work itself. At these rehearsals the symphony was available in score, so that even the slightest triviality would not escape observation, and overall the players would penetrate the meaning and purpose of the composer with greater certainty.[2] And so this most difficult of all symphonies (if, that is, one does not wish simply to play the notes correctly) was performed not only with the greatest accuracy and precision, but also everywhere with congruence and consistency, with grace, neatness and delicacy, and with an accommodation of the specially combined instruments to each other. In short, it was performed just as anyone could wish who had studied the score, even the ingenious composer himself. After this study, and after hearing the work repeatedly at rehearsals and public performances, we would simply like to add to this that the first, fiery, magnificent Allegro, in its astounding many-sidedness within the greatest unity, in its clarity and purity within the most extensive complications, and in its irresistible enchantment throughout its great length, has become and remained our favorite of all the movements. It would seem to us an irreparable loss if Beethoven, through circumstances, caprice or whatever, should be prevented from writing more works exactly in this form, and in this manner, which he himself has created. Finally, for that very reason we recently read with great satisfaction the report from our correspondent in Vienna, that a distinguished, venerable, well-intentioned and very educated society has come together in that imperial city in order to support this original spirit of higher art and to procure the proper influence for his instrumental compositions.[3] May we also, through this announcement, contribute to that! At the very least it has arisen from a firm and calm conviction upon which no considerations of any kind have had the slightest effect, just as we have already frequently stated in regard to this genre of works by B.

NOTES

1. The short characterizations of each movement were republished in Alfred Dörffel, *Geschichte der Gewandhausconcerte zu Leipzig vom 25.November 1781 bis 25.November 1881* (Leipzig: Breitkopf & Härtel, 1884): "Grosse, heroische Sinfonie, compon. von Beethoven, und zum erstenmale in Leipzig aufgeführt: (1) feuriges, prachtvolles Allegro; (2) erhabener, feyerlicher Trauermarsch; (3) heftiges Scherzando; (4) grosses Finale, zum Theil im strengen Styl" (Grand, heroic symphony, composed by Beethoven, and performed for the first time in Leipzig: [1] fiery, splendid Allegro; [2] lofty, solemn funeral march; [3] vehement scherzando; [4] grand finale in part in the strict style).

2. At this time it was still common for orchestral music to be performed without a conductor in the modern sense; the direction was undertaken by the first violinist and/or by the continuo player, who had only their own parts before them. The writer here refers to a copyist's score of the symphony prepared from the printed parts. Score publication was still a rarity; see entry nos. 97 and 116, vol. 1. The *Eroica* was not published in score until 1809, when it was issued in London by Cianchettini and Sperati (Kinsky-Halm, 130). Compare the reviewer's comments at the conclusion of entry no. 149, above.

3. The writer refers here to the concert organization known as the "Musikalisches Institut," "Liebhaber Concerte," "Musikfreunde," or "Gesellschaft der Musikfreunde," which presented twenty concerts in the 1807–08 season (see Morrow, *Concert Life in Haydn's Vienna*, 62–63).

～

151.
"News. Prague." *Allgemeine musikalische Zeitung* 9 (17 June 1807): 610.

Beethoven's *Eroica* Symphony excited our interest; finally we heard the colossal work. I can express no judgment upon this work in a few lines, and many would be out of place in a notice like this one. Therefore let it suffice to recount here, in regard to this product of an artist who is called the musical Jean Paul,[1] this product in which, scorning all fetters, he expressed himself with all the depth and genius of his soul, what an impression it made upon a not uneducated circle of listeners. The first Allegro pleased greatly and was generally recognized as magnificent. The funeral march seemed to many to be too long. The scherzo received general, enthusiastic approval. (The originality and power, together with the pleasing and popular tone that B. bestowed upon it, overcame everything and raised the approval to the point of enthusiasm.) The finale pleased less, and it seemed to me that here the artist often wanted only to play games with the audience without taking its enjoyment into account simply in order to unloose a strange mood and, at the same time, to let his originality sparkle thereby. The performance was exemplary; the tempos were particularly well chosen.

1. On the many comparisons to be found in these reviews between Beethoven and Jean Paul, see, for example, entry no. 24, vol. 1, p. 51.

~

152.
M . . . s. *Zeitung für die elegante Welt* 8 (1807): 276–77.

(Arrangement for piano four-hands by August Eberhard Müller)[1]

(Mentioned: *Prometheus* Variations, op. 35)

This grand, rich composition was recently performed twice as an orchestral symphony in Leipzig with extraordinary effect and has already aroused astonishment in other great cities. It belongs among those few symphonies that, with their spirited energy, set the listener's imagination into a sublime flight and sweep his heart away to powerful emotions. But the connoisseur will only enjoy it as a complete work (and a repeated hearing doubles his spiritual enjoyment) the deeper he penetrates into the technical and aesthetic content of the original work. This symphony is in E♭ major and consists of four movements, the last of which contains the theme in E♭ major upon which Beethoven has already written such striking variations. Since there are so few orchestras complete and accomplished enough to perform such a difficult work suitably, and since even when one has heard it so performed, it is still very interesting to repeat this music to oneself on a good fortepiano, we will be grateful to the publisher and to Music Director Müller for having provided such a complete keyboard reduction so well suited to the instrument, as one could expect from the insights and talents of Mr. M. on the basis of other similar works. The list of distinguished compositions for four hands is not extensive, and accomplished keyboard players will find rewarding work here.

NOTE

1. This arrangement is also praised at the end of entry no. 149.

~

153.
"On Permanent Concerts in Leipzig during the Previous Semiannual Winter Season." *Journal des Luxus und der Moden* 23 (1807): 444.

Of new productions in this genre we heard a symphony by *Gyrowetz*[1] in D major, of brilliant effect, two by *Friedrich Schneider*[2] in Leipzig, which demonstrate much talent and fire, and finally, above all others, *Beethoven's* new grand *Eroica* Symphony, the greatest, most original, most artistic and, at the same time, most interesting of all symphonies. It is a product that will remain an eternal monument to the outstanding genius, the rich imagination, the deep feeling, and the highly developed art of its composer. Indeed, one could offer it as a high ideal of this genre without thereby doing an injustice to the excellent symphonies of *Mozart* and *Haydn,* and without forgetting that this ingenious and grand work of art would itself not exist as it is now if these wonderful earlier symphonies (including Beethoven's earlier ones) had not led the way.[3]

NOTES

1. Adalbert Gyrowetz (1763–1850) was a Bohemian composer and opera conductor in Vienna. Gyrowetz was known for his association with Haydn, whose style he continued to cultivate long after it went out of fashion. He took an active part in the arrangements for Beethoven's funeral.

2. Johann Christian Friedrich Schneider (1786–1853) was the foremost member of a family of musicians, a teacher, and a composer of a large number of oratorios. He is also credited with giving the first performance of Beethoven's "Emperor" Concerto, op. 73. A report on this performance appeared in AMZ 14 (1812), 8.

3. "Whoever wishes to read more about this symphony will be able to instruct himself sufficiently with the thorough, brilliant review in the twenty-first [issue] number of the AMZ from 1807, where this work of art is examined particularly from the technical point of view" (see entry no. 149, above).

~

154.
"News. Vienna." *Allgemeine musikalische Zeitung* 10 (6 January 1808): 239.

(With *Coriolan* Overture, op. 62)

Even more difficult is the grand Beethoven Symphony in E♭,[1] which, conducted by the composer himself, received much approval.[2] The reviewer must, despite all that has been written about this work of art, remain true to the opinion, which he expressed concerning the first performance, that this symphony certainly contains much that is sublime and also beautiful, but that this is also mixed with much that is harsh and all too ample, and could only obtain the pure form of a finished work of art through a rearrangement. A new overture by this composer (who is supposed to become engaged for the theater under very advantageous conditions)[3] is full of power and fire; it was designated as being intended for Collin's *Coriolan.*

NOTES

1. The Mozart G-Minor Symphony, K. 550, had just been discussed.

2. According to Mary Sue Morrow, this review refers to the *Liebhaber* concert of 6 December 1807 (see her *Concert Life in Haydn's Vienna,* 345).

3. This report is cited in Thayer-Forbes, 426, where the reference made here is connected with a petition made by Beethoven, probably in late 1807, to the new management of the Imperial Royal Court Theater. The composer proposed to write an opera every year for 2400 florins plus the receipts of the third performance. Despite this optimistic prediction, his proposal was not accepted.

~

155.

"Brief Notice." *Allgemeine musikalische Zeitung* 10 (10 February 1808): 320.

(Arrangement for piano quartet)[1]

This well-known work, extensively evaluated earlier in these pages, is arranged here with diligence. Even in this form it has as much and as good an effect as is possible for pieces that depend so much on the unique effect of all the instruments, particularly that of the wind instruments in opposition to the strings. All four players must be rather accomplished in order to perform this quartet properly. The engraving is clear and good.

NOTE

1. The arrangement for string and piano quartet was published by Bureau d'Arts et d'Industrie in Vienna; the arrangement was announced in the WZ on 20 April 1807 (see Kinsky-Halm, 130).

~

156.

"News. Vienna." *Allgemeine musikalische Zeitung* 12 (7 February 1810): 295–96.

On 8 September a concert in two parts was given at the Theater-an-der-Wien for the benefit of the theater's fund for the poor. The following pieces were performed. The first part opened with the grand *Eroica* Symphony by L. van Beethoven, No. 3 (E♭ major).[1] It would be superfluous here to say anything about the value of this artistically rich and colossal work, since not only has it already been discussed several times in these pages, but the entire work was thoroughly analyzed and appropriately evaluated in the ninth volume, no. 21, of this *musikalische Zeitung;* indeed, even the technical and mechanical aspects of it were examined and clarified. I will confine myself to the performance alone, which, even though the work is extremely long and seemingly ought to fatigue both artists and listeners, nevertheless came across so well that it was possible to obtain great enjoyment from it.

NOTE

1. Other works on the benefit concert included selections from Mozart's *La villanella rapita,* a violin concerto by Clement, Cherubini's Overture to *Anacréon,* a Nasolini aria, and the "Hallelujah Chorus" from Handel's *Messiah* (Morrow, *Concert Life in Haydn's Vienna,* 357).

~

157.
"Leipzig." *Allgemeine musikalische Zeitung* 13 (23 January 1811): 66.

Twelfth concert. . . . The second half was filled by Beethoven's grand, ingenious work, the *Sinfonia eroica,* to the lively satisfaction of the extremely numerous listeners, who listened with heightened attention until the final chord. It was performed by the orchestra with unmistakable enjoyment and love, with as much precision and fire, and yet also with as much delicacy as it demands if, with its length of fifty minutes, it is to bring about such an effect upon a mixed public.

~

158.
K. B. "Miscellaneous." *Allgemeine musikalische Zeitung* 16 (30 November 1814): 811.

5.
The grave is deep and still
and horrible its brink! etc.[1]

Who has not felt the truth of these words of the poet already in their life? Does not the departure of every citizen of this earth from the "friendly familiarity of being and doing" have in itself something that deeply affects the serious observer? How much more moving is it, then, when an elevated, magnificent spirit departs forever from our midst? In a situation such as this, one should listen to the funeral march from Beethoven's *Eroica* Symphony and sense its effect!—Certainly, a magnificent person is here being led to the grave; these tones tell us so in the clearest possible way. All the pain and all the joys of his earthly life resound once again in our breast, deep and sweet, but only as the gentle voice of an echo, for already they are gone by, and have now fled irretrievably! Assuredly, the departed one now walks in the kingdom of clarity and light—refreshingly soothing melodies tell us this in the language of heaven perceptibly enough—but we remain abandoned at the grave and look up toward that kingdom's nocturnal womb. Life has lost meaning for us; we feel alone; each sensation gradually perishes in the feeling of an interminable longing, and only with terrible resignation can we at last tear ourselves from this place in order to plunge into life's rushing stream and at least to drink forgetfulness from this Lethe![2]

NOTES

1. The quotation represents the first two lines of the poem "Das Grab" (The Grave) by Johann Gaudenz von Salis-Seewis (1762–1834). Although an offspring of Swiss nobility of considerable lineage, Salis-Seewis sympathized with the beginnings of the French Revolution, but soon became disillusioned, took leave from the Swiss guard stationed in France, and returned to public life. He published only poetry, which shows elements of sentimentality and classicism. "Das Grab" was set to music by Reichardt, Zumsteeg, Schubert, and several other composers. See Lawrence Snyder, *German Poetry in Song: An Index of Lieder* (Berkeley and Los Angeles: Fallen Leaf Press, 1995). The quotations within the text are from the same poem.

2. In Greek and Latin mythology, Lethe is the plain or river of oblivion. Dead souls drink of the river before reincarnation, so that they will forget their past lives.

∾

159.

"News, Munich." *Allgemeine musikalische Zeitung* 17 (25 January 1815): 63.

The first concert opened with the *Eroica* Symphony of Beethoven. It had a grand, sublime effect. We are ever more amazed by the creative power of this great composer. Even the dilettante is ever more drawn into its moods, which to be sure are often strange.

∾

160.

"News. Kassel." *Allgemeine musikalische Zeitung* 18 (30 October 1816): 754.

Second concert. *Eroica* Symphony by Beethoven. This ingenious work was very well performed; it was simply found to be too long, even though the last movement was not given until the conclusion of the first part of the program.

~

161.
"News. Berlin." *Berliner allgemeine musikalische Zeitung* 1 (4 February 1824): 41.

The royal general music directorship is to be thanked for the great satisfaction given by the magnificent *Eroica* Symphony of Beethoven, performed with the utmost precision at the concert that it organized on 19 January. The audience, small in number but thoroughly sensitive to art, took up this rare gift with the greatest of thanks, which could be recognized in the loudest possible applause accorded to the creator of these harmonies and to the royal orchestra, which surged forward with genuine inspiration and repeated particularly in regard to the most ingenious scherzo or rondo, throughout which the melody "Was ich des Tags mit der Leyer verdien' "[1] is ingeniously woven.

NOTE

1. The title of this song translates "That which I earn with the hurdy-gurdy during the day." A. B. Marx, who edited the BAMZ and probably wrote this report, also mentions the resemblance of Beethoven's scherzo theme to this old soldier's song in his biography of the composer.

~

162.
"Review." *Berliner allgemeine musikalische Zeitung* 1 (5 May 1824): 163–64.

(With Symphony No. 5, op. 67; Symphony No. 7, op. 92)

The most brilliant part of the concert was made up solely of: *Beethoven's Eroica Symphony,* which was well performed by Concertmaster Möser[1] and a suitable orchestra.

Mr. Möser—whose reputation as a virtuoso sufficed to assemble a sizeable audience, to whom his own person, in his connection with other virtuosos and in accordance with his official position, provides sufficient means for entertainment in the virtuoso style, yet tasteful within that sphere—Mr. Möser nevertheless saw fit to prepare for his listeners a noble enjoyment, and proved in this way that he stands far higher than the most distinguished virtuosos, who only have an understanding of their technique and their concerts. He has revealed himself, through his choice and successful performance of the *Eroica,* as a connoisseur and friend of the highest form of instrumental compositions. As rare as complete performances of symphonies have been until now in Berlin, so much more is it to Mr. Möser's credit to have given such a fine example to his esteemed colleagues. We wish to see now who will be the first to follow him and pay honor to these compositions, which can be called the exclusive property of the German people, and to their greatest of composers. The C Minor,[2] and above all the A-Major Symphony,[3] remain as worthy companion pieces to the *Eroica*. The last, in particular, has been taken up in Vienna with unceasing enthusiasm and has become the delight of all friends of music who have heard it, who have only seen its score, or who have played through it at the pianoforte. Written in a flight of inspiration, it is second to none in depth and exceeds all others in clarity, and would be well suited to open up these new spheres of musical art that abound in Berlin to all those who have only a receptivity to music, and to disclose a shining proof of the splendor and riches of Beethoven's genius.

The orchestra performed extremely well. Its and Mr. Möser's exertions were acknowledged by the most lively applause, which broke out after each individual movement. It was thus demonstrated as well, that the public is receptive to great works (and will assuredly become ever more so) if they are simply not deprived of them.

Something on Beethoven and his symphonies will follow.

NOTES

1. Karl Möser (1774–1851) studied music in Berlin under the concertmaster Karl Haack and became a leading figure in Berlin's music life with his frequent chamber music soirées. He directed a number of premieres of Beethoven's music, including the first Berlin performance of the Ninth Symphony in 1826.
2. The Fifth Symphony.
3. The Seventh Symphony.

≈

163.
12.[1] *Allgemeiner musikalischer Anzeiger* (Vienna) 1 (1829): 199.

(Arrangement for piano quartet)[2]

The copy of a giant tableau; a colossal statue on a reduced scale; Caesar's portrait shrunk by the pantograph;[3] an antique bust of Carraran marble[4] made over as a plaster cast.—One is readily satisfied, however, with a half-accurate silhouette when one cannot have the original. Then fantasy begins its sweet play, and all the world certainly knows the beneficial effects of the powers of imagination and recollection.

NOTES

1. The number 12 refers to an unknown author and is perhaps an editorial code to conceal his identity.

2. The piano quartet arrangement of the *Eroica*, first published in 1807, was reprinted in Vienna by Tobias Haslinger in 1828, probably occasioning this review (see Kinsky-Halm, 130).

3. A pantograph was an instrument for copying on a predetermined scale. Consisting of four light bars connected in a parallelogram form, one end was used to pass over the lines to be copied while the other end contained marking instruments that made the copy.

4. "Carrarischer Marmor" refers to the famous white marble quarried in the vicinity of Carrara in Northern Italy.

~

OP. 56
TRIPLE CONCERTO FOR PIANO, VIOLIN, AND CELLO IN C MAJOR

164.
M . . . s. *Zeitung für die elegante Welt* 8 (1808): 337.

(Arrangement for piano four-hands by August Eberhard Müller)[1]

Among the most recent pieces for four hands, *Beethoven's* grand Polonaise, which appeared under the title *Polonaise concertante à quatre mains pour le Pianoforte par L. v. Beethoven Tiré de l'oeuvre 56* (price twenty groschen), is certain to receive the greatest approval. What ingratiating melody! what sweet, surprising transitions! what an artistic, and yet always charming and interesting treatment and working-out of the ideas! But it would be superfluous to say anything to recommend the most beautiful works of this genius. Only this about this composition: it demands an instrument of expanded compass and performers who are initiated into Beethoven's manner, but it is still perfectly in accordance with the nature of the pianoforte.[2]

NOTES

1. This arrangement by August Eberhard Müller was published by Kühnel's Bureau de Musique in Leipzig in 1808 and consists only of the third movement. Beethoven himself called attention to the polonaise character of this movement by designating it "Rondo alla Polacca." Several subsequent arrangements for piano, both four and two hands, testify to the popularity of this movement, which seems to have quickly outstripped the rest of the concerto in this respect.

2. Because the range of the Viennese and French fortepianos gradually increased during the first decades of the nineteenth century, potential buyers of piano music had to be warned if the music exceeded the earlier five-octave range. For a general discussion of

these changes, see Michael Coles, *The Pianoforte in the Classical Era* (Oxford: Clarendon Press, 1998), 272–80 and plate 11; for the ranges used in Beethoven's piano music, see William S. Newman, "The Range of Beethoven's Pianos," *Beethoven on Beethoven* (New York: Norton, 1988), 57–62. As early as 1803, Beethoven owned an Erard piano with c^4 as its highest tone.

~

165.
"News. Concert in Leipzig. New Year's through Easter. Instrumental Music." *Allgemeine musikalische Zeitung* 10 (17 April 1808): 490–91.

Of the *concertos* and other *solos* heard this quarter, we find the following particularly worthy of being singled out. *Beethoven's* grand Concerto for Pianoforte, Violin, and Violoncello, accompanied by a lavish orchestra; the solo parts played by Mrs. *Müller,* Mr. *Matthäi,* and Mr. *Dozzauer.*[1] In our judgment, and not just in terms of time, this concerto is the last of those by Beethoven in print. In it the composer has loosed the reins of his rich imagination, all too ready to luxuriate exuberantly in its richness, as he has scarcely yet done anywhere else. The work contains such an overflowing mass of figures, and certainly—particularly in the overburdened first movement—of such disparate figures. Beethoven indulges himself here once again—likewise particularly in the first movement—with such learned, scarcely playable and at times even ineffectual difficulties, and also once again with so many of his intricate, bizarre juxtapositions, that overall one might have to feel it as a burden to follow him adequately. So it would be, if one were not also once again surprised by just as many spots that are as well conceived as they are beautiful; if one were not compensated by the far less overburdened third movement, completely new and full of spirit and expression, and thus reconciled as far as possible to the whole. As well as the concerto was played and accompanied, as thoroughly as the public here has been won over to Beethoven's compositions, this one pleased only moderately.

NOTE

1. Elisabeth Catherina Müller (Theodore Albrecht gives her first name as Maria; see *Letters to Beethoven and Other Correspondence,* 3 vols. [Lincoln: University of Nebraska Press, 1996], I, 137, n. 5) was the wife of August Eberhard Müller (1767–1817) (see n. 9 in entry no. 149 above), who, before becoming organist at the Ulrichskirche in Magdeburg in 1789, had married the daughter of his predecessor. She was an accomplished pianist, and they gave many performances together. She was organist in the Ulrichskirche in Magdeburg and performed regularly as pianist for Mozart concertos in the Gewandhaus in Leipzig.

Heinrich August Matthäi (1781–1835) (*New Grove,* 10: 639 gives his first name as Karl) was a prominent violinist in Leipzig; he later became concertmaster of the Gewandhaus orchestra and held that position until his death. He also founded the Gewandhaus Quartet from among the orchestra's leading string players.

Justus Johann Friedrich Dotzauer (1783–1860) was one of the foremost cellists of his generation. He lived in Leipzig and played in the Gewandhaus orchestra from 1805 to 1811. His technical studies are still widely used by cello students.

~

166.
"News. Leipzig." *Allgemeine musikalische Zeitung* 11 (28 December 1808): 204.

Mrs. Müller, together with Mssrs. Matthäi and Dotzauer, also gave a repetition of Beethoven's grand Concerto for Pianoforte, Violin, and Violoncello, which was much more successful than the first production of this extremely difficult work last year—at which time we discussed it at greater length.

~

167.
"News. Leipzig." *Allgemeine musikalische Zeitung* 22 (17 May 1820): 346.

Then Mrs. Neumann-Sessi sang a less than excellent aria from *Sofonisba* by Paer;[1] whereupon followed Beethoven's Concerto for Pianoforte, Violin, and Violoncello, with accompaniment of a large orchestra. So far as we can recall, this work has not been performed here before.[2] It is, however, not one of this master's best compositions. The polonaise-like finale pleased the most and was also the best performed.

NOTES

1. Anna Maria Sessi (1790–1864), Neumann-Sessi after her marriage, was a prominent Italian-born singer active in the German-speaking countries in the 1810s and early 1820s. Her first name is sometimes given as Marianna or Mariane, apparently in confusion with her sister, Marianna Sessi-Natorp (1776–1847), also a well-known singer. She was active at the Imperial Royal Hofoperntheater in Vienna for several years, but later her activities were centered in Leipzig. She interpreted several Mozart roles with great success, including Donna Anna in *Don Giovanni* and the Countess in *Figaro.* Her singing appears to have been universally admired. The aria in question was probably "Io saprei con alma forte" from Paer's *Sofonisba,* which the AMZ describes her as performing elsewhere in concert.

See AMZ 15 (1813), 771; 18 (1816), 8, 93, 122, 513; 19 (1817): 159–60. A biographical sketch appears in Kutsch and Riemens, *Großes Sängerlexikon*, 2729.

Fernando Paer (1771–1839) was particularly well known for his operas. He worked in Vienna from 1797 to 1802 and became concertmaster at Dresden in 1802 where he composed *Leonore, ossia l'amore conjugale*, based on the same plot Beethoven later used in *Fidelio*. A copy of Paer's score was found among Beethoven's papers.

2. The writer was mistaken; see the previous entry nos. 165–66.

$\sim$

OP. 57
PIANO SONATA IN F MINOR ("APPASSIONATA")

(See entry no. 29, vol. 1, p. 59)

168.
"Review." *Allgemeine musikalische Zeitung* 9 (1 April 1807): 433–36.

(Mentioned: Piano Sonata op. 27, no. 2)

Everyone knows how B. customarily treats the grand sonata; and always, though with the greatest variety in regard to details, B. remains on the whole more or less true to his custom.[1] In the first movement of this sonata (fifteen pages in $\frac{12}{8}$ time)[2] he has once again let loose many evil spirits, such as are already familiar from other grand sonatas of his. In truth, however, it is here worth the effort to struggle not only with the wicked difficulties, but also with many a sudden impulse of indignation over learned peculiarities and bizarreries! These oddities of the master's fancy have been discussed so often, however, that the reviewer does not wish to say another word more about them. He will only remark that precisely for that reason he also can say nothing about the details of this entire long movement, because almost everything is saturated by these oddities. It goes without saying that it also is not lacking in spots where one cannot mistake the great artist. Furthermore, whoever can perform this Allegro completely as it needs to be played deserves true respect as a keyboard player!

Many people will probably smile when the reviewer admits that the very simple movement that follows, only three pages long, is more pleasing to his feelings, as well as to his understanding—although admittedly far more art and learning were required to write the former than the latter! This second movement is a very short Andante con moto with variations. One should take note here of the extremely unpretentious, beautiful, noble theme, all of which can even be fit onto one line:

OP. 57
Andante con moto, mm. 1–16

That cannot really even be called a melody? Is it nothing but a succession of chords that are extremely closely related to one another? Does it appear to be nothing at all? Amazingly enough, the reviewer agrees with you! He does not deceive you, though, by saying that in music (as in morality) nothing is less important than "appearing to be something." In return, do him the favor of going to your good pianoforte and playing through this unassuming line in a way that is attractively significant, devoid of all harshness, with the tones appropriately joined together, solemn, swelling, and diminishing, and let thereby everything pretty sound forth for as long as it should. If you do not then feel that music like this little theme and the variations that (but for one) *completely* resemble it, worked out almost entirely in varied settings, with syncopated notes or broken chords, if you do not feel, I say, that such music goes from heart to heart, then—one of us does not have one![3]

The magnificently worked out, characteristic finale is written just as soulfully, but at the same time with great power, solid artistry and masterful confidence. Here is to be found none of the minced, forced quality that is displayed by several other finales by B. of comparable vitality and strength. This Allegro resembles, both in regard to invention and treatment (and also approximately in character), the excellent Allegro in C♯ minor in B's Fantasy in that key.[4] Only a single time does the composer seem to the reviewer to have broken with the seriousness of this character and the austerity of this manner of writing: on p. 21, second system and following, up to the point where he comes back around to the theme.[5] Transitions and passages of filler like this one, which contain not much more than nothing, though certainly cast into the semblance of a form, must certainly be conceded even a great master in free improvisation, but he should not write them down in such highly important pieces. The surprising inversion (though by no means snatched out of the air) that Beethoven himself sets into on p. 24 (Presto) is as new as it is agreeable.[6] This entire finale, although it is by no means easy, is nevertheless not nearly as difficult to play as the first movement—as always, that which is designed in a natural way and worked out according to the principles of art is easier for the accomplished player than that which—well—that which is not so!

Incidentally, this entire sonata extends the range of the pianoforte, and very frequently, up to three octaves above middle C, without the passages that go above the G below that being transcribed, or even being easy to transcribe.[7]

Yet one more small detail! In keyboard music, as elsewhere, *writing out* of the highest notes should be avoided, and things should be arranged in the way that is customarily used to accommodate for lack of space: the passages should be written an octave lower and marked with an 8. It goes without saying that whoever plays *such* music does not see the notes individually, but rather glances in an instant over a whole succession of them: from time to time, however, particularly in those passages that do not retain the same figuration throughout, even the most practiced player will be blinded by the many ledger lines and hesitate uncertainly, until he has had a chance to study the matter further.[8]

NOTES

1. Beethoven divided his piano sonatas with opus numbers into "grand sonatas" and sonatas. The sonatas described on the title pages of the first editions as "Grande Sonate" are ops. 7, 13, 22, 26, 28, 53, and 106. Opus 57 is not, however, described as a "Grande Sonate" on its title page.

2. The reviewer is referring to the original edition, published by the Bureau d'Arts et d'Industrie in Vienna, on whose title page the work is identified both as LIVme Sonata and as op. 57.

On the number 54, which appears on the title page, see Hans-Werner Küthen, "Pragmatic Instead of Enigmatic: 'The Fifty-First Sonata' of Beethoven," *Beethoven Newsletter* 7 (1992): 68–73.

3. The aesthetic goal that music should come from the heart of the composer and move the heart of the listener is discussed in performance practice treatises of the Classical period. See, for instance, Daniel Gottlob Türk, *School of Clavier Playing,* trans. Raymond Haggh (Lincoln: University of Nebraska, 1982), 337. Beethoven himself inscribed the autograph of the Kyrie of the *Missa solemnis* with the notation "Von Herzen—Möge es wieder zu Herzen gehen."

4. This is a reference to the finale of the "Moonlight" Sonata, op. 27, no. 2, which is described on the title page of the first edition as "Sonata quasi una Fantasia."

5. The second system of p. 21 of the first edition begins with m. 167 (the *fortissimo* reiterated Cs in the right hand over an Alberti dominant pedal) and continues through the recapitulation at m. 212.

6. This refers to the final Presto beginning at m. 308. This is not, strictly speaking, an inversion of the theme, but it is a striking conclusion that, as the reviewer notes, is closely related to the rest of the movement.

7. As the range of the piano was being constantly extended during this time, this was a warning to those who owned older instruments with smaller ranges that this sonata would be impossible to play without making drastic rearrangements of those passages that exploit the high end of the keyboard. Beethoven's accommodation to the smaller range of contemporary instruments can be seen elsewhere in his keyboard works, for example in op. 31, no. 3, movt. II, m. 54.

8. The reviewer is referring to passages like those at m. 60, m. 87, mm. 226–27 of the first movement, m. 79 of the second movement, and mm. 264–69 and mm. 341–54 of the third movement. Modern editors, for example, Artur Schnabel, have sometimes used octave markings for these passages.

~

OP. 58
PIANO CONCERTO NO. IN G MAJOR

169.
"News. Vienna." *Allgemeine musikalische
Zeitung* 11 (25 January 1809): 267–69.

(With scene and aria *Ah! perfido,* op. 65; Symphony No. 5, op. 67; Symphony No. 6
Pastoral, op. 68; Fantasy for Piano, Chorus, and Orchestra, op. 80; and Mass, op. 86)

Among the musical performances, which were given in the theaters during Christmas week, that which Beethoven gave on 22 December at the Theater-an-der-Wien is incontestably the most noteworthy.[1] It included only pieces of his composition, and new ones at that, which had not yet been heard publicly and for the most part have also not yet been printed. The order in which they followed one another was the following. (I am intentionally quoting the exact words of the program.)

FIRST PART

I. Pastoral Symphony (No. 5)[2] more expression of feelings than tone painting.
First movement. Pleasant feelings, which are awakened in people upon arriving in the countryside.
Second movement. Scene by the brook.
Third movement. Joyful togetherness of the country people: leads to

Fourth movement. Thunder and storm; which leads to
Fifth movement. Beneficent thoughts after the storm, joined together with
    thanks to divinity.
II. Aria, sung by Miss Killitzky.[3]
III. Hymn with Latin text, written in the sacred style, with chorus and solos.[4]
IV. Keyboard Concerto written by himself (Industrie-Comptoir.)[5]

SECOND PART

I. Grand Symphony in C Minor (No. 6.).
II. Sanctus, with Latin text, written in the sacred style, with chorus and
    solos.[6]
III. Fantasy at the keyboard, alone.[7]
IV. Fantasy at the keyboard, which concludes after a time with the entry of
    the orchestra, and then with the choir joining in as a finale.[8]

It is all but impossible to pronounce judgment upon all of these works
after a single first hearing, particularly since we are dealing with works of
Beethoven, so many of which were performed one after another, and which
were mostly so grand and long. However, I will refrain even more from
making such short, insignificant observations as might be permitted, since
we hope that you will soon hear all of this for yourself, and will impart a
thorough judgment about them to the readers of the *musikalische Zeitung*;
for several of these pieces have already been engraved, and various others will
soon be engraved. In regard to the performances at this concert, however, the
concert must be called unsatisfactory in every respect. Demoiselle Killitzky
certainly has a very agreeable voice, but she nevertheless sang very few notes
in tune and more often she actually sang wrong notes. This seemed, however,
to result from timidity, which will probably be overcome with time. Most
striking, however, was the slip that took place during the final fantasy [mm.
90ff.].[9] The wind instruments were playing variations on the theme that
Beethoven had previously stated on the pianoforte. Now it was the oboes'
turn. The clarinets—if I am not mistaken!—miscount, and enter at the same
time. A curious mixture of tones arises; Beethoven leaps up, tries to silence
the clarinets; but he no sooner succeeds in this than he very loudly and
somewhat angrily calls out to the entire orchestra: "Quiet, quiet, this is not
working! Once again—once again!" And the orchestra so praised must be
satisfied with starting the bungled fantasy over again.

NOTES

1. The performance described here is one of Beethoven's best-known public appearances. The circumstances surrounding the concert and the sometimes contradictory reports
of what happened there are summarized in Thayer-Forbes, 445–49.

2. Beethoven apparently allowed the Fifth and Sixth Symphonies to be "misnumbered" on this program, although when they were published the following year as ops. 67 and 68, the C-Minor Symphony was clearly numbered "No. 5" and the Pastoral Symphony "No. 6." The familiar designation corresponds to the order of composition; although Beethoven worked on both symphonies simultaneously for a while in 1807–08, the C minor was both begun and finished first.

3. This was *Ah! perfido, spergiuro*, op. 65 (see n. 2 in no. 177.)

Josefine Killitzky (also Kilitzky, Killitschgy, later Schulze—1790–1880) was the sister-in-law of Ignaz Schuppanzigh. As a child performer in church, her voice made such a favorable impression that her musical education was subsidized by the Austrian empress. According to Thayer, she had to substitute at the last minute for Anna Milder (later Milder-Hauptmann), a much better-known singer, after Beethoven insulted Milder's fiancé at a rehearsal. The eighteen-year-old was understandably nervous and performed poorly. She later had a successful career and premiered the role of Leonore in Berlin.

4. The Gloria from the Mass in C Major, op. 86.

5. Opus 58, in G major, which was published in August 1808 by the Bureau d'Arts et d'Industrie in Vienna.

6. Also from op. 86.

7. This indicates an improvisation by Beethoven; the German word "phantasieren" literally means "to improvise."

8. The Choral Fantasy, op. 80, was the only piece specifically composed for this performance, apparently in a great hurry because Beethoven needed a rousing finale to what must have been an extremely long program.

9. Thayer-Forbes, 448–49 summarizes the differing reports of what exactly happened here.

≈

170.

"News. Leipzig." *Allgemeine musikalische Zeitung* 11 (17 May 1809): 523.

(Mentioned: Piano Concerto No. 1, op. 15)

Performed for the first time were: a quartet from the little opera *Der Zitterschläger*, with poetry by Seidel set to music by Friedr. Schneider[1] and not yet brought to the stage, a still unpublished concerto in G major for the flute by A. E. Müller,[2] and the newest of Beethoven's pianoforte concertos, in G major, Vienna, Industrie-Comptoir. The quartet was full of life, ably and carefully realized in all voices, and had a very favorable effect. The other works can scarcely be discussed in brief. Let it simply be mentioned here, where we must be brief and leave detailed evaluation to the reviewers, that the concerto by Müller, in regard to invention, working-out, and instrumentation, belongs among the most superior, effective and also most gratifying to the solo player among all those for which we have to thank Music Director Müller. The one by Beethoven is the most wonderful, unusual, artistic, and difficult of all those that B. has written, yet less gratifying to the solo player than, for example, that in C. The first movement in particular will be heard many times before we are able to follow it completely and therefore truly enjoy it. This is, however, less the case with the second movement, uncommonly expressive in its beautiful simplicity, and with the third, which rises up exuberantly with powerful joy. Properly performed, they will find full approval everywhere on first hearing.

NOTES

1. *Opera Composers and Their Works* (R-Z, 1646, from *The Mellen Opera Reference Index: Opera Librettists and Their Works,* ed. Charles H. Parsons (Lewiston: Edwin Mellen Press, 1987), lists a one-act *Singspiel* written by Friedrich Schneider in 1809 with a text by H. Seidel entitled *Der Zettelträger*. This is probably the same work being cited here. There is no indication as to whether the whole opera was ever performed.

2. This was presumably Müller's op. 30, published in 1809 by Peters in Leipzig.

≈

171.
Friedrich Rochlitz. "News. Leipzig." *Allgemeine musikalische Zeitung* 20 (8 April 1818): 259–60.

(Mentioned: Symphony No. 8, op. 93)

Pianoforte concerto by Beethoven, played by Mr. Music Director Friedr. Schneider. (G major. This little-known composition,[1] which is nevertheless one of the most original and, particularly in the first two movements, most brilliant and outstanding ones by this master, was performed by the soloist and orchestra masterfully throughout and with the most beautiful effect, likewise particularly in those two movements.) . . . Symphonies. By J. Haydn. E♭ major, beginning with the drum roll[2] (superbly performed). By Beethoven the newest one, in F major, twice. (It was performed, particularly the second time, entirely as might have been wished and yet pleased less than the other ones by this master. The second and third movements seemed to be received the best.)

NOTES

1. Given its popularity today, it might be surprising to modern readers to realize how little known the Fourth Concerto was during Beethoven's lifetime. The lack of recognition was due not only to the difficulty of the piano part, but also to the fact that pianists often performed their own concertos in public. In 1824 the Berlin critic A. B. Marx, in an important essay titled "Some Words about Concert Life, Especially in Large Cities," expressed his desire to hear the Pastoral Symphony and the Fourth Concerto performed more often: "Must then always new pieces be played? Only worthless compositions should not be heard again, and the preference of the concert giver for such works is the only reason for the ill-mannered craving for the new. An artwork is new as long as it offers nourishment to our mind and heart. Many will prove upon hearing to be old; many will

still be new after a hundred hearings. When so many operas in many cities obtain fifty, a hundred performances, should not a Beethoven concerto deserve ten performances? A few of those attending the concerts will be in the situation to understand such a work completely for the first time, and a few will hear it for the tenth time without finding new pleasure in it. In Berlin we have recently seen an at least closely related example. In Berlin, where symphonic works have been neglected—thereby impairing the sense and education of the public—the *Pastoral Symphony by Beethoven* was nevertheless given *four times* in one winter season [1825] . . . This writer has spoken to many musicians and friends of art who misjudged the sense of the work after the first performance, taking in nothing, trying to see much foolishness in the comical parts, who then after the second performance became conscious of many individual beautiful parts, and finally reached the idea and the magnificence of the whole. Why shouldn't this happen with good concert pieces? What can be more simple than the immortal Adagio in Beethoven's G-Major Concerto? This delighted the writer the first time he read it in score; and after hearing it three times, he still did not dare to presume that he had grasped its entire profundity" ("Einige Worte über das Konzertwesen, besonders in großen Städten," BAMZ 2 [1825]: 350). The translation is from Sanna Pederson, "A. B. Marx, Berlin Concert Life, and German National Identity," *19th-Century Music* 18 (1994): 97–98.

As the first score edition of the Fourth Concerto was not printed until 1861, Marx was perhaps reading the concerto from the piano part of the first edition of the parts, which had been published in 1808. In the first edition of the parts the piano part for the second movement contains the solo part on two staves underneath a reduction of the orchestral part on two staves. In the outer movements, orchestral cues are indicated on the two staves of the piano part.

2. Haydn's Symphony No. 103.

≈

OP. 59
THREE STRING QUARTETS

(See entry nos. 12 and 93, vol. 1, pp. 38, 169)

———————————

172.
"News. Vienna. 27 February." *Allgemeine musikalische Zeitung* 9 (18 March 1807): 400

(Mentioned: Symphony No. 1, op. 21, Symphony No. 2, op. 36, and Symphony No. 3, op. 55)

Beethoven's grand symphony in E♭, which was recently assessed in your pages with such impartiality and propriety,[1] will shortly be performed in company with the composer's other two symphonies (in C and D), along with a fourth, as yet unfamiliar symphony by him, in a very select company, which for the composer's benefit has subscribed to a considerable contribution. Three new, very long and difficult violin quartets by Beethoven, dedicated to the Russian ambassador, Count Rasumovsky, also attract the attention of all connoisseurs. They are deep in conception and marvelously worked out, but not universally comprehensible, with the possible exception of the third one, in C major, which by virtue of its individuality, melody, and harmonic power must win over every educated friend of music.

NOTE

1. See entry no. 149.

～

173.
"News. Brief Notices from Letters." *Allgemeine musikalische Zeitung* 9 (5 May 1807): 517.

In Vienna Beethoven's newest, difficult but substantial quartets are giving ever more pleasure; the amateurs hope to see them soon in print. One also looks forward with pleasure to the best, newest compositions by Eberl. Probably they will come out here (in Vienna), where particularly the Kunst- und Industrie-comptoir is to be commended for its editions of grand, lengthy works.[1]

NOTE

1. Opus 59 was published by the Bureau des Arts et d'Industrie (Kunst und Industrie-comptoir) in December 1807 or January 1808 (see Kinsky-Halm, 141). The publication was announced in the WZ on 9 January 1808 and in the AMZ on 27 January 1808.

～

174.
"News. Frankfurt am Main." *Allgemeine musikalische Zeitung* 23 (21 February 1821): 111–12.

(E minor, No. 2, only. With Trio for Piano, Clarinet or Violin, and Cello, op. 38, or Trio for Piano, Violin, and Cello, op. 70, no. 2)

The marvelous trio in E♭ by Beethoven was performed with a degree of perfection that left nothing to be desired but a da capo. Mr. Baron von Wiesenhütten, one of our most distinguished dilettantes, played the pianoforte part and Messrs. Hofmann and Hasemann the accompanying voices.[1] The second of the three large violin quartets of Beethoven, in E minor, was next. Whoever knows this composition must form a good opinion of a public before which something so significant and yet unpopular can be performed. Everyone listened to the often rather bizarre notes with remarkable silence, an effect that only such a successful performance can bring about. Messrs. Schmitt, Hofmann, Kessler, and Hasemann rejoiced in a loud recognition of their merit.

NOTE

1. Hasemann is described in the AMZ (20 [1818], 857) as one of the foremost players in the orchestra at Frankfurt am Main. His cello playing, it is said, excited astonishment, and he was also a virtuoso on the trombone. His career appears to have continued into the 1830s, as additional references to him continue to appear from time to time. No additional information is available on the other two performers mentioned.

~

175.
Musikalische Eilpost 1 (1826): 163.

(Arrangement for piano four-hands, no. 2)[1]

We list the four movements of the work so that everyone will know which quartet it is: Allegro, E minor $\frac{6}{8}$,[2] Adagio molto, E major $\frac{4}{4}$, Allegretto, E minor and major $\frac{3}{4}$, Presto, E minor $\frac{4}{4}$. An evaluation is superfluous. Beethoven's name guarantees the value of the arrangement for pianoforte. No difficulties are to be found, but neither is it as easy to perform as it appears to be if one only looks fleetingly at the notes. The printing is cramped, but clear.

NOTES

1. The only four-hand arrangement of op. 59, no. 2, published during Beethoven's lifetime is the arrangement by C. D. Stegmann that was published by Simrock in Bonn in 1824.
2. The text reads "Es moll," but this must be a misprint.

~

OP. 60
SYMPHONY NO. 4 IN B♭ MAJOR
(See entry nos. 12 and 93, vol. 1, pp. 38, 169)

———————

176.
"News. Vienna, 16 January." *Allgemeine musikalische Zeitung* 10 (27 January 1808): 286–87.

The marriage of our monarch[1] was celebrated with a sumptuous performance of Gluck's *Armida*, with admittance permitted only by ticket. The appearance of the theater on this day (9 January) was truly imposing. The emperor with his household and the amiable empress in full splendor, the boxes filled with the diplomatic corps, the entire parterre full of ladies in their finery, upon whom many millions of diamonds seemed to sparkle, the unanimous, joyous shout as the imperial pair entered—all this made a unique, truly uplifting impression. As to the opera itself, about which so much has already appeared in your journal, I believe I ought not comment, except to say that it was given in the greatest splendor, with many ballets included, yet without exceptional applause, perhaps because expectation had been raised too high, and it was forgotten that, in order to enjoy the artistic merits of an opera by Gluck, one must not expect to hear a modern opera.[2]

The subject of modern music leads me naturally to Beethoven's newest symphony, in B♭, which was repeated at our local amateur concert under the direction of the composer.[3] In the theater it did not succeed greatly, but here it received a great deal of what seems to me to be well-deserved applause. The first Allegro is very beautiful, fiery, and rich in harmony, and the minuet and trio also have a distinct, original character. In the Adagio one might sometimes wish that the melody were not so much divided up between the various instruments, a mistake that also frequently mars the otherwise rich and fiery symphony in D minor by Eberl.[4]

NOTES

1. The Austrian emperor Francis I (formerly Holy Roman Emperor Francis II) married his third wife, Maria Ludovica of Este, on 6 January 1808.

2. *Armide* by Christoph Willibald Gluck (1714–87) was first performed in Paris in 1777. *Armide* is one of Gluck's "reform" operas, in which the composer challenged the frivolities and inconsistencies of much current operatic music; its single-minded neoclassicism would probably have led even the original audiences to judge the work unusually austere and difficult.

3. Mary Sue Morrow notes that this *Liebhaber* concert dates from 27 December 1807. It had also been performed on a benefit event on 15 November (Morrow, *Concert Life in Haydn's Vienna*, 344, 347).

4. A full review of this symphony, which was published by Breitkopf & Härtel in Leipzig in 1805, appears later in this volume of the AMZ (10 [1807–08]: 747–50).

≈

177.
"News. Leipzig." *Allgemeine musikalische Zeitung* 13 (23 January 1811): 62.

(With scene and aria *Ah! perfido,* op. 65)

The annual concert for the benefit of the aged members and widows of the musical institute opened with Beethoven's Symphony No. 4 (Vienna, Industrie-Comptoir). This as yet apparently little known, spirited work (B♭ major, E♭ major, B♭ major) contains, after a solemn, magnificent introduction, a fiery, brilliant, powerful Allegro, an Andante that is well crafted and charming throughout, a very original, wonderfully attractive scherzando, and a strangely put together, but effective, finale.[1] On the whole, the work is cheerful, understandable, and engaging, and is closer to the composer's justly beloved Symphonies Nos. 1 and 2 than to Nos. 5 and 6. In the overall inspiration we may place it closest to No. 2; the curious individual turns of phrase, by which Beethoven has recently frightened many performers and angered many listeners, and which hinder rather than further the effect, are not used excessively. The symphony, which is anything but easy to perform, was played extremely well and was applauded unanimously. A fitting conclusion, though in a completely different character, was provided by the well-known grand scene: *Ah! perfido, spergiuro*[2] by the same composer, which was once again heard with the greatest pleasure. Faced with these two works side by side, one can hardly restrain the wish that it might be possible for this ingenious, revered Master to be inclined to go farther in *this* direction, and, as he is certainly capable of doing, travel ever higher! Miss Campagnoli,[3] who sang the scene, did not achieve the full degree of expression that it demands and permits, but sang nevertheless with surety, precision, and a beautiful voice.

NOTES

1. Following its two performances at the end of 1807, the Fourth Symphony was apparently only performed once in Vienna during the years 1808–10. The critic's statement that the symphony remained little known is accurate. See Morrow, *Concert Life in Haydn's Vienna,* 347–64.

2. Although published as op. 65, this dramatic scene and aria from the widely used *opera seria* libretto *Achille in Sciro* by Pietro Metastasio (1698–1782) was set by Beethoven in 1795 or 1796 and is thus contemporaneous with the two little piano sonatas of op. 49. The high opus numbers of both works may be explained by their having been withheld from publication until Beethoven's growing reputation led to increased demand for his music during the first decade of the nineteenth century. Published in 1805, *Ah! perfido* was widely performed during Beethoven's lifetime.

3. This was probably one of the two daughters of Bartolomeo Campagnoli (1751–1827), who directed the Leipzig Gewandhaus Orchestra from 1797 until 1818. Campagnoli left his position in Leipzig in order to further his daughters' singing careers. Albertina, the older of the two, was around twenty-two years old in 1818 and would thus have been about fifteen years old when the performance reviewed here took place. The younger daughter, Gianetta, ultimately had the more successful career. It is impossible to determine which one of them sang on this occasion. See AMZ 37 (1835) 566–67.

178.
"Overview of the Musical Productions in Mannheim. Winter Season 1811–12." *Allgemeine musikalische Zeitung* 14 (3 June 1812): 381–83.

(With Symphony No. 5, op. 67 and Symphony No. 6, op. 68;
mentioned: Symphony No. 1, op. 21 and Symphony No. 3, op. 55)

The first evening opened with the Symphony in B♭ Major of the musical *Jean Paul,* Beethoven, which had not yet been heard here *publicly*—a work upon which the composer has bestowed all the originality and energy shown by the earlier productions of his muse, without marring its clarity with bizarreries, such as disfigure many of his works, excellent examples being the Pastoral Symphony and the *Eroica*—a work that in genius, fire, and effect can be compared only to the C-Minor Symphony, and in clarity only to the first in C major, but that in difficulty of execution can be compared to none. It was performed—and this is no insignificant praise—with great power, not a little precision, and not without delicacy; particularly effective were the wind instruments, these positions still being occupied here by such good performers. The impression upon the listeners was as desired. The public applauded each movement, showing once again how responsive it is to a good ensemble. . . .

The third evening was also ornamented, like the first two, with at least one excellent new ensemble work: Beethoven's Symphony in C Minor, which has been heard a few times at the local museum but had not yet been given publicly. It is a stream of glowing fire, which in the first movement appears as a fire held back within itself and never completely breaking out, and in the Andante (more grandiose than tender) seems only to rest in order to prepare for greater expressions of strength. In the $\frac{3}{4}$ time of the finale[1] (a foreboding *pianissimo,* broken only by isolated fortes, which surge forth only to be broken off again, and once again in the key of C minor) it announces ever more the nearing of the final overflowing of its might. Finally, after a long, drawn-out pedal point on the dominant, it unfolds in a magnificent transfiguration with the entry of a broad $\frac{4}{4}$ time in C major, makes its proud way like a triumphal procession with great display of magnificent instrumentation, reaches the highest level of sublimity, and, after a powerful, expansive conclusion that repeats the final chord to the greatest possible satisfaction, leaves the hearer uplifted in a way that can be compared to the total impression of very few other symphonies. With truly unique genius, Beethoven here makes use of the contrast between various time signatures and keys: the first movement built entirely upon a theme of four notes and two tones—the extended rhythms that occur here, and that occur particularly in the Andante—the temporary suggestions of C major that appear in the Andante (to be sure, actually in the key of A♭)[2] in the interpolated trumpet themes, producing at the same time a precipitous upsurge of restrained boldness, the beginning of the finale, still in a minor key, in a somewhat fast $\frac{3}{4}$ time (which yet could not less resemble a *Scherzo*) whose continual piano, subsequent repetition in the gauntest pizzicato (here providing neither Haydnesque humor, nor Beethovenian bizarrerie, nor Jean Paulian *Bocksfuß,*)[3] but rather prudently calculated to elevate the tension, and after all this, finally the simultaneous appearance of all conditions capable of producing the highest satisfaction: the most perfect time, the broadest, most rounded rhythms, the purest and most satisfying tonality.

NOTES

1. Most commentators now consider the finale to begin with the Allegro theme in C major and would label the Allegro in C minor and $\frac{3}{4}$ time as a separate movement. Many movements in Beethoven's music are written so that they *segue* into one another in a continuous fashion. This case is unique, however, in that a significant recall of the earlier C-minor music returns after the final Allegro has begun, creating a very close link between the two movements and leading this observer to describe them as a single finale.

2. Measures 29–37, 78–86, 146–68.

3. German for "goat's foot." In mythology, satyrs and devils frequently had a "goat's foot." The term, which derives from Latin "hircipez," was popularized in literature by Jean Paul Richter to signify the grotesque or perverse.

≈

179.
"News. Milan." *Allgemeine musikalische Zeitung* 15 (11 August 1813): 532.

(With Symphony No. 5, op. 67 and Symphony No. 6, op. 68; mentioned: Symphony No. 1, op. 21)

At Moller's Academy here are now being performed six symphonies, entirely unknown in Milan, and hence also new to Milan, three of which are by Mozart and three by Beethoven. The first one by Mozart (the big one in E♭ major) pleased so much that it was regarded as the paragon of all sublime symphonies. The second, likewise by Mozart (in C with the concluding fugue), pleased as well, but did not create the same *furore*. Finally, the third, also by Mozart (in D, beginning with an Adagio), enchanted everyone.[1] It was given preference over Haydn's symphonies.

All attention was now focused on Beethoven. The one in B♭ major was performed first. It did not please at all. The second symphony, the one in C minor, was revered, and it was compared to the First Symphony by this master, in C major. Finally, the Pastoral Symphony (for the performance of which, by the way, it happened that five instruments were missing) pleased only now and then, and people said: *Si vede il gran genio, ma c'è poco canto.*[2]—Without venturing into further commentary and observations, let me simply observe that people in Italy wish to pass judgment upon Beethoven's music immediately upon first hearing it (and you can easily imagine *how*). His C-Minor Symphony only pleased uncommonly after repeated hearings; probably the same thing will happen with the Pastoral and the Symphony in B♭.

NOTES

1. The symphonies discussed are Mozart's K. 543, 551 (the "Jupiter"), and 504 (the "Prague"), respectively.

2. Italian: "There is great genius here, but little song."

~

180.
"Brief Notice." *Allgemeine musikalische*
Zeitung 16 (30 March 1814): 235–36.

(Arrangement for piano four-hands by Friedrich Mockwitz; with Symphony No. 6, op. 68)[1]

This wonderful work, rich in imagination and full of life, in which, almost as in Beethoven's Sixth Symphony, what serves and what constitutes music are placed close to each other in their furthest extent, bent together, and as much as possible blended—has here been arranged for two keyboard players with insight and diligence, without being made difficult to perform. In those places where the effect is based primarily upon the charm of particular instruments, it can scarcely go farther than to produce a pleasant recollection for those to whom the original is not unknown. The same is true of those places where the very full, richly ornamented but gentle accompaniment of the string instruments is added to very simple, sustained notes of the wind instruments. Apart from these places, the work makes even in this form a distinctive effect and invigorates irresistibly. Paper and lithography are good; the price is affordable. Incidentally, the Beethoven symphonies have now been so widely disseminated that the reviewer scarcely needs to add that this number 4 is the one in B♭ major whose original appeared four or five years ago in Vienna.[2]

NOTES

1. Friedrich Mockwitz (1773–1849) arranged a large number of works by Haydn, Mozart, and Beethoven for piano four-hands, including not only symphonies but overtures and string quartets as well. This arrangement of op. 60 was published by Breitkopf & Härtel, Leipzig, in November 1813.

2. The first edition of the parts for the Fourth Symphony was published in Vienna by the Bureau d'Arts et d'Industrie in 1808, thus six years earlier than 1814. The first score edition was not published until 1823 in an edition by Simrock of Bonn.

~

181.
"News. Kassel." *Allgemeine musikalische*
Zeitung 18 (30 October 1816): 758–59.

Symphony in B♭ Major by Beethoven. That this composer follows an individual path in his works can be seen again from this work; just how far this path is a correct one, and not a deviation, may be decided by others. *To me* the great master seems here, as in several of his recent works, now and then excessively bizarre, and thus, even for knowledgeable friends of art, easily incomprehensible and forbidding.

~

182.
"Concerning the Lower Rhine Music Festival. Düsseldorf on 28 May 1822."[1] *Niederrheinisches Unterhaltungsblatt* 1 (2 June 1822).

At the celebration of the second evening, the first section of the concert began with the grand Symphony of Beethoven in B♭ Major, which is familiar to you, and about which you recently remarked to me in F, that it contained more bombast than substance. In a true sense, and exactly as it must be, it was capably managed, and while I listened to it with contentment, I can say without overstatement that the overture to *The Magic Flute,* with which the first half closed, gripped and transported me.

NOTE

1. For more information on this festival, see entry no. 30, n. 1, vol. 1, p. 78. According to *Die Musik in Geschichte und Gegenwart* [henceforth MGG], ed. Friedrich Blume (Kassel: Bärenreiter, 1949–79), 4: 115, the festival was directed in 1822 by Franz Burgmüller, one of its founders.

~

183.
"News. Berlin, 13 January 1823." *Berliner allgemeine musikalische Zeitung* 1 (28 January 1824): 31.

My neighbor wrote, undisturbed:

4.[1] Grand Symphony by Beethoven, we do not know which number. Introduction and first Allegro good; Andante [Adagio] too fast, the timpani several times too loud; the scherzo completely in the spirit of this often sublime and often bizarre composer; the finale once again played too quickly.

NOTE

1. The number "4" refers to the article section.

184.

Ludwig Rellstab. "Travel Reports by Rellstab.[1] no. 4, Vienna." *Berliner allgemeine musikalische Zeitung* 3 (18 and 25 May 1825): 162–63 and 169.

In this superb locale the miraculous symphony was played with all due fire, which may impress on our minds that we are in close proximity to the still living master, who would be present with a severely critical ear if an extremely unlucky fate had not, unfortunately, excluded him from the paradise that he opens up for us. Simply the awareness of being so near to the creator of this work brought about the sense of his spirit's invisible presence. The work was taken up with seriousness of purpose, and had this been absent, the opening notes of the Adagio would have impressed it on both the listeners and the performers. Like an oppressive storm it slowly and solemnly draws near, obscures the peaks of the mountains, hides the sun, and threatens with light thunder, just as an aroused beast of prey bears its anger at first deep within itself, before springing forth with a loud cry of fury. These anticipations fill us with more terrible forebodings than does the reality of danger. After this effect brought about by the first ten measures, we feel as though everything that follows comes from within ourselves, created out of our own innermost soul, for the oppression that grips our breast is expressed so truly in the notes cast off by the orchestra, as though they were themselves gasps for breath, that the inevitability with which the music unfolds, strange only in appearance, is made clear through the most unmediated of feelings. From time to time the wind instruments give added emphasis, as though a gentle, steadier sigh were urging itself between the uneasy drawings of breath. Now the thunder rolls anew; we fall silent, daring hardly to breathe! Stronger strokes now follow more quickly, anxiety turns at last to pain, the comforting tear breaks forth, and after two flashes of lightning the menacing storm bursts and, with claps of thunder, lit up by the fire of the lightning, the silvery storm of rain rushes powerfully but blessedly down. Out of this bold splendor the irresistibly forward-rushing Allegro [vivace] rises up and carries us triumphantly forward in a full, surging stream. If I were called upon here to give an opinion on this long familiar work, I would undertake to point out that practically no other work of Beethoven shows as effective control of the overall form as in this symphony. The individual movements are so beautifully juxtaposed, everything develops so naturally, as only the most accomplished master would be able to bring about, for: "Only from perfected powers can grace step forth!"

Not only this, but the movements in themselves are so superbly crafted that each is formed perfectly within itself. Let us consider first the Adagio, in which the sweetest and most painful of melodies delightfully nestles against the one motive made, as it were, from bronze, which stands like a pillar around which tender green shoots are growing.

OP. 60
Adagio, m. 1 (with corrected rhythm in brackets)

This simple motive is used to produce the most stunning transition, mounting from the softest *piano* to *fortissimo,* from frightening pizzicatos in the string instruments to the mighty rhythmic thunder of the timpani.[2] It almost sounds like the last thunderclaps of the retreating storm, resounding through the mountains, which faintly continue to threaten, while lovely blue skies and sunlight break through the clouds and the freshened earth smiles in the trembling brightness of the silver droplets. Jean Paul says: the storm has already passed, but the tears remain in the flowery eyes of the trembling earth. I only want to mention further the entrance of the motive after the cadenza, where it truly resembles faraway thunder, which resounds through the mountains with awesome beauty.

OP. 60
Adagio, mm. 60–62

Of the melodic counterpoint that it creates with other motives of the Adagio, of the intricate art with which the whole is put together, I will not speak, but only express the wish that we could once again hear this enchanting work here.

The cheerful, yet frightfully daring minuet stands in opposition to its trio like man and wife. The minuet is agitated like the wild impetuosity of manly anger, the animosity of which draws tears to the eyes—manly tears, like those Achilles shed in his rage over Agamemnon's taunting injustice.[3] The trio, on the other hand, insinuates itself with gentle pleading and seeks to soothe the raging breast. The rhythm is so tender and flowing that we almost seem to see the gentle, wavelike emotions of the pleading beloved. There is also visible a very gentle trace of a smile, which is like the fine thread that binds both pieces together and lets us know that the tender pleas and the stormy anger will both return to the common resting place of inclination and friendly goodwill. Let us listen:

OP. 60
Trio, mm. 90–94

The little motive at the end of this example, following upon the stirring melody, has a slight touch of mischief, which only heightens its gracefulness. No, the word is too strong—rather it is a touch of that good-natured, delicate irony of an unaccustomed indignation, which allows us to predict that it will soon disappear. To show the inimitable amiability with which this melody proceeds, with what devices of art the effect is continuously magnified, either through rhythmic reinforcement or through instrumentation, would belong in a critique, and I have been given room only to show a little imagination. Since I am at the finale of the symphony, I also have arrived at the finale of my imaginative powers.[4] I do not know how to describe how the joyfully mischievous and yet so lovely and graceful last movement of this symphony affects me. It is a continually bubbling, living spring, which rushes gracefully past, sometimes in happy, teasing leaps and sometimes in a wavelike dance, always clear and always deep. Indeed it is so deep that the sun and sky are mirrored in it, and we see through the clear water into the fullness of the universe, which only a great, noble soul can so feel and so return. Full of the deepest, most heartfelt veneration I give thanks to the master, who through great genius created something so wonderful

> And wakened the power of those dark feelings
> Which wondrously slept within the heart.

NOTES

1. Ludwig Rellstab (1799–1860) was an important literary figure as well as an influential music critic. The periodical *Iris im Gebiete der Tonkunst,* which he founded in 1830, helped to fill the void left in the musical life of Berlin by the premature demise of Marx's BAMZ. He wrote the texts of seven songs from Schubert's final song cycle, *Schwanengesang,* although these texts had first been offered to Beethoven, whom Rellstab greatly admired. Rellstab has the reputation of being a musical conservative, but the

sympathetic understanding of Beethoven's style that he demonstrates in this report, the imaginative manner in which he interprets the music, and the abundance of literary references that he employs all show him to have been, at the age of twenty-six, thoroughly in step with the artistic and intellectual climate of the 1820s.

2. The passage in question is apparently mm. 38–49 of the Adagio, in which the two-note dotted figure that had appeared at the beginning of the movement as an accompaniment in the second violin attains an unexpected motivic prominence.

3. The action of Homer's *Iliad* is precipitated when Agamemnon is forced to give up his concubine and in response steals the concubine of Achilles. Enraged, Achilles refrains from drawing his sword against Agamemnon at Athene's request and retreats to the shore of the sea where he weeps and pleads with his mother, the sea-goddess Thetis, to gain Zeus's support for the Trojans so that the Greeks will be aware of the injustice when he withdraws his forces from the battle against Troy, leaving the Greeks vulnerable to defeat.

4. "Indeed, they truly seem to have reached their last breath, if they were ever completely alive."

~

185.
K. Breidenstein. *Bonner Wochenblatt* no. 101 (17 December 1826).

It falls within my purpose gradually to acquaint the local music loving public with the outstanding recent symphonies, and specifically with those of Bethoven. Everyone recognizes the extraordinary nature of Bethoven's achievement in this area, and he is rightly considered to be the founder of a new (that is, the newest) epoch in instrumental music, inasmuch as he uses the materials of his art in a manner that was not yet fully granted to his great forerunners, Haydn and Mozart—although this by no means compromises their originality.

"The instrumental compositions of all three masters (says Hoffmann[1] in his *Fantasiestücke*) breathe a similar Romantic spirit, due to their all having taken possession of the peculiar essence of the art; the character of their compositions, however, is markedly different. The expression of a childlike, happy soul dominates in Haydn's compositions. His symphonies lead us into a vast green meadow, into a joyous, colorful crowd of fortunate people etc. Into the depths of the spirit kingdom we are led by Mozart. Fear surrounds us, but in the absence of torment, it is more a forboding of the infinite.—In this way, Beethoven's instrumental music also opens up to us the kingdom of the gigantic and unmeasurable. Glowing beams shoot through this kingdom's deep night, and we become aware of gigantic shadows that surge up and down, enclosing us more and more narrowly and annihilating everything within us, leaving only that interminable longing, in which every pleasure that had quickly arisen with sounds of rejoicing sinks away and founders, etc." What Hoffmann says here about Bethoven's instrumental music in general is entirely appropriate to the B♭-Major Symphony, which today will be performed here for the first time. Unfortunately, I do not have the space to discuss this in detail; I can only draw attention to a few things. The introduction to the first movement begins with fearfully drawn out minor sonorities followed by staccato ones, and flows with growing brilliance into the onward-rushing Allegro. The theme of the Adagio is as simple as it is original. Two tones (E♭ descending to B♭), which are repeated like the strokes of two unlike hammers, run through the entire movement and are united with the sweetest melodies, taken up first by this, then by that, then by all the instruments. The principal motive in the minuet actually falls into two-four time, but is here forced into three-four, producing a unique, one might say comically indignant, effect. In the trio the wind instruments begin a rich but earnest melody, which seems to be mocked by the violins and other string instruments, inasmuch as they interrupt it with isolated, playful motives, which completely decline participation and, by means of a joyous unisono, contend for victory. The reentry of the minuet both ends and renews this struggle. The full splendor of the combined effect is then developed in the finale.

NOTE

1. Ernst Theodor Amadeus Hoffmann (1776–1822) still ranks as one of the most prominent critics of Beethoven in the nineteenth century. His reviews of works by Beethoven, particularly of the Fifth Symphony (see entry no. 206), did much to enhance recognition of Beethoven's unique accomplishments and to place his music within the context of literary Romanticism. Although he always had a special affinity for music (he changed his middle name to Amadeus in honor of Mozart), Hoffmann was active in virtually every field of artistic endeavor. His fluency with both music and language thus equipped him to be one of the most perceptive and articulate music critics of all time.

Fantasiestücke in Callots Manier (1814–15) comprises prose tales and essays on various themes on music or composers. Hoffmann rewrote the reviews of the Fifth Symphony, which appeared in AMZ in 1810 (cols. 630–42 and 652–59) (see entry no. 206), and of the Piano Trios, op. 70 (AMZ 15, cols. 141–54) (see entry no. 226) for the essay on Beethoven's instrumental music, omitting much technical analysis and the music examples. For more on Hoffmann's music criticism, see Peter Schnaus, *E. T. A. Hoffmann als Beethoven-Resenzent der Allgemeinen musikalischen Zeitung* (Munich: Musikverlag Emil Katzbichler, 1977); and Wallace, *Beethoven's Critics,* 20–26 and 126–43.

This oft-quoted passage, no less familiar today than it was in Hoffmann's own time, first appeared in his review of Beethoven's Fifth Symphony.

∾

186.
"Great Lower Rhine Music Festival 1828, in Cologne."[1] *Cäcilia* 8, no. 31 (1828): 211.

The performance on the second day consisted, as usual, of several pieces. The first was *Beethoven's Fourth Symphony* in B♭ major. There are no words to describe the deep, powerful spirit of this work from his *earlier* and *most beautiful* period.[2]

The performance was adequate to the work. Some details were superbly performed, while others fell below expectation. Particularly the Adagio and the menuetto and trio have their great difficulties. Least praiseworthy of all were the tempos, which at times were too fast and even inconsistent. Excessively fast tempos often obscure the most beautiful effects. The portrait becomes unclear, obscured by mist, even blotted out entirely.

NOTES

1. The director of the festival this year was Ferdinand Ries; he presumably conducted the performance described here.

2. Although at least two three-part divisions of Beethoven's works had been suggested by 1827, the author of this review simply divides the works into an earlier "most beautiful" period and a later apparently less beautiful period. As K. M. Knittel discusses, Beethoven's later works were frequently associated with his deafness and illness and "caused great discomfort for the critics." See her "Imitation, Individuality, and Illness: Behind Beethoven's 'Three Styles,'" *Beethoven Forum* 4 (1995): 34.

≈

187.
Beiblatt der Kölnischen Zeitung no. 11 (22 June 1828).

The second day brought to us first Beethoven's Symphony in B♭ Major. The symphony, about which nothing more can be added to what has already been said in these pages, demonstrated in an unsurpassable performance that nothing more magnificent has ever been written of this kind, nor might ever be written again. The orchestra was truly enchanted, and loud applause rewarded the performers, who showed us instrumental music in its true greatness and magnificence.

≈

188.
M.[1] "Report—Möser's Music Performances." *Berliner allgemeine musikalische Zeitung* 7 (20 March 1830): 92.

(Mentioned: Symphony No. 3, op. 55; Symphony No. 5, op. 67; Symphony No. 6, op. 68; Symphony No. 7, op. 92; Symphony No. 9, op. 125)

The Beethoven symphony was but a repeated testimony to the fulfillment of the highest duty of the artist. It is one of the works of the immortal tone-poet and belongs in the same sphere with Mozart's, Spohr's,[2] and other symphonies in which the composer has not yet risen to a heightened awareness, to a specific idea.[3] One must unconditionally recognize a higher meaning in his Symphonies in C Minor, A Major, E♭ Major, F Major, and D Minor,[4] but one of them also left *some individual matters* still to be desired, which are more perfectly expressed in this symphony. Everyone can sense that whatever drew the poet into his work filled him completely; with love he dedicated himself completely to it; and this *true love* shows him in every moment what is proper, protects him from every foreign admixture, from every mere caprice. His flattering words calm and inspire us just when the time is right; his most powerful storms of sound shake us, albeit to a joyous trembling; he uplifts us even with the sense of his terror and our own weakness, whereas the arbitrary strokes of other works offend us with a sense of blindly raging power.

NOTES

1. Some of A. B. Marx's writings in BAMZ are signed in full and others are only signed, as here, with a "M." See Wallace, *Beethoven's Critics,* 558–59, for a discussion of other reviews signed "M" in BAMZ.

2. Louis Spohr (1784–1859), though today regarded as a minor contemporary of Beethoven, was considered in his own time to be one of the central figures of the early Romantic period in music, equally celebrated for his operas and his instrumental works. At the time this was written, Spohr had composed only three of what would eventually be ten symphonies. These are cataloged in Brook, *The Symphony,* reference volume, 529–30. For more detailed information, see entry no. 36, n. 5, vol. 1, p. 89.

3. The notion that the greatest symphonic works express a single, specific, and comprehensible idea originated in the 1820s, inspired in particular by Beethoven's Ninth Symphony and the extramusical message that it contains, and reached full fruition in the later critical writings of A. B. Marx. For a partial treatment of the origins of this idea and its context, see Wallace, *Beethoven's Critics,* 45–104; and Scott Burnham, *Aesthetics, Theory and History in the Works of A. B. Marx* (Ph.D. diss., Brandeis University, 1988).

4. Symphonies Nos. 5, 7, 3, 6, and 9.

~

189.
"Overview of Events." *Iris* 1 (23 April 1830).

(Arrangement for piano quartet with flute, violin, and cello by J. N. Hummel)[1]

About Beethoven's Fourth Symphony, which is perhaps the most admirable of all his works, we may well be excused from commenting further. We may expect thanks, on the other hand, if we draw attention to the two arrangements cited above, which, having been made by so experienced and gifted a musician as Hummel, can hardly have failed to turn out well. Not everyone has the opportunity to hear the greatest orchestral creations in their original integrity; thus, arrangements of this sort, which make them accessible to smaller groups of players, should be taken up gratefully by all fair-minded persons. Performance of this symphony on the pianoforte alone is not easy;[2] indeed, if one makes strict demands of oneself, it is very difficult. Such a splendid work, however, may indeed require some effort, and one will gladly make the sacrifice in diligence in order to lose as little as possible of the effect.

NOTES

1. This arrangement was published by Schott at Mainz in 1830. Johann Nepomuk Hummel (1778–1837) was an Austrian pianist and prolific composer of orchestral, choral, and chamber works. A student of Mozart, Anton Salieri (1776–1841), and Johann Albrechtsberger (under whom Beethoven also studied), Hummel composed in nearly every genre.

2. In contemporary usage, chamber works for piano and one or a few instruments were described as piano solos with accompaniment. This differs from the modern perspective, according to which the piano tends to be seen as the accompanying instrument.

~

OP. 61
VIOLIN CONCERTO IN D MAJOR

(See entry no. 12, vol. 1, p. 38)

———————

190.
"News. Vienna." *Allgemeine musikalische Zeitung* 9 (7 January 1807): 235.

The admirers of Beethoven's muse will be interested to hear that this composer has written a violin concerto—as far as I know, his first—which the locally beloved violin player Klement performed with his customary elegance and grace at the academy given for his benefit.

~

191.
Wiener Theater-Zeitung 2 (1807): 27.

(Mentioned: Septet, op. 20; Symphony No. 1, op. 21;
String Quintet, op. 29; Symphony No. 2, op. 36)

The superb violin player Clement[1] also played, among other exquisite pieces, a violin concerto by Beethhofen, which was received with exceptional applause due to its originality and abundance of beautiful passages. In particular, Klement's proven artistry and grace, his power and confidence on the violin, which is his slave, were received with loud bravos. The educated world was struck by the way that Klement could debase himself with so much nonsense and so many tricks in order to delight the crowd while still being able, in this first production, to express beauty and sublimity. We do not contradict this opinion. Regarding Beethhofen's concerto, the judgment of connoisseurs is undivided; they concede that it contains many beautiful qualities, but admit that the context often seems completely disjointed and that the endless repetition of several commonplace passages can easily become tiring. They maintain that Beethhofen should use his avowedly great talent more appropriately and give us works that resemble his first two Symphonies in C and D, his graceful Septet in E♭, the spirited Quintet in D Major, and various others of his earlier compositions, which will place him forever in the ranks of the foremost composers. At the same time, however, they fear that if Beethhofen continues on this path, both he and the public will come off badly. Music could quickly come to such a point that everyone who is not precisely familiar with the rules and difficulties of art would find absolutely no enjoyment in it, but, oppressed instead by a multitude of interconnected and overabundant ideas and a continuous tumult of the combined instruments, the like of which will be required for initiation, would leave the concert with only an unpleasant feeling of exhaustion. In general, the public was well pleased with this concerto and Clement's fantasies.[2]

The remaining pieces of music were for the most part received with decided pleasure.

NOTES

1. Clement was known for tricks such as those described in this article, including playing the violin while holding it upside down.
2. The parallel between this passage and the conclusion of entry no. 145 above, the review of the *Eroica* from F, is striking; both begin by describing performances by Clement and then characterize the public's reaction to the latest work of Beethoven in virtually identical words. Because certain passages agree almost word for word, it is possible that the author of this article simply borrowed from the article in F.

~

OP. 62
OVERTURE IN C MINOR TO HEINRICH JOSEPH VON COLLIN'S TRAGEDY *CORIOLAN*[1]

(See entry nos. 12 and 14, vol. 1, pp. 38, 40; 154, vol. 2)

———————

192.
"News. Leipzig." *Allgemeine musikalische Zeitung* 10 (25 May 1808): 559.

Beethoven's Overture to Collin's *Coriolan* (C minor), which was published in Vienna a few weeks ago, is once again a very significant work, written more in the manner of Cherubini[2] than in that of B's previous orchestral works. The character of this overture is grand and serious, to the point of gloominess. It is strictly and learnedly written throughout with great care and unmistakable diligence and is calculated besides to produce much more of a profound than a radiant effect. It must be played in a very assured, clear, and lively manner if it is to attain its purpose; performing it, therefore, is anything but easy.

NOTES

1. Heinrich Josef von Collin (1771–1811) was an acquaintance of Beethoven who wrote several plays on classical themes that were widely performed in the early nineteenth century. *Coriolan* was first performed in 1802, more than four years before this overture was written. Beethoven's overture was likely used at a single performance of the play that took place on 24 April 1807. As these reviews make clear, it was heard from the beginning primarily as a concert piece. The first edition of the set of parts was published by the Bureau d'Arts et d'Industrie in January 1808.

2. It is interesting to note that Hoffmann makes this same comparison. (See entry no. 196, below.) For a twentieth-century commentary on the resemblance between the overtures of the two composers, see Arnold Schmitz, "Cherubinis Einfluß auf Beethovens Ouvertüren," *Neues Beethoven-Jahrbuch*, 2 (1925), 104–18.

~

193.
"News. Leipzig." *Allgemeine musikalische Zeitung* 11 (19 October 1808): 47.

Of music with artistic significance we heard little in these weeks. The first three of the customary weekly winter concerts will be discussed at the end of the first quarter, as has always been the case here. To lovers of first-rate new music, only three of the pieces performed can be provisionally recommended: a magnificent symphony by Andr. Romberg (No. 2 in D Major),[1] which is as artistic as it is coherent, and has a tidiness and perfection in its working-out like few others; Beethoven's most recent grand overture to Collin's *Coriolan* (in C minor), full of inner, powerful life, original harmonic twists and turns, and with a truly tragic effect (but difficult to perform well); and the Quartet in F Minor (pianoforte, violin, viola, and violoncello), so spirited, particularly in the first and last movements, by Prince Louis Ferdinand of Prussia, which in distinctiveness of treatment, in a fire of imagination that actually seems to burn, and deep, melancholy feeling, must be placed next to the works of the greatest artists in this type of music.

NOTE

1. Andreas Romberg (1767–1821), who was particularly well known for his string quartets, belonged to an illustrious family of musicians, several of whom are mentioned

throughout these reviews. *New Grove,* 16: 144–46, details their identities, relationship, and instrumental specialties.

~

194.
"News. Munich. 30 March." *Allgemeine
musikalische Zeitung* 11 (26 April 1809): 480.

On the sixth of this month, a grand concert was given for Mr. Eder, the violoncellist.[1] Born not far from our capital city, he entered very early into the service of the Elector of Trier. Despite grievous changes, he remained in that area and only came here a short time ago. Countless people attended the concert given by this venerated artist; and if his manner of playing and composing bears traces of an outmoded sensibility, his talent and his great skill were universally recognized.

A new overture by Beethoven also achieved the success that it deserved, but it was unable to win universal approbation. We are yet too little accustomed here to the often bizarre sensibility of this original artist. Director Fränzl[2] performed again on this occasion his already familiar concerto with accompanying choirs, harps, etc. An appropriate, ingenious idea! But not entirely new to us! For some time we have heard similar violin concertos in church with the text of the Mass. But placing a work of art in its place, in its proper light, is no ordinary task! It betrays the thinker and connoisseur!

NOTES

1. Karl Kaspar Eder (1751-?) was a Bavarian cellist and a member of the Trier orchestra. In 1802 he published a Symphony for Orchestra, op. 5.

2. Ferdinand Fränzl (1767–1833), the last and most illustrious of a family of German musicians, was active in Munich from 1806 until 1826. The work mentioned here is probably his "concertino" *Das Reich der Töne,* written for violin with the accompaniment of several voices, choirs, harp or piano, and full orchestra, which was published by Schlesinger in Berlin. The AMZ (5 [1802–03]: 307) also gives an account of Fränzl playing another violin concerto that included Turkish music.

~

195.
A-Z. "A Declamatorium and a Grand Concert."
Thalia 2, no. 19 (6 March 1811): 73.

A declamatorium was held on 27 February in the Imperial Royal Court Theater next to the palace. The program opened with the *Overture to the Tragedy Coriolan.* The masterworks of Mr. van Beethoven, even if not always equally valued, are animated by such a spirit, and by such a distinctive quality of melody and instrumentation, that it is difficult to compare them with other compositions. It is certain, therefore, that Mr. van Beethoven is not a composer for the general public. When, as was the case today, there is also a careless production, a continuous noise from the crowd that was still belatedly arriving, and an immodest talkativeness that troubles every friend of art, the artist can seek the reward that he deserves only in the quiet but genuine applause of the smaller number of his admirers and connoisseurs. The gripping seriousness, the elevated style of this overture was the worthiest possible preparation for the sublime *Prayer of Adam to the Messiah,* a selection from the eighth canto of Klopstock's *Messiah,*[1] which was declaimed by the imperial royal court actor, Mr. Brockmann.

NOTE

1. *Der Messias,* by Friedrich Gottlieb Klopstock (1724–1803), the first four cantos of which first appeared in print in 1748 (the final version was not published until 1799, long after Klopstock had lost his importance), was one of the most influential German works of the middle decades of the eighteenth century because of its emotional style and subjective treatment of the subject matter. For Klopstock's importance to Beethoven, see Thayer-Forbes, 246.

~

196.
Ernst Theodor Amadeus Hoffmann. "Review." *Allgemeine musikalische Zeitung* 14 (5 August 1812): 519–26.[1]

Since, according to the once customary, and certainly not too objectionable, arrangement in the theater, every presentation begins with music, so should every truly significant play have an overture, which would fix our feelings exactly as the character of the piece requires. Various tragedies have already acquired overtures, and the ingenious Beethoven has likewise furnished Collin's *Coriolan* with a magnificent work of this type—even though the reviewer must admit that Beethoven's purely Romantic genius does not seem to him to be entirely reconcilable with Collin's predominantly reflective poetry, and that for that reason, the composer will only grip our souls powerfully and prepare us completely for what is to follow if it pleases him to write overtures for the tragedies of Shakespeare and Calderon,[2] which express romanticism in the truest sense. The somber, terrifying character of the present composition, the horror-inspiring suggestions of an unknown spirit world, allow more to be anticipated than is subsequently fulfilled. One truly believes that this spirit world, frighteningly heralded by subterranean thunder, will draw nearer during the play, perhaps Hamlet's armored shade will stalk across the stage, or the fateful sisters will draw Macbeth down to the underworld. More pathos and brilliance would perhaps have agreed better with Collin's poetry. Nevertheless, apart from those expectations that will be aroused only in a few connoisseurs who truly comprehend Beethoven's music, the composition is completely suited to awaken the specific idea that a great, tragic event will be the content of the play that follows. Without having read the program, nobody could expect anything else; no common tragedy can be performed after this overture, but specifically an elevated one, in which heroes rise up and are defeated.

The overture consists of only one movement, Allegro con brio, common time, C minor; the first fourteen measures are nevertheless written in such a way that they sound like an Andante that only leads into the Allegro. This beginning grips and fascinates our feelings irresistibly, an effect that results from the entire idea, but primarily from the original instrumentation. In spite of the *fortissimo* marking, the first two measures are given to strings alone, which strike low C heavily and decisively, and an F-minor chord of a quarter note's duration breaks shrilly from the full orchestra in the third measure. The deathly quiet that follows, the new beginning by the string instruments with the same heavy, terrifying C, once again the shrill $\frac{6}{3}\natural$ on F, the deathly quiet again, the C in the string instruments for the third time, the chord raised to the seventh[3], and now at last two chords by the entire orchestra, which lead into the theme of the Allegro: all of this heightens our expectations; indeed it constricts the breast of the listener; it is the frightful, menacing murmur of the approaching storm. In order to make this comprehensible, the reviewer sets forth the entire introduction:

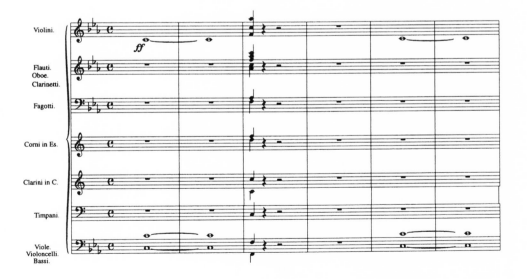

OP. 62
Allegro con brio, mm. 1–14

The principal theme of the Allegro that now enters bears the character of an uneasiness that cannot be quieted, a longing that cannot be satisfied, and as unmistakably as it is conceived in Beethoven's distinctive spirit, it also reminded the reviewer strongly of Cherubini, and the spiritual kinship of both masters became clear to him. Even the further development of the overture is closely related to several of Cherubini's overtures, particularly in the instrumentation.

OP. 62
Allegro con brio, mm. 15–21

The transposition of this theme a tone lower (B♭ minor) right after a one measure rest, is also unexpected and heightens the tension in which we were immediately placed by the opening measures [mm. 22ff.]. The music turns to F minor, and, in the full tutti that now enters, back to C minor, and goes, after the principal theme has been touched upon in a shortened form by the second violin and the violoncello,

OP. 62
Allegro con brio, mm. 40–41

to the first inversion of the dominant of the related major key of E♭, which closes the first section of the overture. Now the second principal theme enters, accompanied by a figure that returns frequently throughout the entire movement, and that is almost always played by the violoncello [mm. 52ff.]:

OP. 62
Allegro con brio, mm. 52–55

F minor, G minor, and C minor are mostly touched upon in the working-out of this theme, until the second part of the overture closes in G minor with syncopated notes in the first violin, against which violoncello and viola perform a new figure in eighth notes [mm. 102ff.]:

OP. 62
Allegro con brio, mm. 102–03

After the close in the dominant, the figure just quoted, with the same accompaniment of violoncellos and violas, leads the music through G minor,

F minor, A♭ major, D♭ major etc., across the length of thirty-four measures into F minor, in which key the beginning of the overture is repeated [mm. 152ff.]. The music turns toward C minor, and the second theme, with the same accompaniment as in the first part, enters in C major [*sic*, m. 178], but goes at once into D minor, E minor, and immediately thereafter back into C minor.

OP. 62
Allegro con brio, harmonic
reduction of mm. 200–02

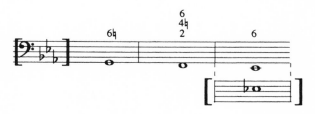

There follows the same figure in syncopated notes with accompaniment of the violoncello, which first brought about the close in G minor, but is now broken off in the following manner [mm. 240ff.]:

OP. 62
Allegro con brio, mm. 237–45

The reviewer has included the oboes, trumpets, and kettledrums, in order to let the reader sense the terrifying effect of the dissonant C that he experienced hearing the overture in performance. The heavy horn note G 8*va*, upon which the second principal theme unexpectedly enters in C major (as quoted above) [mm. 244ff.] also heightens the expectation anew before the conclusion. This luminous C major was, however, a fleeting glance at the sun through a dark cloud; then after four measures the somber principal key returns, and a theme in syncopated notes, similar to the figure that has already been frequently mentioned, leads back to the beginning of the overture, which, however, now appears in a different instrumentation. The heavy C, which first lay only in the string instruments, is now played by the oboes, clarinets, bassoons, and trumpets as well [mm. 216ff.]. Now come short broken phrases, measure-long rests, and at last the music dies out with the following notes:

OP. 62
Allegro con brio, mm. 297–314

The reviewer will mention that he has set down the full score of the conclusion and that the entire remainder of the orchestra is silent, and these heavy tones, this lugubrious note in the bassoon, which sustains the fifth above the tonic, the complaint of the violoncello, the brief strokes of the contrabasses—all are united with deep feeling toward the highest tragic effect, and to the most tightly drawn expectation as to what the rise of the mysterious curtain will reveal.[4]

The reviewer has taken the trouble to give a clear idea of the inner structure of the masterwork, and one may observe from what very simple elements its artistic edifice has been put together. In the absence of contrapuntal turns and inversions, it is primarily the artistic and fast moving modulations that give freshness to the return of the same phrases and sweep the listener powerfully forward. If various contrasting phrases were piled up, the composition, with its modulations that never rest but rather hasten restlessly from one key to another, would have become, like many sections of more recent, imitative compositions, a rhapsody without self-control and inner coherence. There are only two principal themes, however; even the middle transitional passages, the powerful tuttis, remain the same. Indeed, even the form of the modulations remains alike, and so everything leaps out clearly and distinctly for the listener, upon whom the theme impresses itself involuntarily. The reviewer must refer whoever wishes to discover the deep, meaningful instrumentation that truly enchanted him to study the work itself, since the quotation of many individual, ingenious passages would stretch him out too far. Every entry of the wind instruments is calculated and employed to the greatest possible effect. The E♭ horns and C trumpets frequently form triads, which make a deep, thrilling impression.

For several years the violoncello has been an instrument newly acquired by the orchestra; for before that no one had thought of treating it as an obbligato instrument throughout, independent from the fundamental bass.[5] In this overture, too, it rarely goes *col Basso,* but has its own figurations, some of which are not easy to perform. The reviewer concedes that this manner of treating the violoncello is an evident gain for the orchestra, since many a tenor figuration does not sound out enough when performed by violas, which are generally dull-sounding and customarily are played by weak players. The penetrating, original sound of the violoncello, on the other hand, has a decisive effect; in the full tutti, however, the reviewer would not be able to decide to rob the contrabasses of the support of the violoncellos, since the tone of the contrabasses only becomes clear and articulate through doubling at the higher octave.[6] The reviewer is speaking here only of figurations that the violoncello would have to play as middle voice in the tutti; for it goes without saying that it can perform bass figurations for which the double basses can play only the bass notes, since otherwise it is awkward for the latter to play them in the tutti without compromising the effect and clarity of the bass line.

OP. 62
Allegro con brio, mm. 110–11
(with rewritten Contrabasso part)

Apart from this, the overture, like nearly all orchestral compositions of the clever, ingenious master, is a very difficult task for the orchestra, even though there are no extraordinary difficulties in the individual parts. Only a lively cooperation and a deep immersion of each participant in the spirit of the composition, brought about by frequent and diligent rehearsals, can produce the powerful, irresistible effect that the master intended, and toward which he richly employed every means at his disposal.

NOTES

1. Chronologically, this was the second of Hoffmann's five Beethoven reviews in the AMZ; that of the Fifth Symphony had appeared in vol. 12 (see entry no. 206 of this vol.), while reviews of the incidental music to Goethe's *Egmont,* the Mass in C Major, op. 86, and the two Piano Trios, op. 70, were to appear in vol. 15. Although Hoffmann's authorship of these reviews is well established, they were originally published anonymously, like nearly all reviews in the AMZ.

For an extensive discussion of these five reviews, see Peter Schnaus, *E. T. A. Hoffmann als Beethoven-Resenzent der Allgemeinen musikalischen Zeitung* (Munich: Musikverlag Emil Katzbichler, 1977); and Wallace, *Beethoven's Critics,* 20–26, 126–43.

2. The works of Shakespeare and of the Spanish dramatist Pedro Calderón de la Barca (1600–81) appealed widely to the Romantics (in spite of being perceived as diametrical opposites), because of their imposing world images and lyric outbursts of passion: "What pictures, what fire in these very lyrics, romances, and octaves. Not a drama, scarcely an act is without such creations of splendor" (Ludwig Tieck [1773–1853], *Kritische Schriften,* vol. 2, 194f.; Tieck translated Cervante's *Don Quixote* and consulted on the Schlegels' translations of Shakespeare's dramas).

3. Both of these chords are actually diminished sevenths—the first spelled by Beethoven F, A♭, B♮, D, the second spelled F♯, A♮, C, E♭.

4. Hoffmann here calls attention to the fact that his analytical technique, although quite thorough by the standards of the day, is employed selectively to demonstrate the emotional effect of particularly important passages. It is misleading to suggest, as many modern writers have done, that Hoffmann set out to provide a technical or formal analysis of Beethoven's music.

5. The cello's ability to act as an independent voice, not necessarily constrained by the traditional role of continuo instrument, was well established by even the middle of the eighteenth century. Hoffmann is correct, however, in observing that it did not usually fulfill this role in orchestral music before Beethoven. Several of Haydn's symphonies feature brief passages for a solo cello or independent cello section, but Beethoven, in his earliest orchestral works, followed the convention of writing only one part for cellos and basses, with the understanding that the latter were to play it an octave lower than written.

The opening of Beethoven's *Eroica* Symphony may be the first passage in orchestral music to feature the entire cello section independently of the basses as a vehicle for thematic statement, and the sections remain substantially independent throughout the movement, although they are still notated on the same staff. In the second movement of the *Eroica,* Beethoven wrote independent cello and bass parts on separate staves, and from the Fourth Symphony onward, this notation became his standard practice, even when, as was still frequently the case, the parts were most often identical. Even by Beethoven's standards, the prominence and independence of the cello section in the *Coriolan* Overture is highly unusual.

6. Although Hoffmann doesn't say so, this is an accurate description of Beethoven's actual practice.

~

197.
"Concerts." *Wiener allgemeine musikalische Zeitung,* 1 (3 April 1813): 214.

Our capable bassoonist, Mr. Anton Romberg, chamber virtuoso to Prince Lobkowitz, gave on 28 March a musical academy in the Imperial Royal Little Redouten-Saal. The pieces of music performed were few, but they were all the more distinguished either by their solid content or by the high degree of perfection with which they were performed. The Overture from *Coriolan* by Mr. Louis van Beethoven provided the introduction. This classic work is sublime beyond our ability to praise it; every venerator of musical art knows it and pays homage to the genius of its composer. The orchestral players felt the worthiness of their calling on this occasion and executed it with rare precision and expression. Thereupon, Mr. A. Romberg played a concerto in C major by an unknown composer.

~

198.
"The Lower Rhine Music Festival 1824." *Beiblatt der Kölnischen Zeitung* (4 April 1824).

A beautiful celebration will soon return. Exactly the same point in time when the return of spring festively enlivens the universe likewise brings back to the Lower Rhine the magnificent festival that for a succession of years has established here a lively sensibility for art and the veneration of art and supported it with growing love—the annual grand music festival. It is truly a well-calculated idea, or (if only chance perhaps wanted it so), a very happy coincidence, that the annual Society of the Friends of Music has been attached to our locality at the beginning of the most beautiful time of year in order to mix with all their power the hymns of art together with the great concert of nature. The friendly Society, surrounded with great congeniality by blossoming spring, represents for its part, as it were, spring in the kingdom of notes. But its fruitful effect is not limited to the glorification of a particular segment of time, but is revealed already in enduring fruits. How significantly has the cultivation of the noble art of music been broadened since its establishment, how much has the number of public as well as private groups increased, which receive delight and honor from it! For several years, singing societies have been forming in nearly all the bigger and smaller cities, which are all animated by, if not founded specifically by, the competition to participate in the great annual festival. And masterworks, which in previous times could be heard only rarely, in a few places that were known to provide the opportunity and means for them: have they not become common property through the awakening and exercise of talent? Is their enjoyment not being shown by amateur societies everywhere, which certainly achieve varying degrees of success due to varying circumstances, but which here and there undoubtedly render more service through the voluntary combining of private means than used to be performed through an overabundance of public means?

In this way, the Lower Rhine Music Festival has already had the happiest influence on the spread of education. This prosperity has likewise extended to its own advancement; for the growing love of art also brings to the festival itself ever more growth in brilliance and significance. It is to be expected that this mutually conducive interaction will once again be tested in this year's celebration. All the arrangements that have been made already offer the most favorable prospects.

According to the order of succession arrived at by the participating cities, Cologne is the location for this year, and 6 and 7 June are the days of the celebration.

The first day will be distinguished by a new work, which owes its creation to this festival and thus guarantees it an honorable mention in the history of German musical art; for Mr. Friedrich Schneider, Kapellmeister in Dessau,[1] has upon request set to music specifically for this occasion a grand oratorio written by Mr. E. von Groote: *Die Sündfluth*.[2] We may indeed have splendid expectations of the creator of the magnificent composition of the *Weltgericht* and many other outstanding pieces of music; the new work will give new evidence of great mastery.

For the second day works of solid worth have likewise been chosen, namely: (a) the Symphony No. 4 by F. Ries, the Lower Rhine's greatly celebrated master of the pianoforte; (b) two hymns[3] by the ingenious L. van Beethoven, who by his birth likewise belongs to the Lower Rhine; (c) the overture by the same to *Coriolan;* (d) the 103rd Psalm by Fesca.[4]

All the pieces to be performed hence provide worthy, highly rewarding undertakings for a great Society. The most favorable signs already exist concerning the means for the fulfillment of this undertaking. The most gratifying promises of participation are arriving from all sides, so that the number of participants may rise through an appropriate choice to 500. The success of the performance is further guaranteed in particular by the name of the person who is to direct it; namely, concertmaster *Fr. Schneider* will come from Dessau to undertake the direction.

To these inner and most essential components of the festival may be added an auspicious alteration to the location in which it is to be held. The hall Gürzenich,[5] which is so exceptionally well suited for such assemblies, will now not be lacking in those fittings that were still found to be needed at its first reuse by the Music Society three years ago. The city council of Cologne, in order to promote the goals of the Society for its part as well, has appropriated a sum of money toward repairing the ceiling of this majestic hall, by means of which it gains significantly from the acoustical point of view, while this and other beautifications that are to be performed in part give it at the same time the most pleasing appearance.

All circumstances thus seem to be coming together, to prepare a truly outstanding festival for the art of music. Thanks are due to the concord that has brought together such an imposing, generally delightful whole from such individual, disparate parts!

NOTES

1. Schneider was the composer of a large number of oratorios, which he frequently conducted himself at music festivals. The reference below is to his earlier oratorio *Das Weltgericht* (1819).

2. See entry no. 199, below.

3. The "hymns" were selections from the Mass in C, op. 86.

4. Friedrich Ernst Fesca (1789–1826) was a German violinist and composer of symphonies, chamber music, and operas. He also wrote *Lieder* and a number of sacred works for chorus.

5. Named after a prominent local family, the Gürzenich, built in the 1440s, was originally a banquet hall for Cologne's merchants. In more recent years, it has been used primarily as a concert hall.

∽

199.
"News. *The Lower Rhine Music Festival, 1824.*" *Allgemeine musikalische Zeitung* 26 (26 August 1824): 561–67.

From the Rhine. According to the order of succession that exists among the cities of the Society, Cologne was the place where the festival was celebrated during Whitsuntide on 6 and 7 June. The friends of art who had made all the arrangements there in the year 1821 undertook the same task this time as well. They began it in a timely way, for on their request the Cologne city council has already designated, on 31 July 1823, a significant sum for repairing the roof of the majestic great hall, over 12,000 square feet in size, in the Gürzenich commercial house, by virtue of which it must have gained a great deal in regard to acoustics. Much earlier, however—namely right after the music festival of 1821, they formed the resolution of having a poem written by a poet from our fatherland set to music specifically for this festival, and having the performance led by the composer himself. Government-assessor Eberhard von Groote,[1] a capable, deeply feeling poet, acceded to the request to write an oratorio and produced *Die Sündfluth*, which concertmaster Friedrich Schneider in Dessau, the celebrated creator of the *Weltgericht* and of many other outstanding masterworks who has done so much honor to the Lower Rhine Music Festival, undertook to set to music. To this purpose, he received the text as early as March 1823; by the end of the same year the work was finished, and in January 1824 the score had already arrived in Cologne.

The friends of art in Cologne who arrange the festival were guided in selecting and distributing all of the pieces of music to be performed at the festival by the belief that the new work of art, which owed its existence to the festival, should distinguish the first day; and that the second should form a worthy keystone, and at the same time should bring to mind primarily those names that, due to their having long been established as part of the Rhineland's honorable heritage, must be particularly dear to the Rhinelanders.[2] Thus, for this second day were selected: the Symphony No. 4 in F by Ries.—two hymns by Beethoven, or the Kyrie, Gloria, and Credo from his Mass in C.[3]—the Overture by Beethoven to *Coriolan*—the 103rd Psalm by Feska. . . .

The hymns by Beethoven, written in a mood of ascetic inspiration, fully expressed the sensibilities of the listeners; they attested to the greatness of this ingenious composer.

The overture to *Coriolan* by Beethoven, that highly ingenious and difficult to perform tone poem, was given in a most masterly way, but did not have as much of an effect as did the other works upon most listeners. It is somewhat short, and the tragedy by Collin, which is intended to follow it, was unknown to many of them, so that it remained largely incomprehensible. . . .

Undivided applause testified to the fact that, next to the new masterwork by Friedrich Schneider, Cologne was glad to honor the Rhineland's excellent sons, Beethoven and Ries, at this festival; and that in this way, the homemade wreath was decorated by an exotic pearl in a way that was true to the fatherland, while any one-sidedness, which is so fatal to art, was avoided. The Rhineland may look back with exaltation and joy upon this lovely national festival; for a whole national tribe,[4] whose chorus was led this year by the venerable Cologne, has already for years set what is most worthy as its goal, and united itself spiritually to that end in the name of art. The first youthful enchantment produced by this lovely undertaking has not become cold, but rather grown manyfold, and it seems once again to prove the old saying from the time of Swabian art: "Singing and song must be at home on the lovely Rhine."

NOTES

1. "Born in Cologne on 19 March 1789, Eberhard von Groote wrote: *Faust's Atonement with His Life.* Cologne 1816—*Pocketbook for Old German Times and Art.* Cologne 1816—*Tristan by Meister Gottfried von Strassburg.* Berlin, 1821—Contributor to the *Rhenish-Westphalian Almanac of the Muses,* to the journal *Agrippina,* etc." Actually Groote published a medieval text under the title *Tristan von Meister Gottfried von Strassburg mit der Fortsetzung des Meisters Ulrich von Thurheim.*

2. "Beethoven, that hero and true creator of present-day instrumental music and his powerful student Ferdinand Ries were both born in the neighboring city of Bonn."

3. Selections from the *Missa solemnis* (in this case the Kyrie, Credo, and Agnus Dei) were also listed as "hymns" at the Viennese premiere in 7 May 1824.

4. That is, the Rhineland.

~

200.

A. B. Marx. "Correspondence. Berlin, 30 November 1825." *Berliner allgemeine musikalische Zeitung* 2 (7 December 1825): 395–97.

One classic, complete work in an entire concert organized by the royal Concertmaster, Mr. Seidler,[1] and his famous and beloved wife, that is not very much: in a concert that included Merkadante,[2] Pär, and throat variations on a carafe theme,[3] not very much at all. The work, however, the Overture to *Coriolan* by Beethoven, amounts to a lot, and thanks and honor have already come to Mr. Seidler, who was the first to perform it in Berlin, on its account.

The fact that the undersigned attaches such importance to just this work, which was coldly received, while the performers were applauded with genuine interest after each movement by Lafont[4] and Merkadante, may surprise many of the concertgoers. The largest and best portion of the listeners, however, would have been just as stimulated and uplifted by the work in question, if two circumstances had not prevented this from happening.

First, the performance was not suitable for this purpose; the orchestra was too small to give the necessary fullness of sound to such a highly meaningful and passionate work in the full and heated hall. The reviewer took his place in the middle of the hall and found that even the most powerful passages of the magnificently orchestrated composition sounded thin and dull. If a work of this type is to be performed, and a large crowd, which covers the expenses but impairs the sound, can be foreseen, then in *Berlin* the customary concert orchestra could certainly be augmented. It would also have produced a good *effect* if the orchestra had been raised up and the rows of listeners, which muffled the sound, had been further removed. The performers also seemed (if the reviewer understood Beethoven's work correctly) not yet to have grasped all of the composer's intentions; according to the reviewer's interpretation, for example, the last note of the principal theme

OP. 62
Allegro con brio, m. 22

should have been not only sustained, but also strengthened, while the preceding ones should have been correspondingly softer and more fleeting, even if in the parts this note is merely marked tenuto. The cello parts, too,

which are certainly very difficult, but designed to be beautiful and effective throughout (and certainly the right musician does not allow himself to be frightened off by difficulties), should have stood out with greater fullness and impetuosity, to which purpose it would perhaps have been unavoidably necessary to place a greater number of players on the cello line.

Secondly, however, it is certainly not to be expected that a large audience can comprehend such a profound work upon first hearing *without preparation.* Admittedly, if we had reached the point in *Berlin* that has already been attained in *Leipzig,*[5] where *all* the symphonies of Beethoven and of many other masters are performed throughout the year, *then* the public's feeling for such artworks would be more receptive and heightened; then even the most beloved soprano would not be able to undertake a concert without choosing mostly good pieces; then even the *foremost* soprano would have to recognize that with an offering of Merkadante, she will be outdone by every *mediocre* singer who performs Mozart, Beethoven, and other genuine artists. Can the costliest vessel ennoble its content, turn water into *wine*? If Madame Seidler, with her charming voice and great skill, sings pieces by Merkadante, do we hear anything other than a commonplace thing coming from a lovely mouth? But the undersigned has given a judgment on the entire concert (while not having had time to hear everything), and only wishes to speak about the overture.

It seems to have been listened to like everything that is taken to be but a customary introduction to the main event, and that is disregarded apart from a pair of pleasant melodies and some spectacle that signals applause at the final conclusion. Enough has happened in most earlier concerts to make the audience (with the exception of those who, either in themselves or through favorable circumstances, found it possible to prepare themselves in a more elevated way) lower its expectations, and forget that something entirely different matters in an overture, a concentration of the ideas that prevail in the piece, preparing for it and introducing it. Now this task is solved in Beethoven's Overture to *Coriolan* as much as it can possibly be. When we think of the proud, fierce, deeply feeling youth, banned by the people's party, forsaken by the nobles for whom he had taken up battle with them, leading his sworn enemy in a triumphant invasion of Rome, unsusceptible to any reconciliation, deaf to pleading, and then, through childlike love and veneration of his mother in his furious hatred, beaten in his promise of revenge, himself once again banished and wandering forth into forgetfulness and night, or (as other historians would have it) suffering death for his reconciliation under the swords of his suspicious warriors: there we have the content of the overture.[6] Every phrase in it, for example, that quoted before, or this pleading one

OP. 62
Allegro con brio, mm. 56–59

has unmistakable meaning, and the whole is arranged so as to be as momentous and vast as the event itself, and dies out in sorrow and darkness, like Coriolan's life.

So much, at least, could have been suggested to the audience, which, as has been said, cannot guess at such things for itself, and therefore does not discover them.

NOTES

1. Karl Seidler (1778–1840) was one of the foremost German violinists of his day. His wife, Caroline (1790–1872), daughter of Beethoven's friend Anton Wranitzky and niece of the conductor Paul Wranitzky, was a well-known soprano; she was the first to sing the role of Agathe in Weber's opera *Der Freischütz.* See Kutsch and Riemens, *Großes Sängerlexikon,* 2717–18.

2. Giuseppe Saverio Raffaele Mercadante (1795–1870) was a prominent Italian opera composer. Despite Marx's obvious contempt, Mercadante later became an important operatic reformer and a rival of Verdi.

3. "Kehlvariationen auf ein Karaffathema." This refers to a custom, common among university students in the eighteenth and nineteenth centuries, of reciting or singing verse extemporaneously on images etched or painted on the broad base of a bottle of wine with a narrow neck. At the end of each performance, a drink was taken and the bottle passed on until the students were too drunk to continue. The reference here is obviously pejorative.

4. Charles Philippe Lafont (1781–1839) was the preeminent French violinist of his day. He gave a famous joint performance with Paganini in Milan in 1816. His compositions include concertos and other works for the violin and at least one opera.

5. On the performances of the symphonies in Berlin and Leipzig during the 1820s, see Pederson, "Marx, Berlin, and German National Identity," 87–107.

6. Collin presumably based his play, as did Shakespeare, on Plutarch's account of the life of Caius Marcius (186–157 B.C.), called Coriolanus in honor of his victory at the Volscian capital of Corioli. Plutarch tells how Marcius was banished from Rome through an unprecedented usurpation of power by the common people, exercised through the newly created tribuneships, whose establishment he had opposed and sought to rescind. Nourishing an implacable desire for revenge, he placed himself at the service of the Volscian leader Tullus. After several important victories, Marcius was at the point of invading Rome

when his mother, accompanied by his wife and children, begged him to retreat. Coriolanus was then murdered by Volscian conspirators who feared the outcome of his anticipated public defense of his actions. In Collin's play, Coriolan falls on his own sword in the final scene, surrounded by sympathetic Volscian commanders.

~

OP. 65
SCENE AND ARIA *AH! PERFIDO*

(See entry nos. 177 and 263)

201.

Johann Friedrich Reichardt.[1] "Review." *Berlinische musikalische Zeitung* 1, no. 96 (1805): 379–82.

A very lovely scene full of power and expression and just as full of fortunate, moving melodies and brilliant instrumental effects. Up until the Allegro of the rondo, there is no measure, no note, whose effect is not certain, even if the lengthening of the Adagio after the repetition of the theme is perhaps too long and therefore detracts from the impression of this beautiful song. In the Allegro, which begins very pathetically, the more frequent disruptions of the tempo are very detrimental to the effect of the whole. The slower and the more lively tempos alternate seven times, which become all the more tiring because the slow tempo begins and ends each time with the same melody and even in the same key. The tragic effect of the whole, which could be very great in view of the layout and working-out of the rest, is finally completely destroyed by such glaring contrasts. This unfortunate effect is all the more inevitable because the slow melody, which is completely lacking in purity and distinctiveness, forms the greatest possible contrast with the Allegro. In every regard, it is the most glaring contrast of black and red that can be placed together in notes. Admittedly, this is most pleasing to insensitive listeners, who wish only to be shaken up and then once again reassured from time to time, and nothing is more certain than their loudest applause. Should a man of B's genius and artistry, however, have such a goal in mind when working out scenes that are conceived in times of the happiest inspiration, sung with an aroused and uplifted soul? For him to set the goal of arousing the loud hand-clapping of the crowd through commonplace means is hardly worthy of himself and of his art.[2] Mr. B. must now, with that self-respect that is proper to the genuine artist, take into account and not forget that, in those works that are exhibited to the public, he will be counted among those masters whose talent places them among the ranks of those whose every departure from pure good sense and from the proper artistic norms can and must lead to a thousand aberrations. All that is showy, and thus is most loudly applauded by the crowd, will be more easily imitated a hundred times over, before the true beauty and greatness in his works is first completely perceived and utilized for its own benefit. But enough said in this tone to a man for whom we would so gladly reserve our most perfect respect, purely and without qualification.

The friends of singing will certainly thank the publisher for this scene, and for the manner in which it was released; in addition to a complete keyboard reduction, which to a certain degree replaces the score, they will find the accompanying instrumental parts individually engraved, and thus can satisfy their inclinations either in a complete concert or at a solitary keyboard.[3] May several such interesting concert scenes soon be placed in our hands!

NOTES

1. Johann Friedrich Reichardt (1752–1814) was a composer, writer, and editor of the *Berlinische musikalische Zeitung,* with which he helped pioneer music journalism and advocated classical German aesthetics. The BMZ is also one of the first periodicals in northern Germany to publish music criticism on Beethoven. Because of his unorthodox life style, Reichardt was frequently at odds with political authorities and often moved about from post to post. His opposition to Napoleon is largely responsible for the abrupt end of the BMZ. In Germany he is known for his *Lieder,* particularly his musical compositions of Goethe's poetry.

2. "A lovely word from K. W. S. in his correspondence with *Goethe* (see no. 120 of the *Intelligenzblatt der Jenaischen allgemeinen Litteraturzeitung*) is very appropriate here. 'Where ambition is more the motive than love for the thing itself, all skill and wisdom will become ineffective at precisely the point where the innermost mysteries of art begin, which only reveal themselves to a loving enthusiasm.' Mr. B. can certainly relinquish his loving enthusiasm with full assurance that this provides the first and last word."

3. The first edition was published in July 1805 by the Bureau de Musique in Leipzig. As the critic remarks, the soprano part contains a piano reduction, as is noted on the title page (see Kinsky-Halm, 155).

202.

"Concerning Various Musical Performances in Leipzig."
Berliner allgemeine musikalische Zeitung 3 (12 July 1826): 225.

(With Symphony No. 6, op. 68, Symphony No. 7, op. 92,
Symphony No. 8, op. 93, and "Namensfeier" Overture, op. 115)

The symphonies that were performed at the final subscription concerts of this year were (1) the Pastoral Symphony of Beethoven. For those who know how to feel and perceive it, can the easy, joyous life in nature be described in tones more purely, and with an easier flow of feeling, than in the first Allegro? And is there a more heartfelt expression of thankfulness for the returning peace of nature than in the so-called shepherd's song? (2) Symphony by the Abbé Vogler,[1] a work that through its well-known artful simplicity and originality contrasts so laudably with most more recent works of this kind. (3) Beethoven's A-Major Symphony (No. 7), and (4) his Symphony in F Major (No. 8) of which the first, even if it already shows the transition into the later period, yet stands incomparably higher than the latter, having much more significant thematic material, and an Adagio[2] that is beyond comparison. The overtures were (1) to Mozart's *Così fan tutte.* A perfect performance requires a good oboe player, which we certainly have here, but unfortunately not in the orchestra. (2) to *Faniska,* by Cherubini,[3] splendid and effective, and also superbly performed. (3) To *Die Zauberflöte.* (4) A new overture by Beethoven in C (no. 115, published by Steiner in Vienna), introduced by a Maestoso in common time, leading to an Allegro vivace in $\frac{6}{8}$, which flies by easily and fleetingly, but not without power. It was probably composed earlier and has only just been published.[4] (5) A rather affectedly powerful overture by Max Eberwein to Calderon's *Leben ein Traum.*[5] Of the solo pieces, I will mention only the magnificent concert scene by Beethoven, *Ah perfido spergiuro* etc., which still adheres completely to Mozart's manner, and which Miss Queck sang far better than her final aria by Rossini (from *Semiramis*), which lies much too low for her voice and in addition was performed from a very faulty copy.

NOTES

1. Abbé Georg Joseph Vogler (1749–1814) was a German theorist, teacher, organist, pianist, and composer. More recognized during his lifetime for his improvisations than his compositions, Vogler nonetheless composed a large number of stage works, sacred and secular vocal music, and instrumental music. Only three symphonies by Vogler are listed in MGG and the *New Grove:* Symphony in G Major, S. 107 (1779); the "Pariser" Symphony in D Minor, S. 118 (1782; dedicated to Marie Antoinette); and the Symphony in C Major, S. 164 (1799, revised in 1806).

2. The word "Adagio" is used here in the generic sense to designate a slow movement. The second movement of the Seventh Symphony is actually marked Allegretto.

3. Cherubini's *Faniska,* with a libretto by Joseph Sonnleithner, who was also Beethoven's librettist for *Fidelio,* was first performed in Vienna in 1806.

4. The overture "Zur Namensfeier" (the title was not given by Beethoven) was in fact written in 1814–15, though not published until 1825.

5. Max Eberwein is probably Traugott Maximilian Eberwein (1775–1831), a violinist, composer, and member of a prominent musical family known for its associations with Goethe. *La vida es seuño* by Calderón was written in 1635 and provided the major source for a drama of the same title (*Das Leben ein Traum,* 1834) by a friend of Beethoven, Franz Grillparzer (1791–1872).

OP. 66
TWELVE VARIATIONS ON
"EIN MÄDCHEN ODER WEIBCHEN" FROM MOZART'S
DIE ZAUBERFLÖTE, FOR PIANO AND CELLO, IN F MAJOR

203.

M . . . *Allgemeine musikalische Zeitung* 1 (6 March 1799): 366–68.

(With Eight Variations on "Une fièvre brûlante"
from Grétry's *Richard Coeur-de-Lion,* WoO 72)

It is well known that Mr. *van Beethoven* is a very capable keyboard player, and if it were not well known, one could deduce it from these variations. Whether he is equally fortunate as a composer is a question that, judging by these samples, would be more difficult to affirm. The reviewer does not mean to deny that several of these variations were pleasing to him, and he gladly admits that in those on the theme: *Mich brennt' ein heißes Fieber,* Mr. B. has succeeded better than *Mozart* did when he worked on the same theme early in his youth.[1] But Mr. B. is less fortunate in the variations on the first theme, where, for example, he allows changes and rigidities in the modulations that are anything but beautiful.[2] Examine, for example, Var. XII, where he modulates in broken chords from F major into D major:

OP. 66
Variation 12, mm. 40–46

and then where, after the theme has been heard in this key, he suddenly falls all at once back again into F in this manner:

OP. 66
Variation 12, mm. 53–55

Study and listen to such transitions as I will, they are and remain trite, and are and remain all the more so the more pretentious and ostentatious they become. In any case, I will not, however, be the first or only person to have said this to the composer of the above-mentioned pieces. Such a monstrous abundance of variations is now produced and unfortunately also printed, without very many of their composers seeming truly to know what exactly is involved in writing good variations. May I give them a piece of advice, as well as may be done in a small amount of space? Well, then, whoever has spirit and skill to write something good in the area of music—for without these qualities one remains a piece of ringing brass or a tinkling bell—should learn (1) to *choose his theme* from *Joseph Haydn*. The themes of this master are outstandingly (a) simple and easy to grasp, (b) beautifully rhythmic, (c) not commonplace, and capable of further elaboration in melody and harmony.[3] If one wants (2) to have instruction as to how such a well-chosen theme is *to be worked out* (to the extent, that is to say, that instruction can be given about something of this sort): let him study most of all a little work that, as far as I can tell, is little known, and certainly not as well known as it deserves to be, *Vogler's* evaluation of Forkel's Variations on the English Folk Song *God Save the King,* published in Frankfurt by *Varrentrapp und Wenner.*[4] This writing should not be taken simply for an ordinary review; its author, who is just as ingenious as he is learned, shows in it not simply what is to be criticized in these variations and how to improve it, but always why it is to be criticized, why it needs to be improved, and why it should be improved precisely so and not otherwise.

NOTES

1. K. Anh. 285: Seven Variations on "Une fièvre brûlante" from Grétry's *Richard Coeur-de-Lion.* Mozart scholars consider this work to be spurious.

2. Modulations by thirds became a hallmark of Beethoven's tonal language. Arguing that such modulations were a way to relax the rules of eighteenth-century harmony, William Drabkin observes that "third related harmonies occur throughout Beethoven's work, though invariably within a framework of traditional tonal relationships" (*Beethoven Compendium: A Guide to Beethoven's Life and Music,* ed. Barry Cooper [London: Thames and Hudson, 1991], 202).

3. Beethoven's indebtedness to Haydn's skills at varying his initial material is discussed in Jan LaRue, "Multistage Variance: Haydn's Legacy to Beethoven," *Journal of Musicology* 1 (1982): 265–74.

4. Vogler's *Verbesserung der Forkel'scher Veränderungen über das englische Volkslied "God Save the King"* was published in 1793. It consisted of a commentary on 24 *Veränderungen für Clavichord oder Fortepiano auf das englische Volkslied: "God Save the King"* by Johann Nikolaus Forkel (1749–1818), published by Breitkopf & Härtel in 1791. Vogler accompanied his criticisms with his own "improved" version of the variations.

~

OP. 67
SYMPHONY NO. 5 IN C MINOR

(See entry nos. 22, 45, and 50, vol. 1, pp. 45, 101, 125; 178, 179, 226, and 240, vol. 2)

204.
"News. Leipzig." *Allgemeine musikalische
Zeitung* 11 (1 February 1809): 281.

Apart from these pieces the following distinguished themselves: Mozart's spirited, artistic scene with obbligato pianoforte,[1] sung by Miss Schicht;[2] a very lively bravura aria for tenor, sung, and probably written as well, by Mr. Jul. Miller;[3] a free fantasy for the pianoforte by Music Director Müller performed in combination with the last of his great capriccios, and indeed so excellently that we have never heard Mr. M. play with greater mastery; and finally a new, grand symphony by Beethoven (No. 6),[4] which in its fashion, in accordance both with the ideas and with their treatment, once again stands so much apart from all others that even the trained listener must hear it several times before he can make it his own and arrive at a definite opinion. This is particularly true since it is also so difficult to perform that even the most practiced orchestra will not be able to play it for the first time with complete accuracy and according to the composer's intentions. This symphony will be published in several weeks by the firm of Breitkopf & Härtel.[5]

NOTES

1. This was probably "Ch'io mi scordi di te . . . Non temer, amato bene," K. 505, written by Mozart to be performed by himself and the English singer Nancy Storace.

2. According to AMZ 9 (1806–07), 338, Miss Schicht was the daughter of Johann Gottfried Schicht (1753–1823), an eminent conductor and composer who succeeded August Eberhard Müller as Thomascantor in 1810. Her mother was the Italian singer Costanza, née Valdesturla (?-1809). She performed frequently in Leipzig at the end of the first and the beginning of the second decades of the nineteenth century.

3. Julius Miller (1782–1851) was a prominent tenor who composed several operas, including *Der Freybrief, Die Verwandlung, Die Alpenhütte,* and *Hermann und Thusnelda.* He appears to have been a rather remarkable character, although he outlived his fame and died in debased circumstances.

4. "Musik in Leipzig" in AMZ 11 (1809) still mentions the C-Minor Symphony as No. 6 and the Pastoral as No. 5, although in the *Intelligenzblatt* for April, which lists upcoming publications, they are numbered correctly. This notice, which dates from February, probably refers to the symphony now known as No. 5.

5. The first edition of the parts for the Fifth Symphony was published by Breitkopf & Härtel in April 1809, three months after this review. The parts for the Sixth Symphony were published by Breitkopf & Härtel in May 1809.

205.

"Music in Leipzig. Instrumental Music." *Allgemeine musikalische Zeitung* 11 (12 April 1809): 433–37.

(With Symphony No. 6, op. 68; mentioned: Symphony No. 3, op. 55)

Symphonies—by J. Haydn, the one in G major with Turkish instruments;[1] the second to last of those in D major (Andante in G major);[2] the one in C minor;[3] and the older concertante (with obbligato violin, violoncello, flute, oboe, and bassoon);[4] by *Mozart,* the earlier one in D major (Andante in G major);[5] by *Beethoven,* the *Eroica* Symphony (No. 3); and the new one, No. 6,[6] from the composer's manuscript, but which has also just been printed by Breitkopf & Härtel.[7] It was given for the first time at the extra concerts by Mr. Tietz[8] in Dresden, where, however, because of its great difficulties, the performance was not entirely successful. The repetition in the weekly concert went very well (apart from a few small points) and was received with enthusiasm.

The first movement (C minor) is a serious, somewhat gloomy Allegro, which seems to consume everything with fire, while remaining noble, even and firm in feeling as in the working-out; despite many peculiarities, it is handled simply, strictly, and quite regularly. It is a worthy piece, which will give rich satisfaction even to those who adhere to the traditional manner of arranging grand symphonies. The Andante is arranged from the most heterogeneous ideas—gently rapturous and ruggedly military—in a completely original and very attractive way and throughout remains alone of its kind. Everything that appears to be capricious in this wonderful movement nevertheless shows great learning, a confident overview of the whole, and very careful working-out. The scherzando that follows (for a perfect performance of which an orchestra of strong players is hardly possible) we did not, we have to admit, find to be completely enjoyable on account of its all too strange whims. One knows, however, that such products of humor in art are—if this comparison may be allowed us—like the higher refinements of the art of cooking: one must first make oneself receptive through repeated consumption, after which one often becomes all too fond of them.

The finale is such a stormy outpouring of a mighty imagination as can scarcely be found in any other symphony. That which has to do specifically with performance is not so much in question here: however, the power of the emotions that constantly struggle anew with one another, the continually renewed contrasts, which, moreover, are mostly set against one another in the sharpest possible way, the continually returning sense of surprise that is produced by this, as also through the strangeness of the ideas and their completely unusual juxtaposition, sequence, and combination: all this, united with much that is peculiar and very piquant in the use of the instruments, charms and creates tensions in the listener throughout the whole duration of this long movement so thoroughly and so continually anew that it cannot fail to be accorded a brilliant effect wherever it is well performed. A second new, grand symphony by the same composer (No. 5),[9] which likewise has just been printed from the manuscript by Breitkopf & Härtel, and which he himself has titled *rustic* (Pastorale), is a scarcely less noteworthy and peculiar product. A seemingly simple and good-natured pastorale (Allegro, ma non molto), to which the composer himself has given the subtitle: "Awakening of happy feelings upon arrival in the countryside" and which is certainly not lacking in original turns of phrase, even though it is designed in such a way that the principal effect falls upon the later movements, is followed by an Andante con moto. Designated more precisely by the composer as: "Scene by the brook," this is written, in accordance with the ideas, in a manner that is very simple, and in feeling as very gentle and (apparently intentionally) also very monotonous as in working-out. It seems to us, even allowing for that which it is and should be, somewhat too long. The painterly layout of the whole is, however, ingenious, and even a number of closely juxtaposed, jokingly treated copies of particular more ordinary phenomena (especially toward the end) cannot be received by anyone—even if he does not care for such things at all elsewhere—without delighted laughter, since they portray the objects in such an exceptionally striking way, and since, as has already been said, they are only used in a humorous manner.[10] We hold the Allegro no. 3, "Merry togetherness of the country people," interrupted by "Storm and thunderstorm," Allegro no. 4, to be the most excellent movements of this work. They are completely as they must be, with such a newness and abundance of ideas, and such power and effectiveness in their working-out, that one can never hear them without amazement and joy. The bright and completely characteristic joviality in the first of these movements can be compared only to the "Celebration of the wine growers"[11] in Haydn's *Seasons,* and the rushing storm, with all that normally accompanies it, is carried off with such energy and persistence—so much to the shame of those means that are customarily employed to this purpose—that one can truly only be astounded at the riches and artistry of the master. Incidentally, we certainly do not wish to undertake to defend all the harmonies that appear here and in various other places in this work. The whole is suitably and respectably concluded by an Allegretto ("Shepherd's song. Joyful and grateful feelings after the storm"), even though the preceding movements are detrimental to the effect of this last movement in and of itself. In this respect Haydn was more fortunate in his evening scene after the storm (in the *Seasons*),[12] and Beethoven would have been too if he, like Haydn, had made this last movement even a great deal simpler, gentler, and more artless.

The entire work will certainly find much applause everywhere that people approach it without a predetermined opinion, and enter with good will and happy spirits into the intentions of the artist. This can sometimes be facilitated by a word, a suitable label, and to this purpose we will further mention that, rather than a symphony, this composition would much more appropriately be called the fantasies of a composer suggested by those topics that Beethoven mentions.

NOTES

1. Symphony No. 100 in G, "The Military."
The original word "Janitscharen-Instrument" refers to "Janissary instruments," which derived from a band formed by the Turkish sultan's bodyguard (the Janissarism disbanded in 1826). German versions generally consisted of triangles, cymbals, and a bass drum. For a history of "alla Turca music," see Mary Hunter, "The *Alla Turca* Style in the Late Eighteenth Century: Race and Gender in the Symphony and the Seraglio," *The Exotic in Western Music,* ed. Jonathan Bellman (Boston: Northeastern University Press, 1998), 43–73.

2. Symphony No. 101, "The Clock."

3. Probably Symphony No. 95.

4. Hoboken I:105 in B♭. This is the only concertante symphony that Haydn wrote, so it is unclear why the writer makes the distinction that he does.

5. Probably either the "Haffner" or the "Paris" Symphony.

6. Concerning the reverse and incorrect numbering of Symphonies Nos. 5 and 6 at their first appearance, see entry no. 169, n. 2.

7. "A reduction for keyboard four-hands by Fr. Schneider is also forthcoming." The first edition of the parts was published in April 1809.

8. The Dresden violinist Ludwig Tietz is mentioned briefly in *New Grove,* 19: 17. Tietz was a talented violinist with a few published compositions.

9. Actually No. 6.

10. The author probably refers here to the literal imitations of the nightingale, quail, and cuckoo in the coda of the movement.

11. Presumably this refers to the chorus "Juchhe! der Wein ist da," which concludes the "Autumn" section of Haydn's work.

12. This is apparently a reference to the trio and chorus "Die düstren Wolken trennen sich" from the "Summer" section of Haydn's *Seasons.*

∾

206.
Ernst Theodor Amadeus Hoffmann. "Review." *Allgemeine musikalische Zeitung* 12 (4 and 11 July 1810): 630–42 and 652–59.[1]

(Also arrangement for piano four-hands)
The reviewer has before him one of the most important works of that master who no one will now deny belongs among the first rank of instrumental composers. He is permeated by the topic that he is to discuss, and no

one may take it amiss if, stepping beyond the boundaries of the customary critique, he strives to put into words what this composition made him feel deep within his soul. When music is being discussed as a self-sufficient art, this should always be understood to refer only to instrumental music, which, disdaining all help, all admixture of any other art, purely expresses the peculiar essence of this art, which can be recognized in it alone. It is the most romantic of all the arts—one almost wishes to say the only one that is *purely* romantic. Orpheus's lyre opened the gates of the underworld. Music reveals an unknown kingdom to mankind: a world that has nothing in common with the outward, material world that surrounds it, and in which we leave behind all predetermined, conceptual feelings in order to give ourselves up to the inexpressible. How little did *those* instrumental composers who tried to represent these predetermined feelings, or even to represent events, recognize this peculiar essence of music, trying instead to treat that art that is diametrically opposed to the plastic arts in a plastic way! Dittersdorf's[2] symphonies of this kind, as well as all more recent *Batailles de trois Empereurs*, etc. are ludicrous mistakes that should be punished with complete oblivion. In song, where the poetry that is added indicates specific affects by means of words, the magical power of music works like the wondrous elixir of the wise, by means of which various simpletons make every drink delicious and magnificent. Every passion—love—hate—anger—despair etc., such as we encounter in opera, is clothed by music in the purple shimmer of romanticism, and even that which we experience in life leads us out beyond life into the kingdom of the infinite. The magic of music is this strong, and, as its effect becomes more and more powerful, it must tear to pieces any impediment from another art. The height to which composers of genius have presently raised instrumental music has been reached not only through simplification of the expressive means (perfection of the instruments, greater virtuosity of the performers) but through their deep, heartfelt recognition of the peculiar essence of music. Haydn and Mozart, the creators of recent instrumental music, first showed us this art in its full glory; he who grasped it with full devotion and penetrated its innermost essence is—Beethoven. The instrumental compositions of all three masters breathe a similar Romantic spirit, due to their all having taken possession of the peculiar essence of the art; the character of their compositions, however, is markedly different. The expression of a childlike, happy soul dominates in Haydn's compositions. His symphonies lead us into a vast, green meadow, into a joyous, colorful crowd of fortunate people. Youths and maidens glide by in round dances; laughing children, listening beneath trees, beneath rose bushes, teasingly throw flowers at each other. A life full of love, full of blessedness, as though before sin, in eternal youth; no suffering, no pain; only sweet, wistful yearning for the beloved form that hovers far away in the glow of the sunset, comes no nearer, and does not disappear; and as long as it is there, it will not become night, for it is itself the sunset, which illuminates the mountains and the woods. Into the depths of the spirit kingdom we are led by Mozart. Fear surrounds us: but, in the absence of torment, it is more a foreboding of the infinite. Love and melancholy sound forth in charming voices, the power[3] of the spirit world ascends in the bright purple shimmer, and we follow along in inexpressible longing behind the beloved forms that beckon to us in their rows, flying through the clouds in the eternal dance of the spheres. (For example, Mozart's Symphony in E♭ Major, known under the name of *Schwanengesang*.)[4] In this way, Beethoven's instrumental music also opens up to us the kingdom of the gigantic and the immeasurable. Glowing beams shoot through this kingdom's deep night, and we become aware of gigantic shadows that surge up and down, enclosing us more and more narrowly and annihilating everything within us, leaving only the pain of that interminable longing, in which every pleasure that had quickly arisen with sounds of rejoicing sinks away and founders, and we live on, rapturously beholding the spirits themselves, only in this pain, which, consuming love, hope, and joy within itself, seeks to burst our breast asunder with a full-voiced consonance of all the passions. Romantic taste is rare, Romantic talent even rarer: this is probably why there are so few who can strike that lyre that opens up the wonderful kingdom of the infinite. Haydn treats that which is human in human life romantically; he is more in accordance with the majority. Mozart lays claim to that which is more than human, that which is wondrous, and dwells within the innermost spirit. Beethoven's music moves the lever controlling horror, fear, dread, pain and awakens that interminable longing that is the essence of romanticism. Beethoven is a purely romantic (and precisely for that reason truly musical) composer, and this may be the reason that he has been less successful with vocal music,[5] which does not allow for unspecified yearning, but only represents those affects that are indicated by the words as they are experienced in the kingdom of the infinite—and that his instrumental music does not appeal to the masses. Even those masses who do not follow Beethoven into the depths do not deny that he has a high degree of imagination; on the contrary, it is customary to see in his works simply the products of a genius that, unconcerned with the form and selection of its ideas, gives itself over to its own fire and to the momentary promptings of its imagination. Nevertheless, in regard to presence of mind, he deserves to be placed on the very same level as Haydn and Mozart. Separating what is merely himself from the innermost kingdom of notes, he is thus able to rule over it as an absolute lord. The artists of aesthetic measurement have often complained about the total lack of true unity and inner coherence in Shakespeare, while it requires a deeper look to reveal a lovely tree, whose buds and leaves, flowers and fruits all grow from the same seed. Likewise, it is only by entering very deeply into the inner structure of Beethoven's music that *the* great presence of mind of this master reveals itself, which is inseparable from true genius and is nourished by unceasing study of the art.

Beethoven bears musical romanticism deep within his soul and expresses it in his works with great genius and presence of mind. The reviewer has never felt this in a more lively way than with the present symphony, which, in a climax that builds steadily until the end, reveals this romanticism of Beethoven more than any other work of his, and sweeps the listener irresistibly into the wonderful spirit kingdom of the infinite. The first Allegro, $\frac{2}{4}$ time in C minor, begins with a principal idea that consists of only two measures, and that, in the course of what follows, continually reappears in many different forms. In the second measure a fermata; then a repetition of this idea a tone lower, and again a fermata; both times only string instruments and clarinets. Even the key cannot yet be determined; the listener surmises E♭ major. The second violin begins the principal idea once again, and in the second measure the fundamental note of C, struck by the violoncello and bassoon, delineates the key of C minor, in which viola and violin enter in imitation, until these finally juxtapose two measures with the principal idea, which, thrice repeated (the final time with the entry of the full orchestra), and dying out in a fermata on the dominant, give to the listener's soul a presentiment of the unknown and the mysterious. The beginning of the Allegro, up until this point of rest, determines the character of the entire piece, and for this reason the reviewer inserts it here for his readers to examine:

After this fermata, the violins and violas imitate the principal idea, remaining in the tonic, while the bass now and then strikes a figure that resembles that idea. A constantly mounting transitional passage, which once again arouses that presentiment, even stronger and more urgently than before, then leads to a tutti whose theme once again has the rhythmic content of the principal idea and is intimately related to it:

The sixth chord based on D⁶ prepares the related major key of E♭, in which the horn once again recalls the principal idea. The first violin takes up a second theme, which is certainly melodious, but still remains true to the character of anxious, restless longing that the whole movement expresses. The violin carries this theme forward in alternation with the clarinet, and each time in the third measure the bass strikes that first mentioned recollection of the principal idea, by means of which this theme is again completely interlaced into the artistic web of the whole [mm. 58ff.]. In the further extension of this theme, the first violin and the violoncello repeat five times, in the key of E♭ minor, a figure that consists of only two measures, while the basses climb chromatically upward, until at last a new transitional passage leads to the conclusion, in which the wind instruments repeat the first tutti in E♭ major, and finally the full orchestra closes in E♭ major with the oft-mentioned recollection of the principal theme [mm. 83ff.]. The principal theme once again begins the second part in its initial form, only transposed a third higher and played by the clarinets and horns. The phrases of the first part follow in F minor, C minor, G minor, only differently arranged and orchestrated, until at last, after a transition once again made up of only two measures, which the violins and the wind instruments take up in alternation, while the violoncellos play a figure in contrary motion and the basses climb upwards, the following chords enter in the full orchestra:

OP. 67
Allegro con brio, harmonic reduction of mm. 169–80

They are sounds by means of which the breast, oppressed and alarmed by presentiments of the gigantic, vents itself powerfully; and like a friendly form, which radiantly illuminating the deep night moves through the clouds, a theme now enters that was only touched upon by the horn in E♭ major at m. 58 of the first part.[7] First in G major, then in C major, the violins play this theme *alla 8va*, while the basses play an upward-climbing figure that somewhat recalls the tutti passage that began at m. 44 of the first part [mm. 179ff.].

OP. 67
Allegro con brio, mm. 179–86

The wind instruments begin this theme *fortissimo* in F minor, but after the third measure, the string instruments take up the two final measures, and, imitating these measures, string and wind instruments alternate yet another five times and then strike individual chords, always diminuendo and once again in alternation.

    After the sixth chord

OP. 67
Allegro con brio, harmonic
reduction of m. 214

the reviewer would have expected G♭ major in the chord progression that followed, which then, in the manner in which things are done here, would lead back to G major, having been enharmonically transformed into F♯ minor. The wind instruments, however, which strike the chord that follows that sixth chord, are written:

OP. 67
Allegro con brio, harmonic
reduction of m. 215

Immediately thereafter, the string instruments strike this F♯-minor chord

OP. 67
Allegro con brio, harmonic
reduction of m. 216

which is then repeated for four measures alternately by strings and wind instruments. The chords of the wind instruments are always written as was indicated above, for no reason that the reviewer can discern.

The sixth chord

now likewise follows, ever weaker and weaker. This has an unsettling and terrifying effect!—The full orchestra now strikes up a theme that is almost identical to that which was heard forty-one measures earlier,[8] while only the flutes and trumpets hold the dominant, D. This theme, however, comes to rest after only four measures, and the string instruments and horns, and then the remaining wind instruments, strike the diminished chord

pianissimo seven times in alternation. In the next measure [m. 240], the basses then take up the first principal idea for two measures, with the remaining instruments *unisono*. Bass and upper voices imitate each other in this manner through five measures, followed by three measures in unison, and in the fourth measure, the full orchestra, with trumpets and drums, sounds the principal theme in its original form. The first part is now repeated with minor variations; the theme that first began in E♭ major appears now in C major and leads to a triumphant close in C major with trumpets and drums. This very conclusion, however, turns the music into F minor

Through five measures of full orchestra on the sixth chord: clarinets, bassoons, and horns strike *piano* an imitation of the principal idea. One measure of general pause, then for six measures

all the wind instruments resume as before: and now the violas, violoncellos, and bassoons take up a theme that was heard previously in the second part in G major, while the violins, entering *unisono* in the third measure, perform a new countersubject. The music now remains in C minor, and, with small variations, the theme that began in m. 71 of the first part is repeated by the violins first alone, and then in alternation with the wind instruments. The alternations become ever closer and closer, first one measure, then a half measure; it is a driving urgency—a surging storm, whose waves strike higher and higher—until finally, twenty-four measures before the end, the beginning of the Allegro is repeated once again. There follows an organ point over which the theme is imitated until at last the final conclusion follows strongly and powerfully.

There is no simpler idea than that which the master laid as the foundation of this entire Allegro

OP. 67
Allegro con brio, mm. 1–2

and one realizes with wonder how he was able to align all the secondary ideas, all the transitional passages with the rhythmic content of this simple theme in such a way that they served continually to unfold the character of the whole, which that theme could only suggest. All phrases are short, consisting of only two or three measures, and are divided up even further in the ongoing exchanges between the string and the wind instruments. One might believe that from such elements only something disjointed and difficult to comprehend could arise; nevertheless, it is precisely this arrangement of the whole, as well as the repetitions of the short phrases and individual chords that follow continually upon one another, which hold the spirit firmly in an unnameable longing.

Completely apart from the fact that the contrapuntal treatment shows deep study of the art, it is also the transitional passages and the continual references to the principal theme that show how the master did not simply conceive the whole, with all its characteristic features, within his spirit, but thought it through as well.

Like a charming spirit voice, which fills our breast with comfort and hope, sounds next the lovely (and yet meaningful) theme of the Andante in A♭ major, $\frac{3}{8}$ time, which is performed by the viola and violoncello. The further development of the Andante recalls numerous middle movements from Haydn's symphonies, inasmuch as, just as frequently happens there, the principal theme is varied in many different ways after interjected transitional phrases. It cannot be equated with the first Allegro in terms of originality, even though the idea of continually interrupting the transitions back to A♭ major by allowing an imposing phrase in C major with trumpets and drums to intervene produces a striking effect.[9] The transition to C major occurs twice in the midst of enharmonic exchanges:

OP. 67
Andante con moto, mm. 28–30, 77–79

whereupon the grandiose theme enters and then the modulation to the dominant chord of A♭ major is completed in the following manner:

OP. 67
Andante con moto, harmonic reduction of mm. 90–97

In a simpler but very effective way, the flutes, oboes, and clarinets prepare for the third transition to this C major theme:

OP. 67
Andante con moto, mm. 144–47

All the phrases of the Andante are very melodious, and the principal theme is even beguiling, but the very progress of this theme, which goes through

Ab major, Bb minor, F minor, and Bb minor before first returning to Ab, the continual juxtaposition of the major tonalities Ab and C, the chromatic modulations, express once again the character of the whole, and by virtue of this the Andante is a part of that whole. It is as if the frightful spirit, which in the Allegro gripped and unsettled the soul, were to step forth and threaten every moment from the storm clouds into which it had disappeared, and the friendly forms that had surrounded us comfortingly were to flee quickly from its sight.

The Minuet[10] that follows the Andante is once again as original, as gripping to the listener's soul, as one might expect from this master in the composition of that part of the symphony that, according to the example of Haydn, which he was following, should be the most piquant and ingenious of all. It is primarily the distinctive modulations, closes on the dominant-major chord, whose bass note is taken up by the bass as the tonic of the following theme in minor—the theme itself, which always extends itself by only a few measures, that strongly express the character of Beethoven's music, as the reviewer has described it above, and arouse anew that restlessness, that presentiment of the wonderful spirit kingdom with which the phrases of the Allegro assailed the listener's soul. The theme in C minor, played by the basses alone, turns in the third measure toward G minor, the horns sustain the G, and the violins and violas, joined in the second measure by the bassoons, and then by the clarinets, perform a four-measure phrase that cadences in G. The basses now repeat the theme, but after the G minor of the third measure, it turns to D minor and then to C minor, where the violin phrase is repeated. The horns now perform a phrase that leads into Eb major, while the string instruments strike chords in quarter notes at the beginning of each measure. The orchestra, however, leads the music farther, into Eb minor, and closes on the dominant, Bb major. In the same measure, however, the bass begins the principal theme and performs it just as at the beginning in C minor, only now it is in Bb minor [m. 53]. The violins, etc., too, repeat their own phrases, and there follows a point of rest in F major. The bass repeats the same theme, extending it, however, going through F minor, C minor, G minor, and then returning to C minor, whereupon the tutti, which first appeared in Eb minor, leads through F minor to a C-major chord. However, just as it went before from Bb major to Bb minor, the bass now takes up the bass note C as tonic of the theme in C minor [m. 96]. Flutes and oboes, imitated by the clarinets in the second measure, now take up the phrase that was first performed by the string instruments, while these repeatedly strike a single measure from the previously mentioned tutti; the horns sustain G, the violoncellos begin a new theme, which is connected first to a further development of the violins' opening phrase, then to a new phrase in eighth notes (which had not yet been heard). Even the new theme of the violoncellos contains allusions to the principal phrase and is thereby intimately related to it, as it is also through the similar rhythm. After a brief repetition of the tutti, this section of the minuet concludes *fortissimo* in C minor with trumpets and drums. The second part (the trio) is begun by the basses with a theme in C minor, which is imitated fugally by the violas in the dominant, then by the second violin in a shortened form, and then similarly shortened by the first violins. The first half of this part closes in G major. In the second part, the basses begin the theme twice and stop again, continuing forward the third time. To many this may seem humorous, but in the reviewer it awakened an uncanny feeling.—After much imitation of the principal theme, it is taken up by the flutes, supported by oboes, clarinets, and bassoons, over the bass note G, which is sustained by the horns, and it dies out in individual notes, which are struck first by the clarinets and bassoons and then by the basses. Now follows the repetition of the theme of the first part by the basses; in place of the violins the wind instruments have the phrase now in short notes, concluding it with a point of rest. Hereupon follows, as in the first part, the extended principal phrase, but in place of the half notes there are now quarter notes and quarter-note rests. In this form, and for the most part abbreviated, the other phrases of the first part also return. The restless longing, which the theme carried within itself, is now raised to the point of anxiety, which presses powerfully upon the breast so that only individual, broken sounds can escape from it. The G-major chord seems to point to the conclusion, but the bass now sustains the bass note A♭ *pianissimo* through fifteen measures [mm. 324ff.], and violins and violas likewise sustain the third, C, while the kettledrum strikes the C, first in the rhythm of that oft-mentioned tutti, then for four measures once in each measure, then for four measures twice, and then in quarter notes. The first violin finally takes up the first theme and leads through twenty-eight measures in which this theme is continually heard, up to the seventh of the dominant of the fundamental note. The second violins and the violas have sustained the C continually with the kettledrum playing the C in quarter notes; the bass, however, after having run through the scale from A♭ to F♯ and back to A♭, has struck the fundamental note G. Now enter first the bassoons, then one measure later the oboes, then three measures later the flutes, horns, and trumpets, while the kettledrum continually strikes the C in eighth notes, whereupon the music goes directly into the C-major chord, whereupon the final Allegro begins. The reason why the master continued the dissonant C of the kettledrum up to the conclusion is clarified by the character that he was striving to give to the whole. The heavy strokes of this dissonance, sounding like a strange, frightening voice, excite terror of the extraordinary—the fear of spirits. The reviewer has already mentioned somewhat earlier the mounting effect produced by the theme being extended for several measures, and in order to make this effect even more vivid, he will here place these extensions together:

OP. 67
Allegro (III), mm. 1–4, 8–16,
44–48, 53–64

At the repetition of the first part, this phrase appears in the following manner:

OP. 67
Allegro (III), mm. 244–52

Just as simple, and yet, when it reappears in later passages, just as gripping in its effect as the theme of the first Allegro, is the idea with which the tutti of the minuet begins.

OP. 67
Allegro (III), m. 27–28

The full orchestra, to which piccolos, trombones, and contrabassoons are now added, enters with the splendid, triumphant theme of the concluding movement, in C major—like radiant, blinding sunshine that suddenly illuminates the deep night. The phrases of this Allegro are treated more broadly than those that came before. They are not so much melodious as they are powerful, and suited to contrapuntal imitation. The modulations are unaffected and understandable; the first part has, for the most part, almost the feeling of an overture. Throughout thirty-four measures this part remains a tutti of the full orchestra in C major; then, to the accompaniment of a powerful, rising figure in the bass, a new theme in the upper voices modulates to G major and leads to the dominant chord of this key. Now begins yet another theme, consisting of quarter notes separated by triplets, which, in regard to its rhythm and its character, departs completely from what has gone before, and once again urges and impels like the phrases of the first Allegro or of the minuet:

Through this theme and through its further working-out through A minor toward C major, the soul is once again placed into a mood of foreboding, which had momentarily departed from it during the jubilation and rejoicing. With a short, rushing tutti the music turns once again to G major, and violas, bassoons, and clarinets begin a theme in sixths [mm. 64ff.], which is later taken up by the entire orchestra, and, after a short modulation to F minor, the first part concludes in C major with a powerful bass figure, which is then taken up by the violins in C major and then again by the basses *al rovescio*. The figure just mentioned is continued at the beginning of the second part in A minor, and that characteristic theme consisting of quarter notes and triplets enters once again. In shortened and restricted forms, this theme is now extended through thirty-four measures,[11] and in the course of this working-out the character that was already expressed in its original form is thoroughly worked out, to which no small contribution is made by the secondary phrases that are mixed in, the sustained tones of the trombones, and the triplet strokes in the kettledrums, trumpets, and horns. The music at last comes to rest on an organ point G [mm. 132ff.], which is struck first by the basses, and then by the bass trombones, trumpets, horns, and kettledrums, while the basses are performing a concluding figure *unisono* with the violins [mm. 132ff.]. Now, for the length of fifty-four measures, this simple theme from the minuet returns,

and there follows, in the two concluding measures, the transition from the minuet to the Allegro, only in a shorter form than before. With minor variations, and remaining in the principal key, the phrases of the first part now return, and a rushing tutti seems to lead to the conclusion. After the dominant chord, however, the bassoons, horns, flutes, oboes, and clarinets take up this theme, which was at first only touched upon, one after another [mm. 317ff.].

There follows yet another concluding phrase; the strings take up this phrase anew, after which it is played by the oboes, clarinets, and horns, and then again by the violins. The end seems near once again, but with the concluding chord in the tonic the violins take up, Presto (a *più stretto* begun several measures earlier), the phrase that was first heard at m. 64 of the Allegro, while the bass figure is the same one that they struck up in m. 28 of the first Allegro, and that, as has often been remarked above, is closely related to the principal theme through its rhythm, and strongly recalls it. The full orchestra (the basses enter a measure later, imitating the upper voice canonically) leads with the first theme of the last Allegro to the conclusion, which, shored up by many splendid, jubilant figures, follows after forty-one measures. The concluding chords themselves are written in a unique way; namely, after the chord that the listener takes for the last comes a measure rest, the same chord, a measure rest, once again the chord, a measure rest, then the same chord in quarter notes once every measure for three measures, a measure rest, the chord, a measure rest, and then C *unisono* struck by the entire orchestra. The perfect calm of the soul, brought about by various cadential figures following one after another, is abolished by these individual chords, struck between pauses, which recall the individual strokes in the Allegro of the symphony, and the listener is made eager anew by the final chords. They are like a fire, which was believed to have been put out, and which continually strikes out into the heights again in brightly blazing flames.

Beethoven has retained the customary succession of movements in the symphony. They appear to be put together in a fantastic way, and the whole rushes past many people like an inspired rhapsody: but the soul of every sensitive listener will certainly be deeply and closely gripped by a lingering feeling, which is precisely that unnameable, foreboding longing, and sustained in it until the final chord. Indeed, for many more moments after it, he will not be able to depart from the wonderful spirit kingdom, where pain and joy surrounded him in musical form.

Apart from the inner construction, the instrumentation, etc., it is primarily the intimate relationship that the individual themes have to one another that produces that unity that holds the listener's soul firmly in *a single* mood. In Haydn's and in Mozart's music, this unity dominates everywhere. It becomes clearer to the musician when he then discovers a fundamental bass that is common to two different passages, or when the connection between two passages reveals it; but a deeper relationship, which cannot be demonstrated in this manner, is often only expressed from the spirit to the spirit, and it is this relationship that prevails among the passages of both Allegros and of the minuet, and magnificently announces the master's presence of mind and genius. The reviewer believes that he can bring together his judgment about this magnificent work of art in a few words when he says that, ingeniously conceived and worked out with deep presence of mind, it expresses musical romanticism to a very high degree.

No instrument has difficult passagework to perform, but only an orchestra that is extraordinarily confident, practiced, and inspired by a *single* spirit, can venture to perform this symphony; for each moment that is in the least bit inadequate will spoil the whole irreparably. The continuous alternations, the exchanges between the string and wind instruments, the chords that are to be struck individually after rests, and so forth, demand the highest precision, on account of which the conductor should also be advised not, as often does occur, to play along more loudly than is appropriate with the first violins, but much rather to hold the whole orchestra constantly in his eye and hand.[12] The first violin part is useful to this purpose, as it contains the entries of the obbligato instruments within itself.—The engraving is correct and clear. The same publisher has released this same symphony in an arrangement for pianoforte four-hands under the title: *Cinquième Sinfonie de Louis van Beethoven, arrangée pour le pianoforte à quatre mains*. Chez Breitkopf et Härtel à Leipsic (Pr. 2 Rthlr. 12 Gr.)[13] The reviewer is not otherwise much in favor of arrangements; nevertheless, it cannot be denied that the enjoyment of a masterwork, which one hears with the full orchestra, often excites the imagination as much as before in a lonely room, and sets the soul in the same mood. The pianoforte produces the great work like a sketch does a great painting, which the imagination enlivens with the colors of the original. What is more, the symphony has been arranged for the pianoforte with understanding and insight, so that the necessities of the instrument are taken appropriately into account without obscuring the peculiarities of the original.

NOTES

1. This was the first of Hoffmann's five Beethoven reviews for the AMZ. In it, he introduced many of his essential ideas about Beethoven, and, together with the review of the piano trios, op. 70, it later became the basis of his well-known essay "Beethoven's Instrumental Music." First printed in the ZEW, this essay appeared in Hoffmann's *Fantasiestücke in Callots Manier,* which itself became one of the central documents of Romanticism.

Much of this review is incorporated verbatim into the essay, which has long been available in English translation. Since all of the later, more technical passages are omitted, however, the essay gives a rather distorted view of Hoffmann's critical aims. What is interesting about the original review is not simply that it contains a lengthy "analysis" of the symphony, but that Hoffmann structures this analysis so as to support his view that the symphony opens "the gates of the underworld," unleashing powerful emotions that are barely held in check by the more prosaic building blocks of the musical structure. See Wallace, *Beethoven's Critics,* 22–24, 126–43.

2. Karl Ditters von Dittersdorf (1739–99) was a talented composer who is still frequently cited as the epitome of everything that was staid and unimaginative about the Classical style in the hands of minor composers. It is an undeserved stigma, but, as this reference makes plain, it can be traced all the way back to Hoffmann, who was also one of the first to identify the famous triumvirate of Haydn, Mozart, and Beethoven as a stylistic unity.

3. Translator's note: many previous translators have taken the word "Macht" (might or power) as a misprint for "Nacht" (night). Both nouns form distinct metaphors (albeit with different relationships of intensity between vehicle and the metaphorical referent) when used with the verb "aufgehen," which was a common stylistic practice in early-nineteenth-century German prose. We have chosen to stay with the text as printed.

4. K. 543. The name "swan-song" was apparently a contemporary designation that has not survived. In any case, it is no more appropriate to this work than it is to Schubert's final song cycle, since a swan is supposed to sing *only* before it dies. Mozart's Symphony in E♭ Major, K. 543, was composed in 1788, three years before his death. The name may be related to the exalted style of the introduction to the first movement and the subsequent lyrical first theme.

5. Hoffmann was perhaps thinking here of the failure of Beethoven's only opera *Fidelio,* premiered in 1805 and revised in 1806. Aside from the Choral Fantasy, op. 80, and the Mass in C, op. 86 (both works also poorly received at their premieres in 1808 and 1809 respectively), almost all of Beethoven's other vocal works published or publicly performed before 1810 were *Lieder.*

6. That is, a B♭-major triad in first inversion.

7. The horn actually plays this theme at m. 59. The published score, however, contains an extra measure—the current fourth—which was not in Beethoven's manuscript. The first 100 copies of the first edition, too, were printed without this measure; the half-note D with a fermata appeared in m. 4 instead. Since Rochlitz reports that a copy of the score of the symphony was sent to Hoffmann while it was "still in the hands of the engraver," it is likely that Hoffmann wrote his review on the basis of this earlier version, even though the musical examples printed with it give the passage as it appears in modern editions. See Paul Hirsch, "A Discrepancy in Beethoven," *Music & Letters* 19 (July 1938), 265–67; and Kinsky-Halm, 159.

8. Measure 228, which Hoffmann compares to the earlier thematic statement at m. 187.

9. On the double variation form of this movement and its compositional genesis, see William Meredith, "Forming the New from the Old: Beethoven's Use of Variation in the Fifth Symphony," *Beethoven's Compositional Process,* ed. William Kinderman (Lincoln: University of Nebraska Press, 1991), 102–21.

10. Actually Allegro; Beethoven did not call this movement a minuet. In fact, in one of his early sketches, it is the second movement that is labeled "Andante quasi Menuetto."

11. Actually thirty-two measures; Hoffmann does seem to have miscounted here.

12. Hoffmann, in other words, is advising the principal first violinist, who still traditionally "led" the orchestra from his own seat, to exercise a function similar to that of the modern conductor. Like so much else in this review, this highlights the extent to which Hoffmann thought of the Fifth Symphony in terms of a unifying concept that requires intellectual depth and application to understand. It would not simply "emerge" from a technically adequate performance, but must be imposed by an interpreter who is acutely aware of everything the music contains.

13. This arrangement, by Friedrich Schneider, was published in July 1809.

~

207.
"Concert." *Wiener allgemeine musikalische Zeitung* 1 (8 May 1813): 293–94.

(With WoO 2a: Triumphal March in C for *Tarpeja* by C. Kuffner.)[1]

On 1 May Mr. *Ignaz Schuppanzigh,*[2] chamber virtuoso to his Excellency the Lord Count von Razumovsky, gave the musical declamatory morning entertainment in the concert hall of the Imperial Royal Augarten, which was advertised in our last issue. It opened with the grand C-Minor Symphony of Mr. Louis van Beethoven. This outbreak of ingenious imagination, of powerful greatness, this living portrait of high passion in all gradations, up to its most violent moments, and its resolution in triumphant jubilation, is generally recognized as one of the composer's masterworks, which claims the position of a classic in the area of large-scale instrumental music. What fullness and solidity of ideas! What richly effective instrumentation! What true inner genius! Even if the composer sometimes loses himself in the boundlessness of his imagination, even if he also frequently steps beyond the usual proportions in the construction of his periods, this very shaking off of the forms venerated by the older classical composers gives him the opportunity once again to incorporate new beauties. The performance, as is always the case under Mr. *Schuppanzigh's* direction, was very powerful and fiery and, apart from a few spots, precise. Only the beginning of the trio, where the contrabasses and violoncellos intone a fugal passage in running notes on the lowest strings, and the violas answer them, did not stand out. The reviewer has noticed this at every performance of this symphony; the cause of it appears to lie in the difficulty of the passage, which certainly cannot be played otherwise than *staccato* by any contrabass player, by virtue of which the comprehensibility of the passage must suffer.—After this symphony, Mademoiselle Hensler,[3] a dilettante, sang a grand Italian aria by Liverati,[4] her teacher. She showed many promising talents, which allow us to expect an outstanding singer to result from her continuing education under the direction of this very accomplished master. Mr. Mayseder[5] played the new potpourri for the violin that was already heard at his own concert, and in it he developed anew the already famous characteristics of his playing, to which was joined on this occasion an agreeably surprising energy in performance. Mr. Linke[6] played variations on a Russian theme by Bernard Romberg on the violoncello. It is to be regretted that the playing of this magnificent virtuoso was somewhat diminished in this hall by the weak tone of his instrument. The program was completed by the military march that Mr. L. v. Beethoven has written for the recently performed tragedy *Tarpeja*.[7] The declamatory part of the concert was provided by Miss Adamberger,[8] imperial royal court tragedian, who recited two beautiful poems with the greatest truth and naturalness of expression.

NOTES

1. Christoph Kuffner (1780–1846) was a prolific writer with a strong interest in Latin antiquity and published novels, plays, as well as translations of the Latin classics. He received his music instruction from Anton Wranitzky (1761–1819), who was director of Prince Lobkowitz's orchestra. Wranitzky's brother Paul was music director of the Court Theater; he also provided the external source for Beethoven's Variations for Piano on a Russian Dance from Wranitzky's *Das Waldmädchen*, WoO 71. His *Sauls Tod* had been intended as an oratorio for Beethoven. Kuffner was believed by Czerny to be the author of the text of the Choral Fantasy, op. 80, although this attribution is not generally accepted.

2. A prominent violinist, Ignaz Schuppanzigh (1776–1830) performed a number of Beethoven quartets. As the leader of Count Razumovsky's quartet, he gave first performances of several Beethoven quartets.

3. Josephine Hensler (dates unknown) was, according to AMZ 15 (1813): 52, the daughter of the theater director Karl Friedrich Hensler (1759–1825), for whom Beethoven wrote the Overture "Die Weihe des Hauses," op. 124, and the "Gratulations-Menuett," WoO 3.

4. Giovanni Liverati (1772–1846), an Italian opera composer, lived in Vienna from 1805 to 1814 and knew Beethoven personally.

5. Joseph Mayseder (1789–1863) was one of the most significant Viennese violinists in the first half of the nineteenth century. He was the original second violinist of the Schuppanzigh quartet, which played a crucial role in introducing Beethoven's music. According to his biographer, Sonnleitner, Mayseder was particularly well known for his performances of the quartets beginning with op. 127, which were not well received by his audiences. He was also a composer, teacher, and conductor of the orchestras of the Kärnthnerthor Theater and the Hofmusikkappelle. Beethoven met him around 1800 through the violinist Schuppanzigh. Mayseder frequently appears as an author and a subject in Beethoven's conversation books. For a recent study, see Heinrich Bauer, "Joseph Mayseder, ein Wiener Geiger der Zeit Beethovens und Paganinis," *Münchener Beethoven-Studien,* ed. Johannes Fischer (Munich: Emil Katzbichler, 1992), 229–35.

6. Joseph Linke (1783–1837) was the cellist of the Schuppanzigh quartet from 1808. See François-Joseph Fétis, *Biographie universelle des musiciens et bibliographie générale de la musique* (2nd edn. Paris: Firmin Didot Frères, 1873–80), 5, 310–11.

7. *Tarpeja,* by Christoph Kuffner, was first performed on 26 March 1813 at the Hoftheater in Vienna.

The march in question is WoO 2a, a triumphal march in C major, which was written at the time *Tarpeja* was first performed (see Kinsky-Halm, 429).

8. Antonie Adamberger (1790–1867) was the daughter of an opera singer and actress in Vienna. After her mother died in 1804, Heinrich von Collin, the writer, assumed supervision of her education. She married one of the most prominent writers of the time, Theodore Körner (1791–1813), the son of Friedrich Schiller's close friend. Körner wrote several *Lieder* and dramatic roles for her, most notably *Toni.* Antonie was particularly cherished by her contemporaries (e.g., Clemens Brentano) because of her unique combination of beauty, talent, and high moral standards.

~

208.
K. B. "Miscellaneous." *Allgemeine musikalische Zeitung* 16 (8 June 1814): 395–96.

4. It is generally known that father Haydn is the creator, in the most singular way, of a special type of minuet. Through him these pieces were first transformed into little, characteristic pieces of music, which in his beautiful symphonies and quartets often overwhelm and delight all susceptible people in a way that is just as piquant as it is unusual. Meanwhile, the great master himself suspected that this type of piece was capable of yet further development, and thus often expressed the wish that for once a truly *new* minuet would be written.[1] Through Beethoven's genius this wish of the late composer's has come to fulfillment in the most magnificent way. It would be almost superfluous to point to isolated examples, since so many of his works offer the most delightful demonstrations of this accomplishment. Yet I must think here of the truly ravishing minuet by this artist from his C-Minor Symphony:[2] this wonderfully original outpouring of the highest genius. Surely "none of woman born" can hear without a mysterious shudder these tones that tear apart the heart. The dark gateway to the spirit kingdom opens up; its residents come up and mingle among us; their purely rhythmic sounds clash coldly and stridently with the deep, melodic complaints of human nature.[3] A truly horrifying darkness envelops with gloom the colorful kingdom of light and its configurations: then, concluding movement, C major, the sun shines joyously forth, and defeated are the masks and monstrosities of the kingdom of ancient night; light and clarity return, and the most joyous life stirs in every pulse. Thanks to you, great, magnificent artist, that you *wrote* this work from out of the depths of your rich soul. The muse of music herself placed the imperishable wreath upon your head!

1. Haydn's famous statement that someone should try to write a truly new minuet was first recorded in AMZ 11 (1808–09): 740 as part of Georg August Griesinger's *Biographische Notizen*.

2. This again refers to the third movement, which Beethoven simply titled "Allegro."

3. The acknowledged quotation here is from *Macbeth:* "Be bloody, bold, and resolute; laugh to scorn / The power of man, for none of woman born / Shall harm Macbeth" (IV, 1, 79–81). In these phrases, however, the author, like so many others who wrote about Beethoven at this time, is paraphrasing E. T. A. Hoffmann.

~

209.
"News. Leipzig." *Allgemeine musikalische Zeitung* 19 (21 May 1817): 355–56.

(With *Christus am Ölberg,* op. 85)

20 March. Beethoven's Symphony in C Minor was fervently and well performed, although not as perfectly in all details as last year, and was rewarded with loud applause . . . 30 March, Palm Sunday . . . Beethoven's oratorio *Christus am Ölberg;* the solo parts performed by Mrs. Neumann-Sessi, and by the men named above.[1] The work is well known, and, as much as one is amazed by many parts of it, it is not, in our opinion, one of the great master's most successful works.

NOTE

1. Those mentioned were a Mr. Weidner and a Mr. Anacker. The last named may have been Augustin Ferdinand Anacker (1790–1855), later the cantor and music director of the city of Freiburg, a student of Friedrich Schneider, and described by Fétis (*Biographie universelle,* 1, 93–94) as a particular devotee of Beethoven's music. He published much choral music and had an immense impact on the musical taste of students through his very popular music seminars.

Weidner is described in AMZ 19 (1817): 159 as a member of the Leipzig Theater with a sound and powerful tenor voice that is still in need of further refinement.

~

210.
Du Mont Schauberg.[1] "Louis van Beethoven's Symphony No. 5 in C Minor." *Beiblatt der Kölnischen Zeitung* nos. 10 and 11 (20 and 27 May 1821).[2]

Beethoven bears musical romanticism deep within his soul and expresses it in his works with great genius and presence of mind. This can scarcely be felt in a more lively way than in the symphony mentioned above, which, in a climax that builds steadily until the end, reveals this romanticism of Beethoven more than any other work of his, and sweeps the listener irresistibly into the wonderful spirit kingdom of the infinite.

The first movement ($\frac{2}{4}$ in C minor) is a serious, somewhat gloomy Allegro, which seems to consume everything with fire, while remaining noble, even and firm in feeling as in the working-out; despite many peculiarities, it is handled simply, strictly and quite regularly. The beginning of the same up to the first fermata on the dominant determines the character of the entire piece, and there is no simpler idea than that which the master laid as the foundation for it in the first two measures. One realizes with wonder how he was able to align all the secondary ideas, all the transitional passages with the rhythmic content of this simple theme in such a way that they served continually to unfold the character of the whole, which that theme could only suggest. All phrases are short, consisting of only two, three, or four measures, and are divided up even further in the ongoing exchanges between the string and wind instruments. One might believe that from such elements only something disjointed and difficult could arise; nevertheless, it is precisely this arrangement of the whole, as well as the repetitions of the short phrases and individual chords that follow continually upon one another, which holds the soul firmly in an unnameable longing. Completely apart from the fact that the contrapuntal treatment shows deep study of the art, it is also the transitional passages and the continual references to the principal theme that show how the master did not simply conceive the whole, with all its characteristic features, within his spirit, but thought it through as well.

The Andante is arranged from the most heterogeneous ideas (gently rapturous and ruggedly military ones) in a completely original and very attractive way. The lovely and yet meaningful theme (in A♭ major, $\frac{3}{8}$ time) is performed by the viola and violoncello and is varied in many different ways after interjected transitional phrases. It cannot be equated with the first Allegro in terms of originality, even though the idea of continually interrupting the transitions back to A♭ major by allowing an imposing phrase in C major with trumpets and drums to intervene produces a striking effect. All the phrases of this movement are very melodious, but its progress through various keys, and the continual juxtaposition of the major tonalities A♭ and C, the chromatic modulations, express once again the character of the whole, and by virtue of this the Andante is a part of that whole. It is as if the frightful spirit, which in the Allegro gripped and unsettled the soul, were to step forth and threaten every moment from the storm clouds into which it had disappeared, and the friendly forms that had surrounded us comfortingly were to flee quickly from its sight. The minuet that follows the Andante is once again as original as one might only expect. It is primarily the distinctive modulations—closes on the dominant-major chord, whose bass note is taken up by the bass as the tonic of the following theme in minor, the theme itself, which always extends itself by only a few measures—that express the character of this entire symphony and arouse anew that restlessness, that presentiment of the wonderful spirit kingdom, with which the phrases of the Allegro assailed the listener's soul. The minuet passes into the concluding movement (Allegro, $\frac{4}{4}$ time in C major), with whose splendid, triumphant theme the full orchestra enters, to which piccolos, trombones, and contrabassoons are now added. Sunlight, which suddenly illuminates the deep night, breaks in. The phrases of this Allegro are treated more broadly than those that came before. They are not so much melodious as they are powerful, and suited to contrapuntal imitation. The modulations are unaffected and understandable.

The entire finale is a stormy outpouring of a mighty imagination. The power of the emotions that constantly struggle anew with one another, the continually renewed contrasts, which, moreover, are mostly set against one another in the sharpest possible way, the continually returning sense of surprise that is produced by this, as also by the strangeness of the ideas and their completely unusual juxtaposition, sequence and combination; all this, united with much that is peculiar and very piquant in the use of the instruments, charms and stretches the listener throughout the whole duration of this long movement so thoroughly and so continually anew that it cannot fail to be accorded a brilliant effect wherever it is well performed.

Beethoven has retained the customary succession of movements in the symphony. They appear to be put together in a fantastic way, and the whole rushes past many people like an inspired rhapsody; but the soul of every sensitive listener will certainly be deeply and closely gripped by a lingering feeling, which is precisely that unnameable, foreboding longing, and sustained in it until the final chord. Indeed, for many more moments after it, he will not be able to depart from the wonderful spirit kingdom, where pain and joy surrounded him in musical form.

If one wants to bring together a judgment of this magnificent work of art of the master into a few words, one should say only that it is ingeniously conceived, and worked out with deep self-possession, expressing musical romanticism to a very high degree.

We may rejoice to be able to call the composer of this work of art our countryman. Louis van Beethoven was born in Bonn in the year 1772.[3] In the year 1792 he traveled to Vienna, where he has made himself into one of the foremost heroes of art. Himself an instrumental virtuoso, equipped with bold imagination and filled with deep knowledge of the soul of every instrument, touched by playful humor and by Mozart's deep seriousness, he has created his own romantic world of notes, in which imagination, given over to feeling, is always dominant, and determines the sequence of the modulations.

How strongly do we wish this great man life and health, that he may present us with many more exquisite works of music![4]

1. In the 1600s, Gereon Schauberg started a business in Cologne, which published the *Postamts-Zeitung* (1651; later *Die Kölnische Zeitung*). The business eventually came to be known as the "Du Mont Schauberg'sche Druckerei der Kölnischen Zeitung" after it came into the possession of Marcus Du Mont, who married Katharina Schauberg.

2. With slight paraphrases, this article is compiled of alternating excerpts from the AMZ's correspondence section of 12 April 1809 (entry no. 205, above), and from Hoffmann's review of the Fifth Symphony (entry no. 206, above), which has been adapted to convey the essence of Hoffmann's thought without his extensive analyses. Only the two concluding paragraphs appear to be the author's own. Nevertheless, the article offers a striking example of how musicological ideas, published in Germany's most scholarly journal and intended for a specific audience, were extracted and presented to a general public, and it demonstrates how the process of forming public opinion actually took place.

3. On the confusion about Beethoven's birth year, see entry no. 1, vol. 1, p. 23, n. 2.

4. Although such wishes for long life and health are not uncommon in this period, in this case the author may have been responding to the following report in the AMZ from 10 January 1821: "Herr von Beethofen was sick with a rheumatic fever. All friends of true music and all admirers of his muse feared for him. But now he is on the road to recovery and is working actively." According to Beethoven, the illness lasted for six weeks and interfered with his composing. See Thayer-Forbes, 775–76.

~

211.
"News. Magdeburg." *Allgemeine musikalische Zeitung* 26 (6 May 1824): 299.

(Mentioned: Symphony No. 2, op. 36; Symphony No. 3, op. 55)

At the concerts of the Masonic Lodge we heard these symphonies: the great one with the concluding fugue in C major, the G minor, the E♭, and the one in D without a minuet by Mozart,[1] one by Krommer,[2] No. 2 in D and the *Eroica,* and also the last movement from the C-Minor Symphony of Beethoven. It was a strange misconception to perform this last movement, which, as is well known, fits together with the minuet, *without* the latter, as a self-contained piece of music. It may well have been felt that a minuet does not make an appropriate beginning: but in that case, why was the entire symphony not performed? In the intention of serving up to the public one of its favorite pieces, it was not taken into consideration that the seasonings were missing. For upon what is the extraordinary effect of the C-major theme based, entering with all the power and splendor of the instruments, but the sharp contrast that the restless bustle of the minuet forms against it? And does this beginning without preparation sound well as an opening? Through such treatment, a masterwork is unnecessarily fragmented and arouses only longing for that which is missing.

1. Symphonies Nos. 41 ("Jupiter"), 40, 39, and 38 ("Prague"), respectively.

2. Franz Vinzenz Krommer (1759–1831), a Czech composer, wrote about ten symphonies, as well as numerous concertos, various vocal works, and a large amount of chamber music.

~

212.

M.[1] "Berlin, 8 Dec. 1825. First Subscription Concert in the Jagor Hall."
Berliner allgemeine musikalische Zeitung 2 (14 December 1825): 404.

In their first subscription concert the Messrs. Bliesener[2] have shown what they want with their choice of the grand C-Minor Symphony and the new grand overture of Beethoven.[3] With them, they have far surpassed all of this year's previous concerts.[4] The performance, particularly of the C-Minor Symphony, left much to be desired in regard to precision, nuances of *forte* and *piano,* and so forth;[5] nevertheless—do not twenty measures of this symphony, indifferently performed, give more pleasure and sustenance than a concert at which a splendid performance is squandered on poor works, and nothing delights except, perhaps, the personal talents of a soprano, which can be better and more abundantly enjoyed at any opera? We wish that both works would be repeated at a later concert; then we might hope for a more satisfactory performance for the C-Minor Symphony as well. These gentlemen would be very well advised to use the large number of their concerts to prepare their society and the audience for the grandest and most difficult works by means of the symphonies of Haydn and Mozart, which are so much easier, and yet masterly.

NOTES

1. As mentioned above, some of A. B. Marx's writings in BAMZ, as here, are signed only with a "M."

2. Ernst and Friedrich Bliesener, court musicians, began a series of "Ubüngskonzerte" in 1800 at which amateur performers had an opportunity to improve their performance skills. Performances by this orchestra were not normally open to the public. In 1807 they began a concert subscription series that ran through the 1820s. According to Sanna Pederson, "Some of these amateurs, however, participated in the subscription concerts, which did not evidently hold to high technical standards"; see Pederson, "Marx, Berlin, and German National Identity," *19th-Century Music* 18 (1994): 99–100. Pederson translates a portion of this review and puts it in context of Marx's goals on pp. 103–04. For more on the Blieseners and concert life in Berlin, see Christoph-Hellmut Mahling, "Berlin: 'Music in the Air,' " in *The Early Romantic Era,* ed. Alexander Ringer (Englewood Cliffs NJ: Prentice Hall, 1990), 109–40.

3. The reviews of the Bliesener concerts of 8 December 1825 and 11 January 1826 in BAMZ and F do not concur as to the repertory of the programs. According to Marx's review

in BAMZ, the Fifth Symphony and "the new grand overture of Beethoven" were performed on the 8 December concert, and the Sixth Symphony was given on the 11 January concert. According to *Der Freymüthige,* the Fifth was performed on 8 December and the Sixth on 11 January, but a Beethoven overture, "not yet heard here," was played on 11 January. *Der Freymüthige* does not mention a Beethoven overture on the 8 December concert. According to Marx, the complete programs were (1) 8 December 1825: Beethoven's Fifth and a "new grand overture," a duet from Rossini's *Diebscher Elster,* a grand scene from Pavesi, an Adagio and Rondo for flute by Tulou, and Variations for the pedal-harp by Bedard; (2) 11 January 1826: Beethoven's Sixth, a Rossini scena, B. Romberg's Variations for Cello on Russian Songs, a Viotti violin concerto, and a comic aria from *Dorfsängerinnen. Der Freymüthige* gives only the repertory of the 11 January concert as Beethoven's Sixth, the unnamed Beethoven overture ("not yet heard here"), and Étienne-Nicolas Méhul's overture to the opera *Ariodant.*

The identity of "the new grand overture" mentioned by Marx in BAMZ is not clear, though it is likely that *Coriolan* was the work performed. In his review of Seidler's performance of the *Coriolan* on 30 November 1825 in Berlin (see entry no. 200), Marx noted that Seidler was the first to perform it in Berlin and that the audience was certainly not expected to "comprehend such a profound work upon first hearing without preparation." Thus *Coriolan,* though composed in 1807, was "the" new Beethoven overture for Berlin in late 1825.

In the *Freymüthige* review, the phrase "not yet heard here" may mean that the unnamed overture had not been heard yet in the *Bliesener* subscription series. If the overtures mentioned in the BAMZ and *Freymüthige* reviews are one and the same (*Coriolan*), the *Freymüthige* remark that "many admittedly were not yet able to understand [it] completely after a single hearing" would only make sense if the critic is referring solely to the Bliesener's audience, since the overture had already been heard in the Seidler concert on 30 November. The *Freymüthige* critic does echo Marx's comments, in his BAMZ reviews of the 30 November Seidler concert of the *Coriolan* and the 8 December Bliesener concert of "the new grand overture," that repeated hearings are necessary to understand the work.

Although it would not seem to explain the discrepancies in the programs cited here, it should be noted that at least in later years Marx was not the most reliable or accurate critic. Already in 1860 Thayer pointed out that in Marx's 1859 Beethoven biography he quoted other authors without citation, may have plagiarized Otto Jahn, and did not verify his information by consulting surviving sources. See Theodore Albrecht, "Thayer *Contra* Marx: A Warning from 1860," *Beethoven Journal* 14 (1999): 2–3.

4. Given the lower quality of the Bliesener concerts, Marx probably means here that this first concert surpassed all of the 1825 Bliesener concerts, not all of the Berlin concerts of 1825.

5. A similar comment is made about the Bliesener performance of the Sixth Symphony in entry no. 213: "It turned out well, to the extent that the available means would allow."

~

213.
"Concert. Berlin." *Der Freymüthige* 23 (14 January 1826): 44.

Mentioned: Symphony No. 6, op. 68

About Beethoven's F-Major Symphony, which began the concert, we can say the same that we did about the performance of the C-Minor Symphony in the first concert.[1] It turned out well, to the extent that the available means would allow. An overture by Beethoven, not yet heard here[2]—an ingenious tone painting, rich in imagination, which many admittedly were not yet able to understand completely after a single hearing, and Méhul's[3] overture to the opera *Ariodant,* rich in effects, were also included in this concert and were well performed. If the Messrs. Bliesener continue to offer such substantial pieces, and to summon up such beautiful talents, they may expect greater and greater interest for their concerts, which we wish them from the heart.

NOTES

1. On the Bliesener concerts, see entry no. 212, n. 1. The second Bliesener concert of the new season was given on 11 January 1826.

2. Concerning the conflicting reports on the repertory of the first two Bliesener concerts and the identity of this overture, see entry no. 212, n. 3.

3. Étienne-Nicolas Méhul (his name is sometimes given as Étienne-Henri) (1763–1817) was a French composer of operas and symphonies. He was noted for his contributions to the developing art of orchestration. His *Ariodant* was first produced in Paris in 1799.

≈

214.
"Our Concerts." *Musikalische Eilpost* 4 (March 1826).

O, do not chatter to me about changes therein;
As it was yesterday, it will be today.

It struck a quarter to six; I took my ticket and hurried out into the dark, rainy autumn night. From far away the brightly lit windows of the G . . . house already shone festively at me. From all the streets carriages rattled, sedan chairs swayed, dark figures streamed toward the bright doorways, and inside an unbroken succession of richly dressed ladies and gentlemen moved onto the broad staircase. Quickly, with a pounding heart, I pushed my way through the brightly colored crowd. The hall was nearly overfilled as I entered—an effect of the great reputation that had preceded Signora M. I was enticed today most of all by Beethoven's Symphony in C Minor, which, according to the program, would be performed in its entirety, and I had prepared myself for this in an appropriate manner. All the cares and trivialities of everyday life, which swarm around people like flakes of snow, lay shaken off before the door—I was in the happiest, most restful of holiday moods. But alas! Damned be every joy that must be waited for; the devil gets wind of it, and before we know it, he brings about a malicious accident, and we are cheated!—I had taken my seat at a pillar way in the background; just as the conductor gave the signal to begin, my evil demon approached me in the form of the accursed R. . . . He is one of the many who hold themselves to be experts because they can tinkle a bit at the keyboard, are familiar with the triad, have composed some dances with false rhythms, and have, furthermore, a memory that accurately imparts to them the reasoned judgments of the newspapers and other writings. They know no other happiness than to babble forth the notions they have collected; preferably, though, and impudently enough, to men of means.

We were going to hear today the most heavenly symphony of our divine Beethoven, he said to me. God! What a work! "It moves the lever controlling horror, fear, dread, pain. It opens up to us the kingdom of the gigantic and the immeasurable. Glowing beams shoot through this kingdom's deep night, and we become aware of gigantic shadows that surge up and down, enclosing us more and more narrowly and annihilating everything within us, leaving only the pain of that interminable longing in which every pleasure that had quickly arisen with sounds of rejoicing sinks away and founders, and we live on, rapturously beholding the spirits themselves, only in this pain that, consuming love, hope, and joy within itself, seeks to burst our breast asunder with a full-voiced consonance of all the passions." And so it went on! the entire essay from Hoffmann's *Fantasiestücke;* everything that has ever been written or said about Beethoven's compositions he stuffed in front of me, without letting anything disturb him—not even the symphony, which meanwhile resounded through the hall with fresh, magical life. And I had to remain silent! I could not choke his ceaselessly working throat, as much as my fingers yearned to do so; he was, to be sure, the nephew of the Minister, and the Minister was my superior! But inwardly, my offended blood rushed to my heart, like the furious surf against the rocks. Alas, such beastly chatterers about art had already so often spoiled art for me. My mood was gone—I was annihilated, shattered.

The symphony was ended, without my having, in the confusion of the conversation and in my inner fury, taken in a single note. Now Signora appeared; my devil turned to look at her through his glasses; I took advantage of the moment, slipped away behind the column, and pressed myself deep into the other corner of the hall. From there, I could see how he soon began to look for me diligently once again, but in vain; I was too well hidden. It was not long before he entrapped the organist of the M . . . church, upon whom he burst forth just as eagerly, while holding him firmly by his jacket button, probably because he feared that, unimpeded, he might slip away from him before everything had emerged from his heart, or even more from his memory. I was rescued!—In order to escape from all disturbance, I closed my eyes tightly, and then all was once again at peace within myself, and I was the lord of my own mood. And now began the recitative; a magnificent, sonorous voice struck my ear, but, oh heaven and earth! At once there began a soft whispering and tittering in the hall, and next to me somebody was laughing in such a continuous crescendo, that I and everyone else near him had to look and laugh with him without knowing why. What was it, then? Now, then, nothing more than the fact that the singer accompanied her notes with some pantomimes of a peculiar nature. Soon, to be precise, she shoved her long lower jaw, with a row of decayed teeth, so far forward, that her tightly stretched upper lip almost disappeared behind it; then she tugged convulsively at her mouth toward both ears, as though she had bitten a wild pear. Smiling intimately she now leaned toward the audience; then she stared at it again with wide open eyes, head thrust backward proudly and scornfully. Finally, in one passage, she waved with her arms and bent her whole body so frantically back and forth, as though she had been set upon by a swarm of bees, that the whole audience broke into loud, uncontrollable laughter: goodnaturedly, however, applauding furiously at the same time. Oh art! Oh music! Even in the keyboard trio with flute and violoncello that now followed, the devil was not absent. To begin with, the long, pale, pained-looking face of the flutist, who with bespectacled eyes gazed spookily from behind the old music stand out at the audience like Banquo's ghost at *Macbeth,* made such an adverse impression that a pregnant woman withdrew at once, afraid of things going wrong, and then the violoncellist, exactly at the moment in the Adagio that he bent forward with expressive, blinking gestures, was struck on the nose by a broken bow-string in such a way that he drew back as though frightened by thunder, upon which a general laughter once again sounded forth. Now I had had enough. This was the pleasure to which I had been looking forward so much; this was the magic, in which I had hoped to revel, to forget the rude present! No, I could bear it no longer; with the bitterest feelings in my breast I ran out into the gloomy night and chased through the streets in rivalry with the howling wind. Was this then the first time that things had gone this way for me? Death and devil! Once a dandy of a violinist angered me practically to death through his clowning around with twine, with which he filled up the pauses. Soon the fury of the conductor struck me, who raised himself on the music stand like the innkeeper in *Die Mitschuldigen* upon the grandfather stool. Another time the loud, impertinent chatter of those around me drove me nearly to distraction. If some degree of attentiveness was once able to reign in the hall, through a particularly kind divine providence, during a melting Adagio, just then did an old, worn out coquette with varnished over (tinseled) charms rush in through the door, and never stopped clearing her throat, scraping her feet and moving her chair, until she had everyone looking at her. In short, I could remember no concert where such and similar pitiful incidents would not have clouded the appearance of the blessed goddess, and undermined the power that she has over my heart.[1] Dear Heaven! I have always thought of the life and work of a composer as something delightful, elevated, sublime! With passionate and fervent prayer he calls up exalted inspiration, and it comes, drawn through the silent night. Then the world fades for him; the harmonies of the spheres sound forth; all his powers strain to catch the ecstatic sound, to master it, in order to proclaim it to his brothers. Finally he succeeds, and happy, blessed, he cannot wait for the moment when it will sound forth in heavenly charm and blissful splendor. It arrives!—What sounds! What harmonies! What an almighty heaving and roaring; how the notes rustle, sparkle, and flash! His fibers tremble; with transfigured eyes, he looks around himself as proudly as a god, feeling that the whole world must now sink to his feet in love, gratitude, and enthusiasm. And what does he now behold!—A father sent his only son into the world. He hoped for news. Then finally a friend wrote to him: "Your Ferdinand cut the throat of his excellency the lord Minister last week, and was therefore led yesterday morning in a lovely procession to the footstool, and was brought by our accomplished Master Treffegleich[2] with one stroke from life to death."

Poor father! Poor composer!

Soon it was midnight; the wind blew icily upon me. In a nearby cellar, happy drinking songs could be heard; I descended, ordered punch, and threw myself, tired and sorrowful, upon a bench in the corner by the fireplace.

Why so sullen, privy civil servant, asked a familiar voice, and through the billowing tobacco smoke strode toward me the postmaster S., the cellist in our little quartet circle, and a passionate musical amateur.

Why? I cried out; I hurry directly to the gates of heaven; I am opening them, and inside brightly colored Eden smiles at me in a splendid, shimmering, unearthly, magical magnificence; then I awaken, it is a dream, and burning Hell, with its black devilish masks, grins mockingly at me.—Ugh! what a horrible allegory, he cried out. What made you so furious? Where were you?

At a concert!

At a concert? Ah yes, I understand. You promised yourself a magnificent enjoyment, and you were cheated, weren't you? Yes, that is completely to be expected; concerts and enjoyment! He laughed mockingly at this. I have not gone to a concert for twenty years, and it is just as long since I have traveled on the Danube. Hang it all, I cried out, what does the Danube have to do with concerts?

Properly speaking, not much, he replied. And yet it, or rather, an experience that I had upon it, showed me clearly and unmistakably that whoever loves and enjoys music must never go to a concert.

Strange!

Now, listen! I was traveling at that time from Regensburg to Vienna, upon a postal boat, where much colorful company is always found within a narrow space. Among others, I came to know a pair of young musicians, virtuosos on the horn who were going out into the wide world for the first time, and with whom I soon entered into intimate confidence. On a magnificent summer afternoon, and in a happy frame of mind, far from all artistic pretentiousness, they took out their instruments, and played on them in a truly lovely and wonderful way. Indeed, if only one person had listened and paid attention to it. The loud and confused activity that had been going on on the boat all day long did not stop for a moment, and since the crowd always affects the individual, I myself was not able, despite my best efforts, to get into a proper frame of mind, or to obtain any enjoyment. Embittered, almost furious about this, I withdrew to the most remote corner of the boat, burying myself between piles of heaped up bales of merchandise, and cursed the numb indifference of people and their vile contempt for my heavenly art.

Yes, yes, I cried out sullenly, that's how it is all over. They do not understand nor want that which is divine. They cling to the base and commonplace; only coarse material pleasures charm and satisfy them.

So I also believed and decided at that time, he said, but I soon learned otherwise. What, is there then nothing else, nothing at all, in the world besides music that is entitled to our attention? Does music simply need to sound forth, no matter when, no matter where and under what circumstances, for the soul, be it occupied by the most heterogeneous thoughts, to cast everything else away and aside and listen to the notes? No, that is not within anybody's power. If any kind of art is going to take special possession of the soul, then the soul must also be in a special mood for it, must be receptive to it. To awaken and retain this receptiveness of the soul, particularly favorable circumstances must also be present, and above all, all distracting and disruptive influences must be eliminated. When several different phenomena impress themselves upon the soul at the same time, it becomes dazed and confused; it takes in too much, and therefore nothing at all. It is easy to compare it to a lake. Now, when it is peaceful and crystal clear, the blue sky with its golden clouds and the green bank will easily be reflected in it. It only takes a slight play of waves, though, for these pictures to begin to fluctuate and become indistinguishable. If a storm wind whips up the waves, however, the lovely magic will disappear into the foundation that has been so cruelly stirred up. Upon the boat, far too many phenomena were impressing themselves at the same time upon my soul for it to have been able to give any one of them its undivided attention. Simply, the brightly colored shoreline, changing every moment in a continuous transformation, with its castles, windmills, forests, rocks, and villages, gave my eye so much to do throughout the day that no other sense was able to approach the level of enjoyment provided to it. And it is the same way at all of our concerts. All the different workaday connections of our social relationships are thrown so narrowly and colorfully before the eye, and they all excite such various plays of thoughts in the consciousness of those gathered there: where then is there room for that restfulness and passivity of the soul, without which no work of art, but least of all a musical one, can be truly and completely grasped?

Oh, you are only too right, I cried out: the arrangement of our concerts makes any legitimate effect impossible. But how can this be remedied, I asked in a subdued tone.

He shrugged his shoulders. Let us return to the Danube once again, he continued; my story was not yet finished.

I had grumbled all day in my hiding place; as I came out again, the sun was slowly setting behind the distant mountains, and a magically lovely, fragrant evening sank coolly and refreshingly upon the languishing earth. The eye, which during the day was free to glance in all directions, was now bounded by high mountains covered with dark pine forests, which rose jaggedly on both sides, forming a channel into which the river quickly narrowed. Soon deep dusk surrounded us. Isolated stars began to appear in the arch of the heavens; from the shores little lights blinked and glimmered at us cozily, and the boat glided smoothly and peacefully down the quiet river. Then all noise, flirtation, and chattering became mute; a mood settled over the whole company, and the deep, foreboding silence of all nature sank into the hearts of the living, so that all of us, looking quietly and contemplatively ahead, cherished our innermost dreams, and forgot the outer world and all its pretenses. And now, in this very moment, horn tones arose from the wooded mountain nearby, wailing like the last sighs of a hero dying alone. Heavens, what a world of feelings was awakened by those sounds! Ah! they pressed upon the deepest deepness of the heart and awakened the entire slumbering past, so that it sprang forth, as though through magical pictures called up by a magic lantern, many-colored, brightly shining, and then gloomy once again—sweet and melancholic images. Indeed, as the never ceasing waves carried the ship farther and ever farther, and the tones now resounded melancholically only from the far distance, it seemed to me as though they were lamenting words of farewell from my loved ones, from whom I must now depart forever, never to meet again.—A deep, endless longing took hold of me, which at last released itself in hot, flowing tears. And truly, it was not I alone who felt this way; the hearts of the others were similarly moved, as was shown by sighs stealing faintly here and there from their breasts, and by the devout, almost awe-inspired silence of all of them. What, now, can explain the completely different effect that the same instrument had upon the same hearts? Was it not the bright day, with its many-faceted, rich images, which took the power away from my friends' tones; and was it not likewise the night, which veiled all things from the eyes, and the distant, unseen nature of the horn player in the forest, which so facilitated this?

Ah, there is no doubt, I cried out; but how, be it ever so difficult, can we transform the daytime scene upon the Danube, which reappears at our concerts, into the nighttime one?

I believe there would be nothing easier, he responded. Imagine a hall in which, first of all, the orchestra with its people and instruments is hidden from the audience's view by a light curtain; this would put a whole crowd of destructive demons in chains, not to mention how much more atmospheric music becomes when it resounds unseen. Imagine further that instead of the many burning candles there is a single hanging light, which gives forth only as much subdued illumination as wretched decency demands. Furthermore, both sexes could be separated by a barrier, and all doors must be closed at the beginning. What do you think; would not the dim light, full of foreboding, compose the souls of those who entered, purifying away the dross of everyday life and setting into them that mood which alone is appropriate for the enjoyment of art? Would not the springlike sounds, coming as though from another world, lift these poor earthly worms, swimming in the sludge of the everyday world, for a moment at least into the bright, heavenly regions of a more beautiful world?—But alas, as long as the concert hall is nothing but a place for observation and conversation, where everyone finds the usual forms and interests of the day piled up around him, music can never be anything therein but a sermon in the desert, or a painting in a dark chamber!

And were these thoughts not known to you a long time ago, I cried out almost angrily? We would have long since been helped!—Do you think so? he asked scornfully. Yes, yes, my dear privy civil servant; it is easy to tell that you are still young. He took up his hat and cane. Do not go to a concert again, he said, for as long as the venerable Master Schlendrian[3] is still alive, everything will remain the same, and you will be disturbed yet many more times in your must beautiful enjoyment. Good night!

NOTES

1. The muse of art.
2. Literally the name means "strike at once."
3. Literally, Master Humdrum.

≈

215.
"Musical Writings." *Allgemeiner musikalischer Anzeiger* (F) 1 (23 December 1826): 207–08.

Symphony by Beethoven in C. What can and should the reviewer say about this gigantic work? He is far too modest to want to *make a judgment* about it. Let him only be allowed to express his *feelings,* as is allowed to every lay person. That this, like all of *Beethoven's* compositions, is ingenious and original, he acknowledges in full humility. Is everything that is original in art, however, also beautiful? This he doubts. Even if today's symphony was clearer and easier for him to understand than most *more recent* ones by its creator, it nevertheless has many moments that are so baroque and wild that they seem to the reviewer to be not aesthetically beautiful and therefore contrary to good taste. Furthermore, in his perception, the monstrous length of the divisions (components of the work), particularly the nearly *endless* third or concluding movement, is extremely fatiguing.[1] Nothing, he believes, is more harmful than exhausting the listener so that he has no desire left for further enjoyment. A French poet has said:—Le secret d'ennuier est de *tout* dire.[2] This can also be aptly applied to music. One must not rob the listener of the wish that the piece of music might have been longer, necessitating instead the observation that it has been too long. This is particularly the case today, when the eardrum is so overwhelmed by monstrous noise that one runs the risk of becoming deaf.

NOTES

1. Scholars have recently concluded that Beethoven intended the third movement of the Fifth Symphony to have a five-part form, and many modern orchestras perform the movement in this manner. See Egon Voss, "Zur Frage der Wiederholung von Scherzo und Trio in Beethoven's fünfter Sinfonie," *Musikforschung* 33 (1980): 195–99; and Sieghard Brandenburg, "Once Again: On the Question of the Repeat of the Scherzo and Trio in Beethoven's Fifth Symphony," in *Beethoven Essays: Studies in Honor of Elliot Forbes* (Cambridge MA: Harvard University Press, 1984), 146–98. The final version published in the first edition and discussed in this review of 1826, however, is the three-part form. Once again, though, this writer is considering both of the last two movements as a single entity.

2. "The secret of being a bore is to say *everything*."

≈

216.
"Short Notices." *Berliner allgemeine musikalische Zeitung* 4 (9 May 1827): 151.[1]

(Arrangement for piano, flute, violin, and violoncello by J. N. Hummel)[2]

Every expert and friend of art is so filled by the high worth of B's Symphony in C Minor, the greatest masterwork among all the creations in tone that were achieved in this type of music by the high creative flight of this wonderful romantic, that it would be like taking owls to Athens if we were once again to dwell upon it.[3] It would be almost as unnecessary to say more about an arrangement by Hummel than that it is outstanding. With this arrangement the master of pianoforte playing has earned the thanks of many, which we will not miss the opportunity to offer to him publicly. How many smaller towns are there not, which would not be capable of procuring for themselves an enjoyment such as that which such works can afford them, were it not made possible for them in this and similar ways? Even in bigger cities, which rejoice in capable orchestras, one would enjoy that which is magnificent if one heard it publicly more often than is customarily the case, but may also enjoy it gladly within the circle of domestic company. This undertaking can therefore not fail to have a wide distribution. By the way, it is not B's Third, but rather his Fifth Symphony.

NOTES

1. The same article appeared in AMZ 31 (1829): 49.

2. This arrangement was published at Mainz by B. Schott. On the title page it was incorrectly identified as Beethoven's "Troisième grande Sinfonie," although the key and opus number were given correctly.

3. The German original "Eulen nach Athen tragen" derives from the play *The Birds* by the Greek comic playwright Aristophanes (ca. 445 B.C.–388 B.C.). In *The Birds,* Euelypides asks who brought the owls along with the flock of birds to Athens, where the owl was the official animal of the city and was thus already in abundance.

≈

217.
Ignaz Ritter von Seyfried. "Review." *Cäcilia* 10, no. 39 (1829): 174–82.[1]

(Arrangement for piano with accompaniment of flute, violin, and violoncello by J. N. Hummel; mentioned: *Missa solemnis,* op. 123; "The Consecration of the House," op. 124; Symphony No. 9, op. 125; and String Quartet, op. 131)

In our scribble-happy days, when everyone who is able to hold a goose quill between his forefingers is only too anxious to become a writer, merely to be able, with puffed up peacock pride, to crow that Anch' io![2] which is so flattering to his vanity, and already feels himself to be chosen and called from above if he is able now and then to fill up at least a few pages with his scrawl, whether it consists of words or of notes, of his own thoughts or those of other people, of outlooks and opinions that he has reached himself or of mindlessly repeated parrot chatter, whether an old or new, true or false, courteous or rude, wise or foolish thing—in these days at once fertile in quantity and mostly sterile in quality, the custom, one would almost wish to say the rage for arranging (though it should probably often be called deranging) has, I believe, spread to the extent that one fears to perceive therein the devastating effects of an epidemic disease.

Infected thereby, everything falls victim, nothing is too holy; nothing escapes from these iconoclasts, nothing is spared: the greatest symphonies and overtures—masses and church cantatas—oratorios and operas etc. etc. etc. must pay the price, and are offered up to us in the most variegated forms and configurations: as keyboard reductions with and without voices, arranged for military band—as quintets and quartets, trios, duos, and solos for particular instruments, scilicet:[3] violins, guitars, flutes, csákány,[4] etc. (*per parentesin:* the mouth harmonica, vulgo: snout drum offers a not yet cultivated field; take note, my lords!) probably, at last, even transformed into waltzes, galops, polonaises, and ecossaises. It must be adapted without first inquiring very much, considering, or pondering whether the little garment, emasculated beyond recognition, will fit the athlete's limbs or not *c'est ègal!* The engravers hammer away indefatigably upon it, the printers vigorously stir up the urchins of the press, and the publishers—yes, indeed!—they are not likely to come to shame in this way; otherwise they would pass over the opportunity, for these born and sworn enemies of the poor authors (according to Magister Lämmermeier's definition) understand *quid juris,* and as a rule never undertake anything, except where monetary gain will result as a mathematical certainty.[5]

What wonder then that one is completely covered by goosebumps and feels shivers as though from a cold fever any time one hears or reads once again of a new arrangement, and in this case has perhaps committed himself, into the bargain, to contributing a serious word about it.

It is an entirely different matter, however, if the transformation originates with an accredited artistic peer of equal rank, and concerns a masterwork for which we have always harbored the warmest love, the most active sympathy, and for which we are filled with true regard and immeasurable admiration.

This agreeable, most gratifying situation occurs here, inasmuch as Hummel makes us the present of an arrangement of Beethoven's Symphony in C Minor and Mozart's D-Minor Concerto, by means of which not only is the general accessibility of these outstanding tone poems substantially promoted, but a new enjoyment of an entirely individual nature is brought about as well.

While a numerous, well-organized, practiced orchestra is an indispensable condition for the performance of original compositions, here it is possible to obtain a comparable result, only on a reduced scale, with minimal means. Indeed, since all the tutti-ritornellos are included in the principal part, the concerto takes the form of an abstract, self-sufficient solo piece, with the accompanying instruments serving for the most part simply to heighten somewhat the effect of the whole.

Now, it is probably not necessary to bring to attention for the first time the fact that Hummel is recognized as the master of his instrument throughout the entire music world, accustomed to solving every problem, no matter how difficult. Perhaps no one has studied more carefully than he the nature of the pianoforte, which is so little suited to expressive melodic passages. Probably no one has penetrated deeper than he into its most deeply hidden individuality. He knows better than anyone what creates difficulty and what pleases. He knows the crags on which so many are shipwrecked, and like an experienced pilot, he understands how to steer wisely around them. He does not demand more than can be performed, but what he does demand fulfills its potential to the most perfect degree.

So has he now created from out of Beethoven's symphony a genuine, natural keyboard piece, which never gives the impression that it is only the representation of a conglomeration of the most diverse instruments; playable, with the most brilliant effect of virtuosity, through the sensible choice of the most serviceable fingerings. Without sacrificing any of the beauties and merits of its model, it can truly stand by its side honorably and unobscured, even if only as a reduced copy. On closer acquaintance, it can reliably conquer all the more patrons, as the accompanying trio demands lesser powers, so that four united friends of art can create an enjoyment for themselves that otherwise must have been denied them from the original, which is unfortunately so seldom heard.

An even more solid, lasting and consequential use may perhaps arise from the arrangement of the Mozart concerto. Let this be said to the shame of our degenerate times, as for example here in Vienna it would be considered a wicked, unforgivable offense against the *bon ton* for any Mozart keyboard composition to be allowed to be seen any more upon the music desk! Thus has modern vandalism stifled and undermined pure sensibility for true art! If now, by contrast, the matadors among our pianists would once dare to make the attempt, which would involve no fundamental risk, and for the time being were to perform these arrangements by Hummel in the smaller circles, and then, with all the forces at their command, were to perform the original itself, or its equally masterly companion pieces in C, D, and B♭ major, naturally, completely in accordance with the creator's intentions, might not a reaction of the most firmly rooted eccentricity be brought about thereby, good taste gradually be brought back into general honor, and the prevailing, disgraceful frippery be officially banished into its native nothingness? May these heartfelt words not die away as a voice in the desert!!!

Both editions are very good, and the active publishing firm, which through the truly large, uncommonly costly enterprise, undertaken throughout on a corresponding scale, of publishing Beethoven's gigantic works of his most recent life as an artist: the Mass No. 2, the fugal, ceremonial overture in C, the Ninth Symphony with choruses, and the Quartet in C♯ Minor, in full score as well as in parts, keyboard reductions, etc. etc. etc., which none of their colleagues seem to be willing to risk, has already earned the most rightful claim to the gratitude of all friends of art, has also clearly attested here to its glorious striving to promote the good according to its powers, even with sacrifices.[6]

NOTES

1. See also BAMZ 4 (19 March 1828): 90.
2. Italian: "me too."

3. Latin: "namely."

4. According to the *New Grove Dictionary of Musical Instruments* ([London: MacMillan, 1984], 1: 525), the csákány was a Hungarian instrument resembling a recorder. It was apparently invented in the early nineteenth century and was popular in Vienna. An early version of the modern harmonica was also constructed in the 1820s by Christian Friedrich Ludwig Boschmann (1805–64) (ibid. 2, 128).

"Per parentesin": Latin: "in parenthesis."

The last four items of the sentence are various types of dances.

5. "Quid juris": Latin: "what law" or "what right."

6. Appearing in C, this last paragraph is somewhat disingenuous, since the journal was published by Schott, the same firm being praised here so extravagantly. Seyfried is correct, though, that this firm had published ops. 123, 124, 125, and 131 in a variety of different formats. For details, see Kinsky-Halm, 364–65, 368–69, 377–78, and 398–99.

≈

218.

"The Great Lower Rhine Music Festival at Düsseldorf.
Whitsuntide 1830." *Cäcilia* 12, no. 48 (1830): 306–07.[1]

The following day opened with *Beethoven's* Fifth Symphony in C Minor. If unfathomable depth may be ascribed to a human work, then without question it has a rightful claim to this name.[2] Out of a restless forward motion made up of self-consuming longing, out of the nocturnal horror of powerful spirit struggles, the most beautiful melody arises ever new, and it seems as if all love and joy on earth plays around this newborn in a thousand lovely forms. The scherzo, in C minor, in combination with the finale, Allegro in C major, shows in particular such a greatness of conception, such an abundance of ideas, that in this colorful richness the eye is often blinded and the soul almost succumbs. But a powerful, high-minded phrase always awakes striving and earnestness anew. A performance like this one, powerful and tender, is assuredly not often obtained by *Beethoven's* creations. At least we do not recall any comparable one. It is hard to say to which section the prize should be awarded, but the string instruments in particular were of an uncommon excellence.

NOTES

1. According to MGG 4, 115, the Lower Rhine Music Festival in this year was directed by Ferdinand Ries.

2. "*Cäcilia* III, no. 10, p. 171." The reference is to Gottfried Weber's article "Über Tonmalerei," which will appear in vol. 3 of this series. To support his disparagement of *Wellington's Victory*, which he considered unworthy of Beethoven, Weber compared it unfavorably to earlier examples of "Beethovenian fire" like the Fifth Symphony.

OP. 68
SYMPHONY NO. ("SINFONIA PASTORALE," F MAJOR)

(See entry nos. 29, 35, 45, 84, vol. 1, pp. 59, 86, 101, 161;
178, 179, 180, 202, and 205, vol. 2)

219.
"Review." *Allgemeine musikalische
Zeitung* 12 (17 January 1810): 241–53.[1]

This work of B., wonderful, original, and full of life, which can be placed without hesitation beside his other masterworks, was more closely described in the last volume of this journal by the author of the overview of concerts in Leipzig, after it was performed there from the manuscript,[2] and its goals and attributes in regard to aesthetics so thoroughly discussed that the reviewer would need only to repeat this if he did not intend to use the space accorded to him in a different manner. Specifically, he intends this time to bring the other side of the work into closer consideration: the artistic side, in the narrower sense of the word. Let a word more be set forth about this here in order to prevent misunderstandings.

The work contains in symphonic form a painting of country life. "A painting? Is music supposed to paint? And have we not left the time far behind when musical painting was thought to be a good thing?" Indeed, we now have got this fairly well sorted out, that the representation of outer circumstances through music is considered extremely tasteless, and, from the point of view of aesthetic judgment, the person who makes use of such second-hand means to create an effect is taken into little account. These remarks, however, do not apply to the present work, which is not a representation of *spatial* characteristics of the countryside, but much more a representation of emotions that we experience upon seeing things in the countryside. That such a painting is not tasteless, and not opposed to the goals of music, can be seen by everyone who has thought seriously about this art and about the nature of emotions.

Now to the promised closer treatment of the work. And if even a written notice about it can give us no complete idea of the worth of this composition, since, in order to be properly enjoyed, it must be heard, then at least an examining glance that we cast upon it may arouse among the public at large the intention to lend a more attentive ear to the performance, and among thinking musicians may offer the substance and the summons to much that is pleasant and instructive.[3]

The whole consists of five movements, each one of which forms a small whole in itself. The first movement—Allegro, ma non troppo (F major, $\frac{2}{4}$)—

begins with a simple, pleasing melody, which expresses the agreeable feelings that a walk from the city into the countryside excites in people. After the first measures, parts of the theme are repeated, with continually changing accompaniment, and with the wind instruments gradually entering, first quietly, then with louder intonation, in order to show the heightening of the emotions, which bit by bit become lively the nearer the city dweller, seeking relaxation in the countryside, comes to his goal. At m. 53, a new melody enters, which, in a similar manner to the first, beginning with a simple violin accompaniment in eighth notes, followed by triplets with the addition of a flute, and finally by sixteenth notes and the participation of all the wind instruments, superbly demonstrates the feelings of another person growing from weak to strong. Toward the end of the first part, power and active life are found in all the voices, gradually diminishing again toward the close. The second part begins with the two opening measures of the first one, supported by soft, sustained notes in the clarinets, bassoons, and horns [mm. 139ff.]. Then the remaining wind instruments also enter, one after another, supporting the theme, which is performed alternately by the first and second violin, and by the viola and violoncello, which play triplets beneath it, in stronger sustained tones. The transition from B♭ to D major at m. 25 makes a powerful effect:[4] however, the twenty-seven-measure-long stop on the dominant chord is perhaps too wearying to the ear [mm. 163–90]. The composer presumably felt this way himself and tried to remedy it by placing the theme in various voices, sometimes in the strings, sometimes in the wind instruments, with alternating loud and soft dynamics: however, the ear would nevertheless much rather be charmed by a new harmony, which, entering in the fifty-fifth measure [m. 193], comes, in the reviewer's opinion, somewhat too late. At this measure the theme speaks to us in G major, with the second violin playing a charming two-measure countertheme, which is imitated by the violoncello, once again most agreeably. The modulation from G to E major, as the dominant of A [m. 209], is the same as that from F to D major and makes a similar, splendidly surprising effect. The measures that follow, however, due once again to too long a pause upon the dominant chord, E, are disagreeable to the ear to the same extent as the eventual return of the theme, which is now repeated in A major [mm. 237ff.], is pleasing. After the repetition of the same, the artist takes up a different four-measure phrase, so that the ear will not become tired through continually listening to just one phrase,[5] and, by presenting this phrase first simply, then with an accompaniment of sixteenth notes, and finally with the power of all the wind instruments, intensified by a long tremolo of the first violin, leads us back again to the opening theme.[6] This now appears to us as an old friend of whom we can never grow tired, since he shows us his presence in the most variegated forms, and, fearing to become boring, prefers to spend some time apart in order to let us feel all the more deeply the joy of seeing him again. Amid these various means by which the first theme returns, we come, not feeling the least bit of emptiness, with the exception of those places discussed above, to the end of this first number without realizing what a long journey already lies behind us. No. 2, according to the artist's intention, is supposed to represent a scene by the brook. Truly, we do feel everything to which such an out of the way place in nature, suggestive of contentment and peaceful observation, invites us. This entire number appeals to the soul primarily through the awakening of gentle feelings. The choice of the key of B♭ major,[7] the lingering $\frac{12}{8}$ time, the natural excursions into related keys—less surprising, to be sure, but no less pleasing—all of this must *lead* the feeling listener from sensations of lively joy to the restfulness of a more introverted contemplation. The second violin and the viola begin a gentle melody in triplets, which, doubled by the two violoncellos at the lower octave, is superbly brought out. Against this, the first violin plays a short countersubject—appropriate, though, for an introduction, which can never be highly worked out—throughout four measures. At the fifth measure, the accompanying movement in the second violin, viola, and the two violoncellos becomes faster, and we in fact believe that we are hearing the gentle murmuring of a brook. The melody of the first violin becomes more flowing and continuous; the feeling becomes more specific. At the seventh measure, the first clarinet and the first bassoon take up the phrase with which the first violin began. The murmuring motion goes on in the violoncellos and the second violin, and the first, with little trills, seems to suggest the twittering of birds in the shadows around the brook.[8] The horns chime in with their own figure, consisting of syncopated notes, which the two bassoons, and then the clarinets and flutes, take over from them (mm. 23 ff.) in an accomplished and effective manner. After the thirty-second measure, we await the close in the dominant, F; however, the ingenious composer's stock of ideas has not yet been used up. He holds back the conclusion, modulating from C, as the dominant of F, to A, the dominant of D, which he often exchanges with the related dominants, D, G, and C, along with a charming melodic phrase played by the first bassoon and the viola and then in the forty-first measure by the first violin with a varied cello accompaniment. Finally, he fulfills our expectation, which has several times been agreeably deceived, by means of the transition to the dominant of the principal key that first succeeds in m. 50. Now the opening theme enters once again, but in what a different form! The first violin varies the short introductory phrase. The clarinets and bassoons now perform mutually the lovely melody, moving in triplets, which the second violin and the viola, doubled by the violoncello, played at the beginning of the piece. Not yet satisfied with this, the composer adds in that original figure consisting of syncopated notes, at whose first appearance we thought of anything but a resemblance to the principal theme, and surprises us just as agreeably through this connection as we are surprised by an unexpected encounter between our friends, who, one from here, the other from there, find themselves through a happy chance at a common place, where they relay to us with brotherly hearts their various fates, which are united by common interest and the bond of friendship. This whole passage from the fiftieth to the fifty-fourth measure, in this varied but not unrecognizable form, makes an indescribably beautiful effect and gives us an elevated conception of the artist's spirit. The passage that follows (mm. 54–58) is no less beautiful, through its simplicity, than the preceding one was through its artistic combinations. The following four measures were less pleasing to the reviewer; the reason, he believes, is because the seconds formed by the melodies of the first and second violins lie too close together. For the sake of clarity, and in order to authenticate what has been said, let these measures be quoted here:

OP. 68
Andante molto moto,
mm. 58–61

Measures 91–94 displeased the reviewer for the same reason. Everything else is worthy of praise. One passage toward the end of this number, however, deserves to be particularly celebrated, in which the songs of the nightingale, the quail, and the cuckoo are imitated in close succession so successfully that, like a portrait snatched completely from a mirror image, they make everyone laugh. This passage *will not* be censured by anyone, partly for this reason, and partly because, even apart from this special consideration, it is good and agreeable, and *cannot* be censured by anyone. The idea of representing bird songs through musical notes is certainly not new in itself, but the manner in which the artist has sought to represent them belongs to him alone. Specifically, he lets all three bird songs enter in short succession, and then together, so that a charming ensemble is formed of three voices, each of which contains its own song. The passage is too original for a quotation of it here to be misplaced:

OP. 68
Andante molto moto,
mm. 129–32

The reviewer took less of a fancy to the third number, which comprises an Allegro in F major in $\frac{3}{4}$ time, in comparison to those which precede and follow it, due to a lack of variety in harmony and instrumentation, to the violation of metrical unity and to frequent repetition of individual passages. At the very beginning, before we have properly anchored ourselves in the principal tonality of the whole, we are already somewhat ungraciously displaced from this possession in the ninth measure and thrown into D major. Our stay here is also not long, for already at m. 17 our new dominion is taken away from us and the old one given back. At m. 25 we must experience once again this disagreeable *exmissio possessionis,*[9] and only after it has passed can we take a firmer footing for the first time. We do not, to be sure, return so quickly to the principal key; our ear, however, is not so much offended by harsh transitions as fatigued by a unison extending through forty-four measures, which is only hemmed in here and there by a fundamental voice lying in the basses, bassoons, and horns. Only when this stops, and the setting becomes polyphonic, does the continuation gain in variety and interest. The reviewer found the alternate section inserted at m. 91 to be equally fatiguing, partly because of too frequent repetition, partly because of sparse decoration with new harmonies. The alternate section from m. 165 to m. 204 seems to him to have the same defect, in addition to the fact that the shift from $\frac{3}{4}$ time into $\frac{2}{4}$, and the dissimilarity of the figurations in this section to those in the principal section, does too much damage to the continuity of the whole. With all of this taken together, this number can hardly compete for the first position with those that remain.

We find all the richer compensation for this, however, in the two pieces that follow. No. 4 represents a thunderstorm to us in the liveliest colors. This piece is incontestably the most successful of all those in this painting of the countryside and has a sublime effect throughout. As many as are the individual images that are presented to us by such a subject, and as often as other composers have worked it over, sometimes with and sometimes without the greatest success, the form in which the ingenious Beethoven presents us with this imposing natural drama in mimesis is correspondingly simple and new. When composers of a lower rank wish to represent a storm to us, they commonly take the pregnant moment, and, in order to be completely genuine, they do not let the appropriate musicians, namely the drummer and the two trumpet and flute players, catch their breath any more than the listener. When they believe that they have ranted and raved long enough, they break off without warning, so that the entire musical commotion seems more like the ghostly work of a poltergeist, which upon appearing excites all elements at once, but sensing the morning breeze disappears with a violent bang, upon which everything suddenly lies covered with the stillness of the grave.[10] Not so Beethoven. Certainly, the highest level of the hurricane is a subject of his representation; but he as little disdains thereby the lingering approach as he does the gradual receding of the storm. So we sense the distant thunder in the tremolo of the contrabasses and violoncellos in the first two measures; the violins paint for us in the following five measures the faint, restless movement of the wind, of the approaching storm. Little by little the storm draws nearer, and by the twenty-first measure it appears to us in all its dreadfulness with the powerful entrance of all the wind instruments and a four-measure-long drum roll. The high notes of the thrice-struck octaves—F, E, G♭—which the first violin brings out; the uninterrupted cries of the oboes, horns, bassoons, and trumpets, which express the howling storm; the striving sixteenth-note figures in the basses, which imitate the rumbling of thunder; the frequent dissonances, predominantly the diminished-seventh chord with its inversions—a true image of the feelings of horror and terror—everything fills us with great and sublime emotions. However, as gradually as they arose, just as gradually do the violent outbreaks of the storm disappear. Then the violins play in slower motion; the wind instruments play more quietly and sparingly in interspersed solo passages that show cheering glimpses of the sun; the trumpets are completely silent in the last twelve measures and are not heard again before the following number, where they accompany the joyful feelings of the country dweller after weathering the storm. So much for this magnificent piece, designed entirely for effect. To describe all its individual beauties with words would require too much detail, would indeed be impossible. Listen, and you will get to know the composer here in all his greatness.

No. 5 (F major, $\frac{6}{8}$), the content of which has already been described, begins with a phrase that, performed by the clarinet, imitates an alpine cowherd's melody. What can be conceived more naturally, more beautifully, and more in accordance with the character of the country dweller than such an expression of joy? The melody begins in C major, the dominant of F, and is repeated in m. 5 by the horn in an original way against an unprepared $\frac{7}{4}$ chord, which is first resolved on the third eighth note of the eighth measure.[11] If the artist intended thereby to express the different tones of shepherds' instruments from different places in the village, then he has happily obtained his goal. With the ninth measure a simply beautiful theme enters, fashioned from the first measure, which, since it moves only in quarter and eighth notes, paints the first degree of joy exceptionally well. With the seventeenth measure the second violin takes up the first melody and plays it an octave deeper. The first violin accompanies in sixteenth-note figures. This rapid motion, along with the varied accompaniment of the wind instruments, which had previously played half and quarter notes, and now progress in continuous quarter notes, shows us the second degree of joy. At the twenty-fifth measure the viola and the violoncello receive this melody, which the clarinets and horns bring out strongly by doubling it, while the first violin takes over the accompaniment in sixteenth-note triplets; the other wind instruments powerfully support the sustained notes—in short, everything paints the highest degree of happy feelings, which approaches loud rejoicing. At the fifty-sixth measure, the composer leads back toward the principal idea, which appears together with the original, unprepared $\frac{7}{4}$ harmony, by means of a section of the theme played, in parts, first by the violins, then by the flute, oboe, and clarinet. The melody that began at m. 9 also speaks to us anew, but, in Beethoven's characteristic way, with a varied accompaniment, which is now played by the second violin alternating with the viola. Hereupon follows, after a modulation to B♭ major, a fifteen-measure-long interlude [mm. 80–94], the insertion of which removes the principal theme from us for some time so we do not become weary of it. Then it comes back, but only a section of it, which the artist develops in the utmost variety of ways. We even hear the more calculated subsidiary theme again in a different form. Played by the violoncello and bassoon, it is then taken up by the second, and then by the first violin, and continued up to the conclusion, first by itself, then accompanied, in the guise of a countersubject, by the figure that shortly before had served as the new introduction to the principal subject, and ending meaningfully with the opening idea, the melody of the shepherd's horn.[12]

And now enough description of this brilliant product, the hearing of which will surely bring more satisfaction to every educated person than an ever so detailed description can give. May the ingenious Beethoven present us again soon with such a masterwork. But, why does this wish need to be expressed, since the artist, who has as much persevering industry as he does genius, has so far anticipated all of our wishes!

NOTES

1. Kinsky-Halm, 163, holds Amadeus Wendt (see entry no. 240, below) to be the author of this review. This information, however, is drawn from Schindler, who also attributes Hoffmann's review of the Fifth Symphony to Wendt (Anton Schindler, *Beethoven as I Knew Him* [henceforth Schindler-MacArdle], ed. Donald W. MacArdle, trans. Constance S. Jolly (London: University of North Carolina Press, 1966), 155–56). Stefan Kunze, *Ludwig van Beethoven: Die Werke im Spiegel seiner Zeit* (Laaber: Laaber-Verlag, 1987), 118 (following Erwin Kroll, "E. T. A. Hoffmann und Beethoven," *Neues Beethoven Jahrbuch* 3 [1927]: 127) gives Michael Gotthard Fischer (1773–1829) as the author. It has also been attributed to Friedrich Rochlitz and even to E. T. A. Hoffmann.

2. The identity of the manuscript used for the Leipzig performance is not clear. Possibilities include Beethoven's manuscript (now in the Beethoven-Haus); a corrected copy with corrections by Beethoven formerly in the possession of the Gesellschaft zu Lambach (now in Ljubliana, Bibliothek der Akademie für Musik); the copy that was used to engrave the first edition (*Stichvorlage,* now lost); a copy "from the first half of the nineteenth century" in the Archiv der Stadt Bratislava (CHS 320/146); or a conducting score (such as existed in the Breitkopf & Härtel lending library in Leipzig for the Fifth Symphony, now in the Beethoven Center in San José). Since the named concert took place in Leipzig, the last-mentioned score is the most probable candidate. See Kinsky-Halm, 162; and Dorfmüller, *Beiträge zur Beethoven-Bibliographie* (Munich: Henle, 1978), 14, 320.

3. See the sections on Enlightenment aesthetics and criticism in the introductory essay of vol. 1 for the importance of several Enlightenment concepts that inform a number of premises in this article. The idea that a work of art must be "pleasant and instructive" was derived by Enlightenment critics from Horace's statement that art must combine "utile dulci" (utility and pleasure) (*De arte poetica,* line 343).

4. Measure 163. This is actually the twenty-fifth measure of what the author calls the second part of the movement, encompassing what we would now call the development and recapitulation.

5. Measures 243ff. Actually, the different phrase is mm. 9–12 of the original theme.

6. Measures 279ff. This is the recapitulation of modern sonata form.

7. The author's mention of B♭ major as an especially appropriate key to depict "contentment and peaceful observation" is in keeping with several descriptions of the meaning of the key during the Classical period. Around 1784 Schubart described it as a key fit for "cheerful love, clear conscience, hope, aspiration for a better world"; in 1796 Galeazzi described it as "tender, soft, sweet, effeminate, fit to express transports of love, charm, and grace." Four years after this review was written, E. T. A. Hoffmann specifically linked the key to the pastoral: "How joyful are the meadows and forests in spring! All the flutes and panflutes, which during the winter lay frozen in dusty corners, are awake and are recalling their favorite melodies that they are now trilling as happily as the birds." See Rita Steblin, *A History of Key Characteristics in the Eighteenth and Early Nineteenth Centuries* (Ann Arbor MI: UMI Research, 1983), 296–97.

8. For a discussion of this passage in the review and Beethoven's use of bird songs in this movement, see Owen Jander, "The Prophetic Conversation in Beethoven's 'Scene by the Brook,'" *Musical Quarterly* 77 (1993): 508–59.

9. "Exmissio possessionis": Latin: "releasing of possession, property."

10. For three recent discussions of the depictions of storms in music of the Classical period, see Owen Jander, "Genius in the Arena of Charlatanry: The First Movement of Beethoven's 'Tempest' Sonata in Cultural Context," in *Musica franca: Essays in Honor of Frank D'Accone* (Stuyvesant NY: Pendragon, 1996), 585–630; Richard Will, "Time, Morality, and Humanity in Beethoven's *Pastoral* Symphony," *Journal of the American Musicological Society* 50 (1997): 271–329; Roland Schmenner, *Die Pastorale/Beethoven, das Gewitter und der Blitzableiter* (Kassel: Bärenreiter, 1997).

11. The harmony here is actually the combination of two open fifths: F–C in the cellos and C–G in the violas.

12. Measures 260–64.

∼

220.
Friedrich Mosengeil.[1] "Review." *Zeitung für die elegante Welt* 10 (1810): 1049–53.

This work of art, with which, on sufficient examination, probably none of the musical paintings known until now can withstand comparison, falls into five acts. The heading of the

First act, "Awakening of happy feelings upon arrival in the countryside," indicates the point of view of the poet, who, in order to be properly understood, has already added the comment: "more emotion than painting" to the title of his work. His tableau is distinguished from the customary musical ones like the work of a painter who idealizes nature from that of an ordinary copyist of it.

Carried by his imagination into the lovely meadows of an Arcadian shepherd's world, enchanted by its innocent pleasures, he calls his heavenly muse, harmony, down to earth, and surrenders himself to her sweet tones.[2] Just as the "*great voice*" in the Revelation of Saint John commands: "What thou seest, write in a book!" so does his goddess call to this enraptured man: "What thou hearest, make a record of!"[3] Alas, we too have probably perceived, sometime or other, similar tones, as though from out of a distant, long lost homeland, even if only in a poetic dream. But among the millions, it is given only to a few to give back so accurately that which is received!

The tones of the shawms and shepherd's horns from flowering plains are perceptible right at the beginning of this act, and individual sounds from these same resound through the entire poem, holding the listener upon the holy ground onto which the composer has drawn him over to himself firmly until the end. He becomes at home with him in these charming valleys. He sees the flowering, happy forms that inhabit them go by, first near, then far, now singly, then passing by in friendly union, and is happy with them. That which emerges as a solo from the joyous multitude of tones in this first movement belongs for the most part to a shepherd's instrument. Even the old, honorable bagpipe seems to us to grumble distinctly along in several places. Always, however, a charming melody runs through the frolicking tones. Is it not the voice of a shepherdess, who wanders over singing from time to time?

The ingenious *Beethoven,* whose difficult compositions often make the most accomplished musicians fainthearted, is here so easy and comprehensible, so simple and childlike! The breast breathes freely, the heart opens itself up to the purest pleasure, and shuts out all trivial cares.

Second act. "Scene by the brook."

The poet rests by the brook—resting easily upon his lyre, which plays by itself—now feasting his animated glance upon flowers, which bow to the gentle wind, now losing himself in the pure, blue depth of heaven. The soft waves of the brook murmur and splash, and the shadowy alders whisper down through the entire scene.

Whoever can or will not follow the master's flight will perhaps find in this incomparable movement too much reality if, while resting by a stream, he has an ear for nothing but the endless murmuring, and an eye for nothing but the everflowing waves, and he falls asleep out of boredom.

Our poet is *awake*!—In the uninterrupted billows and undulations, wherein string and wind instruments alternate with one another, a delightful abundance of tones is perceptible. In this, just as in the previous act, we hear from time to time the voice of a wandering singer drift our way. But the sweet throats of birds predominate here. They chirp and coo, jumping about in the branches, the quail coaxes us from the ground, and from the heights the sounds of the ascending lark come down to us. At last, nightingale, quail, and cuckoo unite to form a trio, which, as small as it is, nevertheless puts the listener in a mood to forgive the composer for closing the act shortly after. "Something more lovely—he thinks—could certainly not follow this!"

Third act. "Joyous togetherness of the country people."

Apart from the well-known scherzo in the *Eroica* symphony of our master, we know of no piece of music that represents the naive joy of an unaffected nature more magnificently than this third act of the Pastoral.

We see the poet leap up from his lyrical rest by the brook in order to be happy together with happy people, and at once there arrives a joyous crowd of country people, all of whom offer him what he wants. The shepherds come first, cheerfully making music. Their oboes sound to us uncommonly melodious and rustically simple. So does the entire accompaniment. The bassoon joins this shepherds' music, as often as it returns, with three descending notes of the fundamental chord, which have an indescribably agreeable effect.

The cheerful lads swing their beauties around in the lively dance. We hear them rejoice and believe that we ourselves are witnessing the cheerful dance.

But in the midst of the joy, in the *fourth act* a storm that has remained unobserved enters from over the mountains. Scarcely have the basses announced its coming in deep, grumbling tones than we seem, with the anxiously hurrying notes of the second violin, to see the surprised little crowd flee, seeking shelter and a roof over their heads. The joy falls silent, and the scene of happiness now remains open only to the effects of a great, majestic nature. Right at the first drum roll the frightful storm bursts forth.—Are we really mistaken when we believe that we hear the sizzling of the quick lightning, the rush of the pouring rain, and the whistling and howling of the stormwind through cracks and crevices? No, no more than we can mistake the powerful thunderclaps that come ever more abundantly in the midst of these, now crashing down with a heavily resounding report, now fading out in deep, receding murmurs.

Great and wonderful is the Lord of Nature! But not only in those places where the lightning illuminates the storm clouds and its thunder makes the mountains tremble, God's finger is also present where the spirit of a favored mortal, aware of his divine heritage, stands firmly in control in the midst of the wild torrents of powerful tones, and melodiously restrains and unites all these diverse sounds, which, if they flow together without constraint, lacerate the ear and shock the feelings. They must obey his creative will and at the same time give voice to his sublime ideas, where they flow so powerfully and overwhelmingly as in this storm by the *Shakespeare* of the musical world.

The storm rages violently, but it passes quickly and bountifully on. The more gentle drum rolls let it echo from an even further distance. And with this echo, gentle human voices also come to the fore once again. We seem here and there to hear a figure calling to another from its place of shelter, and the

Fifth act (marked "Shepherd's song, joyful and thankful feelings after the storm"), which immediately follows, suffices to persuade us that we were not mistaken. Out of their hollow trees, out of their protective caverns, the gallant shepherds spring joyously forth onto the freshened meadow. There they are again, the friendly, well-known tones of the shepherd's horn (represented in an uncommonly striking way at the beginning of the fifth act by clarinet and horn), and they resound often throughout this entire act as well between the thankful songs of the country people until at the end of the piece, in order to leave behind with the listener an unforgettable memory of their call, which awakens a kind of homesickness, they die out practically without accompaniment.

The art of instrumentation and of distribution of parts can be nowhere more brilliantly proclaimed than here. The depth and tenderness with which the artist is able to express, in this last movement, a joy that differs from that felt in the first three movements by means of an added feeling of religious gratitude are indescribable and heighten the admiration with which he filled us in that which came before.

When it comes to works by great artists and poets—and therefore also *Beethoven's* creations, we have often recalled a word that is spoken by Minelli in Wagner's *Wilibald,* and that will probably only be misunderstood by whoever has not succeeded in perceiving the *divine* in art:

"Religion makes us God's children, but art makes us his friends."[4]

NOTES

1. Friedrich Mosengeil (1773–1839) is described in AMZ 23 (20 May 1821): 392, as a church councillor at Meiningen, "a respected poet and intimate friend of musical art." He wrote a series of verbal declamations to be performed with Beethoven's incidental music to Goethe's *Egmont,* which will appear in vol. 3 of this series.

2. For a discussion of the Arcadian representations and the pastoral style, see F. E. Kirby, "Beethoven's Pastoral Symphony as a Sinfonia Caracteristica," *Musical Quarterly* 41 (1970): 605–23.

It should be emphasized here that Mosengeil's description of the symphony as an Arcadian shepherd's world contrasts sharply with the interpretation of the author of entry no. 219, who set the narrative in the present. As the review proceeds, Mosengeil continues his allusions to Arcadia with an important reference to the poet resting with his lyre by the brook. This image of the poet with his lyre is exactly the image depicted in the important Willibrord Joseph Mähler portrait of Beethoven from 1804, which shows the composer in an Arcadian landscape holding a lyra guitar. See the discussion of the extensive symbolism of that portrait in Owen Jander, "The Radoux Portrait of Beethoven's Grandfather: Its Symbolic Message," *Imago musicae* 6 (1989): 102–06. Later critics (see entry no. 222 below, for example) elaborated on the Arcadian symbolism of the symphony.

3. Biblical reference to Rev. 1:11: "Write on a scroll what you see now."

4. Johann Ernst Wagner (1769–1812) was a minor writer during the age of Goethe. The quotation here is from his novel *Willibalds Ansichten des Lebens,* strongly influenced by Goethe and Jean Paul Richter.

~

221.
"News. Munich." *Allgemeine musikalische Zeitung* 14 (19 February 1812): 125–26.

At the second concert, on 3 December, the Pastoral Symphony of Beethoven, which was new to us, stood out from the rest. Not with injustice may the discovery, as well as the only gradually successful development of those instrumental pieces to which the name symphony has been given, be counted among the most noteworthy creations of the human spirit, which our time, and in particular Germany, reveres, and which has extended the boundaries of musical art.[1] If it is difficult for mere instrumental music, however artistically the master may have ordered things according to aesthetic principles, to excite a specific emotion in the soul of the listener, then the attempts to bring more light into this dark region are indeed worthy of our thanks. We do not wish to undertake to discuss here that which Beethoven has accomplished through his efforts. The path that he has laid out for himself is certainly an eccentric one. He raises us above the commonplace and transfers us, albeit oftentimes rather ungently, into the realm of fantasy. In today's symphony, the first Allegro was the most pleasing, the scene by the brook (Andante), with the quail, the nightingale, and the cuckoo, less so. The peasant gathering (Menuett) and the storm that follow are full of character and greatness. The uninitiated hearer, however, will find it difficult to enter into all these secrets that are closed off to him. In pantomimic dance, we have learned to understand the signs, which are often only arbitrarily applied. The language of music that is utilized here, however, is as yet unknown to most people, which should surprise no one, since so little has been done from its side to clarify it for the common understanding.

NOTE

1. For an important discussion of German nationalism and the growing reverence for German "art music," see Pederson, "Marx, Berlin, and German National Identity," 87–107.

≈

222.
K. B. "Miscellaneous." *Allgemeine musikalische Zeitung* 17 (11 October 1815): 693–94.

That the symphony, this most magnificent development of the self-begetting and self-forming genius of musical art, has been raised to a peak by J. Haydn, Mozart, and Beethoven, is certainly as much beyond doubt as the fact that the last-named artist now rules preeminently among the living as lord and master of this realm. Each one of his symphonies could be brought out with full justification as proof of this assertion. For this time, however, I will only mention with a few words that one which, until now, seems to have found the least acceptance—his Pastoral. Certainly this musical idyll, filled with a poetic spirit throughout, unites in its genre that which older and more recent pastoral poetry have accomplished in theirs. With what wonderful originality is the whole conceived! How firm and true it remains to the character of the individual pieces, and with what boundless imagination is it carried out!

The first movement at once develops our innermost sensibility for all the charms of an abundantly rich, beautiful nature, and of the innocently happy life in its bosom. We feel ourselves removed to that Arcadian world about whose existence Spain's and Italy's poets have sung so enchantingly. The scene by the brook that follows has unnameable grace and loveliness. Dark shadows cover us with a vault of foliage against the glowing light, and, by the rustling of the murmuring forest stream, among the songs of feathered minstrels from the meadows and plains, we feel that we are listening to the tender whispering of heartfelt love. If we have tarried until now upon idealized ground, the musical poet now leads us up on the mountains and into the valleys of the Tyrol and Switzerland to joyous peasant dances. Everything rejoices, exults, and turns around us in the festive round dance. Boldly and freely the hearty son of nature takes hold of the powerful, merry maid. It does no good here to be demure and affected! The powerful impulses of nature are stirred up powerfully and without reserve. But a thunderstorm breaks out and upsets the rejoicing. What a contrast to the lovely and amusing scenes that had come before are these frighteningly sublime ones! What masses! What boldness and freshness in the modulations! And now the close of this movement, as the storm finally recedes entirely into the distance; everything becomes clear and cheerful once again, and the shepherd's flute rises up so amiably, spontaneously awakening through these tones all the emotions that have previously filled our breasts in similar natural settings. It is as if we were seeing, after regaining harmony and rest, the colorful bow of peace spanned across the clouds. The alpenhorn resounds, and the jubilation of the shepherds breaks impetuously forth in order to join itself to the choral celebration of nature in praise of the divinity.

223.

August Kuhn. "Concert in Berlin." *Der Freymüthige* 22 (3 May 1825): 347.

(Mentioned: Symphony No. 9, op. 125)

On the day of repentance, 27 April, Beethoven's Pastoral Symphony and Handel's oratorio *Samson* were performed at the opera house by the Royal Orchestra, the Royal Singers, and the chorus of the opera under Spontini's[1] direction. As regards Beethoven's symphony, it has become clear to us anew how awkward and unsuccessful every tone-painting, even by the most ingenious hand, must appear, and we do not count the work, even in regard to imagination and artistic development, among Beethoven's best productions. Sir Knight Spontini would have prepared a higher enjoyment for us if he had brought Beethoven's newest symphony, with the final chorus "Freude, schöner Götterfunken," to performance for the first time—an undertaking that he, and he alone, would be qualified to give direction to worthily.[2] Today's performance of the Pastoral Symphony, however, was significantly inferior to the last ones at Möser's concert, both in regard to its nuances and to its accuracy in interpreting the often difficult introductions of the most ingenious of all living composers.[3]

NOTES

1. Gaspare Luigi Pacifico Spontini (1774–1851) was an Italian composer whose French-language operas were highly successful in the early nineteenth century. At the time this was written he was serving in Berlin as general music director to Friedrich Wilhelm III.

2. The Berlin premiere of the Ninth Symphony took place the next year on 27 November 1826 with Möser as conductor. One of the problems with this performance of the Sixth may have been that, in the opinion of many musicians (including Mendelssohn), the orchestra "never achieved the level of excellence that could be found in Leipzig, London, Vienna (under Nicolai), or Paris." See David Levy, *Early Performances of Beethoven's Ninth Symphony: A Documentary Study of Five Cities* (Ph.D. thesis, University of Rochester, 1980), 400, 402.

3. As mentioned above, the Pastoral Symphony was performed five times between March 1825 and January 1826 in Berlin. These repetitions of a single work were exactly what A. B. Marx called for in his important essay titled "Some Words about Concert Life Especially in Large Cities," BAMZ 2: 350. See n. 1 to entry no. 171 for Marx's plea for repetitions of the Pastoral Symphony.

‿

224.

"News. Berlin." *Allgemeine musikalische Zeitung* 30 (28 May 1828): 363.

(With String Quartet, op. 132)

To begin with, music director Möser[1] delighted us at his final soirées with Spohr's[2] overture to *Faust,* a new *septet* by Lenß,[3] which did not so much show originality in the gift of invention as it did taste, diligence, and familiarity with the instruments, along with a certain degree of agility in modulation, and further with Beethoven's genuinely romantic Pastoral Symphony, which reminded us at an appropriate time of the joys of country life. Then, at the sixth gathering, we heard Möser's second quartet cycle, along with a very humorous quartet by the always youthfully refreshing, cheerful J. Haydn, a quartet by L. Spohr (in E♭ major), less consummately performed than the very difficult, new quartet by Beethoven in A minor, op. 132, which, with all the individual beauties in its ideas, was not appealing in its total effect, due mostly to the exhausting length of the movements and the rhapsodic manner in which they are worked out. The scherzo was best understood and most favorably received.

NOTES

1. Karl Möser (1774–1851) studied music in Berlin under the concertmaster Karl Haack and became a leading figure in Berlin's music life with his frequent chamber music soirées. He directed a number of premieres of Beethoven's music, including the first Berlin performance of the Ninth Symphony in 1826.

2. Spohr's opera *Faust* was first performed in 1816.

3. AMZ 21 (1819): 874 and 30 (1828): 558, inter alia, describe a Heinrich K. Lenß (1793–1856), who was active as a royal chamber musician in Berlin. Several times he performed horn concertos of his own composition.

~

OP. 69
SONATA FOR PIANO AND VIOLONCELLO IN A MAJOR

225.
K. B. "Miscellaneous." *Allgemeine musikalische Zeitung* 16 (16 February 1814): 123.

(Mentioned: Symphony No. 4, op. 60; Two Trios for Piano, Violin, and Cello, op. 70; and Fantasy for Piano, Chorus, and Orchestra, op. 80)

The thorough reviews of various works of Beethoven in these pages, for example, of the two splendid trios for fortepiano, violin, and violoncello, of the fantasy with chorus, and of several of his symphonies, make the desire for numerous similar evaluations very comprehensible. The master's Symphony in B♭ Major, for example, has certainly already been briefly and strikingly described several times, but has never been extensively reviewed.[1] And does it deserve less than any of the others?[2] But for now, I only wished to have genially recommended to the reviewers of the above-mentioned works Beethoven's Sonata in A Major, op. 69, for fortepiano and violoncello. It is unquestionably a worthy companion piece to those two trios, conceived and felt in practically the same spirit. A superbly rounded whole, full of tender loveliness, like few others, and at the same time genuinely romantic, showing genuine depth of soul! If it is executed by two players just as it should be— for which, however, dexterous fingers and a practiced bow will certainly not suffice in themselves: one may expect the most magnificent effect.

NOTES

1. See the brief descriptions of the Fourth that had appeared in AMZ in entries no. 176 from 1808, 177 from 1811, and 178 from 1812.

2. "Editor's Note. By no means; but reviewers, like sailors, will not let themselves be impressed. With such a well-known master, are not notices, such as the editor provides, satisfactory to at least a portion of the readers?"

OP. 70
TWO TRIOS FOR PIANO, VIOLIN, AND CELLO
IN D MAJOR AND E♭ MAJOR

226.

Ernst Theodor Amadeus Hoffmann. "Review." *Allgemeine musikalische Zeitung* 15 (3 March 1813): 141–54.[1]

(Mentioned: Symphony No. 5, op. 67)

Some time ago, the reviewer wrote a judgment of one of Beethoven's weightiest works: the grand, brilliant Symphony No. 5 in C Minor, and took this opportunity to try to express himself completely regarding the spirit and style of the ingenious master. As a result of diligent study of the work itself, the reviewer made the assertion at that time that Beethoven is a purely *romantic* composer, more than any other has ever been, and that it is for this reason that he has been less successful with vocal music, which does not allow for a character of unspecified yearning, but only represents affects that are indicated by words, rather than being felt in the kingdom of the infinite, and that his instrumental music has not been understood by the masses. Even these masses, the reviewer further said, do not deny that he has a high degree of imagination. On the contrary, they customarily see in his works only the product of a genius that, unconcerned with the form and selection of its ideas, gives itself up blindly to the overpowering fire and the momentary promptings of its imagination. Nevertheless, in regard to presence of mind, he deserves to be placed on a level with Haydn and Mozart since he separates what is merely himself from the innermost kingdom of notes and rules over it as an absolute lord. The reviewer finds all of this to be ever more and more confirmed with each new work of the master that comes before his eyes and ears. These two magnificent trios also demonstrate anew how Beethoven carries the Romantic spirit of music deep within his soul, and with what a high degree of genius, with what presence of mind, he animates his works with it. It must enchant and inspire every true fortepiano player when a new work for his instrument appears by *that* master who is himself a virtuoso on the fortepiano, and thus writes for it with a deep knowledge of what is playable and effective, as well as with an obvious partiality.[2] The fortepiano is and remains an instrument more useful for harmony than for melody. The most refined expression of which the instrument is capable does not give to melody the same agile life, with thousands and thousands of nuances, which the bow of the violinist or the breath of the wind player are in a position to bring forth. The player struggles in vain with the insurmountable difficulty set against him by the mechanism, which causes the strings to vibrate and resound by means of a stroke. On the other hand, there is probably no instrument (with the exception of the harp, which is far more limited) that encompasses the kingdom of harmony with full chords, and unfolds its treasures to the connoisseur in the most wonderful forms and shapes as does the fortepiano.[3] If the master's imagination has conceived a complete tone-painting, with rich groupings, bright lights and deep shadows, then he can call it to life at the fortepiano, so that it steps forth colorful and brilliant from the inner world. The full-voiced score, that genuine musical magic book, which retains within its signs all of the wonders of musical art, the mysterious choir of the most variegated instruments, is brought to life at the fortepiano under the hands of a master, and a piece that, in this manner, is well played in all its voices from the score may be compared with a good copper engraving taken from a great painting. The fortepiano is thus particularly well suited to improvisation, to performing from score, to individual sonatas, toccatas, etc. Likewise, trios, quartets, quintets, etc., where the customary string instruments enter in, belong on this account entirely to the realm of fortepiano compositions since, even if they are composed in the true manner, that is to say genuinely four-voiced, five-voiced, etc., what matters here is solely the working out of the harmony, which in itself excludes the emergence of individual instruments in brilliant passagework. The reviewer, who believes that he is making a very valid assertion here, has for this reason an antipathy to all fortepiano concertos, for here the virtuosity of the individual player must be brought to bear in passagework and in the expression of the melody, while the best player on the most beautiful instrument strives in vain for *that* which, for example, the violinist achieves with little effort. Every solo sounds stiff and insipid after the full tutti of the string and wind players, and one is amazed by the agility of the fingers, and so forth, without the soul being properly addressed.[4]

From that which has already been said in a general sense about the spirit and character of Beethoven's music (as well as from the notion, which for the most part can be held to be correct, that he, the profound master of composition, the virtuoso at the fortepiano, will grasp the most individual spirit of the instrument and write for it in the most suitable manner), the idea, as well as the structure, of his keyboard-trios, quartets, etc. may be surmised, and a misconception is scarcely possible, even if one has never seen and heard works of *this* kind by the master. A simple but fertile and lyrical theme, suitable to the most various contrapuntal devices, abbreviations, etc., forms the basis of every movement; all other secondary themes and figures are intimately related to the principal idea, so that everything combines and orders itself through all the instruments toward the highest degree of unity. This is what the structure of the whole is like; but within this synthetic edifice, the most wonderful images alternate in endless succession, in which joy and pain, melancholy and ecstasy appear next to and in combination with each other. Strange forms begin a joyous dance, as they gently fade toward a luminous point, then separate from each other flashing and sparkling, and hunt and pursue each other in myriad groupings. In the midst of the spirit kingdom thus revealed, the enraptured soul listens to the unknown language, and understands all of the most secret allusions by which it has been aroused. Only *that* composer has truly penetrated the secrets of harmony, who truly is able to use them to touch the human soul. To him the numbers and proportions, which are only dead, rigid arithmetic problems to the grammarian without genius, are enchanted potions with which he conjures up a magical world.

The reviewer must say all of this before the evaluation of the individual trios in order to make it sufficiently clear how inimitably great Beethoven is in his fortepiano compositions. He turns first to the Trio No. 1, in D major, whose beginning he sets down, so that what he wishes to say about it will become clearer.

OP. 70
No. 1, Allegro vivace e con brio, mm. 1–9 (all of the original examples follow the first edition in using treble rather than tenor clef for the cello; see Beethoven's letter of Sept. 4, 1816, Anderson L. 652, for his clarification)

The first four measures contain the principal theme. The seventh and eighth measures of the violoncello part, however, contain the secondary theme.[5] The entire Allegro is woven out of these two phrases, with the exception of a few secondary figures, which are placed in between the working-out of these two principal ideas. It was all the more appropriate to let the idea that dominates the entire movement be played in four-octave unison; it impresses itself firmly and distinctively upon the listener so that he is able to keep track of it, like a brightly shining stream, in the midst of the most unusual twists and turns. Furthermore, the character of the trio, less gloomy throughout than many other instrumental compositions of B., expressing a happy good nature, a joyful, proud consciousness of personal strength and abundance, is already made manifest in this theme. Apart from the canonic imitation of the second theme, there is no further contrapuntal working-out in the first part of the Allegro, which is only seventy-three measures long. The closing idea, which the fortepiano plays first against a unison of the violoncello and violin, and which those instruments then take up against a unison on the fortepiano in eighth-note figurations, is not further worked out, and returns for the first time at the close of the second part, although in a different form. The first part really gives only the exposition of the piece. In the second part [mm. 74ff.], a richly artistic contrapuntal web now begins, which continues until the entry of the principal theme in D major in its original form. The bass of the fortepiano takes up a theme, which, however, appears to be nearly the same as the figure in the second measure of the secondary theme played in the first part by the violoncello, in retrograde motion,[6] and against which the violoncello and the upper voice of the fortepiano alternately perform the shortened principal theme, with the violin entering with an even shorter section of the principal theme in canonic imitation.

OP. 70
No. 1, Allegro vivace e
con brio, mm. 74–82

In the ninth measure, the bass of the fortepiano and the violoncello lead in unison from D major to B♭ major by means of the principal theme, and line up the secondary theme against the principal theme in this key. The secondary theme is then continued by the upper voice of the fortepiano as a steady fundamental bass (organ point), while the violoncello and violin repeat the second measure of the secondary theme in thirds. Now there enters a new theme, which marches up and down the scale as far as the seventh, and which lies alternately in the upper and lower voices of the fortepiano, against which the violin and violoncello continue in alternation the idea from the secondary theme. This idea, only one measure long, is now imitated in the fortepiano and the other instruments until the music seems ready to die out in the close canonic imitation based on it. Soon, however, it becomes more lively once again; the violin takes up the first measure of the principal theme and the upper voice of the fortepiano follows, while the violoncello plays the second measure of the secondary theme. A mighty struggle and fight of all the voices now arises. Two measures—one measure—three notes of the principal theme,

OP. 70
No. 1, Allegro vivace e con brio, violin, m. 81

in exact and in retrograde motion, are now twisted together in canonic imitation. This is the most original, richly artistic section of the entire Allegro, and the reviewer sets it down here for the immediate inspection of the connoisseur.

OP. 70
No. 1, Allegro viciae e con bri
mm. 124–40

Now the principal theme returns in the original key, and we expect, according to the customary arrangement of instrumental pieces of this kind, the return of the first part, now remaining in the tonic at the appearance of the second theme as well. It is not so, however; the ingenious master surprises us with an abrupt turn into D minor, in which key the theme is repeated, whereupon the music goes into B♭ major, and the second theme, which is so lyrical, appears. The chromatically rising bass leads the music into A major and then back into D major,

whereupon the closing theme of the first part follows in a varied form in which the eighth-note figure is carried first by the violin and violoncello unisono, then by the upper voice of the fortepiano, then, however, by the bass of the fortepiano. At the reprise of the second part, the second principal theme is once again repeated in canonic imitation by the three instruments in G major in order to lead the music back to D major, whereupon the movement closes with the first part of the principal theme unisono.

The reviewer hopes, through exact description of the progress of this ingenious, splendid piece, not only to have provided an adequate idea of the trio to those to whom it was previously unknown, but also to have made it easier for the connoisseur, upon hearing or playing the piece, to enter more deeply into its spirit, which even in the various contrapuntal twists centers on a short, comprehensible theme. To accomplish this goal, he also did not hesitate to include the score of the most complicated, difficult part in its entirety. The second movement, a Largo assai ed espressivo, has the character of a gentle melancholy that is beneficial to the soul. The theme is made up once again, in the true Beethovenian manner, of two very simple figures only one measure long, which are shared by the fortepiano and the remaining instruments.

OP. 70
No. 1, Largo assai ed espressivo,
mm. 1–8

These few harmonically rich measures once again contain the material out of which the whole is woven. It is most of all the violoncello figure in the ninth measure, with the countertheme in the fortepiano that combines with it so beautifully, which continually appears in imitation; and the principal theme in the second measure of the fortepiano part also has an interconnecting effect, when it is taken up by the violoncello and further extended.

OP. 70
No. 1, Largo assai ed espressivo,
mm. 26–29

The modulation, however, is not complicated at all, and the reviewer will mention only one other peculiarity that distinguishes this movement and raises it above so many fortepiano compositions. The fortepiano accompanies the principal theme for the most part with a setting of sixty-fourth-note sextuplets, which are to be played *pp* and *leggiermente*.

OP. 70
No. 1, Largo assai ed espressivo,
m. 18

This is almost the only way that even the *tone* of a good fortepiano can be brought to bear in a startling, effective way. Specifically, if these sextuplets are played with an accomplished, gentle hand with dampers raised and with the "Pianozug," there arises a murmuring that is reminiscent of the Aeolian harp and the harmonica and that, united with the bowed sonorities of the remaining instruments, has a completely marvelous effect.[7] The reviewer added to the fortepiano stop and the damper pedal the so-called *Harmonikazug* as well, which, as is well known, moves the manual to the side, so that the hammers strike only *one* string, and from the beautiful Streicher fortepiano tones soared up, which surrounded the soul like fragrant dream shapes and invited him into the enchanted realm of strange forebodings.[8]

The concluding movement, Presto, in D major, once again has a short, original theme, which continually reappears in many variations and meaningful allusions throughout the entire piece while a variety of figures are interchanged.

OP. 70
No. 1, Presto, mm. 1–8

Just as the storm wind drives away the clouds, with light and shadow alternating in a moment, as forms then appear in the restless pursuit and commotion, disappear and appear again, just so does the music rush continuously onward after the second fermata. With an unisono at the fortepiano, against which violin and violoncello imitate canonically a new figure that traverses the scale up to the fifth, the music now turns to A major, F major, etc. There follow imitations of the principal phrase, as for example

OP. 70
No. 1, Presto, mm. 76–79

until the entire theme seems to enter in B♭ major, extended, however, in an original manner, which more than anything else expresses Beethoven's style, which shows itself in final movements primarily through a continuous, ever mounting bustle and commotion. The close of the first part leads back to the first principal theme so that there is no noticeable pause at all separating the first part from the second. This is appropriate to the character of the whole movement, which surges forward with restless agitation. The second part begins with a working-out and imitation of the unisono in the first part. Since it would take the reviewer too far to describe all the new, individual twists and the original structure of the whole second half precisely enough to be understood, which could only occur through examples, he will be satisfied with setting down here, from out of the second half, only one single canonic imitation of a figure in quarter-note triplets, which had not been heard previously, since this is again distinguished with unmistakable traits of the master.

OP. 70
No. 1, Presto, mm. 194–210

Regardless of the good nature that prevails in the entire trio, with the exception of the melancholy Largo, Beethoven's genius still remains serious and solemn. It is as though the master believed that deep, secret things can never be discussed in commonplace terms, but only in sublime, magnificent ones, even when the spirit, which is intimately familiar with them, feels joyously and happily uplifted. The dance music of the priest of Isis can only be a highly jubilant hymn.[9] The reviewer is also convinced that pure instrumental music, when it is meant to achieve dramatic effect through itself as music, and not perhaps for a specific purpose, should avoid the meaninglessly playful, the flirtatious jests.[10] The deep soul looks for presentiments of a happiness that, more magnificent and more beautiful than that found here in the narrow world, carried over from an unknown land, kindle an inward, rapturous life in the breast, which can impart a more lofty expression than mere words, which are only appropriate to captive, earthly joy. The reviewer will reserve the right to return again to this subject at the close of the review of the second trio, to which he now turns. Indeed, he will also take the opportunity to express a justified complaint, which he must raise over the fact that it is so difficult to persuade many good keyboard players to perform Beethoven's compositions.

No. 2. The flowing theme, with a restful character throughout, of the introduction: Poco sostenute [*sic*], in E♭ major, common time, is played by the three instruments in canonic imitation.

OP. 70
No. 2, Poco sostenuto,
mm. 1–6

But already at the twelfth measure there appear in the upper voice of the fortepiano, while the violin and violoncello strike only individual notes, more lively figures in sixteenth notes and sixteenth-note triplets, until again an entirely good-humored, expressive theme leads to the pause on the dominant, whereupon an Allegro ma non troppo, in E♭ major, ⁶⁄₈ time, begins.

Regardless of the ⁶⁄₈ time, which is otherwise so appropriate to playful, joking moods, this movement conveys, in its original form as well as in its many twists and turns, a serious and—allow me the expression—aristocratic character. The reviewer was unintentionally reminded of many of Mozart's compositions with a similar ardor, primarily of the Allegro of the magnificent Symphony in E♭ Major, which is known under the name *Schwanengesang*.[11] He is speaking, however, exclusively about the theme, not about its further working-out and the structure of the movement, in which Beethoven's genius once again steps forth in the most original way. After many ideas taken from the principal theme in the upper voice of the fortepiano and the violin, as, for example:

among other things, there follows in the twenty-first measure a second, magnificent theme, still in the principal key of E♭ major, which is played first by the violoncello to the accompaniment of the fortepiano, and then by the upper voice of the fortepiano and the violin all' ottava. Now the music turns to the dominant, and the theme of the introduction reappears in canonic imitation, albeit rewritten in $\frac{6}{8}$ time, and differently divided among the instruments.

The music is arranged in such a way that it sounds like a chorale that enters unexpectedly, which breaks suddenly into the ornately woven fabric, and arouses the soul like a strange, wondrous manifestation. Only a practiced ear would immediately recognize the music of the introduction, so different does it now appear, and it testifies to the boundless riches of the ingenious master, who fathoms the deepest secrets of harmony, that so many motives can sprout from a single idea a few measures long, offering themselves to him like the magnificent flowers and fruits of a prolific tree. The first part concludes in B♭ major with a triplet figure in the fortepiano, against which the violoncello and violin recall the principal theme, and the conclusion leads without interruption back to the beginning of the first part. In the reprise, the triplet figure is further extended with the violoncello and violin imitating each other, striking first four and then only two notes of the principal theme.

The reviewer will also mention the enharmonic modulation from D♭ minor into B major, in mm. 18, 19, and 20,[12] which, without being in the least bit harsh, like many modulations of this kind in recent compositions, nevertheless has the most striking effect. The master has indicated C♭ major in the fortepiano and violoncello at m. 20, but has already allowed the violin to take up B major.

OP. 70
No. 2, Allegro ma non troppo, mm. 111–13

This was apparently done in order to make the intonation easier for the player after the preceding rests, while the fortepiano, moreover, must be tuned in equal temperament, which allows no difference between B major and C♭ major. The return to G♭ major occurs abruptly with three chords.

OP. 70
No. 2, Allargo ma non troppo, harmonic reduction of mm. 122–24

After the return of the principal theme in the tonic, its further working-out is similar to that in the first part with only minor changes, except that the music remains in the tonic as well after the appearance of the second theme. Even before the conclusion, the introduction returns again in common time. After this has continued for only nine measures, however, the ⁶⁄₈ time and the principal theme appear once again, with an abbreviation of which the Allegro concludes. Regardless of the fact that the elements from which this movement is created are more diverse than one is accustomed to elsewhere in Beethoven's music, the second theme of the Allegro having little in common with the first, while the third seems wholly alien to the theme taken from the introduction, everything does come out in a powerful torrent. The truly musical listener will easily grasp the admittedly complicated course of the Allegro, even if at first there is perhaps much that will be unclear to the unpracticed ear. The following movement, Allegretto, C major, $\frac{2}{4}$ time, has a pleasing, melodious theme and is woven together with contrasting interludes in the minor, after which the principal theme constantly returns radiantly in the major, following the pattern that Haydn established in many Andantes, particularly in his symphonies.[13]

OP. 70
No. 2, Allegretto, mm. 1–4

Even in this Allegretto the master remains true to the genuine style of this type of composition, inasmuch as the music is interwoven through the three instruments to such an extent that only taken together do they give a concept of the whole. Each figure is treated thoroughly, and they mesh together effectively at the appropriate point. Indeed, even the beginning

OP. 70
No. 2, Allegretto, pickup
to m. 1

frequently recurs as the music is worked out further, even more pointedly proclaiming the character of the piece: as, for example, at the end of the first Minore and at the conclusion. In order not to become too long-winded, the reviewer must refer here, just as with the following Allegretto ma non troppo, in A♭ major, $\frac{3}{4}$ time, to examination and study of the work, which will delight and uplift every true musician, as only examples that would go beyond the reasonable boundaries of a review can clarify *that* which he would yet like to say. May he now be allowed to observe that the magnificent theme of this Allegretto,[14] which is, to be exact, the provocative middle movement established by Haydn under the name Menuetto, once again recalled to him the lofty, exalted, aristocratic ardor of similar movements by Mozart.

OP. 70
No. 2, Allegretto ma
non troppo, mm. 1–8

The trio has an entirely original structure, inasmuch as it consists of disjointed phrases in which the violoncello and the violin alternate with the fortepiano.

OP. 70
No. 2, Allegretto ma non troppo,
mm. 57–64

In just this trio, the master modulates with bold confidence in his power and dominion over the kingdom of notes in the following manner:

OP. 70
No. 2, Allegretto ma non troppo,
mm. 96–106

One can see what a wealth of piquant effects the enharmonic system offers. The reviewer, however, would probably express the opinion of every genuine, tasteful musician when he allows the use of such means only to the deeply learned master, and cautions anyone who has not entered into the innermost magical realm of the art strongly against them. Only *that* artist who has bridled the eccentricities of his genius through the most diligent study of the art, who has attained in this manner the highest degree of presence of mind, and who now reigns over the innermost kingdom of notes, knows clearly and securely where he may employ the most striking means that his art has to offer to full effect. The student, or, perhaps, the blind imitator without genius or talent, will make his first mistake precisely at the point where he had intended to employ all his might and power. Everything that the reviewer has already said in his evaluation of the last movement of the first trio applies as well to the concluding movement, Allegro, in E♭ major, $\frac{2}{4}$ time. It is a continuous, ever mounting bustle and commotion—ideas, images chase by in a restless flight, and sparkle and disappear like flashes of lightning—it is a free play of the most highly aroused imagination. And yet this movement is once again woven out of a few short ideas, out of figures that are most closely related to one another.

OP. 70
No. 2, Allegro, mm. 1–11 (this example and the following one were erroneously printed in the original as one continuous example)

The first six measures seem to be only the introduction to the true, simple theme, which first enters in the seventh measure. It is precisely this idea, however, which serves for an introduction, with the striking chords of the violin, violoncello, and the bass of the fortepiano, which is later worked out through the most diverse twists and allusions. After the violin, then the fortepiano in return, have extended the theme further, while the violoncello has sounded only its first measure, with the violin imitating it in notes twice as fast, the introduction enters again at m. 31. A sort of cadenza by the fortepiano in triplets leads to C minor—once again the introduction—a cadenza by the violin in G minor—yet again the introduction—a cadenza by the violoncello. Now follows a new theme in quarter notes, which remains

OP. 70
No. 2, Allegro, mm. 123–61

calmer, but only lasts for a few measures. Then a new storm drives the music toward G minor, G major, C major, until that phrase with which the Allegro began leads again through G minor and G major back to the principal key and to the reprise of the first part. The second part begins with the same figure, and now it is just those isolated chords from the beginning, along with the figure in sixteenth notes, which all three instruments play, imitating one another, giving rise to the most ornate, striking working-out with the most audacious modulations. No clear concept of the original treatment can be obtained without examining the score. The reviewer therefore sets out the entire passage, since in so doing he hopes to arouse greater attentiveness even among those familiar with the trio and to facilitate study of this work of art.

After an interruption of only eight measures, which themselves allude again to the figure from the opening, this enters once again and leads by means of the lovely principal theme back into the tonic. The rest of the structure corresponds to the first part, except that the modulations are changed, and the lyrical middle theme, which in the first half appeared in G major,

OP. 70
No. 2, Allegretto ma non troppo,
mm. 89–93

is not only repeated in C major, but also, when the music returns to the tonic, is further worked out in imitation by all the instruments. It finally appears, shortened, in a sort of close imitation, and now the introduction stormily reappears and, alternating with the principal theme, leads at last to the brilliant, surging final periods with sixteenth notes in all the instruments.

There is no unusual difficulty in the fortepiano parts of these trios, if what is meant is simple virtuosity and back-breaking passagework up and down with both hands, with all sorts of unusual leaps and quaint caprices, for the few runs, triplet figures, etc. must be familiar to any accomplished player. Nevertheless, their performance is, in a certain way, very difficult.[15] Many a so-called virtuoso casts aside the Beethovenian fortepiano composition, effectively adding to the reproach: "Very difficult!" an additional one: "And most unrewarding!"

With regard to difficulty, the correct, appropriate performance of a Beethoven composition requires nothing less than to comprehend him, to penetrate deep into his being, and, in the consciousness of one's own solemn dedication, to dare to enter into the realm of enchanted visions that his powerful magic calls forth. Whoever does not feel this dedication within himself, whoever treats music as a mere pastime, suitable only for taking up time during empty hours, for the momentary pleasure of insensitive ears, or for self-serving ostentation, should certainly stay away. The reproach: "And most unrewarding!" pertains only to such a person. The true artist lives only in the work that he has taken up and now performs, in the manner of a master. He disdains to bring his own personality to bear in any way, and all of his musing and aspiration go only to call into active life, sparkling with a thousand colors, all the magnificent, blessed pictures and visions that the master locked up with magical power in his work, in order that they may enclose each person in brilliant, scintillating realms, and carry his imagination, kindling his innermost soul, on a swift flight into the distant spirit kingdom of notes. That there are few such real artists, genuine virtuosos; that, unfortunately, egoism, loathsome, empty ostentation, is gaining ground, is just as certain as that one will probably encounter few connoisseurs who feel completely aroused and uplifted by the deep spirit of the resourceful master. Since it has become the fashion to use music only incidentally, to drive away boredom among company, everything must be light, pleasing, agreeable, that is to say, without any significance or depth. And since there are unfortunately enough composers upon the earth who only slavishly serve the spirit of the times, there is a great deal of bulk food. Even many musicians who are not entirely bad complain about the incomprehensibility of Beethoven's, and even Mozart's, compositions. The difficulty lies, however, in their subjective imbecility, which cannot be bothered to comprehend and retain the whole in its parts. Thus they are always praising weak compositions for their great *clarity*.

The reviewer has been fortunate enough to hear many of Beethoven's compositions so splendidly played by a spirited lady who plays the fortepiano with virtuosity that he saw clearly how to regard only that which is from the *spirit,* since everything else is from evil. May more fortunate circumstances in the world of art make it possible for publishing firms to release Beethoven's instrumental compositions in score. What an abundant resource for the true study of music would then be open to the artist and the connoisseur! With this wish, the reviewer concludes his essay, in which he has expressed so much that really was on his mind.

1. This was the third of Hoffmann's five Beethoven reviews; much of it was later incorporated into the well-known essay on Beethoven's instrumental music, along with portions of the review of the Fifth Symphony.

2. Hoffmann makes a number of important distinctions here. "Fortepiano" was one of the most commonly used terms for the instrument from which the modern piano was to develop—although an increasing number of fine recordings now testify to the many differences between its sonorities and those of the modern instrument. The older harpsichord, with strings plucked by quills instead of struck by hammers, was still in current use in Hoffmann's time, and many publications still used the generic term "Klavier," which refers to any keyboard instrument other than the organ, when discussing keyboard music. Beethoven's op. 70 was a particularly important milestone in the development of the modern repertory of chamber music for piano with other instruments, since earlier trios had generally followed the pattern set by Haydn, in which the keyboard and cello still retained features of the old-fashioned basso continuo. Here, on the other hand, the piano part is completely self-sufficient.

3. Here, Hoffmann uses the word "Flügel," which refers to the winglike shape of the modern piano. "Flügel" is translated here as "fortepiano."

Beethoven had the mistaken idea that the piano was a German invention and wanted a German name for the instrument. After initially settling on "Hammerklavier" in 1817, he also suggested "Tasten Flügel," "Feder Flügel Klawier" [sic], and "Tasten und Hammerflügel." See Anderson, letter no. 748; Brandenburg, letter no. 1069.

4. Since all five of Beethoven's piano concertos had been composed, performed publicly, and published by the date of this review (the Fifth was published in 1811), it would seem that Hoffmann's antipathy to "all fortepiano concertos" must have extended to them as well. Although no one disputes today that "the soul is addressed" in Beethoven's piano concertos, all five extensively rely on the kind of virtuosic passagework that Hoffmann castigates.

5. The author, in referring to the "secondary theme," does not mean the second key area (which begins at m. 43).

6. Actually, this is an inversion rather than a retrograde, although Hoffmann uses the word "rückgangig."

7. The Aeolian harp was a "zither whose strings are set in motion by the wind. . . . The wind generates different harmonics in each string, producing a chord whose texture changes as the wind rises and falls. . . . It was popular in late eighteenth- and early nineteenth-century Europe and was a frequent subject of Romantic literature." See *The New Harvard Dictionary of Music,* ed. Don Michael Randel (Cambridge MA: Belknap Press, 1986), 14.

8. Hoffmann was evidently in possession of an instrument manufactured by the Viennese firm of Nannette Streicher née Stein, which was founded by the daughter of the well-known Viennese fortepiano maker Johann Andreas Stein. The "Pianozug" (the term "-zug" also refers to organ stop) was a common feature of instruments at this time, and it consisted of a mechanism by which a strip of leather or felt was inserted between the hammers and the strings. The "Harmonikazug" resembled the modern una corda pedal. See *New Grove* 18: 267; and Rosamond E. M. Harding, *The Pianoforte: Its History Traced to the Great Exhibition of 1851* (2nd edn. Old Woking, Surrey: Gresham Books, 1978), 44. The effect described by Hoffmann does not entirely come through on the modern piano, and not just because there is nothing analogous to the "Pianozug" on today's instrument. The tones of the fortepiano, which are at once softer and more harmonically full than those of the modern piano, lend themselves exactly to the sonority that Hoffmann describes.

9. The Egyptian goddess Isis was closely associated with her husband and brother Osiris, whom she partially brought back to life after his murder. Among other things, she represented fertility and motherhood. The cult of Isis became widespread in the world of late antiquity. Although it was suppressed by the Christian church, Renaissance scholars and writers revitalized European interest in the cult of Isis, which gained new life in German literature through the work (*Die Lehrlinge zu Sais*) of Novalis (Friedrich Leopold von Hardenberg, 1772–1801), the most significant writer of the early Romantic period.

10. Hoffmann uses the Italian word "lazzi."

11. Hoffmann seems to have felt that this symphony was particularly representative of Mozart's character as a composer, since he used it both here and in his review of the Fifth Symphony, in similar citations, to typify large segments of his music.

12. Of the second half.

13. For a discussion of the "alternating variation" technique and a list of movements in that form in Haydn's symphonies, see Elaine Sisman, *Haydn and the Classical Variation* (Cambridge MA: Harvard University Press, 1993), esp. 267–68.

14. Hoffmann is now referring to the third movement.

15. For a detailed comparison of the difficulties of the piano music of Beethoven as compared to Haydn, Mozart, and Schubert, see William S. Newman, *Beethoven on Beethoven* (New York: Norton, 1988), 67–76.

≈

OP. 70, NO. 2
TRIO FOR PIANO, VIOLIN, AND CELLO

(See entry no. 174)

≈

OP. 71
SEXTET IN E♭
MAJOR FOR CLARINETS, HORNS, AND BASSOONS[1]

227.
"News. Vienna, Beginning of May." *Allgemeine musikalische Zeitung* 7 (15 May 1805): 534–35.

Last winter a musical institute was formed, which still continues due to careful support, and which in its way is truly perfect. These are quartets, which are played in a private house in such a way that the listener always pays five gulden in advance for four productions. Schuppanzigh, the entrepreneur, knows how to enter precisely into the spirit of the compositions with his superb quartet performance and how to bring that which is fiery, powerful, or finer, tender, humorous, lovely or playful so significantly to the fore that the first violin could hardly be better occupied. His student Mayseder, a very talented young man who has only recently begun to be mentioned in your pages, accompanies him just as superbly on the second violin. Schreiber, in the service of Prince von Lobkowitz,[2] handles the viola with facility and precision. The violoncello is superbly occupied by Mr. Kraft, Sr.; he has a beautiful, full tone, uncommonly great facility and accuracy, and never sacrifices the whole in order to make an effect with his instrument.[3] Naturally, it is only the most excellent, outstanding compositions that such masters carefully study and perform publicly only after several rehearsals. So far, quartets by Mozart, Haydn, Beethoven, Eberl, and Romberg have been played. Sometimes bigger pieces are played as well; among these the beautiful Beethoven Sextet in E♭ pleased most, a composition that glitters with beautiful melodies, a spontaneous flow of harmonies, and a wealth of new and surprising ideas. The clarinet was played with consummate perfection by Mr. Pär, in the service of the princely house of Lichtenstein. This artist, in addition to an extraordinary ease and confidence, has such an extremely lovely and agreeable tone and knows, particularly in playing *piano,* how to soften it to such a tender and enchanting delicacy, that he will truly find few to equal him on his instrument.

NOTES

1. Although written in 1796 or before, this work was not published until 1810: hence the high opus number.
2. Prince Joseph Franz Maximilian Lobkowitz (1772–1816) was a leader of the Viennese court theater and a friend and patron of Beethoven, who dedicated several of his works to him. The first performance of the *Eroica* (1804) took place in one of his private concerts. The prince belonged to one of the most powerful families in Austria. Dating back to 1410, the family held enormous political and military influence until the end of the Austrian monarchy in 1918.
3. The group described here is one of several quartets led by Ignaz Schuppanzigh that were associated with Beethoven's music. This is the only time that Joseph Mayseder and Schreiber (who cannot be further identified) played in the group. According to *New Grove* (16: 871), they were probably still members of the quartet when it introduced Beethoven's op. 59 in 1807. Both Anton Kraft (1749–1820) and his son Nikolaus (1778–1853) have been linked with Schuppanzigh and his quartet activities. In view of Othmar Wessely's statement in *New Grove* (10: 230) that "the assumption in earlier literature that [Anton Kraft] was a member of the Schuppanzigh quartet is to be questioned," it is interesting to note that the correspondent specifically says: "the violoncello is superbly occupied by Mr. Kraft, Sr."
For a discussion of the personnel of the Schuppanzigh Quartet's Beethoven performances, see Robert Winter, "Performing the Beethoven Quartets in Their First Century," in *The Beethoven Quartet Companion* (Berkeley and Los Angeles: University of California Press, 1994), 34–41.

~

OP. 72
FIDELIO (LEONORE)
(See entry nos. 12, 23, 31, 45, and 49, vol. 1, pp. 38, 48, 78, 101, 118)

228.
"News. Vienna." *Allgemeine musikalische Zeitung* 7 (29 May 1805): 572.

At the Theater-an-der-Wien, an operetta with music by Fischer, *Die Ver-wandlungen*,[1] was found insignificant, with many reminiscences in the music. Soon an opera by Beethoven will be brought to the stage. This work, in which Beethoven will appear for the first time as a dramatic composer, is anxiously awaited. In the text Beethoven will agree with Paer,[2] who set the same "Leonore" to music last year in Dresden.

NOTES

1. *Die Verwandlungen* by Anton Fischer (1778–1808) was produced at the Theater-an-der-Wien on 9 May 1805.
2. Paer's *Leonora, ossia L'amore conjugale* was produced in Dresden on 3 October 1804.

~

229.
F-b-t. "Vienna Occupied by the French." *Zeitung für die elegante Welt* 6 (4 January 1806): 12–13.

Fidelio,[1] a new opera by Beethoven, was performed. The theater was not filled at all, and the applause was quite meager. In fact, the third act is very extensive, and the music, ineffective and full of repetitions, did not augment the idea of Beethoven's talent as a vocal composer that I had formed from his cantata.[2] I remarked quietly to my neighbor, whose expressions seemed to reinforce my own judgment, that it is precisely in writing operas that so many otherwise good composers come to grief. He was a Frenchman and sought to explain this by virtue of composition being the highest stage of art, and demanding, furthermore, an aesthetic preparation that, so he had heard, was seldom to be found among German musicians. I shrugged my shoulders and was silent.

NOTES

1. The early versions of *Fidelio*, performed in 1805 and 1806, are sometimes called *Leonore*, to distinguish them from the final version of 1814, which has become standard.

Actually, the opera was presented by the Theater-an-der-Wien from the first under the title *Fidelio, oder, Die eheliche Liebe,* and Beethoven, who preferred *Leonore,* gradually acquiesced. The premiere of the 1805 version had taken place on 20, 21, and 22 November. The original complete title is clear on the playbill for the 1805 premiere; it is reproduced in *Beethoven,* ed. H. C. Robbins Landon (Zurich: Universal, 1970), 88.

2. See F-b-t's report of 7 April 1803, in which he comments quite favorably on the music of *Christus am Ölberg,* op. 85, despite some severe criticisms of the text. See entry no. 87, vol. 1, p. 165.

~

230.

"News. Vienna, Mid-December of the Previous Year."
Allgemeine musikalische Zeitung 8 (8 January 1806): 237–38.

The most noteworthy among the musical products of the previous month was the long-awaited Beethoven opera: *Fidelio* or *Conjugal Love.* It was given for the first time on 20 November, but was very coldly received. I will speak somewhat more extensively about this.

A man having been unjustly and suddenly dragged off to a dungeon through the fierce vindictiveness of his enemy and languishing there under fierce treatment, his death must now hide the shameful deed forever, since here and there something of the crime is beginning to be made known. However, his loving wife (Fidelio) has followed him into prison as the warden's apprentice, has been able to win the trust of the tyrant and finally rescues her husband. The daughter of the warden falls in love with Fidelio and causes thereby a rather commonplace episode.

Whoever follows the development up to the present of Beethoven's otherwise undoubted talent with attentiveness and calm examination must hope for something entirely different from this work than what it offers. Until now, Beethoven had so often paid homage to the new and strange at the expense of the beautiful; one would thus expect above all to find distinctiveness, newness and a genuine, original creative flare in this, his first creation for the musical theater—and it is precisely these qualities that one encounters in it least.

The whole, when it is treated calmly and without prejudice, is distinguished neither by invention nor by its working-out. The overture[1] consists of a *very* long Adagio, which strays into all keys, whereupon an Allegro in C major enters, which likewise is not first rate, and which bears no comparison to other instrumental compositions by Beethoven, or, for example, with his overture to the ballet *Prometheus.* The vocal pieces are mostly not based on any new idea, they are usually drawn out too long, the text is endlessly repeated, and, finally, characterization is often missing as well. The duet in the third act in G major after the recognition scene can serve as an example of this, for the continually running accompaniment on the highest strings of the violin expresses loud, wild rejoicing rather than the quiet, sadly profound feeling of having found one another again under these circumstances.[2] A four-voice canon in the first act[3] came out much better, and an emotional descant in F major where three obbligato horns form a lovely, if often somewhat overly ornate, accompaniment.[4] The choruses are of no effect, and one of them, which signifies the joy of the prisoners over the enjoyment of fresh air, is clearly misconceived.[5]

The performance also was not first-rate. Miss Milder has, despite her beautiful voice, too little passion and life for the role of Fidelio, and Demmer sang almost continually flat.[6] All of this taken together, along, in part, with the present circumstances, explains why the opera could only be given three times.

NOTES

1. At the first performances, Beethoven used the overture now known as *Leonore* No. 2.

2. Quoting this report, Thayer-Forbes, 388, notes: "To understand the criticism of the duet, it must be realized that at the occurrence of this duet, 'O namenlose Freude,' in the 1805 version, the dramatic situation is quite different from that of the 1814 version. In both cases the trumpet calls have heralded the start of the dénouement, and after the end of the quartet, Pizarro exits followed by Rocco. But in the earlier version Rocco, instead of giving a sign of assurance to the reunited pair which signifies that all danger is past, grabs Leonore's pistol with a vehemence which causes her to faint. The recitative and duet that follow are concerned not only with the joy of reunion but the uncertainty still of a joint death, which is not resolved until the entrance of Don Fernando himself."

3. "Mir ist so wunderbar," no. 4 in the original version. Except where otherwise noted, references to this version are based on Willy Hess's reconstruction in *Leonore: Oper in drei Aufzügen: Partitur der Urfassung vom Jahre 1805* (henceforth Hess 1805 or 1806) (Wiesbaden: Breitkopf & Härtel, 1967).

This famous canon is briefly discussed in Robert Haas, "Zum Kanon im Fidelio," *Beethoven-Zentenarfeier Wien*, 26. bis 31. März 1927 (Vienna: Universal-Edition, 1927), 136–37. There he notes that "the technique of this quartet places itself within a line of development which was especially cultivated in Vienna. . . . The result is that through Beethoven a fashionable phenomenon became transfigured, and that his canon is embedded in contemporary Viennese opera, but also, that it surpasses all other contemporary works in spiritual content" (my trans.).

4. Except for the key (E major), this is an adequate description of Leonore's aria "Komm Hoffnung," which in Hess's reconstruction of the original version is introduced by a recitative beginning "Ach, brich noch nicht, du mattes Herz!" This is the way it was apparently performed in 1806. Nottebohm, however, concluded on the basis of Beethoven's sketches that the original aria, performed in 1805 and now lost, was in F major (*Zweite Beethoveniana* [Leipzig: C. F. Peters, 1887], 451–52), and that this was reworked to form the second half of Leonore's 1806 aria. The F-major aria would probably have begun with the words "O du, für den ich alles trug," since the four lines beginning with "Komm Hoffnung!" are missing in the 1805 libretto. This "earwitness" account could be taken as substantiating Nottebohm's view. Willy Hess supports his alternative reading by suggesting that Beethoven instigated the changes in the text during the composition

of the aria, and that it is hardly likely that a different, earlier aria would also happen to feature three obbligato horns and bassoon. The F in this report, he says, may have been a printer's error (*Das Fidelio-Buch* [Winterthur: Amadeus Verlag, 1986], 250). Of course, not every anonymous correspondent has absolute pitch.

5. The reference is to the well-known prisoners' chorus "O welche lust," which in the final version of *Fidelio* both opens and closes the finale of the first act. In the first version, the second act closed at the corresponding point with the aria "Auf euch nur will ich bauen," for Pizarro and a chorus of watchmen. The scene in which the prisoners are ushered back underground was written later.

6. The cast at the first performance was as follows: Fidelio—Pauline Anna Milder (later Milder-Hauptmann); Florestan—Friedrich Christian Demmer; Marcelline—Louise Müller; Pizarro—Friedrich Sebastian Mayer; Rocco—Rothe (first name unknown); Jaquino—Josef Caché; Don Fernando—Weinkopf (first name unknown).

Milder (1785–1838) was still in the early stages of a distinguished career, but Demmer is widely believed to have been inadequate for the role. The exact identity of this Demmer is still in dispute, however. Thayer-Forbes (p. 383) is almost certainly incorrect in identifying him with Joseph Demmer of Bonn (who was a *bass* and after 1775 spent most of his career in Amsterdam). Kurt Dorfmüller, in *Beiträge zur Beethoven-Bibliographie*, 322, reports a communication from Dr. Friedrich Slezak in Vienna identifying the first Florestan as Berlin-born Friedrich Christian Demmer (1786–1838). If this is correct, he can hardly have been past his prime, as has sometimes been suggested, at the time of this performance. While Friedrich Demmer came from a family of very talented actors and singers, he was the most gifted and was able to substitute in roles in the theater and opera without practice. During the later years of his career, he became director of the Hofoperntheater. At the 1806 revival, he was replaced by Joseph August Röckel (1783–1870).

Müller (1779-?) was active in Vienna from 1798 to 1811 at the Kärntnertor theater and the Theater-an-der-Wien. In the latter year she left Vienna in the company of a Russian prince, and the history of her later life is obscure (K. J. Kutsch and Leo Riemens, *Großes Sängerlexikon* [Bern: A. Franche, 1987], 2049–50).

Mayer (1773–1835), husband of Maria Josepha Weber and hence Mozart's brother-in-law, was apparently rather conceited, and Beethoven is said to have written a passage from Pizarro's aria "Auf euch nur will ich bauen," with which the second act ended in 1805, specifically to frustrate him (Schindler-MacArdle, 131–32; Kutsch and Riemens, *Großes Sängerlexikon*, 1905–06).

Caché is mentioned several times in the AMZ and seems to have been universally well regarded. The AMZ (13 [1811]: 84) calls him the librettist of J. von Blumenthal's opera *Don Silvio von Rosalva, der Feenritter,* and this is confirmed in Parsons, *The Mellen Opera Reference Index, Opera Librettists and Their Works, A-L,* 109, which also credits him with the libretto of L. W. Reuling's 1833 opera *Das Küchenregiment.*

Weinkopf is described in AMZ 8 (1805–06): 462 as having a "pure, expressive bass voice," and the public as being "very pleased" with him.

&

231.
"Review." *Der Freymüthige* 4 (14 January 1806).

Little new of significance has been given in the most recent times. A new Beethoven opera: *Fidelio, or Conjugal Love,* failed to please. It was only performed a few times and remained completely empty from right after the first performance. The music as well is truly far below the expectations to which connoisseurs and amateurs felt entitled. As learned as everything in it is, both melody and characterization nevertheless failed to achieve that happy, striking, irresistible expression of passion that grips us so irresistibly in Mozart's and Cherubini's works. The music has several pretty spots, but it is still far from being a perfect work or even a successful one. The text, translated by Sonnleitner,[1] consists of a story of liberation of the kind that has come into fashion since Cherubini's *Deux journées*.[2]

NOTES

1. The reader is reminded again that the original orthographies of names are retained in the translations.

2. *Les deux journées* had been produced in Vienna on 14–15 August 1802. In a conversation of 1823 Beethoven told Julius Benedict that the libretto to the opera was one of the best he knew of (for the historical surroundings, see Winton Dean, "Beethoven and Opera," in *The Beethoven Reader,* ed. Denis Arnold and Nigel Fortune [New York: Norton, 1971], esp. 333–35). Beethoven highly esteemed Cherubini, as can be seen in the draft of his letter to Cherubini of ca. March 1823: "I value your works above all other compositions for the theater. . . . I too am enchanted whenever I hear of a new work composed by you, and I take as much interest in it as I do in my own works—in short I honor and love you" (trans. modified; Anderson, letter no. 1154; Brandenburg, letter no. 1611). On the tradition of the rescue opera (the critic here calls it the liberation opera), see Sieghard Döhring, "Die Rettungsoper: Musiktheater in Wechselspiel politischer und aethetischer Prozesse," in *Beethoven zwischen Revolution und Restauration* (Bonn: Beethoven-Haus, 1989), 109–36.

∾

232.
"A Letter from Vienna to the Editor. 20 January 1806."
Berlinische musikalische Zeitung 2 (1806): 42–43.

(Mentioned: Symphony No. 1, op. 21; *Die Geschöpfe des Prometheus,* op. 43; and *Christus am Ölberg,* op. 85)

It is now rather a long time since you have had a letter from me. The circumstances will excuse me. The storms of war have also frightened away the gentler muses, and Euterpe's[1] lyre had to be silent before the jarring noise of the trumpets and drums, which surrounded us on all sides. But in the midst of the tumult of war there appeared a work of musical art that had long been expected with heightened anticipation, Beethoven's first opera, *Fidelio*.

This ingenious composer had excited expectations of every kind with his first instrumental works, but when his first work for the theater, a ballet, *Prometheus*, appeared, it was not only coldly received by the public, but experts also found much to censure; here and there the music was too learned and often not sufficiently expressive. Soon thereafter appeared the first grand

Beethoven Symphony in C Major, a very successful masterwork. Only after several years did the first vocal composition appear, a cantata, *The Death of Jesus*.[2] Here as well we were not satisfied, and surely with good reason, since most of the pieces were far removed from that sublimity that is indispensable to this genre and that predominates even in Haydn's oratorio, though it is clothed with more radiance by the romanticism of his creations than in the older works of this kind.[3] In this oratorio, however, much is to be found that even borders on the frivolous. In individual songs we were amazed at the talent of the composer, while also finding much completely insignificant. All the more expectantly did we await the first opera, in which B. could show how he was able to assimilate the spirit of a dramatic action and bring it to life.

However, this test as well was not extraordinarily successful. Certainly there are individual details to be singled out, but on the whole it lacks that degree of perfection by means of which individual characters are distinguished and maintained in their individuality until the end, and that freshness of melody that seems to arise from the emotion itself, and, without being affected, surprises us as much by its pertinence and appropriateness as by the charm of the notes, as happens in many operas of Mozart, Reichardt, and Cherubini. From what does this disparity arise? Why is it generally true that so many significant instrumental composers are so unfortunate in their works for the theater?

Apart from the fact that the composer for the theater has more need than any other musical artist to be an aesthetician and that the so-called effect of the voices is difficult to calculate, the instrumental composer might be compared to a lyrical poet and the vocal composer to an epic or dramatic one. The former pours forth only his own ideas and feelings in unrestricted pictures, the imagination here works freely and without constraint, not infrequently bustling about in an unbridled and unfettered way, and often this arouses only obscure feelings in others. In vocal composition, particularly in opera, it is a very different case.

Here a task is *laid out* for the musical artist, namely that he must set off a specific course of action, characters who are individuals and who have their basis outside of his art, and delineate things musically with precision, truthfulness, and accuracy. Will not the imagination find it more difficult to accommodate itself to these restrictions, having become accustomed elsewhere to gratifying all its whims? Will it not, rather, stubbornly insist upon that freedom and so produce many a piece of music that may be pretty in and of itself, but that *in this regard,* in this place, is deficient? The Italian composers, too, used to be accustomed to treating the text only as meaningless syllables until the path to better music was finally opened. These ideas may be further developed on another occasion. Shortly, the promised musical history of the Theater-an-der-Wien.

1. In Greek mythology, Euterpe was the muse of lyric poetry and music.

2. That is, *Christus am Ölberg*, op. 85. The reviewer has probably confused its title with that of *Der Tod Jesu* by Karl Heinrich Graun.

The concern with "war" is undoubtedly related to Napoleon's invasion of Prussia. His eventual victories over Prussia at Jena and Auerrstädt in October 1806 and his triumphant march into Berlin forced Johann Friedrich Reichardt to stop publication of his BMZ and flee.

3. The author is presumably referring to Haydn's *Creation* (*Die Schöpfung*), thereby making the reference to his creations (*Schöpfungen*) a subtle play on words.

~

233.
"Theater and Music in Vienna in the Last Winter Months of 1806."
Journal des Luxus und der Moden 21, no. 5 (1806): 287.

You will recall that *Beethoven* first came forward with his opera *Fidelio* on 20 November, a few days after the French marched in. At that time the circumstances were as unfavorable as they could possibly be; every onlooker fell short of that unbiased frame of mind in which a work of art must be evaluated. At the end of the month of March *Fidelio* was given for the second time, and there were certainly changes, for the action, which had been spread out over three acts, was drawn together into two.[1] In this form, regardless of many intrigues, the opera had its most definitive success. *Beethoven,* whose works are decried by many as too difficult, too deeply felt, learned, and transcendent, showed in this opera that he understands how to bring the most lovely graciousness into the most beautiful balance with strength and an inexhaustible wealth of ideas. The breath of genius enlivens the entire work. Shortly before, the same opera, with music by *Pär, was performed for a select audience at the home of Prince Lobkowitz* with the title: *L'amor conjugale.* Brizzi's[2] singing greatly elevated the entire presentation.

NOTES

1. This seemingly simple statement covers a great deal that is still shrouded in controversy. The drawing together of the first two acts into one is probably the least significant of the changes that were made; indeed, the decision to perform the opera in three acts in 1805 seems to have been made rather late in its gestation. Exactly what changes were made between 1805 and 1806, however, is difficult to determine, since there is no integral surviving score of the 1805 version. Willy Hess's reconstruction of that version is therefore tentative and has been subject to challenge. For an overview of the issues involved, particularly with regard to Florestan's aria from the final act, see Michael C. Tusa, "The Unknown Florestan: The 1805 Version of 'In des Lebens Frühlingstagen,'" *Journal of the American Musicological Society* 46 (1993): 175–220.

2. Fétis (*Biographie universelle*, 2, 76) mentions Antoine (presumably Antonio) Brizzi, an Italian tenor born in Bologna in 1774. He performed several times in Vienna before being called to Paris by Napoleon. He later lived in Munich.

~

234.
"News. Vienna, 2 April." *Allgemeine musikalische Zeitung* 8 (16 April 1806): 460.

The concert for the widows of the local musicians was very mediocre. It was completely impossible to conceive how a symphony by Kanne,[1] which had already failed to please on another occasion, was given the honor of a performance here. A flamboyant young man played a Mozart keyboard concerto with agility, but without precision; and a Salieri cantata on a patriotic text is in truth scarcely worthy of mention.

Beethoven has brought his opera *Fidelio* back on the stage, with many changes and cuts. An entire act has thus gone by the wayside, but the piece has benefited and now pleased better.

NOTE

1. Friedrich August Kanne (1778–1833) is now remembered primarily as a music critic; he was one of the few to appreciate fully Beethoven's late works. He may also have written some of the early AMZ reviews of Beethoven. According to Fétis (4: 474), he published a literary fantasy on Beethoven's death. See Wallace, *Beethoven's Critics*, 16–17, 74–77; *New Grove*, 9: 794.

~

235.
Zeitung für die elegante Welt 6 (20 May 1806).[1]

Beethoven's opera *Fidelio* appeared newly rearranged at the Theater-an-der-Wien. The rearrangement consists in the drawing together of three acts into two. It is incomprehensible how the composer could have resolved to enliven this empty shoddy piece of work by Sonnleitner with beautiful music, and therefore, not counting the lowly intrigues of the honorable man, the effect of the whole could not possibly be such as the musician probably wanted to be able to count on, since the meaninglessness of the spoken parts completely or for the most part obliterated the beautiful effect of the sung ones. Mr. B. does not lack lofty aesthetic judgment within his art, since he understands how to express extraordinarily well the emotions that lie in the words to be set, but he seems to lack entirely the ability to look over and judge the text with regard to total effect. The music is nevertheless masterly, and B. showed what he will be able to achieve in the future on this newly entered path. The first duet and the two quartets pleased particularly well. The overture,[2] on the other hand, was displeasing, due to the ceaseless dissonances and the almost constant pretentious buzzing of the violins, and is more an affectation than true art. Miss Milder as the disguised Fidelio sang the part, which was exactly suited to her lovely though little-trained voice, very commendably; at the end, though, she cannot completely struggle free from the embraces of her rescued husband. Miss Müller also did her best.

NOTES

1. The same article also appeared in *Wiener Theaterzeitung* 2 (22 October 1806): 55–56.

2. For the 1806 revival, Beethoven wrote the overture now known as *Leonore* No. 3.

~

236.
Wiener Theaterzeitung 1 (28 May 1814).

On 23 May was performed for the first time *Fidelio,* an opera in two acts, newly arranged from the French. The music is by Ludwig van *Beethoven.* The receipts were allotted to the opera administrators Messrs. *Saal, Vogel, and Weinmüller.*[1] As the poster made known to us, this opera appeared to us today in a completely new form. The composer has endeavored to rearrange it, it was to be adorned with new musical numbers, and in this manner, as it were, the last brushstroke was to be applied to the painting. We rejoiced, therefore, in a pleasure that was unique of its kind. We were amazed at *Beethoven* in his entire greatness, and what was more, we were amazed at the master along with an abundance of admirers who, before the *Battle of Victoria,*[2] had belonged to his antagonists. At last, the great genius has for once prevailed and is able to rejoice in his works within his own lifetime. A great rarity! A rare greatness for our pace-setting republic in the realm of art! How many great men have lived, who were first spoken about when they were no more; for whose works thousands were paid after their death, while during their lifetime they were unable to save enough to obtain a frugal meal!

The music of this opera is a deeply thought-out, purely felt portrait of the most creative imagination, the most undiluted originality, the most divine ascent of the earthly into the incomprehensibly heavenly. *Beethoven* possesses the power to combine his notes with such magic that, like an ode by *Klopstock,*[3] they powerfully broaden the heart when one enjoys them, and occupy the soul with a succession of thoughts and pictures to which one never gave way before. The reviewer who wanted to divide them up according to their tonalities, even if he were just as arrogant and foolish as Mr. Sperling from Krähwinkel,[4] would only be sending a beetle in pursuit of an eagle!

NOTES

1. At the 1814 revival, Saal, Vogel, and Weinmüller sang the parts of Fernando, Pizarro, and Rocco, respectively. This trio had been at the forefront of Viennese opera since the earliest years of the AMZ. Johann Michael Vogl (1768–1840; his name is often spelled without the "e," although all references to him in the AMZ include it) is now known mostly for his friendship and association with Schubert, whose songs he was among the first to champion. In AMZ 3 (1800–01): 43–44, it is noted that among opera singers currently active in Vienna, Vogl, who is described as a tenor (though this misperception is corrected on p. 625 of the same volume), has a good voice and much musical knowledge. Saal, the bass, is described as a very meritorious singer, who has both true knowledge and great industry; no further information about him is available. Carl Friedrich Clemens Weinmüller (1764–1828) is described as an excellent bass with a very penetrating voice. According to Kutsch and Riemens (*Großes Sängerlexikon,* 3168), his range extended effortlessly from contra D to tenor F. Fétis (*Biographie universelle,* 8, 411) notes that "nobody performed better the principal bass parts in Mozart's *Requiem* and in Haydn's *Creation.*" The remainder of the cast was: Fidelio—Milder-Hauptmann; Florestan—Giulio Radichi; Marcelline—Bondra (first name unknown); Jacquino—Frühwald.

The earliest mentions of Radichi (also Radicchi) appear in the AMZ's Prague correspondence in 1807. This correspondence, AMZ 9 (1806–07): 775, notes that he came from Italy and learned German in order to be able to stay in Prague. His first appearance in Vienna is recorded in AMZ 10 (1807–08): 700 where he is complimented for his "pure, musical, and extremely flexible voice," which "charmed everyone." He continued to perform into the late 1820s. His reviews were always mixed, and he was sometimes criticized for his lack of acting ability.

Miss Bondra, the younger of two singers, presumably sisters, by that name, is described in AMZ 16 (1814): 132 as having sung only minor roles until the year 1814. She continued to perform until at least 1830; the Viennese correspondent in AMZ 32 (1830): 770 describes her as having "no voice any more," and there are no further mentions of her in the AMZ.

Frühwald is probably Joseph Frühwald (1783–1848), who was active in Vienna after 1798. He was supported by Marinelli and Hensler until employed in the court opera theater in 1807 as a tenor until 1821. He was the *Singmeister* for the Gesellschaft für Musikfreunde from 1817 to 1848.

2. *Wellingtons Sieg oder die Schlacht bei Vittoria,* op. 91, written and performed at the time of the Congress of Vienna, probably contributed more than any other single piece to establishing Beethoven as a popular composer during the 1810s. See vol. 3 of this series for the substantial press reaction to this work.

3. The author is undoubtedly making a reference to Klopstock's revolutionary departure from descriptive and reflective expression of Enlightenment poetry and his discovery of the emotional potentiality of lyrical metaphor. Klopstock sought to reinvigorate the linguistic elements of poetry with an irrational and religious penetration into the depths of personal experience in order to intensify the experience of objects and feelings in the reader. The author does not seem concerned with the very complex metrical forms Klopstock employed in his odes, which often conflict with the intended effects.

4. Krähwinkel is a fictitious place name in the narrative "Das heimliche Klagelied der jetzigen Männer" from the final part of the novel *Titan* by Jean Paul Richter (1763–1825). A mammoth novel, which appeared in four volumes (1800–03), *Titan* and the narrative "Klagelied" satirize the feudalistic education and control of the aristocracy that falls prey to its own grotesque titanism.

~

237.
"News. Vienna." *Allgemeine musikalische
Zeitung* 16 (5 June 1814): 420–21.

Court opera theater. On the twenty-third we saw performed (for the benefit of Messrs. Saal, Vogel, and Weinmüller) for the first time at this theater, to great applause, *Fidelio,* an opera in two acts, newly arranged from the French, with music by L. v. Beethoven. When this opera was twice given at the Theater-an-der-Wien several years ago, it was not by any means able to rejoice in a favorable reception. It is thus all the more gratifying to every friend of art to know that the composer has been rewarded for his tenacious persistence and painstaking revision. That there are yet others who are not completely in agreement with the general judgment may be imagined. Some say that the subject (once again a rescue story) is obsolete, and that after so many similar ones served up almost to the point of tedium since the *Wasserträger,*[1] it must be more repulsive than attractive. Others say that the music, from the *vocal* point of view, is surely not as original as must have been expected from this master. For example, the beautiful, four-voiced canon (G major, $\frac{6}{8}$), which had to be repeated,[2] is too reminiscent of the canon: "Sento che quelli sguardi" in *Camilla,*[3] while, again, many other passages are reminiscent of Mozart, etc. We will leave such controversies to themselves, and mention only the following. The subject is the same as that of Paer's *Leonore.* Mr. v. B's music is a very successful work. A few things may not fulfill the expectation that is stretched so high because of his instrumental works, but it is not for that reason a failure, and some other things are truly splendid. One may probably concede to those antagonists that the vocal parts are not always worthy of the most praise, that several reminiscences have crept in, and so forth; the whole, though, remains interesting, and the connoisseur is compensated for a few weaknesses by a number of genuine masterpieces, so that every unprejudiced listener will leave the house satisfied. Apart from the overture—which, newly composed for this purpose, was first given at the second performance[4]—most of the musical numbers were briskly, indeed even tumultuously, applauded, and the composer was unanimously called out after the first and the second acts. Mrs. Milder-Hauptmann (Fidelio) was granted this honor as well. Otherwise, Mr. Weinmüller (prison warden) and Miss Bondra the younger (Marzelline) contributed especially to the success. Mr. Vogel's performance (Pizarro) was not to be improved upon, but this role seems to have been written more for a genuine bass, and Mr. V.'s baritone is lacking in depth and power. We would have preferred to see Mr. Wild[5] in place of Mr. Radichi (Florestan); in this way the whole second act would have gained in interest. The choruses went well, and the orchestra preserved its old reputation. This opera has until now been repeated only once, namely on the twenty-sixth. The new overture (E major) was received with thunderous applause, and the composer was again called out twice at this repetition.

NOTES

1. That is, Cherubini's *Les deux journées.*
2. In other words, the quartet, "Mir ist so wunderbar," was encored, in the literal sense of the word, due to its success with the audience at the performance. This was a standard performance convention of the time.
3. *Camilla, ossia Il sotterraneo* (1799) by Ferdinando Paer.
4. This would have been what is now known as the overture to *Fidelio*.
5. Franz Wild (1791–1860) was a well-known singer who left behind a famous description of Beethoven's conducting. See entry no. 135, n. 4, vol. 1, p. 222.

~

238.
"News. Vienna." *Allgemeine musikalische
Zeitung* 16 (6 August 1814): 550.

Theater by the Kärntnertor. The directorship of the Imperial Royal Court Theater granted to Mr. v. Beethoven, as the composer of the beloved and masterfully revised opera *Fidelio,* a benefit performance on the eighteenth, for which he newly composed two more arias and inserted them into the first act.[1] The first aria was accorded to Mr. Weinmüller (prison warden) and made no great effect, even though it was performed diligently by this fine artist. The second aria, with four obbligato horns (E major), is beautiful and has great artistic worth, and was performed with power and feeling by Mrs. Milder- Hauptmann (Fidelio). Yet it seems to the reviewer that the first act has now lost in regard to quick pacing and, drawn out by these two arias, was extended to unnecessary length. Due to the indisposition of Mr. Vogel, Mr. Forti[2] took over the role of the governor and succeeded in it perfectly. Mr. van B. was again accorded the honor of being called out after the first and after the second act.

NOTES

1. The two "new" arias performed at the benefit of 18 July were apparently Rocco's "Hat man nicht auch Gold beineben," which had been omitted from the 1806 performances and was now restored with a revised text, and Leonore's "Komm, Hoffnung," which was rewritten and provided with a new introduction, "Abscheulicher! wo eilst du

hin!" (Thayer-Forbes, 587–88). The scoring actually features three horns and bassoon. Nottebohm has suggested that at the earlier 1814 performances, the version of the aria from 1806, beginning with the recitative "Ach brich noch nicht, du mattes Herz!", was used (*Zweite Beethoveniana*, 306).

2. Anton Forti (1790–1859) was born in Vienna, despite his Italian sounding surname. His voice had such a wide range that he sang tenor parts as well as baritone ones; among the latter were Don Giovanni (his performance of this role is described in AMZ 13 [1811]: 562) and Figaro (both Mozart's and Rossini's). His interpretation of Sarastro is discussed in AMZ, which states that "although this singer's bass is not to be compared with the tones of our Weinmüller in its lowest range, he nevertheless pleased in general with his extremely flexible voice, agreeable manner, and tasteful delivery" (14 [1812]: 559). Kutsch and Reimens credit him with creating the role of Pizarro at the 1814 *Fidelio* revival, but as these articles make clear, he only substituted for Vogl at a later performance. See Kutsch and Riemens, *Großes Sängerlexikon*, 975–76.

~

239.
"News. Leipzig." *Allgemeine musikalische Zeitung* 17 (5 April 1815): 242.[1]

The *opera company* of Mr. Seconda[2] gave, in this second quarter of their visit, various good pieces, which they have prepared with diligence and care. Foremost among these are Paer's *Camilla* and Weigel's *Uniform*,[3] which had long gone unperformed, and Beethoven's *Fidelio,* which had not been seen here before. The last-mentioned opera was given not in the master's rearrangement, but in its first form, as it appeared on stage in Vienna as *Leonore*[4] and then was published at Leipzig in a keyboard reduction.[5] It is truly to the honor of the company that it performed this difficult music with so few mistakes and such confidence. The work, full of spirit and power, met with well-deserved, distinguished applause. We will say nothing further about it, since it is known at many other theaters, and a detailed essay has been promised to us on the subject.[6]

NOTES

1. This performance, which presented the "first" version of *Fidelio,* was presumably the one that prompted Amadeus Wendt's lengthy essay (see entry no. 240). From Wendt's description, it is clear that what was performed was not the three-act version of 1805, but an adaptation of the 1806 version that was divided into three acts. See Wendt's description of the performance and the accompanying notes, below, for further details.

2. The reference here is to the Seconda Opera Troupe founded by Franz Seconda (1755—after 1817). In the following entry Wendt refers to Seconda as Joseph. E. T. A. Hoffmann was the director of the troupe from 1813 to 1814.

3. *L'Uniforme* by Joseph Weigl (1766–1846) was first performed at Schönbrunn Castle in Vienna in 1800; it was written for Maria Theresia, second wife of Emperor Franz II, who herself sang in the premiere.

Weigl was an extremely popular composer of primarily light opera in the first few decades of the nineteenth century. As its repeated mention in the reviews below serves to emphasize, his *Singspiel Die Schweizerfamilie* was one of the most successful works of its time.

4. The writer was mistaken; the opera was performed from the first under the title *Fidelio.*

5. The Breitkopf & Härtel keyboard score of 1810 was made by Carl Czerny from the 1806 revision. See Kinsky-Halm, 177. The title there is "Leonore/Oper in Zwey Aufzügen."

6. This is a clear reference to Wendt's essay, which was indeed one of the longest articles devoted primarily to a single musical work ever to appear in the AMZ. Much of the Leipzig correspondence was written by Friedrich Rochlitz, who at this point was still the journal's editor.

240.

Amadeus Wendt.[1] "Thoughts about Recent Musical Art, and van Beethoven's Music, Specifically His *Fidelio.*" *Allgemeine musikalische Zeitung* 17 (24 May, 31 May, 7 June, 14 June, 21 June, and 28 June 1815): 345–53, 365–72, 381–89, 397–404, 413–20 and 429–36.

(Mentioned: Symphony No. 3, op. 55; Symphony No. 5, op. 67; Symphony No. 6, op. 68)

HIGHER MUSICAL ART.

If for all the other arts there is something at hand that, through the magical glance of genius, is lifted for the first time, ennobled and transfigured, from the ground of reality and seems to be placed in the paradise of ideas, then musical art almost seems *itself* to be *conceived* in this land, and speaks, like the world spirit, through storm and thunder, as well as in the gentle breezes of spring and in the whispering waves of grain, a magical language, which is only comprehensible to those whose hearing discloses, not an abundance of outward noises, but the inward parts of the world and the most secret depths of the heart into which no mortal eye can see. The ingenious musical artist is an initiate of heaven; in invisible signs he proclaims his visions, audible to every ear that is open, but not *perceptible* to every one. Those *less favored,* to whom musical art is, in the exact sense, only *sounding* art, create for themselves through pleasing combinations of notes a language that strikes the ear easily and comprehensibly, increases the charm of living, and agrees completely with Kant's notorious description of music.[2] For this art can be further called an ingenious play of sensations when the notes are regarded according to the impression they make on the physical senses and are combined, either changed or unchanged, to agreeable effect, with a thoughtful but facile selection of phrases and idioms through which the musical spirit of the times is expressed.

VOCAL COMPOSITION. OPERA COMPOSERS.
TWO PRINCIPAL CLASSES OF THE SAME.
SOUL PAINTING IN MUSIC.

Music practices its perfect, invisible power in instrumental music as its own sovereign. It is here, however, that it most easily degenerates, for those who do not know how to control the spirit of the notes with the magical wand of genius, into an *artificial play* with *notes,* whose outward context is more easily perceived than their inward, spiritual connection. Accordingly, the lack of one kind is customarily obscured behind the other. When music consequently appears to be limited by being combined with poetry, it becomes at the same time more specific, more understandable—indeed, we might even say more human—through this combination. The poet becomes the expounder of its heavenly visions; he lends to the listener the thread upon which he descends into the subterranean depths that higher musical art opens up,[3] so that its wings may carry him back into the happy, clear kingdom of heaven in which notes powerfully prevail. The poetic composer takes up the text, which is just as much *given* as it is *chosen,* as the painter does an ingenious sketch, painting it out and animating it into a living whole through the richness of notes.

Here, however, he distinguishes himself from the ordinary vocal composer as does the *painter* from the *dyer.* It is not difficult to find a pleasing melody for a lyrical text that *does not contradict* the situation it describes; even a wealth of ever so lovely and charming melodies and of the most artful harmony is in this case only a brilliant coloration of established outlines. The truly ingenious and poetic composer, however, excites in the soul of the listener exactly *that feeling* that agrees completely with the situation that the poet allows to be contemplated and imagined visually. He gives, as it were, the *feeling itself,* inasmuch as he calls it forth through corresponding successions of notes, since the poet seeks to awaken it in the imagination more indirectly, through description of the situation. That which is *nameless* and *inexpressible* in the situation, which poetry only allows to be surmised at the boundaries of its territory, is proclaimed by *his* notes. Apart from this, the composer and the poet walk hand in hand, not in the sense that their productions are simply at one, running on *next to one another,* but that they permeate and complement one another in alternation; the one is interpretation and clarification of the other, and the most beautiful unification of the arts takes place between the art of notes and that of poetry, when, like *observation* and *feeling,* they are bound together into a complete representation of rich moments from life. But even a relatively mediocre poem, if it only provides an inducement to musical art to individualize the feeling of an interesting moment from life, can live through notes, gaining charm and deep interest.

But herein can be seen just that significant distinction among composers, specifically among opera composers, which determines the greater or lesser *aesthetic* worth of their products, according to whether they are merely *colorists* (dyers), that is, giving the text an agreeable or brilliant coloration, or *soul painters*, that is, such as can give it the *appropriate* coloration, which the *sensible* and *genuine musical poet* would see and demand spiritually, so to speak, in outlines he determines. Composers like Paer,[4] for example, concern themselves very little with their text; if they did not already, of their own accord and as a rule, accept poor opera texts to set, their musical character would compel them even to desire such texts in order to have the power to jump around with them as arbitrarily as possible. When they follow the poet, it is always just in *general*. They have only one color for every sort of emotional stirring, for example, hate, love, joy; the variations lie more in the outward variety of the configurations of notes. If, therefore, the poet perhaps describes the condition of love in a very general way, they apply in *just as general* a way their customary coloration for tender love, for rapturous feelings, without being able, thereby, either to distinguish their works internally through a genuine variety of consistent characters or to distinguish them from each other or from operas by others. For all the variety of their individual melodies and harmonies, such a uniformity still occurs in the whole that, with slight variation of the text, the principal numbers would do just as well in any opera of the same type. The succession of musical ideas for such composers is fundamentally determined by a true association of melodies, which cannot always occur without reminiscences. These melodies have simply been *placed together* by the composers more or less appropriately, and wherever an agreeable or piquant melody or modulation occurs to them, even if it is a dancelike one in the midst of a mood of deepest grief, and least of all with the purpose of *elevating* it, or a sentimental and melancholic one in a situation of the most unreserved happiness, then they are not able to give these up through a glance at what is necessary. They let themselves deviate from the scattered meaning, or probably even more, from the serious goal of art, through awareness of their public and of the expected effect upon the crowd. Their creativity never proceeds from a comprehensive, fundamental treatment of the material that is given to them to be unfolded musically by means of its organic development. This can only occur when the artist has grasped the idea of the whole, has conceived within himself the dominant mood, which the work of art must bring forth as a total impression, holds it firmly with enthusiasm, and thus finally forms and completes the details in the spirit of the whole, and, as it were, *out of the whole*. Their operatic compositions develop outward from the details and consist of details placed together. They are probably concerned with each detail making up a whole, and all that matters for them in this regard is that the individual piece sounds well and agreeable in itself—

that is to say, without regard to and apart from the dramatic whole, with which it should nevertheless stay in direct connection. They follow thereby the customary style of operas and opera pieces, perhaps with an incidental glance aside at their suitability for the concert. Never, though, does their spirit rise up to a concept of the whole. An abundance of opera pieces, for example, those of Paer, of which we are almost automatically reminded here, gain fundamentally and unendingly from this separation, because of the mostly arbitrary treatment of the text. In a concert, where one is reminded only generally of the situation being described by the disconnected text—and where, particularly since one has heard countless times the "Idolo mios," "Ricordati di me," and so forth, one finds no particular motivation to place oneself in the particular setting in which the text belongs—an agreeably performed song, an aria in which the violin plays concertante, and so forth, is pleasing for the most part *merely* because of the *music*, which, in its proper place, could often strongly displease the connoisseur. And yet many regard it as the distinguishing mark of a good work of theater music when its pieces also bring forth a perfect effect when performed in concert. We will not deny that the effect in concert can often correspond to the effect on the stage. Nevertheless, they are quite distinct, as may be judged by the fact that, on the contrary, we would have to place the greatest operatic compositions (many by a Mozart, Gluck, Salieri, et al.) far below the main arias, duets, trios, and so forth from every Italian opera if we overlooked the fact that each piece of music in a truly dramatic work must be *subordinated* in its working-out and significance to the whole and remain dependent upon it. The effect in concert, on the other hand, demands a brilliant working-out of the details, and whatever stands out individually in this way must feature a certain brilliance of virtuosity or otherwise a strongly marked individuality.

A composer who, on the other hand, we would call a musical soul painter (Mozart was one in the most perfect sense, inasmuch as not only each one of his operas, but for the most part each section of them as well, has a distinct character, which impresses itself vigorously and inalterably upon the spirit) animates even the less distinguished poem by virtue of the fact that, where the poet has only portrayed love, hate, doubt, etc. in *general*, he, with an ingenious glance at the given situation, expresses and communicates the very *specific love,* the *specific hate* and so forth, so that his work in tones is powerfully developed into a lively tone *painting.* That this specificity of the situation, which the ingenious composer is able to bring forth, cannot be exhausted by means of words and is therefore something inexpressible, we have already suggested above. Nevertheless, it is recognized by every connoisseur of music who is capable of grasping and feeling a Mozart's *Don Juan, Figaro,* and so forth. We believe that we have already sufficiently indicated the character of this higher class of dramatic composers by means of this contrast, so that an extensive description is not necessary.

BEETHOVEN'S MUSICAL CHARACTER.

The above thoughts were occasioned by the work of a master whose rich, colossal spirit, kindled by Mozart and Haydn, has, so to speak, built up a cathedral into the clouds from out of romantic instrumental music. There is hardly a living composer who can surpass him with regard to abundance of great and serious musical ideas, which seem to have been conceived, not through studying or listening to the works of others, but by lifting himself up into a realm that has not previously been entered. There is hardly anyone who can surpass him in boldness of fantasy, whose flight takes us (as in the *Sinfonia eroica*) now onto the battlefield, where the golden hopes of nations and a glorious, heroic time perish, while another celebrates the day of their resurrection, now into the womb of joyous nature, and into the happy rows of rejoicing shepherds, as in the Pastoral Symphony. In so saying, we by no means wish to defend descriptive or painterly music, to which Beethoven, like his teacher Haydn, seems to incline, for, apart from various eruptions of a joking mood, Beethoven remains what a musician can and should be, a painter of feelings; and, as feeling is generally not without thought, the states of mind that the fantasy of the ingenious composer portrays in notes can also be objectified as *pictures*.[5] He *sees* the circumstances whose states of mind he describes, and the vividness that his tone-pictures have for him in their arousal and formation can certainly often reach the point that he seems to have intended to describe something visible, fixed in place and time. In fact, however, Beethoven's music is so little description of what is real and given that it rather bestows upon every feeling an indescribable, unaccustomed degree of fervor and profundity, and the scrutinizer of the soul who is knowledgeable of music can rightly perceive in Beethoven's music what a *scope* and *variety* of feelings the human heart is capable of. Indeed, if one wished to measure Beethoven only on this basis, then it is perhaps here that he would stand out ahead of all his musical contemporaries. His variety of feeling is immeasurable, his sounds always proclaim a joy that has never been felt or enjoyed; that which is above or below the earth is joined to earthly sounds, and it always appears new and inexhaustible. But one will soon notice that in his musical representations, the *grand* and *colossal* predominate. We might call him the *musical Shakespeare*[6] by virtue of the fact that it is just as possible for him to describe and express in notes the deepest abyss of the struggling heart as the sweet, loving magic of the most guiltless soul, the harshest, deepest pain as delight that rejoices to the height of heaven, the most sublime as the most lovely.[7] Even so, however, his spirit still inclines with *excellent* love to the representation of the most pensive seriousness, fiery enthusiasm, and sublime splendor, and sets the highest affections into harmonic motion. We account for this on the basis that Beethoven's genius, under *Haydn's* and

Mozart's direction, first beheld musical art in the brilliance of instrumental music; to develop it further with an original spirit was for him the next task of his life. His deep, ingenious study discovered the hidden spirit of every instrument, and if various contemporaries of his understand only how to employ this or that one to advantage, to use it with effect, we know no other living composer apart from him, and perhaps Cherubini, who understands how to employ every instrument according to its individual spirit in such original variety and wonderful combinations. Whoever has gained this power over the spirits of the notes must necessarily also feel a powerful impulse to practice this mastery. This can only happen in the most elevated way in instrumental music, which, in turn, is not to be set into motion on account of every *triviality,* but only by *significant* and *powerful stirrings* of the soul. Where he makes use, though, of the entire power and fullness of instrumental music, then that which is unheard of in music becomes possible, and a transcendent power descends upon man, so that in such moments he can imagine himself the inhabitant of a higher world. All instruments must be united, indeed the master himself controls them with the same power as the virtuoso his individual instrument—not for a powerless lament, nor for feeble sentimentality, to be glossed over by a semblance of power, nor (as could be the motto of various recent instrumental composers, who set the hallowed trombones and all instruments into motion to pay compliments to a commonplace flute concerto) in order to do *little with much,* but to bring together the manifold powers of music in an unheard of, gigantic impression in order to fulfill the promises of the romantic spirit in music, which were given to us first of all by Mozart. And in fact, instrumental music also seems to have reached its highest brilliance when, as with Beethoven, all the instruments in a work, indeed all the instruments of the whole orchestra, must play together like the individual virtuoso upon his instrument. No individual stands for himself here; all of them form, as it were, a living universe of notes in unending exchanges and combinations. We believe that we have thus described Beethoven's greatest instrumental compositions. Only a layman, or a musician who misunderstands the power and significance of his art, however, could make this a reproach to the master. For, as overall the difficulty of musical performance does not decide against the worth of the composition, as long as the difficulty is only a *relative* one (for otherwise we would have remained with Hiller, Benda, Vanhall,[8] and so forth instead of progressing to Mozart, Haydn, and Cherubini) thus is the law of art: *out of little much,* also not the *highest* of art, otherwise the lighter types of music, for example, songs with keyboard accompaniment, would be the highest, and Italian music would *unconditionally* earn preference over German. On the contrary, there must be a type in every art that makes use of the artistic means given in their entire range, and thereby must show the most far-reaching impression that its art can make.

REPROACHES OF DIFFICULTY AND INCOMPREHENSIBILITY.

As pertains to musical difficulty, many among us can still recall the time when in many orchestras clarinets were still missing completely,[9] and trombones were missing everywhere, and when instrumental pieces had to be painstakingly rehearsed, which nowadays every small orchestra plays without effort practically at sight, while others were set aside as unplayable, which are now enjoyed everywhere. Indeed, it is particularly well known and within recent memory that Mozart's music was at first indignantly set aside by many orchestras, and for those who prefer Italian music to everything else, it still has a bad reputation. Even worthy men like Hiller, after hearing Mozart's *Così fan tutte,* had to say from their restricted point of view at that time, that something could yet come of this man, but that he worked too bombastically. We should not forget here that there are spirits that hurry ahead of their times with the wings of genius, and only expect complete and profound understanding of their work from a later time, perhaps even from posterity. *This is shown by Kant's* example in philosophy, or Klopstock's, Schiller's, and Goethe's example in poetry, whose first appearance was so little favored by the public that the commonplace critics of that time treated and handled them as their equals.[10] Even the already mentioned example of Mozart bears witness to this, whose *Don Juan* and so forth nowadays offer a musical and theatrical feast to the musical public every time, while earlier the sinister spirit that prevails in this sublime opera seemed to people to go out of bounds. To the spirits of this kind van Beethoven belongs as well. Various of his instrumental compositions (apart from those already mentioned, for example, the great C-Minor Symphony) have already established this, and his *Fidelio*—we dare to prophesy this—will establish it in the future the more it is enjoyed, and approached from all sides, in masterly performances, which it demands as much as it deserves them. For it is the true distinguishing mark of great works that, enjoyed repeatedly, they are ever more pleasing and reveal ever richer enjoyment through contemplation of the endless beauties that are included in the whole, just as the observant eye always finds and discovers more and more worlds in the cloudless sky.

ABOUT GENERAL COMPREHENSIBILITY, ITALIAN MUSIC AND MORE RECENT GERMAN MUSIC. ABOUT INSTRUMENTATION AND A REPROACH OF POWERFUL SCORING.

It is the opinion of several, however—and here we touch upon the second point—that good music must appeal to and win over practically everybody, and they call that being generally comprehensible. If musicians and those knowledgeable about music maintain this, then they forget that, even with a perfect hearing and much musical inclination, they could neither play nor understand the works of Haydn, Mozart, and others, and that they at first had to lift themselves up gradually to the state of musical cultivation at which they now find themselves. If ordinary musical amateurs express it, then we find nothing to reply to, for they certainly know what *they* are most fond of. In art, as in life, we duly recognize that which is superficial and agreeable where it belongs, and when it accurately indicates the required frame of mind; for the domain of nature and art is endless and, through its inexhaustible variety, extends far beyond one-sided theory. We enjoy as well the fleeting dance that excites all our nerves. We can by no means, however, elevate to the norm that in which art appears only as superficial play, and cannot reveal its unlimited powers, without foolishly restricting its range. This would certainly be the case, however, if we demanded in an indeterminate way that every piece of music be generally attractive and comprehensible. More strictly speaking, therefore, the requirement must be stated rather in such a way that every genuine work of musical art of whatever genre, while agreeing completely with the frame of mind that it is supposed to express, must attract the broadly knowledgeable musical expert through ingenious variety, and invite repeated enjoyment, and thereby will it become ever more comprehensible. Only the most superficial dance, however, or merely melodic and rhythmic music, can become *generally* comprehensible—no work of greater fullness and significance can. One must therefore either be consistent and declare the type of music in which the most accessible melody prevails to be the highest one, or else look at Italian music, which is pleasantly captivating and more lyrical, as only one type *alongside* the more learned German music and value it as such, just as experts on the art of *poetry,* for all that they value simple folk poetry and the naive folk song, do not reproach Schiller and Goethe because their works are not perfectly comprehensible to the lower classes without further education and practice. It is for this reason that mankind is capable of being educated, capable of rising to ever greater heights, so that he may not restrict himself to one monotonous sphere of life and regard whatever is serviceable there as the highest model. But the words are scarcely necessary here, for the works of the richer type of instrumental composition have already gained such an ascendancy and are so closely related to the character of the German people that it is hardly to be feared that Italian music, particularly in its *current* condition, can still hold up the powerful flight of German music—even though its most recent masters, particularly Paer, have nourished themselves principally on the German spirit with regard to fullness of harmony and richness of modulation.

Others hold the artificial development of instrumental music to be a corruption of art, which is not without a plausible basis, inasmuch as the *highest* development of a thing holds, at the same time, the seed of its decline. They maintain, accordingly, that all that presupposes deeper study, and therefore all so-called *learned* music, contradicts the character of a work of art. Several words need to be said about this, in so far as this has not been touched upon above. Just as there is natural and art poetry, both of which must be looked at as two types standing next to one another in value, one could also admit two different types of music in regard to the degree of culture of musical art generally as well as with particular nations and individuals, which correspond to these types of poetry. Natural music, as we might call the first of these, would be the type in which those elements of musical art that work directly and immediately upon perception and the senses, and that are thus also communicated and developed by people first of all, and without higher culture, as a gift of nature—melody and rhythm—are the predominant and unmediated expressions of simple sensation.[11] *Art music,* on the other hand, could designate that which can only be based upon deeper knowledge of the relationships of notes and of instruments—notably, however, upon the practice and use of dissonant intervals, as the expression of variegated and more complicated circumstances and emotions—and which is thus distinguished by a perfect development of harmony. Thus it might be appropriate for the more recent music in general to be called art music, inasmuch as it presupposes study of harmony along with perfection of the instruments, in contradistinction to the music of the ancients, and, further, for *German* music to be so called in contradistinction to the less artistic *Italian* music. The highest goal of musical art is not determined through these types alone, or through the predominance of melody or harmony in general—for in such a relationship between the two, one cannot achieve what is obtainable by the other. Genius, however, gives to the elements of its art more or less *equal weight.* Thus German music does not commonly achieve naïveté, simple loveliness, and grace, nor *Italian* music the bold sublimity and intellectual depth of the *German.* A Mozart, however, succeeded in concealing the deepest secrets of harmony through melodic grace and expressiveness. To the *Italian,* therefore, German music, even that by Mozart, necessarily seems *bombastic,* while to the *German,* Italian music seems *empty.* In one, for all the melody, the harmony often comes away empty-handed, while the other stifles the melody with fullness of harmony, dissonances, chromatic progressions, and monotonous figurations. In Italian musical art, *song* predominates (for song demands melody); in the German, harmony (which is not simply *accompaniment*), and with it instrumental music, for while the former can only be fully developed by means of the latter, so, on the other hand, does the latter obtain its highest perfection only by means of the first. Song, in itself, is innate in people; the instruments are the products of art, and artificial music arises as a concomitant of their development. The human throat is not capable of *that* dexterity that human beings show in the play of the instruments. Instrumental music is in itself, therefore, already a more artificial music; it is even more so with regard to the richness of harmony, which the musical artist is able to open up through the instruments. Accordingly, where it becomes *dominant,* song, as well, will be easily *dominated* by it; a fullness and splendor will manifest itself in this world of notes, which excites the artist all the more to strive for the highest and deepest effect. If to this is added, as with the Germans, the inclination to be less easily satisfied with agreeable form, so far as to run the risk of degenerating into formlessness, in order to fathom the meaning and significance of things, and to penetrate inquiringly into their inmost depths, to weigh the near and the far, the highest and the deepest, the scientific spirit, the thoughtful profundity, and finally the dissemination of great ideas and the general movement of the fate of the people, which imparts to all arts a great impetus, then is it clear why German music in more recent times has taken on that serious and sublime character through which ultimately song may well have suffered and at times have been covered up by harmony. Even Mozart was reproached for bombastic instrumentation; is it any wonder that this reproach by the lovers of agreeable, flowing song is now heard even more, since meanwhile instrumental music has become even more developed? Only there may now be discerned as well a covering up of the voices through too prominent accompaniment, and certainly at every point, or only at those points, where the fastest motion somewhat excuses this; and lack of melody generally, due to the ascendancy of harmony. No reasonable musical artist will accompany the song always and without reason with the full orchestra, for whoever does this will only defeat his own purpose and cancel the effect by striving after effect. But painting and portraying circumstances of the highest agitation through the power of instruments must at least be tolerated in opera, unless it happens that the action of the opera, or something that is necessary to understanding it, occurs in a piece of polyphonic music, as happens in various Italian operas; for here the text must necessarily stand out or else the spectator will not know what has happened, and his enjoyment of the music will be disturbed.[12] The powerful instrumentation, painting the situation from many sides (it is, after all, always only an accompaniment), is opposed by song, the principal matter. It is inappropriate for the servant to become the master; indeed, why would a text be necessary if it could not be understood because of the clamor of the instruments? We may add that it is self-defeating always to hide the song to such an extent that it is entirely unheard, and that the growing custom, among the Germans as well as the French generally, of using the most powerful instrumentation possible harms the singers and must bring vocal music to ever greater disadvantage by setting back the art of singing. This judgment, however, does not apply to those musical numbers in an opera that forcefully portray agitated scenes, which are understandable to the spectator through the course of the action or otherwise by means of powerful instrumentation; for here, even with the *weakest* accompaniment, countless words are lost because of poor singers, so that the rule against obscuring the song need not restrict the composer to the degree that his instrumentation must allow *every* word to be heard. Indeed, in light of the customary texts, rendering them inaudible by obscuring the voices is less of a loss than it would be to forego a masterly harmonization. Even apart from this fact, however, without considering the libretto we may still certainly not concede what is customarily held to be established fact when the relationship of poetry to music is under discussion: that the accompanying one is always the *servant,* song and melody the master. The fact that, with the *most beautiful* agreement of both, melody and harmony, song and the so-called accompaniment are *one, can already demonstrate the opposite.* Without a *dramatic* whole, it is also harder to understand the text; in a musical oratorio, for example, the text, and with it the song, must be brought out, although more of the significance of a *Lied* depends upon it. When therefore an ingenious composer, like Beethoven in Pizarro's bass aria,[13] uses strong instrumentation, the instrumentation certainly provides a perfect accompaniment to the emotions of the singer—but it establishes a unity with the voice, and since the situation is understood from what has preceded, it is not important to hear *every word,* which, with a strong voice and if the singer only enunciates clearly overall, is also not impossible. The highly characteristic music takes the place of the missing word; the melody of the voice, instrumentation, and text clarify each other mutually.

GERMAN SONG AND ITALIAN SONG STYLES.

If one nevertheless pursues the reproach deeper, which, particularly in regard to Beethoven, may certainly be refuted, one will find that it arises primarily from those who value the Italian song *styles* (we intentionally do not say Italian song) above all else. These are styles quickly learned with little practice, requiring neither sensibility nor soul, and are certainly not in themselves agreeable to hear, and which yet say everything in the same way, and, like worn out phrases and metaphors in speech, eventually had to become so repugnant to the more versatile and good-natured German that he created for himself his own, more variegated song, not without taking into account the better lessons of the Italians. He also does not seek to dominate everything with his song, but understands how to subordinate himself as necessary to the spirit of the music just as the actor does to the dramatic whole to which his character belongs. Finally, how is the text not mistreated by Italian music, for example, in the bravura arias and the brilliant parts where one hears it in such a mangled way that it is just as good as if nothing at all were said and *no text* were heard? The Germans have appropriately sought to put an end to this offense by simplifying the song and giving the text more significance.

It thus seems to us that a virtue of the more recent German music lies in the fact that we no longer are unconditionally in need of Italian song. But we also recognize the danger of one-sidedness, and therefore the efforts of friends of art are being aroused everywhere to support and develop solid and genuine song through performances dedicated to it. We give song its due; we acknowledge the difference that exists between instrumental and vocal music with regard to the melody of both. We also admit, therefore, that the great instrumentalist is not at the same time a composer of song, and that, if it is true that the greatest composers now living are instrumental composers, song is not always favored by them. We do not wish, however, that *one* kind of song should obtrude everywhere and in the most disparate forms when it is not adequate to the scope and diversity of their characters. The character of the *Beethoven* opera under discussion, for example, is far too big and inclusive for *Italian* song to predominate in it; nevertheless, only a biased person will maintain that the roles of this opera are lacking in *song*. On the contrary, we see in the treatment of the text a poetic spirit that is entirely lacking in the most popular composers, and the treatment of the voices shows what this ingenious instrumentalist can accomplish in a unique way for the theater and opera singing, after this great effort, if he only finds a poet who is congenial to him. But certainly the original resists the great multitude, which gladly clothes itself with the same cut!

ON THE PREVAILING DIRECTION
OF MUSICAL THOUGHT IN THE MORE RECENT MUSIC,
PARTICULARLY IN REGARD TO BEETHOVEN.

We will move on to another point, which is closely related to that just touched upon, and in regard to which the most recent music differs significantly from the older. This point has to do with the progress and the arrangement, or what is generally called the inner economy, of the piece of music, and the principle by which this is determined. In the time *before Haydn* and in the first period of his life music was still so formalized, a chosen theme was developed in such a determined and organized manner, and the composer in general was so strongly subject to the outward laws of custom, to which even the better ones paid their tribute, that one could say that matter-of-fact reason dominated musical composition. We do not deny the positive or negative advantages that were connected with this. Those arts that immediately assume a reality above which their works rise toward the ideal begin with the crudest imitation, in which the urge to copy seeks its fulfillment; at first it has to do only with objects and their manifold forms. To raise them toward the ideal through freedom is reserved for the more elevated *spirit,* if the drive of the outward forms for structure has become powerful. Music, which has *no* model in nature, or no object with whose outward imitation it begins, has, in regard to its line of development, *this much* in common with all other arts; its beginning is the practice and development of *fundamental forms*. In music, these are first unconsciously present in the national melodies of a people and are first consciously developed and put to a variety of uses with the growth of culture and the perfection of the instruments, which, as it were, makes the relationship between notes *visible*. It was the church that first laid claim to musical art; in its service musical art long maintained the distinguished character of simplicity and of sustained, solemn motion, which corresponded to the first deeper study of the relationships between notes. Indeed, even as the theater opened up to music a broader sphere of operations, churchly decorum and simplicity as well as theoretical endeavors still prevailed for a long time, even on the stage. While in the process, the study of harmony was extended knowledgeably in all directions to such an extent that pieces of music often seemed more to be examples and exercises in harmony than harmony a means to an end; those means were nevertheless mastered whose freer use would open up an endlessly rich world of notes, fulfilling the foremost requirements of such an art. For the foundation of a freer musical edifice was, as it were, being laid, or the sketch (the scheme) was being drawn that can only gain a comprehensible connectedness and context in relation to a prevailing, and therefore returning, fundamental idea; thus, the variegated arrangement and development of a theme was made into an inviolable duty. Since a deeper understanding of musical art at first had to be won *gradually,* however, the appealing and agreeable aspects of the folk melodies were relied on first. Everything lived in the kingdom of consonance, and dissonance was used only sparingly as a spice for this simple diet. Striving for power and fullness, for sublimity and bold expression, could not yet predominate in this period. Childlike simplicity, naïveté, innocence, a striving to express sensation in accordance with nature without excess or arbitrariness, clarity, order, and comprehensibility are the positive side; uniformity, stiffness, methodical emptiness, and dryness are the negative side of *Haydn's* musical art. Haydn himself, an extensive description of whose musical characteristics does not lie within our plan, belongs to the period being described by virtue of his love of musical order, the methodical and systematic nature of his works, which—particularly the earlier ones—often even have the appearance of following a predetermined plan, and the childlike simplicity of his melodies. By virtue of the richness of his ideas, however, the inexhaustible versatility of their working-out and in the use of the instruments, he can be seen as the founder of a more recent musical epoch. His joking, humorous essence never lost sight of the intended design. Mozart took an even bolder path. With him, reflection about his works, which the experienced connoisseur can for the most part perceive in Haydn's works, never, or only very rarely, shines forth. Yet Mozart also remains worthy of the highest admiration and is on the whole unsurpassed in this area, so that, with his freest harmonic progressions and with the abundance and fullness of his harmonies, a lack of context, an arbitrary, affected connection, or a harsh modulation is never to be perceived, but always the most profound, most soulful association of musical ideas. His productions can truly be called organic in that all of the details contained in them develop by necessity out of the whole; and yet they show the freedom of every true work of art. They are the products of a profound spirit, and yet nothing betrays their origin; surrendering to them, we live in a special, invisible world, and only the reentry of our thoughts into reality, after the disappearance of the notes, reminds us of the artist and his skill. If in Haydn's works, fantasy often seems to us to be subjected to the control of reason, in Mozart's compositions the two are so unaccountably united that they almost never appear *individual* and *separate*.

Here now is the point from which musical art since Haydn and Mozart has at times progressed ever further, and at times has gone astray into the realm of unrestrained caprice; the point in regard to which almost all more recent composers remain behind Mozart, although we believe that Mozart's brilliant instrumentation and his highly imaginative harmonies have been the primary cause of this. For these offered something that could be regarded as the magically powerful blossom of the more recent German musical art, since nothing like it had been discovered and made available in the earlier musical art of the people. The primary effort of the composer now became to raise this blossom to ever new heights; in the process, however, musical art has taken a completely fanciful path. For in order to develop the wonderful power and effect of instruments ever more, it was necessary to make use of them in the most multifarious combinations and exchanges, which could only be sufficiently motivated by a romantic and fanciful play of ideas. It is *Beethoven* who has made the primary contribution to this and has thereby had a powerful effect upon the most recent period of music. Himself an instrumental virtuoso, endowed with bold fantasy and a deep knowledge of the soul of each instrument, touched by Haydn's joking humor and Mozart's deep seriousness, he developed his romantic world of notes in which fantasy, given over to feeling, is *dominant* throughout and determines the progression of the modulation. Harmony appears here in the most original combinations and twists, but there is no context that would not be possible in this sphere, no harmonic combination and no connection of dissonances that could not occur where the highest degree of feeling and the most powerful contrasts are brought to the fore; indeed, this flight seems to have no written rules.

If other more recent composers cannot hold fast to any idea and do not carry anything through, due to babbling and striving after piquant and appealing details, but rather are only superficially carried away by melodies that they have truly just hit upon, then Beethoven's works have the appearance of being without plan or form for the opposite reason. His spirit probes, sunk in the depths of feeling, into a fullness of harmonies, from out of which he raises himself up above the earth like a radiant bird and extends his boundaries into the clear ether of heaven.

The arts of today necessarily require that each work, in order to be grasped as something whole and to bring forth a *total impression* by *gradually* impressing itself upon the soul, should point during the temporal sequences of its development to a dominant idea and character. This occurs, first, when these sequences develop one thing out of another with necessity and without caprice, and second, when all other sequences by which the work of art develops are controlled by a fundamental idea. In music this is the foundation of the requirement that a theme (a fundamental idea) should be adhered to, and, according to the degree of greatness and significance of the work, worked out to a greater or lesser extent (not according to any learned *rule,* however). A piece of music that is called a fantasy is mostly free from this duty since a production of this kind, whether it is brought forth on the spur of the moment or written down in this same spirit, can only recognize a freer course of musical ideas, the moods and the unrestrained emotional expression of a spirit endowed with art. For this very reason, though, it stands on the borderline of music and of art. For art should represent that which has been perfected in any way. Perfection, however, is not without measure, as the Graces are not without a cestus;[14] the measure is at once limitation and form, limitation that is adhered to by the artist who works according to the spirit of his art and who wishes to distinguish his work from the irregular and uninspired fantasies and dreams of those who are uneducated or as yet undeveloped. Musical fantasy is for the most part forgiven for sins against form and rules if a great spirit controls it; it is a delightful product if the technical assurance of the master brings it unintentionally but universally to light. But to carry this character of fantasy over into other works of music, and thus *to make musical fantasy dominant in the domain of the world of notes,* can only lead to great mistakes. An effusive wealth of ideas and an inexhaustible originality can thereby be made manifest, but clarity, comprehensibility, and order, by means of which the work of art becomes a work, not of momentary moods, but of continuous enjoyment, will often be missing. Here it is that I will speak also of Beethoven's *great mistakes,* for I do not intend to become his eulogist, feeling myself neither called nor justified in doing so, but rather to evaluate impartially his influence on the most recent musical art and his character according to my ability and insight.

Many works of Beethoven, for example, various symphonies and sonatas of his, can only be understood and evaluated as *musical fantasies.* In them, even the attentive listener often completely loses sight of the fundamental idea; he finds himself in a magnificent labyrinth, where on all sides luxuriant foliage and wonderfully rare flowers draw attention to themselves, but with no thread leading back to the restful homeland. The artist's fantasy flows further onward without stopping, points of rest are seldom offered, and the impression made by something earlier is not infrequently obliterated by what comes after; the fundamental idea has completely disappeared, or else it only shimmers to the fore from out of the distant darkness in the flow of the agitated harmony. These works will always remain original and highly interesting because they proceed from an *ingenious* musical artist. There are also immortal works by Beethoven in which we see how magnificently this master can subdue the forces that struggle in different directions and hold together the outpouring of ideas in the most beautiful proportion. Furthermore, this predominance of musical fantasy is more easily tolerated in instrumental pieces, where Beethoven has for the most part made use of it, than in vocal music, which must conform to the idea being expressed.[15] Finally, in the area of art as well, we do not confuse the elevation above a specific style, which mostly arises from the examples of great masters of an earlier time through the continuous custom of imitators, with arbitrariness and whims that also disdain the necessary form, even when they are clever. The first can be taken for granted with a bold spirit like Beethoven, and every genius is only practicing his inborn freedom when he shatters the restraints of idle custom. However, we can by no means fail to recognize, in taking an unbiased look at the most recent musical art, that Beethoven's example in this area has caused great damage, and his powerful spirit has manifested a very detrimental influence upon the art so that other artists of lesser endowments, and such as believe themselves to be artists, have sought to introduce *musical fantasy everywhere* without study of the rules or technical assurance, even into those types of instrumental and vocal music whose nature is for the most part antithetical to it, unconditionally demanding deportment, character, and specific, clear working-out: for example, opera pieces, songs with accompaniment, dances, etc. We name no one, but the connoisseur will easily know the difference.

BEETHOVEN'S MANNERISM.

Another tendency of *Beethoven's* is closely connected with this: the *searching* and striving for the unusual, a tendency in which Beethoven has much in common with Cherubini. Both, instead of being wonderful, are often *strange;* both touch at times upon monotony and bizarreness, and become thereby, as well as by a prodigal use of dissonance, devoid of melody, Cherubini considerably more so, however, than the much richer Beethoven. It is a common saying, repeated to a disgusting extent with regard to great spirits whose striving is misunderstood, that they fly away too high and ascend into regions where it is difficult to follow them, or, like Icarus, fall back to earth.[16] We would like to apply this saying to Beethoven in a certain sense. We believe that specifically his searching can be explained thus. There is a bold flight of fantasy that in itself carries the foundation of its downfall and a straining of the feeling, which does not admit of a long duration and with closer contact with reality must necessarily become languor; and there are, further, times when the more bold the flight of genius is, the more glaring becomes the contrast of reality with the sublime ideal, and the first of these strives inimically in every moment either to elevate or to disturb the harmonic balance of the creative forces. As often as it succeeds in the latter, as often as the enthralled spirit awakens from its inner world of fantasy and its exalted visions disappear, just as often does searching reflection enter, making a reasonable effort to regain the lost paradise, the blessed harmony of the creative powers that were within its sight. Although only the rich spirit finds nothing *commonplace* even in *seeking,* herein lies also the source of the *mannerism* from which we cannot absolve our master, even though it is a mannerism not of weakness, but of power. If, after all this, we may venture a comparison, we would call *Beethoven* the Jean Paul of musical art.[17] Both unite and represent in their domain the fundamental aspirations of German art in an original way. Both illuminate their own sphere with bold flashes in a way that is inexhaustible, clever, and interesting; but the flight of their fantasy often strives beyond that which is considered to be the form and limitations of a work of art, and does not allow clarity and completion, which proceed from undisturbed harmony of the creative powers. After such an unrestrained flight, Beethoven often appears to be a metaphysical brooder in the kingdom of musical art; charm yields to vented power; he looks with a firmly fixed gaze upon that motion that the motion of great thoughts has left behind in his innermost being; he repeats a simple musical figure as if he thought nothing of it and in heightened expectation of that which, as it were, will arise or return from the monotonous striking of steel.[18] His originality loses itself thereby, however, in strangeness and caprice. We will not deny, though, that Beethoven can free himself from this mannerism when he *wants to;* his spirit is too great and original to find it necessary to *strive* for originality and, in place of it, to seize upon caprice and strangeness, into which a too-little controlled susceptibility to outward circumstances may also lead him astray. We also know a significant number of his works that stem from pure harmony of the creative powers, that are perfectly self-contained, and that bear within themselves neither that fantastic formlessness nor this unmusical opposition of seeking and finding, so that that comparison as well is not applicable to them. We feel all the more moved, however, and called upon from pure love of musical art, to the consideration of which we gladly surrender ourselves, simply following the established opinion and conviction relentlessly and without bias, to explain that musical art, upon which Beethoven now exercises so powerful an influence and which is as much indebted *to him* as *he to it,* would be even more grateful to him if he strove more *generally* for the honor of musical art more than for the honor of *his* art, and only sacrificed to it devoutly in hours of undisturbed consecration.

ON BEETHOVEN'S *FIDELIO* IN GENERAL.

After these opinions on the more recent German musical art, with which at the same time we may combine the attempt to characterize Beethoven's music, we will stick to the consideration and evaluation of his (as far as is known to us) *first* opera and beg of those, to whom the forthcoming judgment concerning it might seem too little motivated or biased, that they look back over the above ideas, in which the principles that guided us in this judgment are contained, or else to refute them with the same impartiality with which we impart them. We will consider the fate of this opera only in passing, since this can naturally have no influence on an artistic judgment. For the fact that this opera, previously called *Leonore* because (upon its appearance in Vienna) it was not *generally successful* (the expert knows what an expression of this kind means), was rearranged by the poet and the composer and christened *Fidelio* (which some see as meaning that Beethoven's music—*mirabile dictu*[19]—did not dare to make an appearance next to *Paer's Leonora*!!!!), can only adduce musical baseness against this original work.[20] Supposing, that is, that some consideration were to be given to this lack of success and the reason for it were found only in the *music,* although the text and subject of this opera, with which people, under the guidance of Paer's music, were already acquainted to the point of saturation, must have contributed as well, and that, furthermore, this music displeased both *connoisseurs* and educated friends of art *in general* (superficial dilettantism cannot come into consideration here), then even this would not be a disgrace to the composer, as examples of later *rearrangements* are to be found in all the arts, and here the master entered for the first time into a great sphere that until now was new to him, where it is important to become familiar with theatrical effect and to take it into account without being enslaved to it, and where at the same time he had to prove himself in a *larger* context as a *vocal composer*. Here, however, the contrary, which is customary with great geniuses, seems to have taken place—namely, that rearrangements of works of genius do more harm than good—and this rearrangement itself seems to proceed more from a change in the text and in the order of the scenes, which here and there appeared necessary, than from any necessity to change the *music*. For, apart from the overture, the changes in the pieces that have been retained seem to be completely unessential to the extent that they are not connected with this transposition of the scenes. Since the dramatic content of the opera gains little from this transposition of the scenes, and indeed the disparity between the acts is only increased, we would advise every director rather to allow this opera to be performed essentially in the original arrangement, and are certain that through the repeated enjoyment of accurate and enthusiastic performances of it on the part of the singers as well as the orchestra true friends of music will ever more generally acknowledge it, and ever more thankfully entrench its name in the national shrine where Mozart's divine operas sparkle. At the very least, even now no unbiased musical expert will deny it a place next to Cherubini's *Lodoiska*,[21] to which it is related in several respects. We have mentioned the above only to prevent misunderstandings, and at the same time to specify the point of view of the following evaluation. It rests, namely, upon four attentive hearings of the *original* arrangement, which, in consideration of the theater (at the winter performances by Joseph Seconda's company in Leipzig)[22] and the orchestra, was performed very worthily and with visible love, in comparison with the text and keyboard reduction of the *more recent* arrangement,[23] of which we will take notice here and there to the extent permitted by the partial understanding that it provides. In Vienna, as is well known, the *second* arrangement was ratified with the most extraordinary applause, perhaps with more regard for its theatrical aspects than for the music. Only the expert who was in a position to see and hear both arrangements, and to compare the full scores, would be able to give a perfect judgment here.

ON THE THEME AND SPIRIT OF THIS OPERA.

The story of the opera is that of a noble woman who rescues her husband, who has been overthrown by a court intrigue and placed in the deepest dungeon as a state prisoner as a result of the inhuman revenge of the governor of the state prisons, from assassination, through which the governor strives to remove him from the sight of the minister who is visiting the prison, and who naturally brings about poetic justice in the end. By means of the confidence, which, disguised as a young man, she has won from the dungeon master she finally discovers her husband after great exertion. This subject, with the single insignificant episode of the dungeon master's daughter falling in love with Leonore (disguised as Fidelio), and the father wishing to make his assistant Fidelio into his son-in-law in order to ease the burden of his old age, is *outwardly*, that is, in relation to dramatic and scenic *variety*, very deficient; *inwardly*, however, that is, in regard to the active description and elaboration of the situations that occur that is *possible* here by means of poetry and music, it is endlessly fruitful. This last, to be sure, is only true for the more deeply penetrating poet and composer. Now, as regards the German arranger who has discovered this subject, we cannot exactly tell what in this arrangement is exclusively his; we only recall that the Italian arrangement has no more variety. The German text, however, at least has *this* great advantage over many other opera texts: it is written throughout in fluent verses and in a noble tone; it does not, like many opera texts, make a travesty of the music; and it also has more ideas and fewer stereotypical phrases than the Italian. Therefore, it was not a hindrance to the deeply penetrating composition. The principal mistakes of the arrangement relate to the ordering of the scenes, in which the arranger (as far as we know, the esteemed Sonnenleithner in Vienna) unfortunately allowed himself to be too constrained by the original. Meanwhile, we would like to maintain with near certainty that it was not the arranger but *Beethoven* who happened upon this subject, feeling himself, through inner abundance, full of power and a true calling to enliven this material, since, moreover, in regard to *dramatic* arrangement and certainly for *music,* it is far less inviting to the *poet* than to the *composer.* And, in fact, Beethoven has breathed upon this material with his music a higher, almost unworldly life, so that even if the story is only taken from bourgeois life, *this* faithfulness, this courage, which Beethoven's Leonore demonstrates, this fiery wrath of the governor, at last this high spiritual peace for the suffering one, this pure heartfelt effusion of Marcelline etc.,[24] in short, this energetic manner of feeling, which Beethoven has given to the various characters, seems to come from the inhabitants of a more powerful planet from which he has stepped down and lifts up this *bourgeois* scene with magical power into a more powerful and romantic world. And nevertheless, that which these people feel more strongly and powerfully is taken only from the *human breast* and is related to every one of us, and this heroic feeling descends upon us like a strengthening consecration.

Yes, great beloved master, your notes do not give voice to soothing sentimentality, but only to deeply energetic feelings; your expression is not to be measured by the customary operatic standards; your work did not arise from recollection of a hundred others or from skillful combination of beloved operatic turns of phrase garnished with a few new melodies or modulations. To you, commonplaces are a strange and arbitrary fashion. You stride boldly forward on the path that was opened by Mozart, your great master. Characteristically, and with primal power, a spirit controls the whole from beginning to end, revealing you characteristically and anew in every *cadence,* astonishing us in every sequence! You draw out the spirits that dwell in the instruments, and they serve you with a wonderfully singular expression, each according to its characteristic abilities. Your song is a language of the heart, pure declamation of feeling, and therefore the song predominates more in your work than the singer! But your expression is not the expression of feeling alone; in your hands notes are the expression of deep thoughts, and so you awaken thoughts as well and describe what no poet is capable of describing. Your work is not one of those that conforms gracefully to the meaning, that rushes flatteringly by the ear and only touches the surface of the feelings with a light breath. Thoughtful and deeply felt, it intensifies the spirit's attention so as to understand the language of a higher life and instills that which is portrayed with unaccustomed meaning!

Indeed, I have never come across any opera in which the music excites such a deep interest for the story and leads the attention so powerfully toward the situation being described. Whether, in a greater context as well, Beethoven as a dramatic composer would be able to describe similar but different characters and circumstances, and different types of material, as exhaustively as he has described the individual matters of this opera, is a question that can only be suitably answered when the master has composed *several* operas, to which end we wish that he may find good poets. We do not doubt that he can, although we can scarcely believe him capable, with this unrestrained flow of fantasy and of fiery feeling, of the clarity and facility of ingenious characterization that the profound Mozart demonstrated in his various operas, even in subsidiary characters. We must recognize, however, that the vocal pieces in this opera, while they are mostly very demanding for the singers because of their powerful instrumentation, are virtually free from the reproach that we touched upon above, that is from the mannerism of affectation and strangeness, and, as we will show in detail, even have a fluency of song of which, under the influence of a prejudice, we would not have believed this master capable before we heard this opera. Admittedly, it is not the *customary* style of dramatic singing, which has its own determined standards, but a characteristic, expressive one, like that of Cherubini, and yet more fluent and melodic than his. The declamation is truly masterly down to the details in a way that is rare in more recent theater music.

I have heard several people say, though, that the impression made by this music is all too shocking and oppressive. Specifically, those who hold up that which is pleasing and easily understood or a lightweight display that charms and moves the outward sensibilities as the measure of all greatness in musical art *must* naturally express themselves thus. However, the deeper masterpiece may also demand that it be received repeatedly, attentively, and without prejudice, with a complete submission of the soul. Whoever finds this *impossible* may pass *no* judgment upon it. We wish to concede, as well, that the music of this opera strains the nerves of many with a gentle nature. We have heard this even from some people who call Shakespeare, who added the harshest dissonances of life into the many-voiced choir of his great dramas and his gigantic work, magnificent. Whether the composer can achieve the same effect with his dissonances as the poet can with *his* is admittedly another question, which can only be answered through a deeper comparison of poetry and music, and which consequently cannot be decided here. Only this much is certain: that everywhere that great powers are able to develop, great contrasts are also at hand; Beethoven, however, has conceived of his material in a way that is truly great and has lifted it above the level of ordinary life. This judgment leads accordingly to an incongruity, or rather it leads to the fact that one can understand the maximum through the *poetry*, without finding it in the *music*, and the purely poetic meaning is not sufficient to pass anything other than a layman's judgment upon music. Indeed, we find that our master is most to be compared to the great Shakespeare in that, like him, he is capable of eliciting from the human breast that which is most terrifying along with that which is most cheerful, that which is most powerful and tragic along with that which is most tender and joyful. The part of Marcellina, her duet with Jacquino, and most of all her wondrously sweet duet with Fidelio, and, finally, also the duet of Florestan and Leonore, establish this sufficiently. If, though, the terrifyingly sublime and frightening predominates here, this is due primarily to a failing of the text: namely, that the few cheerful situations do not alternate vigorously enough with the gloomy ones, so that the easy and more pleasing parts were until now concentrated in the first scenes of the first act, while the gloomier sections were crowded into the other half. Even according to a one-sided impression, however, which ignores the opera as *a whole,* this judgment is still untrue by virtue of the fact that every bitter memory and every painful feeling at last dies away in the highest rejoicing and delight. This is our opinion of the whole and of the impression that we received upon hearing it repeatedly. In order to discuss the details, we must first say something about the ordering of the text.

ON THE ARRANGEMENTS OF THIS OPERA.

Now, according to the first arrangement, the action of the opera is divided into three acts. Of the first two, however, only the conclusion of the first act falls at a genuine dividing point in the action (it ends, namely, after revealing the governor's orders for Florestan's death). The ordering of this same act, however, was uncomfortable by virtue of the fact that, first, two canons and then two uncommonly demanding bass passages follow immediately upon one another.[25] The second was very empty of action, inasmuch as the only significant moment contained in it was the fulfillment of Leonore's wish to accompany the old man into the deepest dungeon; the governor's command, however, was only repeated. The scene at the beginning of the second act, where the prisoners enjoy the fresh air, was a mere contrivance that the arranger had added, perhaps in order to get one more chorus, but which we would not like to dispense with due to Beethoven's masterful description of this situation.[26] Both acts were able to be transformed into *one;* the smallest evil to come about thereby was that the first became disproportionately larger than the second: for this had to remain unchanged, since the scene needed to focus on the culminating stages of the action in the dungeon in order to maintain interest in that which was highest and most frightening. It was a greater evil that several magnificent pieces of music perhaps had to be sacrificed thereby.[27] In our opinion, the first act now needed to be arranged throughout in such a way that the audience's attention remained continually directed upon *Leonore. She* had to be seen as the focal point of its action;

the danger of being discovered could mount, or at least the moments that stand in the way of her plan to reach her husband could be brought forward more by the poet. Accordingly, in order to give a meaningful conclusion to the first act, the two moments mentioned above needed to be connected, and the action needed to be carried forward to the point where, on the one hand, the governor demands angrily that the old man carry out his command as quickly as possible, and on the other hand, at the same time, Leonore's wish to accompany the old man into the dungeon is granted. Both moments needed to take place in the finale.

In the more recent arrangement, these moments have, to be sure, been brought closer together, as in the Italian version (in which the *marriage of Marcelline* is given too much prominence), and the repetition of the terrifying command is more strongly motivated. However, inasmuch as it was attempted to bring that contrived scene more closely into the context of the action and the anger of the governor about the freedom that has been granted to the prisoners, the command to lock them up once again and the lament of the prisoners over the loss of this blessing are allowed to be heard at the conclusion of the finale; the primary action is obscured by the secondary action, and the governor's repeated command is only an incidental memory. This also brought about a major change in the music in regard to the first concluding number (the *second* in our arrangement). The music of the prisoners' lament is certainly very moving, but the earlier conclusion (that of the second act in the first arrangement) was far more brilliant and powerful. It would perhaps have been better only to announce the governor's angry command or to have it carried out by soldiers, and then allow the prisoners' lament to be heard. Thereupon Rocco (the dungeon master) would reveal his conversation with the governor to Leonore and announce the granting of his wish. Pizarro (the governor), angry over the delay, would then immediately demand the speediest possible execution of his secret command, and thus the act would conclude with the highest agitation of the emotions.

CHARACTERIZATION OF *FIDELIO* IN DETAIL.

Now to the individual pieces of music. In the second arrangement, Beethoven has exchanged the overture that he wrote earlier for this opera for another one (in E major—it is found in the Vienna keyboard reduction as well).[28] Full of grand and bold ideas, full of deep feeling, but with no obvious unity, indeed, thrown together in the most arbitrary and strangest way with affected modulations that disturbingly inhibited the flow of rich fantasy, and at the same time immeasurably long, that overture must have given a great deal of offense. What is more, one of its most prominent features, the entry of the trumpet (which announces the minister's arrival at the point of highest danger), only becomes comprehensible at the end of the opera and cannot be seen as contributing to the overture, since the rhythmic, melodic, and harmonic context is completely disrupted and disturbed through too harsh a transition. Therefore, this trumpet signal appears only a frivolity that is completely extraneous to the deep seriousness of the overture as a whole. The master may have come to understand all this later, and therefore have put this overture aside. All the same, we hold this to be a loss, for, on the whole, the mood that prevailed in the older overture was in our opinion more in agreement with the character of the opera than the new one, which seems to have but little connection to it. Indeed, the first one seemed to be the fresh and unmediated product of the total impression brought about by perusal of his musical creation. If it had been possible for the master to hold together better the abundance of melodic and harmonic phrases in this overture, to combine the deep but disconnected ideas that strive restlessly to separate from one another, into beautiful symmetry, and to soften the traces of that bizarre mood, then we would gladly dispense with the shorter overture.

No. 1 (in the older arrangement) is Marcelline's aria: "O wär' ich schon mit dir vereint." Merely by glancing at the part of Marcellina, one notices that the German arranger and composer have treated it somewhat more importantly than did the Italian. For it was essential that, if this subordinate figure were to fit into this *painting, planned out with deeper seriousness,* it had to be brought closer to the more noble fundamental tone of its palette. Easy, joking cheerfulness, teasing, but already covetous tenderness are the fundamental traits of this maiden in the Italian arrangement, which Paer rendered as exceptionally charming and melodious.[29] An unprejudiced, thoroughly naive maiden, ripe for love and living in dawning hopes of it, stands before us *here;* gentle self-avowal, accompanied with a stolen sigh, which dissolves in the trusting hope of an inexpressibly sweet joy, is expressed in her first aria, which begins in C minor and concludes in C major. The corresponding motion of the violins that accompany the simple song expresses particularly significantly the excitement of the maidenly heart, which like a spring blossom strives to emerge from its disguise into the light of the joyful day.

Jaquino's (the prison warder) clumsy declaration of love interrupted by knocking at the door, Marcelline's virginal resistance, and his dismay are contained in the second, very originally and outstandingly well-declaimed duet.[30] In the more recent arrangement this is the first, the aria the second number, and in the last mentioned, the text is changed in one place in a way that does not improve it, and the music is shortened by a pair of measures to the disadvantage of the rhythm.[31]

The duet is followed in the original arrangement by a very lovely trio for Rocco (the dungeon master, Marcelline's father), Jaquino, and Marcelline. "Ein Mann ist bald genommen," which stands as No. 9 in the Härtel[32] keyboard reduction, is, however, omitted in the Viennese keyboard reduction according to the more recent arrangement.[33] In any case the reason for this was that the piece that follows, which, however, could have been added later, was more significant in relation to the action, which in general was to be compressed and shortened. Whoever has heard this trio just once, however, will certainly not want to dispense with it. The good counsel of the experienced old man, who simply dismisses the scornful Jaquino, Jaquino's regret, Marcelline's breathing more freely at the thought of Fidelio, all of this is blended into a charming harmony and spoken plainly and simply, without artificial ornamentation of the singing.

Now follows the canonic quartet "Mir ist so wunderbar," which is just as short, between the above-mentioned and Fidelio, who has just come in. Its beautiful, simple theme, introduced by the meaningful viola ritornello, and varied with the most diverse accompaniments, illustrates in a lively way the anxious mood of the maiden betraying love, of the embarrassed Leonore, of the perplexed Jaquino, and of the expectant father. Hereupon follows the dungeon master's comic aria, "Hat man nicht auch Gold beineben." If any piece is to be set aside in order to shorten the whole, it might be *this one*. The music certainly fulfills its purpose, but the beginning of the Allegro is somewhat commonplace, and the old man himself, in whose character we glimpse such outstanding traits, loses uncommonly much because of the money morality that he has to recite here—however much it may be in the character of commonplace jailers.

Rocco offers to Fidelio his daughter as a wife; Fidelio begs the old man to allow him to go with him to the government prison in order to lighten his task and assures him of his courage and his resolution. In this situation comes the magnificently worked out trio between Rocco, Leonore, and Marcelline: "Gut Söhnchen, gut! hab immer Mut!"—strength and gracefulness are beautifully melted into one, the voices are set very melodiously, the harmony is fluent and natural throughout; the highest ardor of loyal souls is expressed in the lively modulations and in the melismatic repetitions of the Allegro (particularly at the words: "I consented to the sweet obligation; it cost bitter tears!").[34]

After this trio, if we are not mistaken (in the Leipzig keyboard reduction the pieces are not in the right order), there comes in the old arrangement the wondrously sweet duet between Marcelline and Fidelio with obbligato violin and violoncello in which the former develops on the dream of her union with Fidelio and builds graceful castles in the air that rise up to heaven.[35] The flow of the melody that illustrates this is untroubled and "clear as a mirror," like Marcelline's heart—and as her wishes rise urgently from her breast, so do the accompaniment and the song mount; the words rush forth like the expression of one who, in the sweet intoxication of feeling, can scarcely catch her breath. Leonore only quietly interjects the words: "How painful to have to deceive her!" The whole is full of life and feeling.

Pizarro (the governor) arrives; the tyrant receives the news that the arrival of the minister, who will inspect the government prisons, is near. What if he were to find Florestan, who he had been told was dead, still in chains? Pizarro had given orders to let Florestan slowly starve; now he can remove him from the minister's eyes only by a quick murder. The storm of diabolical revenge rages in the aria,[36] accompanied by the full orchestra. After six introductory measures, which perform the role of a prolonged upbeat, it first enters in the fundamental key of D minor, then lumbers forth in snakelike coils, as it were, through many different keys, falling back after several striking dissonances into D major, where the chorus of watchmen enters and accompanies it until the end. In the more recent arrangement a measure has been removed from the beginning; but, on the other hand, seventeen measures are added to the chorus, in which the same dissonance is maintained through a succession of notes for four measures.[37] The singer must make an effort to be heard through the instrumentation, as he must if this aria is to be effective, and, in order to give adequate motivation to *this* inner tumult, he must show an extremely forceful nature in his entire performance from his first step upon the stage. Is the ear not all too strongly set upon here by harsh dissonances? We are not able to resolve this question, for being accustomed to the highest degree of attractiveness makes an unbiased judgment difficult in more recent music, as it does everywhere.

Rocco comes, and Pizarro urges him to carry out the murderous attack of which his soul is full: "Now, old man, you must hurry, you will succeed" etc. Hereupon opens up the powerful, *characterful* duet in A major between Pizarro and Rocco. Pizarro's restless urging (the key of which cannot yet be distinguished), his promise, the old man's interrupted questioning: "Just say quickly how I can help!", the demand for steadfastness, the urgent "Speak," the frightful "Murder!", Rocco's numbness, all is unsurpassably described. And now, as the dark plan ventures forth into the light of day, how beautifully are the words "What! Just listen to me! You tremble? Are you a man?" declaimed. The bass carries the rising melody; Pizarro urges: "We may not delay at all; it is the state's responsibility to get rid of this bad subject quickly." Rocco, in his horror, does not know how to utter anything but the cry: "Sir!"; his limbs tremble, he falters before the terrible command. Pizarro, however, is already rejoicing in his heart. Both are superbly expressed at the magnificent moment in G♯ major and by the modulation into C♯ minor. Fearfully, in terrifying dissonances and slow motion, the old man replies: "No, Sir, to take life, that is not my duty!" In a decisive tone (in D major), Pizarro replies "I will sink to doing it myself, if you lack the courage," and orders the old man to climb down into the deepest dungeon to the man "who is scarcely alive, and trembles like a shadow," and quickly to dig a grave in the cistern. The description of these words, Rocco's quick interjection (mostly in recitative) "and then, and then?", and the reply "then I will quickly sneak into the chamber in disguise; a blow, (pause) and he will be silent" (these last words accompanied by the violins pizzicato) elevate this duet to one of the foremost character pieces of more recent music. Furthermore, the last five pieces (treated as separate pieces) are unique to the German arrangement, which, particularly through the last of these, has given the composer an excellent opportunity to show the power of his art. Here, in the performance that we saw, ended the *first* act.

The *second* act was introduced by the original march in B♭ major,[38] which comes before the governor's aria in the *more recent* arrangement. In this more recent arrangement Pizarro's departure is immediately followed by Leonore's magnificent scene, after which comes the prisoners' chorus. There the latter begins the second act and Leonore's aria follows.[39] This chorus, performed by a large enough group, as was the case in Vienna, must have a stirring effect. The voices gradually enter: "O what joy to breathe easily in the free air!" The instrumental accompaniment plays around them like the fluttering of gentle winds, and in between comes a terrifying recollection of the dungeon, which obliterates hope once again. "Freedom!" With this call, lifted up by a powerful modulation, all nerves tremble; but the surroundings command restraint.

We lack the words to describe Leonore's heavenly scene. For this same situation, Paer composed a very superior scene in his own manner, which, however, will bear no comparison with *this one*.[40] The *fervor* of the melody in the vocal line, the magnificent flow of the harmony, the original accompaniment of the obbligato horns, which penetrates all the nerves with a sweet terror, and, what is more, the appropriate, emotionally rich key (E major)[41] all this works together to describe rapturously and inimitably the sweet consolation of hope, the deepest longing, blessed recollection of past days, and the unbounded courage of the loyal wife. Apart from two shortenings of the Adagio, of which only the first makes sense to us, while the second seems to destroy the lovely characteristics of the melody,[42] the beginning of the scene was altered as well, namely by the inclusion of another *recitative*. The reason for this was to situate it in its assigned place in the more recent arrangement. The arranger has, however, come closer in this way to the Italian text: "Abscheulicher, wo eilst du hin" etc., is like the Italian: *Esecrabil Pizarro, dove vai?* (Execrable Pizarro, where are you going?)[43] As regards the music, though, we would not wish to exchange this new, longer recitative for the older, shorter one ("Oh do not break, you tired heart"), since this one is intimately better connected to the aria, while the new one modulates a bit uncertainly. The small alteration in the Allegro also does not meet with our approval at all.[44]

There follows the little finale of the second act (in C major), opened by Leonore's and Rocco's conversation.[45] Rocco recounts that Pizarro has allowed the marriage of Marcelline and the introduction of Fidelio into the prison along with giving the order to dig the grave for the government prisoner in the dungeon. This conversation is magnificently declaimed and here and there gently recalls Mozart without being an imitation, for example, in the cry of the most joyous astonishment: "Yet today, yet today!" in which Leonore breaks forth after the recitative that speaks of that permission, and at the cryptic words: "*We are both digging his grave*"—"Oh, let's not linger here any longer" etc. The individual passages contain, for all the shortness of the whole, a very effective intensification—the vigorous joy of Leonore over the fulfillment of her wish, the ominous dread after the assignment is begun in the agitated Andante in § time, where the slurs performed by the accompanying wind instruments, particularly the clarinets, produce the most gripping effect; the anxious convergence as Marcellina reports to them Pizarro's threat, in a yet more agitated passage (Allegro molto), which modulates very beautifully with a discontinuous accompaniment, the thunderous entry of Pizarro, who demands the hasty completion of his command: all of this is superbly described and raised up to the very highest level of effectiveness. We have already touched upon the fact that in the more recent arrangement this finale is augmented at the *beginning* by the prisoners' chorus, which has been placed immediately before this conversation, and at the *conclusion* by the meek lament of the prisoners, whom the governor commands to be locked up once again ("Farewell, you warm sunlight"). As moving as this last chorus is, the tension is suspended by it, and the conclusion seems to us, as we have already said, somewhat insipid. This addition now makes it necessary to alter somewhat the final Allegro molto, and to interpolate several measures containing Rocco's defense of having indulged the prisoners in this way. This moment as well, although it is well declaimed, we do not hold to be of the foremost effect, again for the reasons mentioned above.

The third act, which shows Beethoven to be a master of the monstrous and frightening, begins with an introduction in F minor, which is followed by Florestan's aria. In the introduction we already seem to feel the terrifying arousal of a suffering human soul in the bleak darkness of the deepest prison, the heavy sighs that interrupt the deathlike silence, the cold horrors that flutter through this place; our heart is filled with fear and pity[46] before we catch a glimpse of the suffering one.

The curtain opens, and Florestan expresses his feelings and ours in the recitative and in the aria that follows it. *Paer* wrote an aria for the same situation with *obbligato violin* and *viola,* a truly good concert aria that, however, apart from the introductory recitative, which is not easy to understand, does not engage the situation nearly as deeply as does Beethoven's composition. What is more, the Italian arranger, in the spirit of Italian theater poets and composers, did not allow anything but the customary tenderness in familiar phrases to be expressed in this situation. In the *German* arrangement, the force of religious submission and patience that arise from a clear consciousness is brought significantly to the fore, along with the sorrowful recollection of the wife; this differentiates this scene somewhat from the customary treatment of similar situations. And this is also beautifully expressed in the music, by means of which the terrifying aspects of the situation are moderated in the most *noble manner*. The composer did not produce an extended concert aria dressed up with brilliant roulades, which would only have distracted from the situation being portrayed; he had a much higher goal in mind. A simple and melodious Adagio in A♭ major, upon which there follows, with the recollection of Leonore, a more agitated section in F minor with arpeggiated accompaniment, which, growing ever slower at the close, is finally given over to the violoncello, and loses itself in the weakly sustained F-minor chord, encompasses the entire situation. We seem to hear how, after the final arousal of feeling, which powerfully summoned up memories, the exhausted strength of the terribly suffering man draws, unnoticed, ever nearer to dissolution, which the Italian arrangement only tried to express in a succeeding recitative, apparently in order not to disturb the popular style of the aria.[47]

Now, it is noteworthy that Beethoven retained the introduction and the first section of this aria without any *very* essential alteration, but worked out the second according to a new text. The first text of this section was perhaps somewhat disconnected and did not bring the recollection of Leonore clearly enough to the fore; the new one is more poetical. In composing this section (in F major), Beethoven was certainly true, on the whole, to the idea and manner of treatment mentioned above, but the composition seems to us both in regard to modulation and to accompaniment to be, for *this* master, so commonplace and ordinary that we would in no way wish to sacrifice the first arrangement of *this* section. On the other hand, it must be admitted that the recitative that precedes the first section is here undertaken and developed in a much more significant way, and the changes in the *first* section are fortunate as well.

Meanwhile, Leonore and Rocco enter the dungeon with lantern and tool and now follows the harrowingly beautiful duet, "Nur hurtig fort, nur frisch gegraben!" while they make the grave ready for Florestan. The more recent arrangement has the advantage here that the words that are spoken by both of them before this work[48] have been set in melodrama.[49] The few notes that have been added here show how much our master can do even with very little; the part that recalls the conversation between these two people in the second act is handled particularly well. The duet itself (in A minor) is once again, as the scene demanded, entirely without vocal ornamentation and artificial turns of phrase and is accompanied very gently by the string instruments and, as often as the theme returns, by the trombones. The sustained chords of these latter instruments cut to the quick; one feels that one is standing here at the abyss of the grave where another world is opening up. The violins, which play throughout nearly the whole piece in triplets, and the predominant figure in the original basses, which seems to burrow ever deeper, point out the monotony of this work, which echoes throughout the bleak vault, as well as the vocal melodies do the uneasiness of the old man who has been driven to this work, and the anxiety of Leonore (who continually looks around, just in case she might be able to recognize her husband in the prison), and the excruciating restraint of most terrifying feelings.

Now, here a voice has also been heard from Prague:[50] "When we proceed from the fundamental principle, the only one (?!) that allows opera to take its proper place in the world of art, that song must enter in where feeling is heightened, then it is a perceptible failing of this work (which, however, can mostly be blamed upon the poet) that precisely the most gripping scene in the whole piece, the scene where Leonore digs the grave for her beloved husband, has been tossed off entirely in prose without music." In accordance with what has been said before, it must be repeated here that it is untrue that this gripping scene has been tossed off without music, for we have spoken of just that gripping duet that belongs here, and that the correspondent must not have heard. Or has he perhaps expressed himself incorrectly, and did he wish to say, in the sense of customary Italian opera, that where feeling is heightened, there must be an aria or in general *a lot* of singing: even, therefore, at this place, where the wife is digging a grave for her beloved husband? First, Leonore's feelings have certainly been intensified to a high point, but cruel necessity commands her at the same time to be *quiet* in order not to betray herself; thus, it was important here to express as well the stifling restraint of feelings through *melody*, not, however, with *a lot of singing*. By *no* means could an *aria* have been placed here. For, not truly knowing *whose* grave she is digging, even if the spectator knows it, Leonore sings even to herself: "Whoever you are I will rescue you; by god, you shall not be a martyr!" etc. The duet is finally so gripping in effect, and the situation so exhausting, that one could scarcely wish for another piece at this point. Thus, the correspondent has either not heard this duet or has not grasped its significance. By the way, even *Paer* has in this situation only a similar duet, whereby admittedly somewhat *more is sung, but less is expressed.*[51]

Florestan rises up from his exhaustion. The work has been completed. Florestan begs the dungeon master to alleviate his misery; Leonore recognizes him. Rocco calls upon Fidelio to give him a remnant of wine from his bottle; Leonore does this hastily, without being recognized by her husband. With an expression of the most moving gratitude, Florestan opens the trio that follows here, in A major, in which Beethoven has masterfully developed the beautiful principal idea, and has shown that at the appropriate place he is also capable of placing charm before power and touching upon all strings of the human heart. Perhaps the short dialogue that comes before this trio, from the important point where Leonore recognizes her husband, could be set in melodrama. In Paer as well, by the way, this recognition also falls *outside* of the trio.[52] It is impossible to convey, however, how beautifully Beethoven has bound together into such a luminously and gently appealing portrait the welling up of the deepest pity in Leonore, the anxious, cajoling pleas with which she besieges the old man to be allowed to give the bread that they have brought along to the poor prisoner, the old man's apprehensive resistance "That is impossible!" etc., the thankful emotion of Florestan over the pity that Rocco and the unknown youth have found for him, which is so profoundly expressed in the words: "You will be rewarded in a better world," and in the agitated cry: "Alas that I cannot reward you!" Here as well, as in the preceding pieces, nothing has been altered.

Rocco goes out and gives the signal, while Leonore calls out to her husband with yet another word of comfort. Pizarro enters in disguise and orders the young person (Fidelio) removed. There begins the fearful quartet in D major ("Er sterbe!"), which, as it were, expresses the struggle of virtue and a peaceful conscience with all the horror of death. In the entryway, where Pizarro announces himself as enemy and avenger with the fatal sword, the very difficult vocal part has been somewhat altered in the second arrangement to the advantage of the declamation;[53] otherwise, everything has remained unaltered. (At the words: "See here, you have not deceived me," A appears in place of F$\sharp$ in the Viennese keyboard reduction, probably due to a printing error.) Leonore, protecting Florestan, steps quickly forward with a pistol; the old man holds her back anxiously; Pizarro casts her aside with the cry: "Madman." She again steps between Florestan and the tyrant. The exclamation: "First kill his wife!" fills everyone with astonishment; fear and love drive her to despairing resistance; as the tyrant raves ever more violently, the instrumental storm rages ever faster; everything is in agitation and uproar. Then the trumpet signal resounds from the tower, which announces the arrival of the minister—a terrifying pause—and again the trumpet call.[54] Everyone looks around with wonder; Pizarro raves fruitlessly, Florestan and Leonore defy his fury, the old man is nearly overwhelmed with fear. Pizarro hurries frenziedly away. Terror has reached its highest level in this frightful night piece, and therefore a number of very harsh, dissonant chord progressions can be more easily justified. The German arrangement and Beethoven's music have the advantage here over the Italian in that Pizarro's storming in upon Florestan and Leonore's coming between them fall in the quartet itself and are described by the music, while there the quartet begins with Leonore's subsequent explanation that she is Florestan's wife.[55] We will forego further comparison, due to shortness of space.

Rocco hurries off after the governor, and on the way out he wrests the pistol from Leonore; Leonore sinks to the ground exhausted and unarmed. Florestan is restrained from coming to her aid by his chains. She finally recovers, as though from a bad dream, and every other feeling disappears in the ecstasy of recognition. This latter is incomparably expressed by the duet in G major that follows.[56] In the more recent arrangement, for no reason that we can perceive, the recitative in C major, in which Florestan summons his wife back to life, and Leonore's reawakening is described, and, further, how after a bad storm nature is calmed once again, has been left out.[57] Probably all of this is now spoken. We would rather have seen the earlier moments, which follow immediately after the scene of the quartet, set in melodrama or in recitative as well so that this recitative with its oboe solo would form the gradual transition from the quartet into the surging duet of the husband and wife. The high-rising theme, repeated by the instrument in the highest tones, the continuous rolling of the accompaniment, describe, vigorously and without extraneous ornamentation, the joy of recognition, and the mutual immersion of the faithful spouses in one another. Here the German arrangement once again has a significant advantage over the Italian, in which this situation was passed over fleetingly in recitative dialogue. The Italian arrangement, on the other hand, in order that Marcelline, who does not see her Fidelio return, and knows nothing about his gender, should not be entirely forgotten, allows her to enter the dungeon with a *key stolen* from her father. Leonore urges her to run to the minister to inform him that Florestan is still sitting here innocently confined, and assures her of her deepest love. This occurs in an affectionate duet.[58] The *German* arranger could not believe Leonore *capable* of this *deception* and could not endure the unpoetical insertion of this episode by means of which Leonore was only debased.

But the anxiety of a frightening departure returns. Then voices are heard from above (a short passage without instrumental accompaniment);[59] the crowd of people, with the minister at the head, streams in to the rescue. The orchestra accompanies this commotion in the older arrangement with a roaring passage.[60] Thereupon follows the short recitative of the minister, who, after the fall of the governor, allows Florestan to be released, and hereupon the inexpressibly beautiful song in F major: "O Gott, o welch' ein Augenblick!" The most blessed reassurance, the most comforting peace are breathed in these notes, which, blended in many ways through all the voices, rise up to heaven like a prayer from a full heart. The links of this passage and the entry of the chorus have a particularly beautiful effect. After a short dialogue in which Pizarro is led away and Marcelline, seeing Fidelio's transformation, accepts Jaquino's hand, there follows the splendid final chorus, which praises the wife's faithfulness: "Wer ein holdes Weib errungen,"[61] and so forth. The whole is treated as a rondo, the theme appears in manifold transformations—once even accompanied by a choral unison, the excitement increases, the rejoicing of the instruments becomes ever greater, and if it seemed earlier that the master had reached the highest level of power and effectiveness, he now rises at last up to a higher one, a heaven of pleasure and ecstasy seems to open up, blessed joy seems to climb down to earth, and life has fought through to the magnificent victory over death.

In the more recent arrangement, this call of the voices from above is not to be found; in place of the transitional music the duet is immediately followed by a march, which leads into the newly added chorus: "Heil sei dem Tag." This march seems to us, even when amplified by a crescendo, unbearably monotonous, and the chorus, in which an excerpt from the earlier march forms the principal idea, seems for Beethoven to be almost *poor*. Also, the musical connection in the Maestoso that follows, where Leonore and Florestan are brought forward, the minister has them released (the scene presumably takes place outside of the dungeon), and Pizarro's plan for Florestan is discovered, does not seem natural and fluent enough. This is particularly to be observed where the more recent arrangement goes back into the older one (shortly before the beautiful melody in F major, which has remained unchanged). In the concluding song as well, nothing has been altered.[62]

We would give preference to the earlier version here as well, but with the modification that after the acclamation the scene should change, and thereupon should come the chorus "Heil sei dem Tag!," and *all* sections from the duet on should be bound together into a whole by intervening recitatives, not simply in order to have a finale, though, for it should be done not to fit the customary style (there are indeed finales whose sections, although following immediately upon one another, are nevertheless not related, and have no *necessary* connection); but rather because the prosaic dialogue in between these pieces stands out all the more harshly the more deeply Beethoven enters into the situations and raises them above what is customary.

By the way, we certainly sympathize with Beethoven for the fact that, with this first operatic composition, he hit upon a subject whose theatrical arrangement, in order to be more generally effective, seemed to require, and still required, many poetic and therefore musical alterations, although, in thinking about what he has done with this material and has made out of it from a musical perspective, we must cry out with Schiller:

Let plastic arts breathe life, I demand spirit from the poet, but only *Polyhymnia* expresses the *soul!*[63]

NOTES

1. Wendt (1783–1836) was a philosophy professor at Leipzig and the author of a number of books on musical topics. Largely on the strength of this essay, he is considered one of the most important of Beethoven's contemporary critics. For more on Wendt and his contributions to the AMZ, see Wallace, *Beethoven's Critics*, 26–35, 57n. See entry no. 26, n. 1, vol. 1, p. 56.

2. In the *Critique of Judgment,* Kant had discussed music entirely in terms of mathematical relationships between notes, creating a model for aesthetic discussion that, in its stilted abstraction, is indeed remote from the reality of music as practiced. Kant also saw the appeal of music as limited to the pleasure provided by agreeable sounds. Many Romantic aestheticians, Wendt among them, sought to break away from this model by describing the effects of music in idealistic, rather than mathematical or functional, terms.

3. This recalls Hoffmann's famous statement that "Orpheus Lyra öffnete die Thore des Orcus." Whether Wendt was familiar with Hoffmann's writings is not known, but, given the frequency with which Hoffmann is quoted and paraphrased in these documents, it is quite likely that he was. Hoffmann's *Fantasiestücke in Callots Manier,* which contain the most familiar version of his Beethoven criticism, were recently published at the time Wendt wrote this article.

4. "We do not impugn hereby the other merits of this master, for example, the variegated, lyrical melodies, and speak in the above context only about the majority of his compositions."

5. Wendt's theories about musical painting have direct parallels in Beethoven's letters and conversations: Charles Neate recounted that Beethoven once told him that "I have always a picture in my mind when I am composing, and work up to it"; Ries reported that Beethoven often had some "special object" (einen bestimmten Gegenstand) in mind when composing; and Beethoven wrote on some sketches for the Pastoral Symphony that "all painting, if carried too far in instrumental music, is lost—; Even without description, one will recognize the whole *more as feeling than as tone-painting*" (see William Meredith, "Conceptions of the Creative Process," *The Sources for Beethoven's Piano Sonata in E Major, Opus 109* [Ph.D. diss., University of North Carolina, Chapel Hill, 1985], 514–24).

6. Wendt seems to have been one of the first writers to compare Beethoven to Shakespeare in this way, although the comparison would later become common enough. For Wendt, though, as the reader will soon observe, the comparison does not indicate unqualified admiration of either Beethoven or Shakespeare. Compare entry nos. 14, 45, and 49, in vol. 1, pp. 40, 106, 122.

7. "What a contrast between the wonderfully sweet, pensive melody to Goethe's 'Ich denke dein,' or the melancholy *Adelaide,* and the titanic battle in the so-called *Sinfonia eroica,* which is no mere fist fight!"

8. Johann Adam Hiller (1728–1804), a noted composer, also wrote several treatises on singing and one on the imitation of nature in music, published in 1754 (see the introductory essay in vol. 1, p. 5).

Johann Baptist Vanhal (1739–1813) was a Czech composer who was prominent in the musical life of Vienna, where he knew both Haydn and Mozart.

It is impossible to tell which member of the extensive Benda family Wendt is referring to. For details of their identities and relationship, see *New Grove,* 2: 462–66.

9. On the history of the clarinet during this period, see Albert Rice, "The Classical Clarinet, 1760 to 1820," *A History of the Clarinet to 1820* (Ph.D. diss., Claremont Graduate School, 1987), 241–307.

10. The author's claim is too vague to know which poetry he is referring to. When Klopstock's religious epic *Der Messias* appeared in the *Bremer Beiträge* in 1748, it was greeted by the Swiss critics as the symbol of literary rebirth. Goethe (1749–1832) and Schiller (1759–1805) also enjoyed much success with their early writings, Goethe achieving the status of a European celebrity. The early successes of all three led to long and stable careers; Klopstock in Copenhagen (1751–70), Goethe in Weimar (1775–1832), and Schiller in Jena (1785–1805). It is true, however, that after his long absence from the literary culture of Germany, Klopstock's later poetry showed little in common with changing tastes and was met with much indifference. Goethe and Schiller also became isolated from the growing popularity of trivial literature and the evolution of the Romantic movement during their ten-year period of literary collaboration (1795–1805).

11. The categories "natural music" and "art music" are direct reflections of Friedrich Schiller's concept of "naive" and "sentimental" poetry. See entry no. 6, vol. 1, p. 31 ("Something on Sentimental and Naive Music") for the earliest discussion of both concepts in music criticism.

12. In other words, in an operatic ensemble, where different characters may be simultaneously singing different texts, or different portions of the same text, the orchestral accompaniment must be kept to a minimum.

13. That is, "Ha! welch' ein Augenblick," in which the fullness of the orchestration does indeed make it difficult to understand the text.

14. In Greek and Roman mythology, Aphrodite, Venus, and the Graces (sister goddesses of beauty and charm: Aglaia, Thalia, and Euphrosyne) wore a cestus, or girdle, as a protection of virginity.

15. "One or two hymns of Beethoven, in our recollection, are guilty of this error, inasmuch as the harmony, which is rich in fantasy, rushes along with the text restlessly, and without clear development of a fundamental thought."

16. This refers to the familiar story of Daedalus's son, Icarus, who, carried away with the wings designed by his father, flew so close to the sun that the wax holding his wings together melted and he fell to his death.

17. On the many comparisons between Beethoven and Jean Paul, see entry no. 24, in vol. 1, p. 51.

18. "To prove what has been said, we need only refer to the earlier overture to *Fidelio*." It is not clear whether Wendt is referring to *Leonore* Overture No. 2, or to No. 3, which is the one he presumably heard at the performance in Leipzig.

19. Latin: "wondrous, wonderful to say."

20. Like the Leipzig correspondent who described this performance, Wendt was apparently also under the impression that *Fidelio* was first performed under the title *Leonore*. It is entirely possible that he is correct, though, in suggesting that the Theater-an-der-Wien preferred the title *Fidelio* because it helped distinguish Beethoven's opera from the familiar one by Paer.

21. Cherubini's *Lodoïska* was first performed at Paris in 1791. Basil Deane writes in *New Grove* that the libretto for this work "is in the popular tradition of the rescue opera, established by Grétry's *Richard Coeur-de-Lion* (1784), but the scope of the musical setting transforms a picturesque and anecdotal type into a genuinely heroic one. For Grétry's arias and simple duets Cherubini substituted a wealth of formal structures. His many ensembles serve to carry the action forward, and his dramatically evolving finales are comparable in size with those of Mozart (whose operas were virtually unknown in France at that date). Whereas Grétry's harmony and texture are elementary, Cherubini employed his harmonic resources dramatically, and gave the orchestra an important role; and while Grétry's approach precluded depth of character, Cherubini presented his characters with realism. *Lodoïska* opened up a new vista for opera composers by demonstrating that areas of human experience outside the restricted fields of historical or mythological grand opera and comic opera could be given serious treatment. In it Cherubini moved as far from the classical legends of Gluck as he did from the world of 18th-century comedy. In spite of its remote geographical setting, *Lodoïska* was relevant to the turbulent Revolutionary world; it set an example eagerly followed by such French composers as Étienne-Nicolas Mèhul and Jean-François Le Sueur and provided a model for Beethoven's *Fidelio*" (see *New Grove*, 4: 206, 210).

22. As indicated in the preceding entry, the founder of the Seconda Opera Troupe was Franz Seconda.

23. Wendt was presumably working from the keyboard reduction by Moscheles, published by Artaria in Vienna in 1814.

24. Again, all texts preserve original orthography. Generally, the orthography today is Marzelline.

25. The two canons were probably "Mir ist so wunderbar" and the imitative trio "Gut, Söhnchen, gut," which were nos. 3 and 4 in the 1806 version. The bass passages are presumably those in Pizarro's aria "Ha! welch ein Augenblick" and in the duet "Jetzt, Alter, jetzt hat es Eile," for Pizarro and Rocco, which were nos. 6 and 7.

26. As will become evident below, the second act in the performance heard by Wendt began with the march in B♭, written to introduce the aria "Ha! welch ein Augenblick." This was followed by the beginning of the original second-act finale (the first-act finale in 1806), which, like the first-act finale in the 1814 version, began with the prisoners' chorus "O welche Lust." At the conclusion of the chorus, Leonore's scene, "Ach brich noch nicht" and aria "Komm, Hoffnung" were interpolated in what must have been a rather jarring manner, given the key transition directly from B♭ major into E minor. The act then concluded with the remainder of the 1806 finale.

27. Missing from the 1814 version were two complete numbers from the original, the trio "Ein Mann ist bald genommen" for Marzelline, Jaquino, and Rocco (no. 3 in 1805) and the duet "Um in der Ehe froh zu leben" for Marzelline and Leonore (no. 10 in 1805). Various portions of other pieces were also altered or dropped, including most conspicuously the original conclusion of the "O welche Lust" finale, which was more focused on the principal action and provided a considerably more dynamic ending to the first part of the opera. Wendt's comments in the remainder of this paragraph reflect his dissatisfaction with the 1814 finale.

28. This is the piece now known as the overture to *Fidelio*. Since the performance Wendt heard was clearly adapted from the *Fidelio* of 1806, it is likely that the overture he heard was Leonore No. 3. It is impossible to confirm this, however, or to ascertain whether Wendt was familiar with Leonore No. 2, which seems to match the description given below more closely.

29. The text of Marzelline's corresponding aria in Paer's *Leonora* reads: "Ah! quel che per te sento / Potessi palesar? / Ma dirlo una Zitella / Non può che per metà. / Ah! venga quel momento, / E tutto ti dirà. / Oh quante cose belle / Con te ben mio sarà." See Willy Hess, *Das Fidelio-Buch,* 366, in the Italian libretto, p. 4.

30. "Jetzt, Schätzchen, jetzt sind wir allein!", no. 1 in the 1814 version.

31. If Hess's reconstruction is correct (Hess 1805, 80), the music at the end of the aria was restored to something resembling its original form in 1814. In 1806 (Hess 1806, 169), two measures were added to the conclusion and the original third measure from the end was altered rhythmically. This was apparently the way that Wendt heard the aria. The concluding line of the text originally read "Ja, ja, ich werde glücklich seyn" (Hess 1805, 80).

32. Actually, this is Breitkopf & Härtel.

33. As noted above, this trio was dropped from the 1814 revision. It was no. 3 in the hypothetical 1805 version (Hess 1805, 102–12) and no. 10 in that of 1806 (Hess 1806, 18–28). Kinsky-Halm, 177, also indicates that it was the ninth item included in the 1810 keyboard reduction.

34. "Marcelline's words 'Du darfst mir auch ins Auge schauen, der Liebe Macht ist auch nicht klein' disfigure the text."

35. From this and other statements by Wendt, it is evident that the performance he heard was arranged with a very free hand, and it did not resemble any of the published versions or hypothetical reconstructions. According to the latter, the duet "Um in der Ehe froh zu Leben" was no. 10 in 1805 (Hess 1805, 193–207) and no. 9 in 1806 (Hess 1806, 11–17).

36. The title of the aria is "Ha! welch ein Augenblick!"

37. The second complete measure in the original version of this aria was omitted in 1814. The seventeen (actually sixteen) added measures are mm. 88–103 of the revision; mm. 94–97 feature a sustained augmented triad C#–F–A.

38. As noted above, this placement of the march was unique to the version heard by Wendt.

39. As noted above, Leonore's scene and aria were apparently inserted directly into the first-act finale of the 1806 version in the performance Wendt heard. They would have followed m. 178 of Hess's 1806 version.

40. The corresponding scene in Paer's opera is act I, sc. 5, beginning with Leonora's words "Esecrabil Pizarro! dove vai?" (Hess, *Das Fidelio-Buch*, 373–74, in the Italian libretto, pp. 34 and 36).

41. The author's references to Beethoven's choices of keys reflect the common belief of the day that different keys signified different emotional qualities. Although there was not widespread agreement on the meanings of each key, E major was described by several Classical period authors as appropriate for the depiction of "noisy shouts of joy, laughing pleasure and not yet complete full delight"; "exalted heavenly life; women and their sweet passions"; and courage and strength. See Rita Steblin, *A History of Key Characteristics*, 252–54.

42. The orchestral introduction to "Komm, Hoffnung," which originally featured an elaborate bassoon passage and thirty-second-note runs in the first two horn parts, was shortened by five measures in the 1814 version (cf. Hess 1805, 209–10; in Hess 1806, this passage is retained, but Leonore interjects, "sprechend oder singend," the words "O Hoffnung, o komm! Hoffnung! O komm!" before the beginning of the aria proper). The vocally ornate passages beginning at mm. 39 and 57 of Hess's 1805 reconstruction were also shortened and rewritten. (Measures 49–52 and 66–67 of the 1814 version: an elaborate vocal cadenza at the last-mentioned point originally preceded the Allegro con brio, which began not in E but with a deceptive resolution to C major.)

43. In fact, in the version of Paer's Italian libretto published in Dresden in 1804 and reprinted in Hess, *Das Fidelio-Buch*, 372 (p. 35 of the German translation), the German translation of this scene begins with the words "Abscheulicher Pizarro! wo gehst du hin?— was denkst du?—was hast du vor?", which are strikingly reminiscent of the 1814 *Fidelio* text at this point.

44. This alteration, which is hardly small, involves the complete omission of the digression to C major described above—twenty-two measures of music in all—and the rewriting of much of Leonore's vocal line.

45. In Hess's reconstruction, the 1806 finale does continue in C major after the prisoner's chorus; the conclusion, however, is in B♭, the same key in which the entire finale began. (Compare Hess 1806, 29–36.)

46. Here the author is applying concepts of dramatic emotions that were at the focal point of all major theories of aesthetic tragedy in the eighteenth and nineteenth centuries: "fear" and "pity."

47. The Italian text of this scene, including the introductory and concluding recitatives, reads as follows: "Ciel! che profonda oscurità tiranna! / Qual eterno silenzio! o come io sono / Separato dal tutto, e in tal momento / Nell'Universo gia mi veggo solo! / Dunque il mortal mio duolo / Termine non avrà, nè'l mio soffrire? / Frà questi ceppi rei dovrò morire? / Per meritarmi un si fatal destino / Numi che fec'io mai? / Le trame disvelai / D'un tiranno, d'un mostro. / Ecco la colpa mia. Ah! quest'abisso / Non è de'mali miei certo'l maggiore. / E'tormento per me peggior di morte / L'esser privo di te dolce consorte. Dolce oggetto del mio amore / Io ti bacio e stringo al seno: / Tu sei vita a questa core, / Tu sostieni l'alma in me. / Deh quel ciglio rasserena / Cara Sposa e ti consola. / Sia conforte alla mia pena, / Che fedele io moro a te. / O Giustizia, mi reggi e mi difendi - / Ma—indebolir mi sento - / Io vacillo—l'orror—la fame—il freddo / Fan tutti intorpidire i sensi miei - / Vieni o morte—t'invoco—ti desio - / Termina tu pietosa—il viver mio" (see Hess, *Das Fidelio-Buch*, 380, in the Italian libretto, pp. 60 and 62).

48. The reference here is to the work of digging the grave.

49. There seems to be an unquestioned assumption that this scene was performed in melodrama in 1805 as well, although there was apparently no melodrama in the 1806 version, which was the basis of the version heard by Wendt. The original melodrama is one of the few passages in the opera that Hess was unable to reconstruct, even tentatively, from surviving sources of the 1805 *Fidelio*.

50. "In no. 51 of this year's *Morgenblatt*. This reviewer's further allegations have, we hope, been adequately touched upon at various points in this article. Only when he asserts that the ingenious composer has been misled by the abundance of ideas flowing forth from his rich spirit to pile these up in disproportionate abundance, so that *no thought is adequately worked out, and emerges in full clarity,* does one come to believe that the correspondent must either have measured this original work by the wrong standard (for example, that of a mediocre composer), or else was at least not *entirely*—present during a great portion of this opera, even during the last-named duet. Besides, not every piece can be worked out to the same degree—see, for example, Salieri's highly dramatic Axur" (*Axur, re d'Ormus,* first performed in Vienna on 8 January 1788).

51. The duet, in act II, sc. 2, of Paer's *Leonore,* begins with the words "Da bravo, via lesto; Si viene di gia," and contains the following words of Leonore: "O misera vittima, / Qualunque tu sia, / Salvarti pretendo / Da morte sì rià, / Giammai soffrirò / Che tanto delitto / Si compia, nò, nò!" (Hess, *Das Fidelio-Buch,* 381–82, in the Italian libretto, pp. 66 and 68).

52. The corresponding trio in act II, sc. 2, of Paer's *Leonora* begins with Florestan's words "Che l'eterna provvidenza vi profonda i doni suoi!" (Hess, *Das Fidelio-Buch,* 384, in the Italian libretto, p. 76).

53. Pizarro's line in the 1814 version is actually considerably more angular and difficult to sing than that in Hess's reconstruction of the 1805 version of this quartet, which was included in the version of 1806 with only minor revisions.

54. "Here is repeated the passage that appeared in the earlier overture, and that is therefore less effective in the more recent arrangement."

55. The corresponding quartet in Paer's *Leonora* begins with Leonore's words "Quell'orfanello abietto, che in me vi stà presente."

56. The title of the duet is "O namenlose Freude."

57. This passage, beginning with Florestan's words "Ich kann mich noch nicht fassen," appears in Hess 1805, 418–25, and Hess 1806, 65–71.

58. The text of this duet reads as follows: Marzelline: "Volentieri o mio carino, / Vado, corro a precipizio, / Ma dei farmi in pria il servizio / D'accertarmi del tuo cor." Leonore: "Ah mia cara, il tempo vola - / Tutto dirti or nor poss'io, / Và, se vuoi l'affetto mio, / Và, se brami un dolce amor" (Hess, *Das Fidelio-Buch,* 389, in the Italian libretto, p. 96).

It is somewhat hard to understand why this deception should be seen as any more reprehensible than those practiced earlier in the opera.

59. Hess 1806, 84, mm. 6–15. In Hess 1805, 454–56, this same choral passage, to the words "Zur Rache, zur Rache! Die Unschuld werde befreyt, Gott schützet die gerechte Sache und straft die Grausamkeit," is accompanied by three trombones.

60. Compare Hess 1805, 445–72, and Hess 1806, 83–98.

61. This line was lifted from Schiller's "An die Freude," which formed the basis for the choral movement of Symphony No. 9.

62. This statement is hardly accurate; all three versions show significant differences throughout this finale.

63. These lines are a quotation of Friedrich Schiller's epigram "Music," which appeared together with other epigrams in periodicals during the late 1790s. Polyhymnia was the muse for music.

$\sim$

241.

Clemens Brentano.[1] "First Performance of *Fidelio* by
Beethoven."[2] *Berlinische Nachrichten von Staats-
und gelehrten Sachen,* 124 (17 October 1815).

(Mentioned: *Wellingtons Sieg,* op. 91)

A terribly difficult opera; it is not at all to be brought off; the orchestra
is in despair because of the difficulties; the chorus members fall like flies
from overwork at the rehearsals. In Vienna as well, it is only given very
rarely; this work is the emptiest, most nonsensical bombast; it is a task for
young people to rehearse two such operas every year, and the conductor
must catch consumption from anger, and the violinists St. Vitus's Dance in
the fingers, and the wind players become paralyzed in at least one lobe of
their lungs, while the singers are turned over like gloves! So said everyone
who wanted to have connections, patrons, an ear at the rehearsals! I heard
many musicians say this as well! Oh, you cunning, good people! Without
much noise, without prior proclamation, for this is none of our business,[3]
Fidelio appears on the stage, the first opera by Beethoven in Berlin. The
house is rather empty; for those who are there, it is very empty, for these are
the admirers of the eccentric Beethoven, who was supposed to have created
such a shrike with this opera.[4] A few clever people are among the spectators;
they have come only to see the know-it-all Mr. Beethoven break his neck.
They repeat everything mentioned above. A new voice is raised; it must have
been one such as are to be found everywhere; it can be heard here and there:
I revere Beethoven, but the opera is very difficult, though splendid; but it
will fail, the whole orchestra and all the singers have spread the word to do
everything possible to make it fail.—Why?—From envy, nothing splendid
should arise.—So?—that would indeed be a terrible kind of spite. But quiet,
leave to us the lot of the beautiful upon the earth to fall beneath the hooves of
the bright, luminous Pegasus![5] Oh, you cunning, good people! How you have
astonished us! What joy you have given us! *Fidelio* is performed—masterfully
performed—our excellent Weber[6] conducted and held everything together
like a man of honor, like a friend of all genius. I do not like the theater, such
as it is in the world today—but today it cheered me to the core. Today I felt
what it is capable of when chance demands of it something magnificent, and
that something can avail itself of talent and the best intentions. The opera
may be difficult in instrumentation and melody and choral writing; this is
said of everything that here and there demands one exertion after another
from the performers, who have tended customarily to go clearly in only one
direction. It sounded, though, like it was easy; it made a noble, simple, grand

impression throughout; everything was understood and felt, and the terrible strangeness consisted mainly of the fact that this evening it was not cousin Michel who moved us, but rather, it often seemed to be the archangel Michael himself, and we all could understand him; he was not too high for us, he was just good enough for us. This is, however, the task and the triumph of art, that it makes the higher realms human; thus do the gods come down to earth, so that we can love them and are encouraged toward heaven. Thank you, good solitary one, Beethoven, solitary in yourself and among your notes, for your work. Thank you, gifted Weber, who honestly and capably wants the best, and all of you, you excellent artists; you have sent forth a multitude of hearts, who love the best, enchanted and moved. Even if the opera is difficult, you performing artists, then it has also become a great honor to you—a step forward, an elevated, ennobling pleasure connected with such work, oh then only yet more difficult; you undertake it truly and present it, all to the general exaltation. Mrs. Schultz[7] sang superbly throughout with beautiful passion; all others have done their part as honestly as possible according to their powers. The whole went splendidly, and will always go more splendidly. If I were the foremost of singers and had no role in such a magnificent work, I would join the chorus. In the good fight the most magnificent join the lowest ranks; this gives a victory, which glorifies everyone. In Beethoven's *Wellingtons Sieg,* the honorable Salieri brought joy by leading the chorus of French drums, Weigl that of the English, and all the virtuosos of Vienna made up the orchestra.[8] There is a greatness in art that, like blessedness, knows no rank. With this work a similar rumor was heard, but the sacred wave, the ebb and flow of genius carried them all blessedly along; all were one; there were no longer any artists, indeed no Beethoven, and the spirits that swam above the wave descended upon everyone. The work came alive; it was created and experienced. In this way alone is a work of art of the highest sort accomplished, for contrary to our business, a good portion of our business must be brought along.[9]

Next a few words about the second *Fidelio,* which always yet would be the first, without thereby making the first into the last.[10]

NOTES

1. Clemens Brentano (1778–1842), brother of one of Beethoven's greatest admirers, Bettina, ranks as one of the most famous poets of the German Romantic era. He was well acquainted with the leading philosophical, literary, and religious figures of his time, carried on significant correspondence with them, and was active in periodical publications; but among his most outstanding creations are his lyrical poems, which are alive with personal expressiveness, musical sound effects, and fresh and powerfully suggestive metaphorical imagery. He also wrote a number of articles and essays on contemporary music.

Brentano's greatest known expression of admiration for Beethoven is the famous poetic cycle *Nachklänge Beethovenscher Musik,* written on the occasion of the first performances of Beethoven's *Wellingtons Sieg oder Die Schlacht bei Vittoria* (see op. 91, vol. 3).

2. The first performance of *Fidelio* in Berlin took place on 11 October 1815. In the first performance, Josefine Schulze-Killitzky (1790–1880) played the role of Fidelio. In the second performance she was replaced by Anna Milder-Hauptmann (1785–1838); see the next entry.

3. The original text has "unser Verkehr," which refers to the noisy and boisterous, as well as anti-Semitic, performances by Karl Boromäus Alexander Sessa (1786–1813) and Ferdinand Alois Wurm (1783–1834) in the play *Unser Verkehr*. The enthusiastic public reception of Wurm's performances underscores Brentano's muted reference here to the "real business" of art. See also entry no. 246.

4. The German text has "Neuntöter" (literally ninekiller), which describes the ability of this type of shrike to imitate all possible calls of songbirds in order to capture prey, i.e., here, the audience!

5. Pegasus is the winged horse of ancient Greek legend, who, by striking his hoof upon Helicon, was able to drive the inspiring source of the muses, Hippocrene, up out of the earth. The image frequently serves as a metaphor for artistic inspiration.

6. Bernhard Anselm Weber (1764 or 1766–1821) was a prominent conductor of opera in Berlin from 1792. Although he composed several operas himself, he is credited in *New Grove* primarily for his interpretations of the music of other composers, particularly that of Gluck, whose operas he performed widely. As this citation makes clear, he also contributed to the dissemination of *Fidelio*. See AMZ 23 (1821): 255–60, for a biographical sketch of Weber.

7. Josefine Schulze was the married name of the hapless Miss Killitzky who bungled the performance of *Ah! perfido* at Beethoven's 1808 "Akademie." Many entries in the AMZ's correspondence section testify to her extremely successful later career, of which this performance was clearly one of the highlights.

8. Various witnesses testify that the orchestra at the first performance of *Wellingtons Sieg*, op. 91, consisted of some of the foremost Viennese musicians (see AMZ 16 [1814]: 70) and a number of distinguished visitors. Thayer-Forbes mentions Dragonetti, Meyerbeer, and Anton Romberg (p. 565) and quotes a notice in the WZ signed by Beethoven and naming Salieri, who "did not scruple to beat time for the drummers and salvos," as well as Spohr and Mayseder (p. 567). See vol. 3 in this series for several eyewitness descriptions of this performance, including an even more complete list of the participants.

9. Again, the reference is to the play *Unser Verkehr*.

10. The reference here is to a poem that Brentano was writing and that carries the title "Zweite Aufführung des *Fidelio* von Beethoven. An Frau Milder-Hauptmann in der Rolle des *Fidelio*." See the next entry.

~

242.

Clemens Brentano. "Second Performance of Beethoven's *Fidelio*. To Mrs. Milder-Hauptmann in the Role of Fidelio." *Berlinische Nachrichten von Staats- und gelehrten Sachen* 125 (19 October 1815).

If you have perhaps acknowledged life to be
A theatrical rehearsal, then triumph on the boards
Certainly seems feeble to you; above praise,
You must be satiated with the world's approval.
It doesn't help you, when the curtain of life is raised,
To have been called out here upon the stage;

Here called out, there called back in,
The peaks of one side are but steps on the other.

Therefore do not be angry; my praise does not concern you.
It may please or displease you.
Not what you did, but what God did through you,
That is what moved me so deeply; that to me was genuine.
Heaven knows that I am no devotee
Of the species of warbling actors;
To most of them I impute only blame,
In order to pay homage to the cultivation and grace of your genius.

Would bizarreness be the tyrannical Pizarro,
Who would keep Beethoven, the lord of more profound art,
Prisoner from us like Florestan?
No, routine and jealousy of theatrical favor
Have supplanted him, but not in vain
Did his sacred ardor break the old spell of song.
Springing to you from its chains and from the deafness of the masses,
They hear him singing *more tenderly*[1] as Fidelio.

To him who hears his song resound from a *tender* breast,
It is but a fountainhead of comfort, which springs from the prison wall
Of Time through the magic of the *tender* muse,
To whose thirst the hand of a *tender* angel presents
The beaker, so that he drinks notes blessedly,
I say blessedly, since on the brim
Of the goblet of sound he joyfully touches the spot,
Where the lips of *tender* grace toasted the fountainhead of comfort.

NOTE

1. The original has "milder," which is a word play on the name of the singer.

~

243.
"News. Berlin." *Allgemeine musikalische
Zeitung* 17 (15 November 1815): 771.

Fidelio, opera in two parts, from the French by F. Treitschke[1] with music by
Mr. v. Beethoven, was performed for the first time on 11 October, and since
then has been heard several times with steadily mounting applause. Since
various reports from Vienna, and then also a detailed review of this opera,

have already appeared in the *musikalische Zeitung*, I will content myself with announcing that it was performed here superbly, and also that no trace of the great difficulties involved in its execution was to be seen or felt in the extremely successful representation under the direction of our conductor Weber. Nearly every number was received with the loudest applause; the following, however, were most generally pleasing: the magnificent overture; Marzelline's (Miss Sebastiani[2]) aria: "O wär' ich schon mit dir vereint" etc.; the quartet for Marcelline, Leonore (Mrs. Schulz), Rocco (Mr. Wauer[3]), and Jaquino (Mr. Rebenstein[4]): "Mir ist so wunderbar" etc.; the trio for Rocco, Leonore, and Marcelline: "Gut, Söhnchen, gut" etc.; Pizarro's (Mr. Blume[5]) aria with chorus: "Ha, welch ein Augenblick" etc.; the duet for Pizarro and Rocco: "Jetzt, Alter, hat es Eile" etc.; Leonore's recitative and aria: "Abscheulicher, wo eilst du hin" etc., and the finale. Likewise in the second act, the trio for Florestan (Mr. Eunike[6]), Leonore and Rocco: "Euch werde Lohn in bessern Welten" etc.; the quartet for Pizarro, Florestan, Leonore, and Rocco: "Er sterbe, doch er soll erst wissen" etc.; the duet for Leonore and Florestan: "O namenlose Freude" etc., and the finale.

NOTES

1. Georg Friedrich Treitschke (1776–1842), stage manager of the Kärthnerthor-Theater, was engaged to make substantial changes in the text of *Fidelio* at the time of the 1814 revival. He was also director of the Hoftheater and wrote numerous operas (eighty-four) and *Singspiele* in addition to poetry.

2. The singer Constanze Sebastiani is mentioned several times in these reviews, but she cannot be further identified. Again, all original spellings are retained.

3. The lengthy career of Johann Gottfried Carl Wauer (1783–1857) is extensively documented in the AMZ. His "beautiful bass" voice is first described in AMZ 9 (1806–07): 340, and he later became particularly successful in the role of Leporello, one of his first performances of which is documented in AMZ 26 (1824): 695. He participated in the first performances of *Der Freischütz* and sang the role of Kühleborn at the first performance of E. T. A. Hoffmann's *Undine*. He continued to perform until 1852, when he celebrated the golden anniversary of his first appearance on the stage. See also Kutsch and Riemens, *Großes Sängerlexikon*, 3151.

4. The tenor Ludwig Rebenstein (1795[88?]-1834) began his career as an actor before beginning to cultivate his voice. In AMZ 11 (1808–09): 784, he is criticized for having too little voice and musical education. His acting ability is confirmed, however, in AMZ 14 (1812): 546–47, where his vocal training is attributed to A. W. Iffland of the Berlin opera. He later attained considerable success and also participated in the first performances of *Der Freischütz* under the composer's direction. He died at the height of his career. See also Kutsch and Riemens, *Großes Sängerlexikon*, 2419.

5. Heinrich Blume (1788–1856) is described by Fétis (*Biographie universelle*, 1, 449) as a "dramatic singer esteemed in Germany." His favorite role was that of Don Giovanni, which he frequently sang in conjunction with Wauer's Leporello. The AMZ (11 [1808–09]: 46) describes his first appearance in Berlin, when he sang Uthal in Méhul's opera of the same name; his singing was called very powerful, but not beautiful. He sang the roles of Huldbrant and Caspar, respectively, at the premieres of E. T. A. Hoffmann's *Undine* and of *Der Freischütz* by Carl Maria von Weber. See Kutsch and Riemens, *Großes Sängerlexikon*, 290–91.

6. The tenor Friedrich Eunicke (1764–1844) also participated, together with his wife, Therese Eunicke-Schwachhofer (1774–1849), and daughter, Johanna Eunicke (1800–56), in the first performance of Hoffmann's *Undine.* He was also known for his performances as Tamino in *Die Zauberflöte,* Belmonte in *Die Entführung aus dem Serail,* Don Ottavio in *Don Giovanni,* and Rinaldo in Gluck's *Armide.* See Kutsch and Riemens, *Großes Sängerlexikon,* 873–74.

≈

244.
"News. Berlin." *Allgemeine musikalische
Zeitung* 17 (13 December 1815): 839.

On 12 November the Royal Orchestra gave a concert for the benefit of the orphans in the Friedrichsstift, whose fathers have died for the fatherland.[1] Beethoven's *Fidelio* formed part of the content of this beautiful concert. The magnificent overture, the canon (performed by Mrs. Milder-Hauptmann, Miss Sebastiani, and Messrs. Rebenstein and Wauer), and the duet (by Mrs. Hauptmann and Mr. Eunike) were heard with great applause.

NOTE

1. The reference here is to the defeat of Napoleon at Waterloo.

≈

245.
"News. Vienna. Overview of the Month of December."
Allgemeine musikalische Zeitung 18 (31 January 1816): 75.

Hoftheater. A rheumatic ailment that befell our favorite, Wild, deprived us of the enjoyment of many hoped-for novelties. We saw, therefore, on the eleventh, a repetition of Beethoven's *Fidelio,* which was brought back upon the scene for the benefit of Mr. Radicchi. Mrs. Campi[1] had to replace Mrs. Milder-Hauptmann for us. As much as we treasure the rare artistic talent of the former, which is in a real sense nearly unique, and value it appropriately; as much as we thankfully acknowledge her praiseworthy efforts to abstain in this composition from all superfluous passages of bravura, and must openly admit that she accomplished everything that we were reasonably entitled to expect of her in this role in accordance with her individuality; she was nevertheless unable, even for a moment, to cause her predecessor to be forgotten. The rest of the cast was as before, and—almost inexplicably—the reception was very cold; the house itself was far from being half filled.

1. Antonia Campi, née Miklasiewicz (1773–1822; it is not clear whether she married or merely changed her name) was a Polish-born soprano of considerable renown who was resident in Vienna in the late 1810s and early 1820s. She was known particularly for her stunning virtuosity in the coloratura style, a fact that this critic recognizes in a backhanded way. She was known for her interpretation of the Queen of the Night in *Die Zauberflöte*, Donna Anna in *Don Giovanni,* and Constanze in *Die Entführung aus dem Serail.* See Kutsch and Riemens, *Großes Sängerlexikon,* 435–36.

∾

246.
Amadeus Wendt. "On a Few *Singspiele* at the Leipzig Theater." *Leipziger Kunstblatt für gebildete Kunstfreunde* 1 (1817–18): 332.

Along with the little *Singspiel: Die Junggesellenwirtsschaft,* which, translated from the French by Treitschke and staged with the very agreeable music of Gyrowetz[1] (it has also been given in several places under the name: *Das Frühstück der Junggesellen,* with music by Nic. Isouard[2]), entertained us highly this year through the comic power of Mr. Wurm[3] in the role of Freudental, and likewise the lively ensembles, particularly of Mr. Klengel[4] and the younger Miss Böhler,[5] we also rejoiced in repetitions of the *Schweizerfamilie*[6] and of *Sargino,*[7] and likewise of the newly rehearsed *Fidelio* of Beethoven, particularly in the guest performance of Mrs. Eberwein from the archducal theater at Weimar.[8]

The reviewer has formed the following opinion about this splendid artist in the course of her representations of Emmeline, Sophie, and Fidelio. Mrs. E. belongs among the most deserving female singers on the German stage. She certainly does not have a big voice, as the Italians say, no brilliant bravura, which in its floridness does not know how to maintain a proper proportion; her voice, which is pleasant, particularly in the middle range, is only of medium power and fullness, modest range, and a degree of skill appropriate to it, and she is therefore less suited for the big and colossal than for the average sort of affective song. This, however, she fills out with unique perfection. Her delivery is so perfectly suited to the emotionally gripping that even her voice (as we have particularly noticed in the most affect-filled pieces in *Fidelio,* for example, the quartet in the second act) seems to receive a growing and pervasive power simply from the feeling that she is expressing. With a prudent sensibility she even penetrates the spirit of the various compositions and individualizes her delivery according to their character, so that we were never once disturbed by a stylistic incongruity, nor, on the other hand, did we ever find the delivery to be empty. If this, and the intelligent confidence of her delivery, is a rare excellence for a German female singer, then the combination of expressive and practiced singing with intelligent acting in which an easy, pleasing deportment predominates is an even greater and rarer one on German stages, and it is pleasing to find performance and declamation conveyed with the same sensibility that the composer conveyed in his music. This is particularly true in *Fidelio,* where the artist's soulful acting, accompanying her singing, brought forth several deeply gripping moments (for example, when her long cherished wish to go down into the prison is granted, particularly in the expression of the words: "ich folge dir bis in den Tod," and in the dungeon scene). And this we call an excellent German female singer. The appreciation of our public was unfailing; it was demonstrated by the artist being called back three times.

As regards the further casting of the operas just mentioned, Mr. Weidner, as Jacob Friburg, showed himself in a more favorable light than previously, particularly in regard to his singing; likewise as Montigny in Sargino; as Jaquino, however, he lacked the easy, naive acting that distinguishes the younger Miss Böhler as Marzelline. Mr. Wurm, as Paul, had already made this role his own; Mr. Weyrstedt and Miss Mollard[9] (Emmeline's parents) were adequate. But on the whole, the opera *Sargino,* in which the artistic fervor of Mr. Klengel as Sargin particularly deserves due appreciation, was more perfectly cast. Mr. Siebert[10] displayed his voice splendidly as Knight Sargino and contributed to the polyphonic vocal pieces with great energy.— In *Fidelio,* apart from Mr. Klengel, who once again sang the part of Florestan with artistry and feeling, we saw all the remaining singers struggle with the greatness and difficulty of the music (particularly in regard to entries and the accuracy of intervals), but at the repetition many an error was improved, and in this regard we must praise such a difficult undertaking, particularly the diligence of the younger Miss Böhler. The orchestra played under the attentive and firm direction of Music Director Schneider with great fire; the chorus sang firmly, and many pieces came into their own upon repetition (for example, the terrifying, great duet while digging in the dungeon).

The author of this report has already expressed his judgment of Beethoven's music for this opera at length in the *Leipzig musikalische Zeitung* (nos. 20–26, 1815).[11] He is still persuaded that since Mozart's *Don Juan* no greater music has been written for the stage; but his opinion of Beethoven's second arrangement, which at that time was only provisionally expressed, has now been perfectly borne out by a twofold hearing, namely, that this music has gained in a few places, but has lost overall. In the older version, for example, the conclusion of the first act was simpler and yet more effective; the old overture was longer, to be sure, but more appropriate in character; an insignificant aria for Rocco has been added in place of an agreeable little trio; also, Florestan's aria was simpler and more appropriate to his situation, and the introduction to Fidelio's aria in the first act was also more singable.

The final conclusion took place in the prison, which was festively lit up by torches, and filled with joyous crowds of people when the rescuing cry came from above. The concluding sections were connected more loosely, but also more simply, and led more quickly to the conclusion; now Florestan is first dragged up into the light of day, then the scene changes, and a section that is somewhat unclear in performance has entered between. But the music still has an effect that gives great proof of its excellence: it gives to the subject matter, which in itself is monotonous and restricted, an uncommon interest, and raises the action with colossal power into the realm of fantasy.

NOTES

1. Adalbert Gyrowetz (1763–1850) was a Czech composer resident in Austria. His *Die Junggesellen-Wirtschaft* first appeared in 1807.

2. Nicolas Isouard (1775–1818) was a Maltese-French composer of a large number of operas. It is difficult to tell which of these is being referred to here, although it might be *Le Déjeûner des garçons* of 1805, cited in Robert Eitner, *Biographisch-bibliographisches Quellen-Lexikon der Musiker und Musikgelehrten der Christlichen Zeitrechnung bis zur Mitte des Neunzehnten Jahrhunderts* (Leipzig: Breitkopf & Härtel, 1900–04), 5, 253.

3. The comic talents of the tenor Ferdinand Alois Wurm (1783–1834) are attested to in the AMZ as well. He was one of the most popular comic characters in Berlin and did 100 performances of the play *Das Hausgesinde* in two years. However, he left the service of the Royal Theater in Berlin due to a criminal investigation for his comic portrayal of the Jew Jakob in *Unser Verkehr,* which resulted in his being sentenced to a year of confinement and to banishment (see AMZ 17 [1815]: 840). He found success in the same type of roles in Leipzig in 1817 and retired from the stage at thirty-four a very wealthy man.

4. August Gottlieb Klengel (1787-?) studied theology at Leipzig, then became a tenor at the Gewandhaus concerts. His voice was described by Fétis as having "a beautiful and powerful sonority," and he was noted for his acting ability. See Fétis, *Biographie universelle,* 5, 55.

5. Christine Böhler (1798–1860) is described in AMZ 20 (1818): 249 as "an agreeable, always welcome figure" and is particularly praised for her acting ability. See Kutsch and Riemens, *Großes Sängerlexikon,* 729–30. See also *Carl Maria von Weber: Writings on Music,* ed. John Warrack (Cambridge: Cambridge University Press, 1981), 365–66.

6. *Die Schweizerfamilie,* by Joseph Weigl (1766–1846), premiered in Vienna in 1809 and enjoyed widespread popularity.

7. *Sargino, ossia L'allievo dell'amore,* by Ferdinando Paer, premiered at Dresden in 1803.

8. Singer Henriette Hässler (1797–1849) was the wife of German composer Franz Carl Adalbert Eberwein. They were both members of Goethe's circle in Weimar. See Kutsch and Riemens, *Großes Sängerlexikon,* 818.

9. Georg Friedrich Engelhard Wehrstedt (1786–1841) was a distinguished bass who performed widely throughout Germany. The AMZ (20 [1818]: 249) (his name is here spelled Wehrstädt) credits him with a "resonant, sonorous bass voice" and praises him for the confidence and quality of his acting and diction. Here he is once again mentioned in connection with Miss Mollard, who "performs small vocal roles with diligence." See Kutsch and Riemens, *Großes Sängerlexikon,* 3161.

10. Franz Siebert, principal bass at the Prague opera, was apparently another singer/actor prized for his comic talents; AMZ 22 (1820): 336 recounts how, at a concert in

Vienna, he covered his face with his hat, held his nose, and hummed a set of variations in imitation of a bassoon. See also Warrack, *Carl Maria von Weber*, 383.

11. See entry no. 240 above.

~

247.
"News. Karlsruhe, in July." *Allgemeine musikalische Zeitung* 22 (25 October 1820): 729–30.

As concerns the opera *Cantemire* by concertmaster Fesca, it is very gratifying to us that such a favorable announcement about it has already appeared in these pages.[1] We can only confirm what the public has loudly and unanimously proclaimed; we count this music among the most beautiful manifestations of art in our time. It has the advantage over the opera *Fidelio,* the only one from more recent times that can be compared to it in terms of inspiration and depth, of a greater variety of emotions, from the serious and terrifying to the restful, friendly, and affectionate, as the picture is not drawn, as it is there, so somberly in black upon black. For all the stamp of originality, the composer has evidently not lost sight of Mozart's spirit, and may every more recent opera composer keep that genius firmly in sight in order not to stray from the true path! Mozart's name, along with Shakespeare's, will rise higher with the centuries, while many who are highly celebrated already see the brilliance of their empty fame extinguished during their lifetime.

NOTE

1. *Cantemire* by Friedrich Fesca was first performed at Karlsruhe on 27 April 1820. The article mentioned here was published in the correspondence section of the AMZ in the issue of 24 May 1820, 356–58, and describes that performance.

~

248.
"Concerts in Berlin." *Zeitung für Theater und Musik zur Unterhaltung gebildeter, unbefangener Leser: Eine Begleiterin des Freymüthigen* 1 (14 September 1821): 152.

The magnificent Symphony in E♭ Major by Mozart[1] and Beethoven's overture to *Fidelio* alone probably make up for a dozen of our favorite desultory evening conversations, and yet—an empty hall!

NOTE

1. This symphony is probably K. 543.

249.

"New Items. Imperial Royal Theater by the Kärtner-Thor."
*Allgemeine musikalische Zeitung mit besonderer Rücksicht auf
den österreichischen Kaiserstaat* 6 (9 Nov. 1822): 713–16.

Fidelio, the only opera that we have from our celebrated master *Ludwig van Beethoven*, has finally reappeared upon the stage after a long absence. The committee, which keeps an eye on German opera—which in our time is not exactly flourishing—has done it an exceptional service by reviving this distinguished work. It has made known to the public its regard for the celebrated composer and has satisfied the expectations of the friends of beautiful music. This is the third time that *Beethoven's* work has reappeared upon the stage, and we candidly acknowledge that the performances in which Mrs. *Milder*, Mr. *Weinmüller*, and Mr. *Vogel* undertook the principal parts were the most outstanding.

The great music, so distinguished by intensive beauties, musical richness, and particularly by beautiful instrumentation, will always excite the interest of all feeling people, particularly those who are musically educated, and therefore its success will be assured. It will give particularly great enjoyment, however, to those who, since the first or, even more, since the second performance, have learned to embrace the work with complete love, and have known how to familiarize themselves with all the beauties that it contains by getting to know the keyboard reduction published by Mr. *Artaria* and Co.[1]

All music that so distinguishes itself from the customary opera music through such deep content and such an artistic arrangement, and that all but deviates from the customary through such an artistic interweaving of the orchestral voices, through the audacity of the transitions and modulations, demands a truly exact familiarity in order to be valued in all its beauty.

One may imagine that the countless admirers of the great master, who marvel at the depth of his inventive spirit in his keyboard compositions, were present to marvel once again at the beauties of this work, which is well known to them, at a public performance.

Mr. *Forti* portrayed the commandant of the fortress, Miss *Schröder*[2] Fidelio, Mr. *Haizinger*[3] Florestan, Miss *Thekla Demmer*[4] the daughter of the dungeonmaster, Mr. *Zeltner*[5] her father, and Mr. *Rauscher*[6] the young prison assistant.

The role of Fidelio was given with a degree of skill that was certainly not unexpected from Miss Schröder, but that, in regard to the difficult role, was truly astonishing. For she not only performed this role, which is distinguished by much difficult intonation and rich figurations of the most noble style, with a beautiful, exuberant voice and exceptional precision, but she also knew how to impart to her acting such a degree of life that acting and singing seemed to be melted together into a beautiful unity, and the not easy task of portraying this character was solved by her in a truly satisfying way. The pure and sonorous high register of her voice was shown off exceptionally triumphantly in the second act, in the great duet,[7] and yet even more in the duet: "O namenlose Wonne!"[8] She also handled the finale of the first act in a truly excellent way. After Fidelio we must touch upon the role of the dungeon master, for its gripping importance demonstrates the attention that the composer paid to the first interpreter of this role and master of dramatic singing, Mr. *Weinmüller,* when this work first appeared. Mr. *Zeltner,* who once showed us quite unexpectedly his genuine suitability for the role of Richard in the *Schweizerfamilie,* and who could later only appear in various small roles, stood out in this role with truly exceptional power and skill. His voice showed itself to be exceptionally sonorous, and his precision and capability in performance found much opportunity to prove themselves.

The good nature of the old man and his conscientiousness in duty that we nevertheless continually observe give the character many fine shadings, which in regard to music demand a many-sided effort. Mr. *Zeltner* showed great fluency in dialogue and motion. He knew his role in all its individual parts. His singing was effective and yet by no means disturbed the necessary freedom of the principal characters by untimely impressions and appearances.

Mr. *Forti* portrayed the governor. Tone and bearing, aspect and gesture, speech and singing, everything was truly appropriate and in accordance with the character; the aria of the commandant, however, demands an exceptional power and depth in order to make the singing heard through the harmonic richness of the accompaniment, and Mr. *Forti* had scarcely recovered from an illness.

The scene in the dungeon was very excellently acted and sung by him.

Mr. *Haizinger* sang the role of Florestan with diligence and precision. We do not deny that many notes in the vocal part lie too deep for his uniquely formed instrument; however, he still knew how to conserve his sonorous power and distribute it appropriately. The aria of Florestan also demands much acting. Mr. *Haizinger* knew how to bring the most significant moments to the fore and particularly excelled in the duet with Fidelio before the close of the second act.

Great was the enthusiasm of the public for this beautiful piece of music, as well as for the canon in G in the first act. Both are masterpieces of musical invention. The beautiful, weighty chorus of prisoners moved every feeling person through its declamatory and musical solidity.

The choral singers and orchestra members felt completely the beauty of the moment, in which through able collaboration they were able to bring *Beethoven's* work closer to success. The beautiful, *splendidly arranged* duet—this expression can only astonish the uneducated—at the digging of the cistern likewise brought about a splendid effect with its intensive beauty. We will discuss the performances that followed in the next issue.

NOTES

1. Artaria published a keyboard reduction by Ignaz Moscheles in August of 1814. An alternative version without voice parts and text was also published.

2. Wilhelmine Schröder-Devrient (1804–60) became one of the foremost sopranos of her time and was particularly noted for her performances of the role of Leonore. Wagner, after hearing her sing the role in 1835, allegedly wrote to her that her performance had awakened in him his calling as an opera composer. She later was the first to sing the roles of Adriano in *Rienzi*, Senta in *The Flying Dutchman*, and Venus in *Tannhäuser*. See Kutsch and Riemens, *Großes Sängerlexikon*, 2670–72.

3. Anton Haizinger (also Haitzinger) (1796–1869) made his debut at the Theater-an-der-Wien in 1821 as Gianetto in Rossini's *La gazza ladra*. In 1823 he was the first to sing the role of Adolar in Weber's *Euryanthe*. He also sang the tenor part in the first performance of Beethoven's Ninth Symphony and of three numbers from the *Missa solemnis* at the famous Akademie of 7 May 1824. Fétis (*Biographie universelle*, 4, 203–04) recalls that he was associated with Schröder-Devrient in memorable Paris performances of *Fidelio*, *Euryanthe*, and *Oberon*. He later performed with her at Covent Garden as well. See Kutsch and Riemens, *Großes Sängerlexikon*, 1221–22.

4. Two Miss Demmers are mentioned repeatedly in the AMZ, Josephina, or Josepha, and Thekla, who later became Mrs. Kneisel.

5. Zeltner is also cited in the AMZ (18 [1816]: 730) for his performance of Narko in Cherubini's *Lodoïska* (see entry no. 240, n. 21 above), which was not well received. He continued to perform into the 1820s, but these *Fidelio* performances may have been the high point of his career.

6. The Viennese debut of Jakob Wilhelm Rauscher (1802-?) is noted in AMZ 23 (1821): 310f., where he is noted for his very successful performance as Ramiro in Isouard's *Cendrillon* (Nicolo's *Aschenbrödel*). He also participated in the first performance of Weber's *Euryanthe*. He later traveled widely and was still active in the 1840s as a court opera singer at Würtemberg. At this time, the AMZ's Hamburg correspondent said that, apart from the fact that Rauscher was well past his prime, he demonstrated his artistic accomplishments in such a way that his vocal weaknesses were forgotten (AMZ 49 [1847]: 567). This performance thus stands at the very beginning of what was to be a long and distinguished career. See Kutsch and Riemens, *Großes Sängerlexikon*, 2411.

7. Presumably "Nur hurtig fort."

8. The actual title is "O namenlose Freude."

≈

250.
"Overview of the History of the Imperial Royal Court Theater to the Year 1818; Particularly in Regard to Opera."[1]
Allgemeine musikalische Zeitung 24 (22 May 1822): 337.

Of the seven new operas we find only Beethoven's *Fidelio* worthy of mention: this work, which, even if it is less theatrical, is nevertheless splendid, with a richness of new ideas and heartfelt expression, attracting the knowledgeable friend of music ever anew; which also soon found acceptance at all good theaters in Germany and will long retain it.

NOTE

1. The section excerpted here describes the operas produced in the year 1814.

~

251.
"Diary of the Viennese Stage. November 1822." *Wiener allgemeine Theaterzeitung* 25 (9 November 1822): 539.

The third (*Burgtheater*)—*Kärntnerthor.* Beethoven's masterwork in the area of opera, unfortunately his only creation of this type, has once again appeared upon the scene, been studied with exertion and diligence, performed with the greatest success, and received with lively pleasure.[1] The administration of the Imperial Royal Court Opera Theater celebrated the blessed name day of her majesty the most merciful mother of our country[2] with a performance of *Beethoven's Fidelio* and began the presentation by singing with heartfelt sympathy the folk song "God save Franz,"[3] with the whole theater illuminated. The performance of the overture already showed with what zeal the study of this opera had been carried out. It made such a general and lively impression that its repetition was noisily demanded; the second time as well it was played with the same precision. The part of Fidelio was portrayed by Miss *Schröder* with such diligence, such exertion, such fire, that although we are accustomed to only the most vital and brilliant performances from her, she nevertheless surprised us. This young talent is on her best way to becoming a completely outstanding declamatory singer. Her voice increases daily in power, her delivery in accuracy and effect. It only remains for her, in order not to be hindered in any way from the perfect delivery of every declamatory vocal part, primarily to establish a uniform delivery of all her sounds and a similarly clear sounding of all her intervals, even in the faster notes. It cannot be said too much that Miss *Schröder* as Fidelio surpassed not only herself, but all the expectations of the public. The repetition of the duet gave proof of the power and endurance of the young singer in that she sang up to the last note extemporaneously with Mr. *Haizinger,* despite the monstrous exertion of the preceding quartet. Miss Schröder was unanimously called out at the end of the opera, and Mr. *Haizinger* appeared with her. This diligent singer portrayed the part of the imprisoned Florestan with all due attentiveness, and although his voice and manner of singing make him more suited to high bravura parts than to solemn and declamatory singing, he nevertheless played his part honorably, and particularly sang the above-mentioned duet with overpowering fire. The portrayal of the prison warden by Mr. *Zeltner* was admirable. This part is a test by fire for the singer; whoever, like Mr. *Zeltner,* is not led astray from the most beautiful and correct performance by the difficult intonation, has passed it with all honors. With regard to acting, as well, Mr. *Zeltner* distinguished himself to the greatest advantage. Mr. *Forti,* as the governor, sang the duet with Rocco, the prison warden, in the first act particularly beautifully; in the quartet in the dungeon he was barely audible. Miss *Demmer,* as Marzelline, and Mr. *Rauscher,* as Jaquino, held their own adequately, and contributed particularly to the beautiful performance of the magnificently canonic quartet in the first act; this caused so much pleasure that it had to be repeated. The choruses, too, were sung with all precision to general satisfaction.

NOTES

1. The opera was performed on 3 and 4 November, 2 and 17 December, and 3 and 18 March 1823. See Thayer-Forbes, 811–12.

2. This apparently refers to Caroline Augusta, Franz's fourth wife, as of 1816, according to C. A. Macartney, *The Hapsburg Empire* (New York: Macmillan, 1969), 212. In Catholic areas, the birth or baptism of an infant was frequently dedicated to the saint whose name was given to that day.

3. That is, "Gott erhalte Franz den Kaiser," Austria's national anthem, which is not actually a folk song but a composition of Joseph Haydn; the melody also appears in the second movement of his "Kaiser" Quartet, op. 76, no. 3.

∾

252.
"Opera." *Wiener Zeitschrift für Kunst, Literatur, Theater und Mode* 136 (12 November 1822): 1101–02.

At the Imperial Royal Court Theater at the Kärntnertor was performed the evening before the most exalted name day of her majesty the empress and queen: *Fidelio,* in two acts, from the French. Music by Ludwig von Beethoven. (Newly placed upon the scene.) Before the opera the festive song "Gott erhalte Franz den Kaiser!" was sung.

The administration of the united theater could have hit upon no more worthy choice than this one, through which a work valued by all admirers of German tone poetry was brought back into the repertory: a work that belongs among the classic manifestations of dramatic music in all ages. The mass of people were certainly blinded at first by the richness of the idea, the brilliance of the harmonic ornamentation, and the depth of the conception; but those who understand art, and those well acquainted with the powerful spirit of harmony, saw light and clarity everywhere and demonstrated it so conclusively that it has become light for everyone. Even if the melodic part of this composition does not make any great demands on the perfectibility of the throat, singing it is nevertheless no easy task since the energy of the expression and the power of the declamation have to be taken all the more into account. A stage that dares to produce such a work honorably will rightly be considered among the first in the nation. Admittedly, classic works of dramatic poetry are given relatively indiscriminately, but here there is another factor involved, and in the kingdom of music, particularly if a work like *Fidelio* is to be dared, there is less room for mediocrity than elsewhere.

In the overture a new world full of great and enticing phenomena already opens up; the brilliant genius of fantasy swims over the depths, agreeably ordering and uniting the grand images and forms, the abundant masses of harmony that intertwine with and cross one another. The orchestra affirmed its old reputation, and this first piece of music already had to be repeated, for the enthusiasm of the crowd cannot be restricted by any consideration of the difficulty of the performance; this difficulty only increases the enticement even more.

The singers at first seemed still to be constrained by a commendable lack of trust in their own powers, but, excited by the sympathy of the public, they soon acquired more and more confidence, and during the course of the production there gradually developed a caloric,[1] which, diffusing with quick growth, particularly in the second act, led to a true fire of enchantment. The performance of the four-voice canon in the first act, sung by Miss Schröder (Fidelio), Mr. Zeltner (Rocco), Miss Th. Demmer (Marzelline), and Mr. Rauscher (Jaquino), already made a favorable impression and was realized by the singers with a happy unanimity. The performance of the trio was somewhat more uncertain. Mr. Forti (Don Pizarro) was received with particular distinction; he brought about a powerful effect in his aria, without strain, and gave the demands of singing their due, here as always. The appearance of Miss Schröder as Fidelio in itself commended her, but the singer commended herself even more by the simply touching expression in the Adagio of the aria; the transitions in the Allegro were very clearly marked, and the sonorous elevation of her voice at the conclusion had an agreeable and gripping effect. The ever vigorous imagination of the tone poet seems to have taken a new, higher flight in the prisoners' chorus. The heart of the listener is not dejected by the expression of their sorrowful lament; it is affected much more by the spirit of faith and trust that prevails in these sounds of lament, by the nobility of feeling that prevails in it. The precision in the performance of the prisoners deserves loud recognition.

The second act, very rich in effects, begins with the aria of Florestan, which Mr. Haitzinger delivered very impressively, supported by the flexibility of his voice and the fortunate application of his extensive high register. The recitative seems to make the greatest demand on his diligence. Where declamatory expression is altogether necessary, the middle range still lacks substance. It was in this act that Miss Schröder, through the energy of her acting and singing, carried the sympathy of the gathering with her from step to step in moments that followed one another in quick succession. This vigorous effectiveness came particularly to the fore in the quartet and in the moment when Fidelio throws herself between Pizarro and Florestan in order to snatch the murder weapon from him. Overall, anxiously troubled love and agonizingly tense expectation were described with the language of ingenuous nature; if, therefore, the harmony of the singing sometimes succumbed to feelings intensified to the point of passion, the surprising power of the expression and the fire of the portrayal abundantly made up for that which was missed. The power, aroused to the point of passion, mounted from one scene to the next and seemed to spread its influence all around. The voice acted powerfully and effectively throughout with secure intonation, and at the same time the singer earned the praise due to an almost completely understandable enunciation of the text. One does not expect just to hear every single word, but here and there an indication of what is being spoken about in this and that significant moment. One's pleasure remains only imperfect when one hears only inarticulate sounds, and if, moreover, the same hindrance that gets in the way of the clarity of the text causes the notes to take on a variety of forms as well, then even the most excellent singing always suffers serious harm.

Mr. Nestroi[2] acquitted himself rather well in the person of Don Fernando. His voice still has a somewhat weak effect in polyphonic pieces. The duet between Leonore (Fidelio) and Florestan was repeated on demand. The tenor competed favorably with the soprano, who was more and more deeply excited by the rewarding success. The entire magnificent finale placed the listener in an enthusiastic frame of mind all the way to the conclusion, which was expressed by the two principal characters being called back out. Leonore appeared once again with Florestan upon the stage. The second performance was attended by the celebrated composer in a box in the first tier.

NOTES

1. A liquid substance whose presence was once believed to be the cause of heat.

2. Johann Nepomuk Eduard Ambrosius Nestroy (1801–62) is described in AMZ 24 (1822): 671 as "a treasured dilettante." Of his interpretation of Sarastro in *Die Zauberflöte*, the Viennese correspondent wrote, "he speaks correctly and his voice is sonorous, only not strong enough for this part in its lowest notes." AMZ 34 (1832): 387f. describes his role in creating *Der gefühlvolle Kerkermeister*, a parody of Cesare Pugni's ballet *Adelheit von Frankreich*, with music by Adolph Müller (1801–86). He wrote up to forty-one librettos for Müller and several for other composers, including parodies of Wagner's *Tannhäuser* and *Lohengrin* set to music by Carl Binder (1816–60), the former of which was revived at the Theater-an-der-Wien as recently as 1927. Another probable Wagner parody, *Der fliegende Holländer zu Fuß*, was set to music by Müller. See Kutsch and Riemens, *Großes Sängerlexikon*, 2094–95. Nestroy's librettos are partially cataloged in *The Mellen Opera Reference Index, Opera Librettists and Their Works, M–Z*, 546.

In spite of the judgment in AMZ, Nestroy's historical fame in Austrian culture rests on his unsurpassed contribution to the Viennese folk theater with his highly cherished works such as *Einen Jux will er machen* or *Das Haus der Temperamente*.

~

253.

"News. Vienna. Overview of the Month of
November. Kärthnerthor-Theater." *Allgemeine
musikalische Zeitung* 24 (25 December 1822): 837.

After all too long a rest, Beethoven's magnificent *Fidelio* once again arose,
radiant like Phöbus,[1] on our musical horizon, and the music committee deserves the most heartfelt thanks of all friends of art for this thoughtful choice,
which loudly proclaims the praiseworthy endeavor of bringing recognized
masterworks to performance to the enduring adornment of the repertory,
when, due to regrettable economic considerations, a private undertaking,
against inclination and better persuasion, is all too often required to pay
tribute to the degenerate contemporary taste. The representation of this
classic opera was in all parts appropriate, fast paced, full of life, and in
agreement with the spirit of the genuinely poetic tone poem. The role of
Fidelio is one of the most distinguished accomplishments of Miss Schröder;
Miss Thekla Demmer plays Marzelline charmingly; Messrs. Haizinger—
Florestan, Zeltner—Rocco, Nestroy—Don Fernando, Rauscher—Jaquino,
Forti—Pizarro—are praiseworthy with regard to singing and acting. Although the noisy instrumentation sometimes incommoded the last mentioned, his fiery performance was effective in the principal moments, and
the enchanted public loudly expressed its thanks for the beautiful artistic
enjoyment by not only rewarding each one with loud applause, but also
causing the overture, the canon, and the jubilant duet in the dungeon to
be repeated.

NOTE

1. "Phöbus," "the radiant one," was an epithet of Apollo in Greek mythology.

~

254.

Fz. "Theater in Berlin. 15 June: 'Fidelio,' Opera in
Two Acts, Music by Beethoven." *Zeitung für Theater,
Musik und bildende Künste* 3 (21 June 1823): 97–98.

(Mentioned: "Adelaide," op. 46)

However indisputable it may be, that *Beethoven's* music opens up the kingdom of the gigantic and immeasurable, that it moves the lever of fear, of
terror, of horror, of pain, and awakens just that endless longing that is the
essence of romanticism; it is not therefore any less true that these powers

can be preeminently ascribed only to his instrumental music, and that he has always been less successful with vocal music, perhaps because it does not permit the character of indefinite longing.[1] Despite the grandiose and ingenious conception of the subject, the accurate description of the various characters and affects, the voices still remain all too subordinate, nearly making a mockery of all singing in comparison to the orchestra, to which all of the brilliant highlights of the composition have been given. It is to be regretted that such beautiful, splendid voices must work themselves flat and tired in the struggle against every type of string and wind instrument without emerging independent and predominant a single time. How gladly one would wish, moreover, for various of the rhapsodically interjected ideas to be worked out and further extended, and that it had pleased Beethoven generally in the genre of dramatic music to be, for once, less *Beethoven* than to be his own *Fidelio*—as he has indeed, in his smaller vocal pieces, for example, in *Adelaide,* proceeded from his own individuality with such beautiful success!

In the performance of the opera in general, one could certainly hear that it had taken a long rest and had just arisen from sleep for the first time. Many specifics were nevertheless highly exquisite, above all Mrs. *Milder* as Fidelio. We must mention, however, a bad habit of the esteemed artist, and assuredly with the very well-intentioned plea that she may give it up just as soon as possible, since it is so disturbing in her singing, and it often touches us as with an ice-cold hand at the most beautiful moments. It is, namely, a frequent, unbearably loud coughing and throat-clearing, always repeated during the rests, which we at first took to be an effect of the winter cold, but which now appears to be continually necessary to the singer in order to purify her instrument and gather up new powers for that which follows. Mrs. *Milder* perhaps does not know what a negative impression this bad habit makes on the listeners, and after we have hereby made her attentive to it, we believe confidently that she will take the well-intentioned pauses to heart, and from now on will not further sour the pleasure that her singing imparts to us with melismas and fermatas of this kind, which are not to be met with in any singing school. Mr. *Stümer*[2] partially lacks the power needed for the part of Florestan, and replacing him with Mr. *Bader*[3] would be to the advantage of the opera. Several of the higher notes of each singer seemed to us after some time to be strikingly rough and hoarse, and operas like *Fidelio* are not designed to help a voice out. If we disregard his out-of-tune singing, Mr. *Wauer* played the part of the dungeon master with steadiness of voice and with praiseworthy acting, and Mr. *Blume* played the villain Pizarro very impressively and accurately without awakening the aversion of the spectators more than is necessary for this character. It was up to us to make the agreeable observation that the directorship had finally cast the part of Marzelline differently, namely with Miss Leist,[4] and, what is more, surprised us very much, since—horribile dictu![5]—Constanze Sebastiani was named on the program. This circumstance had almost frightened us away from visiting the opera. Miss Leist performed her by no means easy task very happily and for the first time showed, particularly in the ensembles, such confidence that we would very much like to recommend her above both of our budding female singers, who every time roll the stone of Sisyphus in a genuine pleasure game, fattened with bravura arias, though without turning an eye toward the conductor, and have truly practiced their diverse little treasures, to which almost alone their entire artistic accomplishments are confined, more than a hundred times previously. The chorus of prisoners went very well and was also applauded; the final chorus, however, limped a bit. Mr. *Devrient* the younger[6] lacked any kind of suitable appearance for the little part of the minister, and his singing in no way compensated for this lack. Our splendid *Beschort*[7] should not have given up the role.

NOTES

1. Obviously, the writer is paraphrasing E. T. A. Hoffmann. See entry no. 206.

2. Heinrich Stümer (1789–1856) is described in AMZ 13 (1808–09): 59 as having a beautiful voice, trained by the Italian composer and teacher Vincenzo Righini. The AMZ (13 [1811]: 655–56) mentions his vocal purity and facile passagework, but says that his voice is rather weak and can barely be understood in polyphonic pieces. Stümer spent virtually his entire lengthy career in Berlin; among its high points were his appearances as Max in the first performance of *Der Freischütz* and as the Evangelist in Mendelssohn's famous 1829 revival of Bach's *St. Matthew Passion*, mentioned in AMZ 31 (1829): 258. His wide repertory also included major roles by Gluck and Rossini. See also Kutsch and Riemens, *Großes Sängerlexikon*, 2878–79.

3. Carl Adam Bader (1789–1870) is described by Fétis (*Biographie universelle*, 1, 213) as "one of the best tenors in Germany," although "the partisans of Italian music disputed his title of singer, and claimed that he only deserved success for his acting." In view of the weakness of Stümer's voice described in the previous footnote, it is understandable that this writer would have preferred the more accomplished Bader in the role of Florestan. See also Kutsch and Riemens, *Großes Sängerlexikon*, 127–28.

4. This singer is first mentioned in the AMZ (17 [1815]: 772) for her performance as Josabeth in Poissl's *Athalia*. The Berlin correspondent in AMZ 19 (1817): 260 praises her in enthusiastic terms, saying that her acting is never bad and is often warm and thoughtful, her voice is pure and agreeable, but that her performance is marred by her evident nervousness. This writer had obviously noted this problem as well, since he praises her here for overcoming it.

5. Latin: "horrible to say."

6. Eduard Philipp Devrient (1801–77) was the younger brother of Wilhelmine Schröder-Devrient's husband Karl Devrient. He was a student of Carl Friedrich Zelter and a friend of Mendelssohn and was better known as a theater historian than as a singer. See Kutsch and Riemens, *Großes Sängerlexikon*, 729–30.

7. Jonas Friedrich Beschort (1767–1846) was one of the many singers from this period who also performed with equal success on the nonmusical stage. As an opera singer, he was known for his interpretations of Don Giovanni and of Orestes in Gluck's *Iphigenia in Tauris*. It is not clear if he did sing the role of Don Fernando at an earlier performance of *Fidelio* or if the writer simply wished that he had sung it on this occasion. See Kutsch and Riemens, *Großes Sängerlexikon*, 247–48.

~

255.

Fz. "22 July: *Fidelio,* Opera by L. v. Beethoven." *Zeitung
für Theater, Musik und bildende Künste* 3 (28 July 1823): 118.

Miss Schröder, from the Royal Court Theater at Dresden, concluded her guest appearance upon our stage as Fidelio. Whoever did not yet know until now what this part truly is, and what can be made of it when singing and acting are united in comparable splendor, must have had this made clear today. The young artist celebrated a triumph such as we have not frequently experienced, although we have seen much that was successful and magnificent in the area of music and drama. The deeply felt, sincere and unassuming, youthfully fresh, abundantly flowing life of her singing, which further distinguishes itself through a variegated, silvery pure intonation, and the gripping moment when Leonore, daring the ultimate in order to rescue her dear husband, holds off the raging governor with a pistol, inflamed every soul. The spirit of unity, unanimity, and context that dwelled in her entire performance, and in which the true inner calling, the true divine spark, can be recognized, spoke for the future mastery of the singer, which she will truly achieve as soon as she becomes less of a beginner in regard to theatrical deportment and becomes yet more at home upon the stage. Miss Schröder is certainly an outstanding figure among female singers; such a distinguished mimic talent is seldom found together with such singing abilities as this foreigner possesses. May she then step forward on the praiseworthy path of cultivating both equally, an effort that will be all the more rewarding in our time, when most female singers entirely neglect their acting in their struggling and striving for gigantic vocal bravura, because of which (while opera has become mostly a concert, in which the scenery serves only incidentally as a means to this end) so many older *Singspiele,* which proceed from that good old epoch when the singer had to be an actor as well, can no longer please. Miss Schröder was called out at the conclusion of the opera; this distinction, when it still truly is one, could not easily be more deservedly bestowed upon anyone. We say nothing further about the performance of *Fidelio;* on the whole, it was comparable to the one that we reported on in no. 25 of the *Theaterzeitung.*[1] We were not at that time entirely satisfied with Mr. Stümer's (Fernando) singing and acting.[2] Today, however, the artist pleased us entirely, and particularly in the beautiful duet: "O namenlose Freude," where, warmed and carried away by the fire of his fellow performers, he accomplished something very superior. Mr. Gern[3] played the minister in place of Mr. Devrient.

NOTES

1. See entry no. 251.

2. Mr. Stümer actually played the role of Florestan.

3. This is probably Albert Leopold Gern (1789–1869), the son of the well-known bass Georg Gern (1757–1830), who was probably no longer performing at the time this was written. The younger Gern, who also had a bass voice, is described in AMZ 25 (1823): 767 as a comic actor, and he is mentioned several times in this capacity in the 1820s. See AMZ 32 (1830): 250–51; Kutsch and Riemens, *Großes Sängerlexikon*, 1077–78; Fétis (*Biographie universelle*, 3, 463) incorrectly describes the two Gerns as brothers.

~

256.
"News. Dresden, from April to the End of June." *Allgemeine musikalische Zeitung* 25 (13 August 1823): 526.

New productions at the German opera included: *Fidelio,* opera by L. v. Beethoven (3).[1] It was cast as follows: Fidelio, Miss Schröder.—Marzelline, Mrs. Haase.[2]—Don Pizarro, Mr. Sibert.[3]—Rocco, Mr. Keller.[4]—Jaquino, Mr. Wilhelmi.[5] We owe great thanks to Miss Schröder, who is now the foremost female singer in our German opera, for having at least given cause for this magnificent opera finally to be heard here once also. This magnificent work, full of power and character, and richly, very richly scored, will admittedly not please the great masses as much as do many superficial, fashionable compositions; but it will long outlive these. The role of Fidelio seems entirely suited to Miss Schröder, who in her acting and singing inclines primarily to the heroic and tragic; she played it with all the fire, power, and expression of her beautiful, youthfully fresh voice, so as to cause us to wish all the more that she would see fit to moderate her power more and learn to use her voice better. But this adjustment will probably be made in due time. She was called out unanimously at the conclusion of the opera. It scarcely needs to be observed that, in addition, the orchestra performed this rather difficult music splendidly. We can only wish that in the future the very long final song could be somewhat shortened.

NOTES

1. This apparently indicates that the opera was performed three times.

2. In AMZ 28 (1826): 704, the premature death of Mrs. Haase on 30 July 1826 is lamented as "a genuine loss for our stage, for seldom will so much grace and loveliness be found united with a beautiful voice."

3. This is probably the same Franz Siebert whose unusual mimic talents are described above in n. 10 of entry no. 246.

4. AMZ 14 (1812): 256–57, describes Keller as "one of the foremost tenors [*sic*] in all the German theaters of today." He seems to have been known mostly for comic roles, and in AMZ 15 (1813): 269, his character acting is singled out for praise. When he first sang in Vienna, AMZ (22 [1820]: 671) noted that he came from Breslau, and that a significant reputation preceded him. From then on, virtually every time he is mentioned he is singled

out for extraordinary praise; Leporello seems to have been one of the few roles he did not do well, although he did better as Bartolo in *The Barber of Seville*. His appearance as Rocco was consistent with the sort of roles he seems to have preferred.

5. Wilhelmi is described in AMZ (16 [1814]: 666) as having a beautiful voice that deserves to be more diligently cultivated; his acting ability is described in more positive terms. Bad reviews predominate, however, in later issues, with occasional good ones indicating that he may have taken some of the criticisms to heart (e.g., AMZ 20 [1818]: 472). Jaquino may have been his last role, since he is not mentioned again in the AMZ.

~

257.
S . . . i "Beethoven." *Morgenblatt für gebildete Stände* 17, no. 265 (5 November 1823): 1057–58.

(Mentioned: *Missa solemnis,* op. 123)

Ludwig von Beethoven belongs among those men whom not only Vienna and Germany, but Europe and our entire age revere. With Mozart and Haydn he makes up the unequalled triumvirate of more recent music. The ingenious depth, the constant originality, the ideal in his compositions that flows from a great soul assures him, despite Italian clangor and modern charlatanism, of the recognition of every true admirer of the divine Polyhymnia. Nothing about his works here, only about his personality![1]

He has recently finished a mass, which he is publishing by subscription. Apart from his imperial highness and eminence, the Archduke Rudolf, Ludwig XVIII subscribed as well. A symphony, quartets, a biblical oratorio, sent to him by the American consul in the English language from the United States, and perhaps also an opera (poetry by Grillparzer) are yet to be expected.[2]

NOTES

1. In accord with the principles of selection as stated in the preface, a section of personal anecdotes has been omitted. Although *Fidelio* is not explicitly mentioned, this article was written in response to a performance of the opera.

2. The list of works in progress is remarkably accurate, suggesting that the report came from someone close to Beethoven. The Ninth Symphony would be premiered on 7 May 1824. Prince Galitzin had requested "one, two or three new quartets" in November 1822, and Beethoven had agreed to write them in January 1823 (the first was not actually completed, however, until February 1825). Beethoven had received the libretto of the oratorio *Der Sieg des Kreuzes* (The Victory of the Cross) in October 1823; the work was commissioned by the Gesellschaft der Musikfreunde in Vienna in 1819, and Beethoven was thinking of using it also for the commission from the Handel and Haydn Society in Boston. In February 1823, Beethoven got in touch with Grillparzer to ask him for a libretto; Grillparzer had two different stories in mind initially (*Drahomira* or *Melusine*), but *Drahomira* was rejected because Grillparzer "did not want to give Beethoven the opportunity to step closer to the extreme limits of music . . . in partnership with material that was semi-diabolical." On the Boston commission, see Otto Kinkeldey, "Beginnings

of Beethoven in America," *Musical Quarterly* 13 (1927): 220–21. On the history of the Grillparzer collaboration, see Thayer-Forbes, 842–46.

~

258.

Ludwig Rellstab. "From the Estate of a Young Artist. A Musical Sketch. Excerpts from Edmund's Diary." *Cäcilia* 4 (1826): installment 13, 5–8.[1]

It should be a happy omen for me that the first day of my stay offered me a joy of which I would not for my life have deprived myself. As I walked in the gate, my glance fell upon a placard. I read: *Fidelio* for the evening. People may have taken me for an idiot, with such consternation did they look at me (for I certainly do not know what I did in my joy). I thought: let them be astonished, how can it hurt you? With what feeling did I sit before the curtain until the first stroke of the overture began!

The entire opera often seems like a wonder to me. It seems to me as though a person has created it who struggles longingly for a strange something, for a heavenly beauty, whose existence he only suspects, but cannot capture it. In the moment that he grasps it, it disappears, and he strives and exerts himself anew. Then he sinks back and allows himself, in apathetic despair, to be satisfied with the worldly, of which he is lord. But suddenly the hand of the heavenly vision offers itself of its own accord and proclaims itself to him in sounds coming down from above, which he wonderingly perceives and longingly records. A musical revelation lies therein. Is there not a legend about a painter who had to paint a portrait of mother Mary and sought the form in vain within himself, which would express the holy nature? One night, as he broods sleeplessly over his task, a shimmer of light from his studio suddenly penetrates his eyes. He rises from his bed, goes over, and quietly opens the door. A stranger is sitting at the easel, diligently painting at his portrait. Full of wonder, the artist approaches and looks over the shoulder of the working one; and behold, the portrait, which he has sought for so long within himself, is being painted by him in vivid colors upon the canvas. Then he wishes to address the stranger, opens his lips and awakes, blinded by the rays of the morning sun. Now, still glowing from the sight of the vision, he hurries to the easel and completes his work to his satisfaction. So do individual passages in *Fidelio* appear to me, namely two duets, perhaps the most elevated that there are of this type. The first, where Leonore must prepare the grave, the other where she, her dearly won husband at her heart, breaks out into the weeping jubilation of rapture. When the terrifying introduction of the first duet begins, when the dark figure murmurs in between in the bass, like the hollowly resounding earth falling upon a coffin, we are seized by an oppression that even holds back tears. But, as Leonore strikes the inmost depths of our hearts in the heavenly sweet melody with the words: "You should not have to lament," the stream of tears then breaks forth warmly and consolingly. And when she further exclaims more loudly, "By God! I will rescue him! I will break his chains!" and the sublime trumpet calls sound in between, like the rejoicing over certain victory, who then might still doubt that the great woman will accomplish the feat? In these measures the outcome of the opera lies as necessary as any conclusion ordained by heaven. If her feat were capable of failure, these words would not have been given in this way. Such confidence, such tenacity, such audacity in the consciousness of the right are never, ever wrong! We ourselves, with everything that we undertake in God, have in our breast a voice that tells us whether we are called to accomplish greatness, or to fall as a sacrifice to it. Leonore must triumph. Whoever still doubts this point does not understand a note of the sublime work.

I had a marvelous proof of the truth of my emotions. My glance had already rested several times upon the figure of a young maiden who sat in a box not far from me with an expression of the deepest, innermost attention. At every gripping passage I turned toward her; she was to me like a confidante to whom I could impart my bliss. More than once I was disappointed in my expectation. At this duet, however, it was as though, by means of the notes, we were being led by a higher power. At the moment when Leonore's "You should not have to lament" resounded, when I felt as though tears were irresistibly arising in my eyes, she too was overcome and placed her hand over her big, gentle eyes in order to hide the tears that she could not restrain. My glance went up to her face. At the first blow of the trumpet upon the powerful C a blush of joy flowed into her pale cheeks, and her eye blinked through the half-extinguished tears with luminous joy, as though she wanted to say: "God be thanked! now it is overcome, he is saved!"—Truly this unknown woman has a gentle and beautiful soul. And now, you song of rejoicing among the tears, you wondrous greeting of bliss from beyond. "O namen-namenlose Freude!" Quiet! My heart is breaking in the quivering urgency of bliss, in the storm of delight!

NOTE

1. These excerpts come from a lengthy (42 pp.), novella-like contribution by Rellstab, which he claims to have compiled from papers left behind by the now-deceased, orphaned son of a pastor. Brought up to love the arts, "Edmund" was turned over to the care of a harsh and unsympathetic uncle at the age of eleven after the death of his parents. Whether or not he has any basis in fact, Edmund certainly exhibits the impressionable, emotional nature typical of German Romantic heroes. The passage translated here describes Edward's arrival at the town of "L." after leaving home.

259.
"News about Music in Munich's Royal Court
and National Theater. 17 October." *Münchener
allgemeine Musikzeitung* 6 (10 November 1827): 94–96.

It is well known that this opera exists in a double arrangement by the same master, and under two different titles. In the first arrangement it was called *Leonore,* was divided into three acts, had a different overture, and as it was longer overall, it also seems to be differently put together in the arrangement in which it was performed here. There is not room here to undertake inquiries into the unique qualities of each of these arrangements, but in regard to music, we have undeniably lost more with the first than is gained with the second, or could be gained. Who can forego the overture to the first arrangement without regret? and the beautiful trio: "Ein Mann ist bald genommen etc." The first overture was, it is true, if we apply the customary standards—but is there really one for Beethoven, other than that which he sets himself?—too long, and intricately involved; but surely more in the character of the whole work than the new one, which certainly could not arise from it as it should, like the first one does, or the one to *Don Juan*[1] (See Hoffmann's *Fantasiestücke,* vol. 1, p. 85).[2] But, things not being different, we can therefore only thankfully rejoice at what has nevertheless remained to us: an elevated work of musical art of the German school, whose immortal substance is inspired with all the feeling that dwells within him, with his language itself for ideas. Here, as in his instrumental compositions, the great master has shown that he rules omnipotently over all the magical devices in the kingdom of notes. As though from an inexhaustible spring, his heavenly genius brings to life idea after idea, ever new and more and more beautiful, and surely it is not his fault if we are not able to grasp all the genuine brilliance, all the loftiness and once again endless depth.

As difficult as it is for the reviewer, he can yet just as little conceal that the above must be asserted today, for the entire conception and performance of this weighty work has never seemed to him so unsuccessful as it did today. Even the overture was anything but well performed by the otherwise so distinguished orchestra. With few exceptions, *Beethoven* has seldom written for the voice with great skill and success; his home ground was instrumental composition, and very naturally so. Here, in our skillful times, there are no constraining fetters, here genius can rule freely, raising itself up into the highest regions with the wings of an eagle, without asking whether an e or an i in the words of the texts coincides with the highest obtainable height. Here it is not necessary to ask whether musical and word accents fall together, and so forth. Thus, the orchestra part in *Fidelio* is by no means only a supporting, accentuating accompaniment; it is at least coordinated with the voice and therefore demands throughout just as careful, refined application of nuance as though it were a solo part. Today, however, not a trace of this was to be found; indeed, the orchestra was not even discreet. We need only recall specifically the often entirely unabashed horns, the trombones, which were several times entirely incorrect, and regret these failings all the more since they could easily have been avoided by a careful, diligent effort. Such works demand study, and *one* indifferent rehearsal cannot suffice even with the most distinguished orchestra. How little Beethoven's intention is generally understood is shown, for example, by the performance of the magnificent prisoners' chorus "O welche Lust, etc.," at the beginning of the finale of the first act. The whole situation and just as strongly the whole incomparable composition expressly call for a continuous piano from the singers, and at the same time for an articulation just as subdued, which rises only to a more lively, but never fiery, expression. Therefore the composer has indeed chosen only a limited range, no jubilant heights, no fast motion, but rather long, simple notes. When, however, this chorus is also taken and presented according to its significance, then the effect is extraordinary. The reviewer, at least, who has often heard *Fidelio* very magnificently performed in Berlin, believes that no music, no situation in any other opera, is capable of exciting such deep emotion, such painful sympathy, as this. Not so here; the tempo was too fast, and "O welche Lust" was sung just like "O welche Lust, etc."[3] We cannot let it go without mention that the simply beautiful choral solo: "Wir wollen mit Vertrauen etc." was performed simply but purely and with feeling by a very good tenor voice, since all too often small secondary parts of this sort are treated entirely too lightly when given to singers of the first rank; for this reason, the part of the minister could have been put into other hands today as well. If, under such circumstances, *Fidelio* does not please, or at least has only a small audience, it is no wonder, even if it were possible for the parts of *Fidelio, Florestan, and Rocco* to be even better cast than they were today with Miss *Schechner*[4] and Messrs. *Löhle*[5] and *Staudacher*.[6]

The fact that Miss *Schechner* chose just this opera for her second debut is a beautiful proof of her individuality as an artist, namely, that she inclines chiefly toward the high tragic. Thus, she has developed, both in acting and in singing, an outward physical power, which in individual moments was genuinely stirring. Mr. *Löhle* endures the struggle with his somewhat unnatural, unvocal part as happily as is to be expected from such a strong-voiced, thinking artist, and we have already hinted that the role of *Rocco,* which was a first-rate success for Beethoven, was given a first-rate performance by Mr. *Staudacher*.

Mr. *Fries*[7] is all too strongly charged and *sings* too little; thus, he has only the right to demand that it be said: "he does not exactly ruin anything," while not denying him the praise of having a highly serviceable artistry if this fault were corrected, as could easily be done. Mr. *Schimon,*[8] as well, was really delightful in the first scene, and Mrs. *Hölken*[9] attains what is possible for a voice that is somewhat weak in the upper range, which admittedly is quickly overwhelmed next to a *Schechner*. Mrs. *Hölken* is very diligent and not without talent; if she is not, or doesn't need to be, raised above the sort of role that is appropriate to her voice, she can always be assured of the applause of sensible people.

NOTES

1. That is, *Don Giovanni.*

2. The author is probably referring to the four-volume publication of 1814/15 or 1819 with a foreword by Jean Paul.

3. In other words, the chorus was performed as though the opening words, "O welche Lust!," set the emotional tone of the whole. The actual situation shows prisoners who have been set free briefly from their dungeons, expressing their joy at breathing the fresh air, only to be driven all too quickly back underground at the end.

4. Anna [Nanny] Schechner-Waagen (1806–60) is described by Fétis (*Biographie universelle,* 7, 443–44) as a "celebrated actress of the German opera." Noted for her performances in *Fidelio,* as well as in *Iphigenia in Tauris* and *La Vestale* and as Donna Anna in *Don Giovanni,* she was forced by illness to retire in 1835 from a burgeoning career. See Kutsch and Riemens, *Großes Sängerlexikon,* 2612–13.

5. Franz Xaver Löhle (1792–1837) is described by Fétis (*Biographie universelle,* 5, 334–35) as a "distinguished German tenor" who received a lifetime contract at Munich beginning in 1819. He was also the composer of a substantial number of songs and religious works, and the author of a singing method based on the educational principles of Pestalozzi. See Kutsch and Riemens, *Großes Sängerlexikon,* 1751–52.

6. Staudacher is described by the Leipzig correspondent in AMZ 23 (1821): 219 as a genuine dramatic singer with an agreeable baritone voice. The correspondent also praises his clear pronunciation and the genuineness of the emotions that he communicates. The Munich correspondent notes in AMZ 35 (1833): 507 that Staudacher is entirely committed to grasping not only the materials and mechanics of the stage, but its poetry as well.

7. Fries is described by the Berlin correspondent in AMZ 21 (1819): 761 as a former member of the Court Theater in Hannover, with a voice that is accurate as to intonation and rhythm, but is nevertheless disagreeable, with no low notes or secure high notes. In AMZ 20 (1818): 720, the Munich correspondent notes that Fries, who is now described as being from the theater at Nürnberg, sang the duke in *Camilla,* and that "his acting, which was good in itself, was not enough to make up for such mediocre singing." This writer seems to have noticed similar failings nine years later, and there is no evidence in the AMZ that Fries ever overcame them. In fact, the Viennese correspondent reports in AMZ 22 (1820): 216 that Fries performed Don Giovanni "in such a way that we never want to see him again"—surely one of the most negative comments ever to appear in the AMZ's correspondence sections.

8. The Viennese correspondent in AMZ 23 (1821): 8 notes that "a young beginner, Mr. Schimon, tried himself out as Carl in Agnes Sorel, without arousing significant hopes." In AMZ 27 (1825): 360, the correspondent from Kassel describes Schimon as an outstanding painter who formerly worked at singing only as an amateur. Although he did not have much success in Kassel with his interpretation of Max in *Der Freischütz,* he apparently was more successful in at least one other role.

9. Little information about Mrs. Hölken can be garnered from the few times she is mentioned in the AMZ—in fact, in AMZ 28 (1826): 7, her name is given as Hölker, although

this is later corrected. In general, this cast seems to have been by far the weakest yet to undertake a performance of *Fidelio*.

~

260.
"News." *Allgemeine Musikzeitung zur Beförderung der theoretischen und praktischen Tonkunst, für Musiker und Freunde der Musik überhaupt* (Offenbach) 1 (8 September 1827): 158.

A correspondent from Vienna in the *Berliner musikal. Zeitung* says: The concert that was given today, in order that a monument to Ludwig van Beethoven may be built from the proceeds, was so little attended because the music to be performed at it was too good and too beautiful. He means: if an Italian coloratura singer had been invited, and allowed to coo "Sorte sebondamini" and such like, the power of magnetic attraction would not have been missing, and the thing would have turned out very differently from a pecuniary point of view.[1] But—but—but—he adds, let whoever will try to swim against the current! The voice of the individual gets out of tune in the desert! It is this way everywhere!!!—Still always a rather general complaint. How can it be remedied, though?

NOTE

1. Although it is not specifically mentioned, this report is about the opera.

~

261.
"Repertory of the City Theater at Aachen."
Stadt-Aachener-Zeitung 243 (11 October 1828): 78–81.

Thursday, the second, for the first time: *Fidelio*, grand opera in two acts by Treitschke. Music by L. Beethoven.

Until now, Aachen's countless admirers of the immortal Beethoven only had the opportunity to be astonished at this powerful spirit in his instrumental compositions. All the more excitedly did they await the performance of this dramatic composition, which has the reputation of being one of the acknowledged, gigantic works of the master. The content of the opera is essentially as follows:

Don Pizarro, governor of a Spanish state prison, has unjustly seized his opponent Florestan and lets him pine away in a dark underground dungeon, a sacrifice to the most gruesome revenge. Leonore, Florestan's wife, who suspects her husband's horrible fate, has known how to obtain entrance to this state prison in a man's clothing, under the name Fidelio, with the intention of freeing him or dying with him, and as an assistant to the dungeon master, Rocco, how to win his favor and unlimited trust. Her steadfast inquiries and her moving sacrifice remain long unrewarded, until finally the following event, which should have hastened Florestan's utter destruction, crowns her tireless striving with a happy success, and makes her the instrument of her husband's rescue. This same Pizarro, informed that the minister Fernando will visit the state prisons in person, decides, in order to guard against any betrayal of his misdeed, to kill Florestan. He gives to Rocco the assignment of murdering him, and, when Rocco recoils from doing this, Pizarro quickly resolves to carry out the murder himself. Rocco is to bury the body of the murdered man in a cistern, the remains of which are found in Florestan's dungeon. Rocco, incapable of performing this task that he has accepted alone, due to the weakness of age, chooses Fidelio as his assistant with Pizarro's consent. Florestan's dungeon is entered so that the dreadful task may be fulfilled; there Fidelio recognizes her half-dead husband by the light of the lantern and pounces upon the tyrant with her loaded pocket pistol as he is about to plunge the dagger into the breast of the sacrifice of his revenge with scornful triumph; forced to delay the moment of revenge, he now tries to destroy both of them, as the minister appears in the state prison and turns over Pizarro to the punishment he deserves.

Apart from the aforementioned principal figures belonging to the action, the secondary characters of Marzelline, the daughter of the dungeon master, and of the doorkeeper Jaquino are also episodically developed in it, and the jealousy of the latter toward Fidelio, along with Marzelline's love for him, brings several happy scenes into the tragic seriousness of the plot, which are very welcome as points of rest. This subject has often been treated dramatically in Spain and France, and the German stage also possesses a similar one in Zschokke's *Iron Mask*.[1] Since, however, these dramas could never achieve a lasting value upon the stage, it was a fortunate idea on the part of the poet to have turned the interesting material into an opera, and thus, with the dramatic part of it, which serves only as a vehicle for music, to have furnished a thread on which the great composer could line up his pearls.

A few general and specific observations on the music of *Fidelio* by a theoretically and practically trained musical connoisseur, whose judgment carries all the more weight as he is intimately familiar with the spirit and manner of Beethoven's music, and has frequently had the opportunity to become familiar with this opera through splendid performances, may be appropriate here.

As in all of his works, Beethoven's powerful spirit grips us also in *Fidelio* and carries us off to the kingdom of the gigantic and the immeasurable, which opens itself up to his thundering sounds. His music moves the lever of fear, of terror, of horror, of pain, of joy, love and hope; it fills our breast with a full-voiced consonance of all the passions and awakens just that interminable longing that is the essence of romanticism. When discerning people maintain that this opera is designed more for the knowledgeable judgment of the connoisseur than for the great masses, and that its beauties only reveal themselves after a very deep study of Beethoven's music as a whole, this is true insofar as this musical creation is certainly not designed for the general public for the satisfaction of everyday feelings, for the easy requirements of superficial conversation. Rather, its magnificent melodies, although now and then covered for unpracticed ears by an almost overpowering fullness of instrumental accompaniment; its nuances and effects; the clarity and power with which the passions are expressed with musical sounds; the prolific fantasies of the composer speak at last to every educated soul, to every thoughtful listener, grip his feelings deeply and inwardly, and lead him into the wonderful spirit kingdom where pain and joy, portrayed in sounds, surround him. Since, however, our ear cannot comprehend such a broad stream of sounds all at once, which loses its restfulness and clarity by rushing through a narrow, stony valley, and, at the first performance, the listener divides his attention generally between the drama, the music, and the performers, the purity, depth, and beauty of musical works of this kind cannot be grasped and felt even through repeated hearings.[2]

Of the sixteen numbers of the opera, including the overture, which all are worthy of the highly celebrated, ingenious composer, we content ourselves here to single out the overture, the canon (no. 3), the aria with chorus (no. 6), the recitative and aria of Leonore (no. 8), the finale of the first act, recitative and arietta of Florestan (no. 10), the trio (no. 12), the quartet (no. 13), the duet (no. 14), and the finale of the second act.

The overture in E has long been recognized, among us as well, as a masterpiece of Beethoven's genuine, individual style of writing; it not only introduces us to the upcoming action in a worthy, highly characteristic way, but, in its extremely large-scale design, working out, and unique instrumentation, it has a truly overwhelming, transporting effect. The canon, no. 3, is a magnificent four-voiced piece for two sopranos, bass, and tenor, free and flowing in melody, clear and natural in its accompaniment and on the stage, as well as away from it, of an enchanting effect. The aria with chorus of Pizarro in D minor and D major, "Ha, welch ein Augenblick!" fills us with horror and dread, which is raised even higher by the unisono of the bleak chorus of the watchmen, which interrupts it: "er spricht von Tod und Wunden." The performance of it demands, all the same, the greatest possible exertion of the singer's powers, if he wishes to be heard through the instrumental accompaniment that rushes away on the wings of doom. The recitative of Leonore: "Abscheulicher, wo eilst du hin?" and the aria in E that follows it: "Komm Hoffnung, daß den letzten Stern etc." are full of sadness and sublimity and bear witness to the wondrous creative power of the composer in the ingeniously masterly union of melody and harmony. The obbligato horn accompaniment is highly effective, but nevertheless obscures the voice of the singer in the Allegro. In the finale, no. 9, the theme of the prisoners' chorus "O welche Lust in freier Luft" and the arrival of Pizarro, which is being prepared in the accompaniment, are magnificently laid out and developed. The second act offers so many beauties piled up upon one another that, in alternation, they almost overdazzle us: the introduction, recitative and aria of Florestan "In des Lebens Frühling Tagen [*sic*]," where the lovely theme is touched upon by the oboe; the trio, no. 12, for tenor, soprano, and bass; the quartet for two basses, tenor, and soprano, wonderful beyond all measure, which first oppresses and unsettles the listener's breast, threatening annihilation with a presentiment of the monstrous, and surrounds him with deep, dreadful night, through which the signaling trumpet penetrates like a radiant form and illuminates it.[3] The composer has brought about an effect here similar to that by which Handel in the oratorio *Samson* and Haydn in his *Creation* portray the origin of light. Finally, the finale, whose splendid theme glows like blinding sunlight, and in whose concluding section singers, choruses, and orchestra unite in exultant joy: truly, whoever is not gripped and irresistibly swept away by all this, neither Beethoven's nor any music at all is written for them!

Of today's first performance let it only be observed for now that, regardless of the highly difficult vocal pieces, the representation was not entirely unworthy of the subject. The audience, seized by Beethoven's gigantic spirit, bestowed upon every number the most thunderous applause and called out Mrs. Fischer[4] (Fidelio) at the conclusion of the piece. The orchestra distinguished itself favorably today not only through precision and care, but also through enthusiastic ensemble playing, for which great praise is due to director Telle,[5] as to all participants. Our warmest thanks to the directorship for bringing into the repertory an opera whose every performance will be a festival for Aachen's music loving inhabitants.

NOTES

1. Heinrich Zschokke (1771–1848) was a novelist, political journalist, and successful writer for the stage. Although regarded today as a minor literary contemporary of Goethe, he wrote dramas that during his lifetime were considered equal to Schiller's. The tragedy mentioned in the text, *Die eiserne Larve* (1808), was popular in Berlin and also performed in Hamburg, Cologne, and Aachen (1827).

2. Much of this paragraph is once again a paraphrase of Hoffmann. This widespread plagiarism shows just how influential his ideas were.

3. Once again, Hoffmann is being paraphrased here.

4. Of Caroline Fischer-Achten (1806–96), Fétis (*Biographie universelle*, 3, 264–65) reports that she was born in Vienna and gave several successful performances in Paris, "but after the arrival of Mrs. Schröder-Devrient, she lost a great deal from being placed in comparison with that great actress, whose voice was less beautiful than that of Mrs. Fischer, but who had the advantage over her of an eminently dramatic talent." Fischer-Achten was particularly known for her interpretations of Mozart roles. Three of her

sons, Ludwig, Emil, and Karl, also became singers. See Kutsch and Riemens, *Großes Sängerlexikon,* 943–44.

5. Friedrich Wilhelm Telle (1798—after 1861) completed keyboard instruction under Cherubini in Paris 1816 and returned to Berlin as music director of the new Königstädter Theater with C. W. Henning. During the years 1825–27 Telle was music director of the Mageburg theater and thereafter music director in Aachen. He wrote operas, ballets, music for plays, *Lieder,* and keyboard music.

❧

262.

"Brief Notices." *Allgemeine musikalische Zeitung* 31 (4 February 1829): 88.

(Keyboard reduction without text, by J. P. Schmidt)[1]

The strange amateur practice, originating in Vienna and now very widely disseminated, of playing grand operas without singing is probably only explicable on the basis of a wish to bring to memory in the most comfortable way and to some extent to enjoy again the pleasure that was felt at the performance of these operas upon the stage. If this is to be achieved hereby, to the extent that it can be, it is necessary to have familiarized oneself with the opera rather precisely, and the reduction must be made with skill and diligence. The latter has happened in this instance; and we must extend our hope to them and to the opera that the former is the case with very many musical amateurs with regard to this opera. Engraving and paper are very good.

NOTE

1. The keyboard version reviewed here was made by J. P. Schmidt and published in Leipzig by Breitkopf & Härtel in August 1828.

❧

263.

"News. Bremen, 31 March 1829." *Allgemeine musikalische Zeitung* 31 (1 July 1829): 432–33.

(Mentioned: *Ah! perfido,* op. 65)

Two operas met with extraordinarily great applause here last winter: Beethoven's *Fidelio,* performed here for the first time on 18 February 1829—not in the theater, however, but in the concert hall, organized by Mr. Grabau,[1] followed by Rossini's *Siege of Corinth* upon the stage. Both have become favorite operas of our public, and the latter would be repeated even more often if the great Turkish drum in it did not make too much noise for feminine nerves, which is not the case in Weber's *Oberon*. *Fidelio* is now being prepared at our theater as well and will soon be performed for the benefit of the soprano Miss Buscher.[2] If this opera is well performed and staged, it will win over all others, since it is so richly endowed and Beethoven has long been the favorite of our friends of music, and rightly so. We already knew the bravura aria from it: *Ah perfido spergiuro,* a masterpiece of musical art, but not well translated into German as "Abscheulicher" and "I follow my inner impulse" (a harshness, instead of: "I follow my impulse").[3] Miss Henriette Grabau sang this aria for us at that time; this time, however, her younger sister Adelheid sang it very expressively in the part of Leonore (or Fidelio), while her brother, Mr. Georg Grabau, performed those of Florestan and Jaquino, Miss Buscher that of Marzelline, and dilettantes the three remaining roles. The great hall was filled to the bursting point, and thus repetitions are soon expected. There is only one voice concerning the great inner purity and the noble, genuine style of this ingenious opera; the subject of the poem is not to the greatest advantage, but about this the composer can do nothing.

NOTES

1. The activities of the tenor Georg Grabau, his "Gesangverein," which included up to a hundred singers (AMZ 26 [1824]: 146), and his family—including three sisters: Adelheid, Henriette, and Marie—are reported on extensively in the AMZ, primarily during the 1830s. The performance described here was followed by a second performance on 25 November, described in AMZ 31 (1829): 842. Henriette seems to have had the most successful career; she is already praised in AMZ 27 (1825): 96 for her "customary skill" and is mentioned as being an accomplished pianist as well as a singer. It is not clear whether the Georg Grabau mentioned below is the director and impresario himself, which would make the three ladies his sisters, or whether the impresario is the father of all four.

2. The text actually has "Sängerin": female singer.

The promising career of the singer Meta Buscher may have been cut short by opposition from her pastor. The AMZ (30 [1828]: 631–32) reports that her operatic debut was rendered notorious by his having advised her that not only all theater performers, but all theatergoers as well would be subject to eternal punishment. This had the effect of bringing out a large crowd in her support, but in AMZ 33 (1831): 58, it is reported that she is no longer appearing in operas, and her name is never mentioned again in the AMZ.

3. The writer seems to have confused Leonore's aria with the much earlier *Ah! perfido.*

~

264.
Vollweiler. "Review." *Cäcilia* 10 (1829): installment 37, 46–47.

(Arrangement for keyboard and violin by Alexander Brand)[1]

Since the admirers of Beethoven so seldom have the chance to enjoy this opera in performance, Mr. Brand has earned great recognition in this regard from the lovers of Beethoven's music, in that he provides, with the present edition, an agreeable opportunity for those who do not yet know the opera itself to make a preliminary acquaintance with it, and for those who have heard it, the liveliest recollection, and, as it were, renewed enjoyment of it, performances being so infrequent.

Whoever is familiar with Beethoven's manner of writing will admit that it is no small task to melt down a Beethoven opera to two instruments.— Mr. Brand has solved the problem very successfully. His main goal seems to have been, not to give the mere letter, but rather the spirit of the music.[2] He has not, as is frequently the case in arrangements, tried only to pile up all the figures contained in the score on top of one another, which usually makes performance unnecessarily difficult and confuses the meaning; rather, he knew how to bring out exactly that which portrays the meaning most precisely, and has carried this over to his two instruments so well that he shows thereby a masterful knowledge of them, for several pieces have such a good effect that they could be taken for original compositions for pianoforte and violin. One can see from the whole work that Mr. Brand has not proceeded mechanically and at a mere commission from the publisher, but rather with diligence and love for the material.

Performance is certainly not very difficult, but it demands players who are already accomplished on both instruments.

The publishing firm has spared nothing toward a beautiful presentation of the work, and it contains only a few printing errors, which are so insignificant that everyone at all accomplished will see for himself how to improve them.

NOTES

1. This arrangement was published by Schott at Mainz in 1828.
2. A reference to 2 Cor. 3:6.

∾

265.

Richard Otto Spazier.[1] Berliner allgemeine musikalische
Zeitung 6 (20 October 1829): 357–60 and 364–67.

Spontini's La Vestale, one of the principal repertory pieces, which in Dresden alone and then in all Germany, has laid claim to the inner circle of performances by the existing Italian opera society (so that if, unfortunately, not even any of Mozart's operas are performed, they too are still held hostage by it), was recently brought out in the spring and in the course of the summer, achieved by the members of the German opera, splendidly cast, in successful presentations with the most favorable reception on the part even of the greater public, and, what is more important, with visible participation of the court. Now, accordingly, toward the end of August, *Beethoven's Fidelio* appeared as well on the German opera stage and was heard by an unusually full house with great attentiveness, sometimes even with enthusiasm. This opera was already staged six years ago under *Maria v. Weber's* direction, only, however, at the express demand of the leading lady, who had chosen it for her debut role.[2] It then disappeared, despite the fact that the actress was the mainstay of our German opera, and after its first presentation it did not appear again on the stage despite the pleasant recollections of its performance, which remained enduringly vivid in the souls of so many. This time, however, it was rehearsed with no ulterior motive, repeated again after several days, and seems on the way to becoming a favorite with the public. Whoever knows the circumstances under which the German opera in Dresden has had to operate since its inception, in competition with a rival, which for many years had monopolized the interest of the public, but otherwise enjoying support and patronage, with no means seeming too costly, no task too great for its maintenance, and which thus tried, successfully, to keep as much as possible within its possession, so that German art was always forced to clothe itself with those rags that the other had left behind and, as has rightly been said elsewhere, had to run like a humble beggar in pursuit of an arrogant rich man in its own fatherland: whoever knows the situation will rightly take phenomena like those mentioned above as harbingers of a new dawn, which now, thanks to the persistent efforts of the men who influence the dissemination of art in Germany, is beginning to break forth upon the long overclouded artistic sky of a city gifted with quite rich resources. There can be no question that, in a capital city that is not over-populated, two institutions of this kind cannot remain permanently side by side, and that throughout the time of their coexistence one of them must drive the other one into the background. Thus, from the very beginning a deadly struggle had to rise up between them. Whether M. v. *Weber* led this struggle to the honor of German art with all the energy available to a man of his calling, whether he always struggled with equal persistence with all the means that he alone had at his disposal—a first-rate company and a *diverse,* selected repertory— whether, apart from *Freischütz,* which was in many regards offensive to the previous king, and *Euryanthe,* which is still inaccessible to the broader public, he used these means *more often* to occupy himself with the works of other masters, so that the court, accustomed only to Italian music, and likewise the public that imitates it, might become friendlier to German music, and more ready to support it, we cannot dare to decide this completely, since it is not to be denied that many external circumstances have worked to the advantage of his successors. Among these are, apart from the death of a monarch who, despite the most distinguished musical education, was to German music what Frederick the Great was to German literature, a long, very ably used absence on the part of the conductor *Morlachi,*[3] who seems to have had no fear of his less well-known rival, and finally the deterioration, which has been noticed everywhere for several years, of new Italian opera music, which is endlessly repeated by the Italian theaters, even in other countries, with an unspeakable uniformity and poverty of repertory. Thus it has come to the point that at this moment the personnel of the Italian opera company is so impoverished that, even for *Rossini's* operas, to say nothing of those by others, it must be supplemented by German singers. Under these circumstances, it may well be expected that with persistent striving, with capable use of this momentary crisis in repeated, variegated activity, the members of the German opera will succeed in forming a first-rate whole, including a principal deep bass singer, who has been missing until now, and in winning a final, decisive, lasting victory, obtaining for German art the last territory in the fatherland that had been occupied by false, foreign art, thereby creating an all too painfully missed opportunity for German artists, creative, representative, and performing alike, to see their accomplishments come to life before the people. For it was only the collision with the Italian stage, and not any lack in musical sense in general, which was responsible for the fact that, until now, Dresden always remained closed to so many German composers and singers. Thus, the blossoming and flourishing of a German artistic institution is more important, and the ultimate complete elimination of this foreign entity from one of Germany's capital cities is not just a local, but well-nigh a national interest.

As long as *Fidelio* is available for the judgment of the world of art, observations about a masterwork that stands *next* to the highest products of human genius among all peoples and in all times can be as little superfluous as are those that are rightfully renewed almost every year about *Antigone, Leom, Faust, Don Juan,* etc., even if these serve no other purpose than to call those forms ever anew before the soul, clearly and consciously, in their proper eminence. No intellectual phenomenon, however, has probably yet given rise to so many points of view as this masterwork, the solitary example of a rounded artistic creation, bearing all the marks of highest perfection, without any earlier or later works of the same kind by its creator. It is a lofty, isolated peak, which stretches far into the heavens with no intervening foothills or ridges. For the other great, immortal creations of this master, his instrumental compositions, are, according to their nature, as entirely distant from *Fidelio* as, perhaps, a Pindaric ode from a drama.[4] They require such different kinds of abilities that only rarely does a *Mozart* or a *Goethe*—creators of so many offspring of the same kind, succeed in combining them. It is not possible that the master was only struck by a solitary lightning bolt in one moment of his rich and steadfast productive life, which would never again erupt from the blessed clouds onto his head. This is the tragedy of this master's fate; like an immense, distant star, his light only began to disseminate upon the earth as he himself was preparing to leave it!

Truly, the *case* of Beethoven, which many believe to be already long closed, can only be completed when his only drama has begun to take its proper place before the people. Those who declare uncontrolled imagination and extravagant bizarreness to be his characteristic, and who therefore assign him the vast, unlimited, indeterminate, twilight domain of instrumental music as his exclusive sphere, let them step up to the stage and show us another example in which Phoebus has led and reigned in the horses before his sun chariot in a more powerful and controlled manner. Let them show us a work in which a master has subordinated every individual thought, every idea and every strength to the whole with greater sacrifice of all that subjective egoism that strives to call attention to itself. Even more, let them show us a work in which every means serves more to clarify the principal themes and bring them into relationship with each other, instead of obscuring them, the principal condition of drama; in which the characters are more sharply distinguished from each other, conceived, maintained, and consequently more developed until the end through music, both in melody and harmony; where light and shadow are more economically divided; where the effects are prepared in advance with greater simplicity, so that the power of the highest peaks can yet remain within the bounds of truly Greek beauty,[5] and even in the most powerful moments still flatters the ear without confusing it, allowing the character traits that it reveals to descend so stirringly through the ears and into the soul! With regard to the interpretation and consequent development of the characters, we need only refer to the point where it comes most sharply to the fore at its two greatest extremes, those of *Pizarro* and the *jailkeeper*. How clearly, genially, simply, peacefully, and melodically do both singing and accompaniment pass by in all the scenes where the last-mentioned is the principal character; how shadowy and unpredictable do both become when Pizarro enters with his air of malice. At some points in his role, indeed, this ignoble air rises to such extraordinary heights that, in the half chaotic confusion, we can only hold onto the racing thread of the harmony with the greatest effort; yet the ear is never numbed, and the boundary into disorder is never crossed, so that we are always clearly aware of the means by which the sinister nature of a clouded mind is stamped oppressively and urgently upon our soul. In this regard, the duet in the scene where Pizarro suggests murder to the jailkeeper, when these elements encounter each other alone, without any mediation, as do Leonore and Florestan when they come together later on, in the second act, is a masterpiece of musically dramatic blending of contrasting elements into one, at once bipartite and yet a harmonically effective whole. Just as recognizable is the contrast between Fidelio's passion and the feeble singing of the emerging Florestan. Less striking, perhaps, yet just as carefully maintained rhythmically and tonally, are those between the faithful wifely love of Leonore and the mere *being in love* of the jailkeeper's daughter in her subordinate nature, and likewise also between the more commonplace good nature of the jailkeeper and the more noble, elevated goodness of soul of the minister who finally arrives. As regards the use of means, the simplicity and the endless fidelity to nature, we must point to that infinitely moving scene where the grave is dug in the cellar. Not since *Gluck's* wild chorus in the first act of *Iphigenia in Tauris* has this dimension of genuine horror been so well recognized and portrayed,[6] with the basses used there strengthened by the contrabassoon. Yet these highlights, like those outstanding individual moments, "I am his wife"[7] etc., are perhaps less to be singled out at this point, in part because by themselves they make too many demands upon the listener, in part because Beethoven has something in common in this or that manner with this or that predecessor, even if not to the same degree. Where he is at his greatest in *Fidelio,* and perhaps stands alone, is, among other things, in his so masterfully dramatic treatment of the chorus, the like of which has not been seen before him. In this he has established a model that, when it is properly and generally recognized and valued, must contribute to leading opera to a degree of perfection in this regard, which, in spite of all recent progress toward capturing the essence of dramatic music, it is still seriously lacking. Since *Don Juan*[8] it has certainly been more and more understood how to create an interaction between the chorus and the other actors, how it can be used itself as part of the action, and how, with the help of music, we obtain an advantage over Greek drama, which only allowed the chorus to act through the medium of the chorus leaders, and thus only through personalities who emerged from it, and who thus ultimately became individuals under a different name. Until now, meanwhile, even in the dramatic passages, where the chorus entered the action in alternation with the principal personalities, its music has been portrayed as a single individual and not also as a multitude of people, that is, in so far as the latter is perceived not merely in a diversity of voices. It had not been allowed to divide up into its parts, and thus to be visibly drawn into the *action* as a multitude; that is to say, the chorus generally all began at the same time and sang the same ideas at the same time from beginning to end.

For this reason it attains in many instances a quality that is not only very awkward but at the same time unnatural, since in the first regard it acted not within itself, but rather all together in relation to a personage or place outside of itself, while in the second regard, a unified group, beginning one and the same thought at the same time, could only sufficiently motivate individual moments of strong emotion, unless the situation itself allowed for a *song* of some kind to be sung by a crowd, song being understood here in its broader meaning. Beethoven transcended these limitations in the chorus "O welche Lust" in an extremely ingenious way. It seems extremely natural to us that, upon stepping out from a dungeon, individuals should break out into this exclamation, that they should inspire others and at once should be themselves inspired, until all are expressing the same thing. While this incitement and imitation are carried through the entire chorus, a reciprocal action is also masterfully portrayed at the words "They are listening to us," maintaining the individuals in continuous action. Thus, we find here a breaking apart of the chorus, which, according to the composer's will, can represent both individuals and the multitude at the same time. Thus does it come about that, through the seemingly dissonant entry of the second voice at the interval of a second, and through that of the third at the fourth, and of the fourth at the fifth, a dissonant chord that, separated in terms of time, harmonizes in the spirit, if not in the ear, of the listener, the master portrays the randomness of the entering voices, which could be heard very well in voices that were only speaking, and thus raises the illusion to the highest level with no appearance of artificiality or calculation. Through this doubly ingenious treatment of the words, which thousands of others would have allowed to be sung in the customary choral manner, the composer at once achieves a fourfold purpose. He creates an artificial setting that captivates the mind and spirit in the most powerful way, provides by this means something that is customarily lacking elsewhere, an extremely lively mutual interaction among the chorus, while at the same time, by means of this device, opening up the understanding of each listener to the artificial setting, making what is artificial seem to be the height of naturalness, and thus succeeding in moving us to tears in two ways that have probably never happened before: first, by means of a chorus in a stage work; and second, by means of a piece of music that is exceedingly difficult. Pages could be written about this chorus alone.

Apart from these few observations, we would like to spend a while trying to determine the reasons that initially set up *Fidelio* for such an astonishingly dreary fate, inasmuch as this is the best way to indicate the essence of this work along with that of others that were more easily received, and likewise the earlier and present condition of dramatic music. It is customary to say that the music in *Fidelio* is too difficult, and therefore incomprehensible to the masses in performance, and to find in this the reason for its failure to get through to them. This seems to us, however, to be beside the point. Where is this difficulty to be found? Is it not rich in simple, indeed pleasing, singable melody? Is not the instrumentation simple enough that an ear that is only somewhat practiced can, upon first hearing, listen continuously to both melody and harmony, grasping and effortlessly following them even as far as the unique courses taken by each individual instrument? Are not the characteristic motives recognizable, clear, and open?—The problem is that despite all of this, it is indeed unspeakably difficult to *perform Fidelio* well— not, let it be understood, if according to its demands it is performed as are other operas—precisely because the sacrifice of every individual outstanding secondary charm, with very few exceptions, makes it from beginning to end a single great *ensemble*, varying only quantitatively and in the number of persons: in a word, because it is *entirely* and *only dramatic*. The *desire* to listen to such an ensemble first of all with attentiveness and participation, the inclination to regard it with satisfaction: at the time when *Fidelio* appeared, the public, not excepting even the most educated, was entirely lacking in these sensibilities from the outset. Does not *Don Juan* itself, with the exception of Gluck's works, the most dramatic German opera before *Fidelio,* owe much of it success initially among the greatest part even of the educated public to a mass of half-episodic scenes and interpolated arias, those of Zerlina as well as the bravura arias of Anna, Elvira, and Ottavio? Mozart, struggling with a persistent wish for popularity, did not disdain those motives, secondary charms, and isolated enticements, in order that they might bring his greater genius forward to the superior members of the people, and was it not only many years later that the more elevated aspects of *Don Juan* first began to be esteemed and valued even by the foremost citizens of music's kingdom? The second, more powerful reason, albeit the consequence of the first, is that, in the present situation of opera everywhere, even a somewhat adequate cast was lacking in order *to be able* to perform *Fidelio.* How long has it been that we, who still stand enslaved to Italian opera music, miss seeing actors, and not simply singers, upon the stage? Even today, ensembles always receive the relatively weakest performances. In them, the singer's freedom is restrained, his attention always occupied by rests and sudden entries, his movements conditional on those of his fellow players and singers, his actions orienting themselves toward theirs. Thus, he must overcome at once countless difficulties that are entirely lacking in solo singing. Most importantly of all, this most difficult task is also the most thankless from the point of view of showmanship. If a singer does his part ever so well, he is only one member of the complete chain, and even if the public makes its approval known—which, moreover, happens more rarely—he receives it only incidentally. This, however, is not sufficient to his artistic vanity, which is after all excusable. For this reason, he always prefers to see operas performed where he more frequently takes the stage by himself and snatches away a bravo for himself alone. Just take a look at *Fidelio.* With the exception of the lead, there is no role that is grateful in this way, and even it is only so in isolated moments. Even here the female artist must have recourse to so-called stage tricks in order to draw attention to herself. Here, the actors, to whom the composer so magnificently subordinated himself, are for the most part required to make the same sacrifice of their own personalities so that all may contribute to a whole. Where, even today, are many such artists to be found together? So there was lacking not only ability but also will on the part of performers. For one individual is of very little help here. By contrast, look at *Don Juan.* Much in it is so self-contained that it can truly stand by itself and work satisfactorily independent of the rest. A poor Don may be made up for by a truly good Leporello, a miserable Elvira by a good Zerlina, and so forth. But the individual parts of *Fidelio* are so interconnected that with a poor Fidelio the whole opera completely fails, and with a good one, most of it passes by without effect if the others are poor, while the rest seems slow-moving and boring by comparison. Where, in all of Germany, was even a Fidelio to be found at that time? Now, to be sure, the situation is in many ways different. The more elevated, dramatic portion of the operas of Mozart and others has already been capably assimilated, while among more educated people the sensibility for purely dramatic music thus awakened has set it off so sharply from concert music, that we come before the stage with other expectations, just as, for this very reason, we encounter entirely different performers upon it. (Surely the false extreme of Rossini contributed to this in a negative way, in that after the initial intoxication it made us yearn all the more for the real thing, while the most recent, so dramatically lively, French operas certainly contributed positively.) Thus, the time will come for *Fidelio*, and through it for Gluck, who has always remained unfamiliar to the public.

A further hindrance for *Fidelio* was the pure tragic quality that continues to the end, despite the earlier predominance of much lighter material, and which in earlier times would have been nowhere less expected than in opera. This viewpoint was strengthened by those older aestheticians, who of all people had precisely the smallest sensibility for the musical in general, to say nothing of the high meaning of dramatic music, as can be seen from almost all their textbooks, which either completely overlook music or treat it like a game and, in the manner of the late Müllner,[9] immediately declare opera to be nonsense. It was once again *Don Juan* that contributed most to the awakening of that sensibility to music's potential for deep tragedy, though admittedly not until many years after it appeared. Its great influence upon the shaping of our music is still not sufficiently appreciated, despite all the wonderful things that have already been said about it. At first it certainly was well received for the most part because of its lighter elements. In a real sense Weber's *Freischütz* could then be placed before all others; in its tragic quality, along with much that is excessive and not beautiful, and which panders too much to the desire of the lower classes to taste the finer sensibilities and sounds, the demonic element nevertheless seems to have been far more deeply conceived than in earlier ghost and devil operas.

Apart from the fact that the subject perhaps drags somewhat toward the end of the first act, which, however, the poet could not avoid through an additional complication, these are perhaps the reasons why the perennial fate of every new, great, and original creation of a genius, that of truly arriving too early for its time since it is only through time that we are able to work our way up toward it, struck *Fidelio* too severely and for too long. With the help of many predecessors and a few successors, we have now nevertheless come so far in relation to it that perhaps its turn may soon come to take its part in the further development of the musically dramatic among our public, composers, and actors. Deep, reverential thanks to the master, who through sacrificing himself in the splendid artistic sense brought forth a star upon the horizon of our artistic heaven, which may lead us to that which alone is true; deep sadness to his memory, that he did not experience the light that it cast here below! The performance in Dresden gave this contributor the further opportunity to confirm the soundness of these observations. "I am curious," said a high-ranking person in his presence to one of the actors, "I am curious to see what kind of an impression *Fidelio* will make on me after six years, for I have made much progress with regard to German music," and he joyfully expressed his enchantment after the performance.

Finally, this time we owe to the actors, who under such circumstances contributed so much to making *Fidelio* a lasting repertory piece in Dresden, a consideration and the thanks of a special mention. In accordance with the nature of the thing, Mrs. *Schröder-Devrient,* who, through her masterful portrayal of Euryanthe, has become known even elsewhere as one of the foremost German stage actresses in opera, made the biggest contribution here. In the last act her passionate, ardent performance transported us to the point of enchantment. Unfortunately, she still adheres to the old ways of singers to the extent that she too often harangues the public through stage tricks, provoking them to express their approval at the close of each number, whereby, particularly in *Fidelio,* much of the illusion is destroyed. The listeners are nevertheless to blame for this, since it is only in this way that the deserved applause can be wrung out of them, and at this price we often gladly gain the overall effect of this masterwork. Apart from *Schechner,* whom we have not heard, she may be the only one who at this time is capable of victoriously gaining for *Fidelio* the position that is due to it. As far as the other actors are concerned, they could only be less pleasing, due to the difficulties that have been pointed out, which apply primarily to them. However, they certainly deserve praise and thanks for gladly and enthusiastically doing everything possible to perform their difficult tasks adequately. It is nearly impossible to do everything that is demanded here the first time around; certainly they will learn more and more with each new performance, and what they gain from this experience will be of all the more service to them elsewhere. This last is one of the primary benefits of performing works of this kind repeatedly. Mr. Wächter,[10] as Pizarro, has the most difficult task, all the more so as, along with the preeminent member of our German opera, to whose beautiful voice it largely owes its revival, he is generally less adequate to this type of role, since as a baritone he is lacking the necessary penetrating low notes, and his most beautiful sounds lie in the range that approaches the middle notes of a tenor. As good as his acting was, the dungeon-master was also lacking in strength of voice, as was particularly noticeable in the beautiful canonic quartet in the first act. The ease and versatility of Mrs. *Wächter* and Mr. *Rosenfelt*[11] served them well in their scenes; Mr. *Bergmann's*[12] ailing tenor voice was entirely appropriate to Florestan, and Mr. *Risse*[13] sang the indescribably beautiful passage where the minister commands Leonore to remove the chains so well that its effect was not lacking, and these few notes moved us to tears for the second time in this same work. With them our feelings for the opera should come to an end, since the following commonplace conclusion only appears naked.

May the music director *Reißiger*[14] seek ever more to captivate firmly the interest of the public, which has already been so vigorously awakened, along with that of the court, which, as far as we can perceive, is very well disposed toward him, through a rapid succession of such solid performances as this. For, as he probably knows best, that particular victory alluded to above has not yet been completely won. Enemies not lacking in skill and established factions still conspire against him. May he above all not allow himself to be disappointed and dispirited by reports, in all probability venal, which undervalue the accomplishments of Germans compared to those of Italians, and which, to be precise, are bound to occur in a very incomprehensible manner with regard to *La Vestale*. He and his performing artists cannot help noticing that attention and quiet acknowledgment of their striving will not fail to accrue to them, and noticing that it has been specifically acknowledged that we owe to them the first performances of the great Beethoven symphonies in Dresden.[15] However, just such public recognition certainly causes difficulty under such circumstances, and for this reason, since this contributor lives for the hope that German music in all its aspects will from now on receive more powerful impetus here, he is glad to acquiesce in the request of the editor of a respected paper to take up again the remarks begun earlier, but later broken off, about music in general and individual works in particular, as may be occasioned by their performances heard on the spot, in order to set them down here in a continuous sequence. May this lead to rich recognition, for the office of a reporter who merely lays blame and complains of his poverty is for him, as for his readers, useless and unsatisfying.

NOTES

1. Dr. Richard Otto Spazier (1803–54) was editor of *Nürnberger Blätter für öffentliches Leben, Literatur und Kunst* (1830–31), but soon became preoccupied with the publication of political essays concerned with the fate of Poland (*Ost und West,* 1835). His failure to engage the interest of Germans in a revolution for the freedom of Poland embittered him, and he went into exile in Paris where he spent the next two decades writing essays on music and translating Spanish literature. He returned to Leipzig at the end of his life.

2. For Weber's changing attitudes toward Beethoven's music, see Karl Laux, "Das Beethoven—Bild Carl Maria von Webers," *Bericht über den Internationalen Beethoven—Kongress, 10–12. Dezember 1970 in Berlin* (Berlin: Neue Musik, 1971), 65–69.

3. Francesco Giuseppe Baldassare Morlacchi (1784–1841) was conductor of the Italian opera in Dresden from 1811 until his death. His personal rivalry with Weber paralleled that of the companies they directed.

Frederick the Great, like many intellectuals of the early Enlightenment, considered French culture to be vastly superior to German and therefore made French the predominant language of the court. The Prussian king's low opinion of German is expressed in an anecdote attributed to him that he preferred to speak French with intelligent men and reserved German for his horses. He did write a history of German literature, *De la Littérature allemande* (1780), in which he advocates French neoclassicism as a model for German literature.

The king of Saxony during Weber's tenure as director of the Court Theater in Dresden was Friedrich August III, who lived and died in the city of Dresden (1750–1827).

4. Pindar (522 or 518 B.C.–442 or 438 B.C.) has been celebrated by Greek, Roman, English, and German poets as the creator of encomiastic poetry.

5. See the introductory essay in vol. 1 (p. 21, n. 36) for the role that the art historian Johann Joachim Winckelmann played in creating the ideal model of beauty based on Greek antiquity: "noble simplicity and quiet grandeur."

6. This is presumably a reference to the opening scene of Gluck's opera, which depicts a violent storm.

7. "I am his wife." Leonore's first line when she reveals her identity and steps between Pizarro and Fidelio is "Töt' erst sein Weib" (First kill his wife). She continues: "Ja, sieh hier Leonore! Ich bin sein Weib, geschworen hab' ich ihm Trost, Verderben dir!"

8. That is, *Don Giovanni.*

9. Although Amadeus Gottfried Adolf Müllner (1774–1829) received his training as a lawyer (1798, University of Leipzig), he devoted his life to literature and edited several literary journals (e.g., *Literaturblatt zum Morgenblatt,* 1820–25, and *Mitternachtsblatt,* 1826–29), in which, however, his vitriolic criticism involved him in vicious feuds, which spilled over into his personal life and contributed to the early deterioration of his health.

10. Johann Michael Wächter (1794–1853; Fétis gives his birth date as 1796) sang at the Dresden Hofoper from 1827 until his death. He was known for his interpretations of Mozart's Figaro and of Scherasmin in Weber's *Oberon,* but from a historical perspective, the high point of his career came in the 1840s with his appearance in the premieres in two Wagner operas as Orsini in *Rienzi* and as the Flying Dutchman under the composer's direction. His wife, Therese Wächter-Wittmann (b. 1802—see this entry below), sang the role of Mary in this same production and appeared at Dresden in a variety of mezzo- and soprano roles. See Kutsch and Riemens, *Großes Sängerlexikon,* 3121–22, Fétis, *Biographie universelle,* 8, 391.

11. This singer, who originally came from Pesth, is mentioned several times in the AMZ. After appearing as Prince Ramiro at a Viennese performance of Isouard's *Cendrillon* (*Aschenbrödel*), he was praised for his "smooth, flexible voice," particularly in its upper range, and his stage presence, but the correspondent added that he seemed to possess little musical knowledge. See AMZ 17 (1815): 354–55.

12. Johann Gottfried Bergmann (1765–1831) was for many years the leading tenor at the Dresden Hofoper, in which capacity he worked closely with Carl Maria von Weber. In AMZ 26 (1824): 388, his interpretation of Adolar in *Euryanthe* is deemed "very praiseworthy, particularly in the gentler sections of the music." The reference here to his "ailing" voice may simply reflect his age at the time of the performance.

13. Carl Risse (1810–?), though still young at the time of this performance, became one of the leading basses at the Dresden Hofoper, where he also participated in the premieres of *Rienzi* and *The Flying Dutchman.* See Kutsch and Riemens, *Großes Sängerlexikon,* 2469–70.

14. Karl Gottlieb Reissiger (1798–1859) was Hofkapellmeister at Dresden from 1828 until his death. As the author implies, he was known as a champion of German music.

15. For a general account of Beethoven's relationship to and the reception history of his works in Dresden, see Hans Volkmann, *Beethoven in seinen Beziehungen zu Dresden: unbekannte Strecken seines Lebens* (Dresden: Deutscher Literatur, 1942). There is no detailed study of performances of the symphonies in Dresden in the first half of the nineteenth century.

Index of Names

Cologne: Du Mont Schauberg'sche Drukkerei der Kölnischen Zeitung, 118; Gürzenich, 81–83

Comini, Alessandra, 10, 13

Czerny, Carl, 114, 185

Demmer, Friedrich Christian, 174–75

Demmer, Joseph, 175

Demmer, Josephina, 235

Demmer, Thekla, 233–35, 237–38, 240

Devrient, Eduard Philipp, 242–43

Devrient, Karl, 242

Dittersdorf, Karl Ditters von, 111; *Batailles de trois Empereurs,* 96; symphonies, 96

Dotzauer, Justus Johann Friedrich, 43–44

Dragonetti, 225

Dresden: Royal Court Theater, 243

Du Mont, Marcus, 118

Düsseldorf: Lower Rhine Music Festival, 132

Eberl, Anton, 18, 53; string quartets, 171; symphonies, 17–18; Symphony in D minor, 55

Eberwein, Henriette. *See* Hässler, Henriette

Eberwein, Traugott Maximilian, 89, 231; *Das Leben ein Traum,* 89

Eder, Karl Kaspar, 71

Eunike, Friedrich, 227–28

Eunike, Johanna, 228

Eunike-Schwachhofer, Therese, 228

Fesca, Friedrich Ernst, 81–83; *Cantemire,* 232

Fischer, Anton: *Die Verwandlungen,* 172

Fischer, Michael Gotthard, 140

Fischer-Achten, Caroline, 254–55

Forkel, Johann Nikolaus: *24 Veränderungen für Clavichord oder Fortepiano auf das englische Volkslied "God Save the King,"* 91

Forti, Anton, 183–84, 233–34, 237–38, 240

Francis I, 54–55

Franz II, 184, 237

Fränzl, Ferdinand, 71

Frederick the Great, 258, 266–67

Der Freymüthige (F), 119–20

Friedrich August III, 267

Friedrich Wilhelm III, 147

Fries (singer), 249–50

Frühwald, [Joseph?], 181

Galeazzi, 140

Galitzin, Prince, 245

Gern, Albert Leopold, 243–44

Gern, Georg, 244

Gluck, Christoph Willibald: operas, 55, 188, 219, 225, 242, 263–64; *Armide,* 54–55, 228; *Iphigenia in Tauris,* 242, 250, 261, 267

Goethe, Johann Wolfgang von, 88–89, 144, 191–92, 218, 231, 254, 259

Grabau, Adelheid, 256

Grabau, Georg, 255–56

Grabau, Henriette, 256

Grabau, Marie, 256

Graun, Karl Heinrich, 178

Grétry: *Richard Coeur-de-Lion,* 219

Griesinger: *Biographische Notizen,* 2

Grillparzer, Franz, 89, 245–46

Groote, Eberhard von, 82–83; *Die Sündfluth,* 81–82

Gyrowetz, Adalbert, 36, 231; *Die Junggesellenwirtschaft,* 229, 231; symphonies, 35

Haase, Mrs. (singer), 244

Haizinger, Anton, 233–36, 238, 240

Handel, Georg Friedrich: "Hallelujah Chorus" from *Messiah,* 38; *Samson,* 146, 254

Hanslick, Eduard, 12; *Vom musikalisch-Schönen,* 7–8

Hasemann (violoncellist and trombonist), 54

Haslinger, Tobias, 42

Hässler, Henriette, 229–31

Haydn, Joseph, 2, 18, 36, 57, 59, 64, 91, 96, 110–11, 149, 162, 189–90, 192, 196–98, 245; Concertante, Hoboken I:105, 93, 95; "Gott erhalte Franz den Kaiser," 237; minuets, 114–15, 162; *The Creation,* 177–78, 181, 254; *The Seasons,* 94–95; piano music, 170; string quartets, 147, 171; Quartet,

Moller: Academy, 58

Morlachi, Francesco Giuseppe Baldassare, 258, 266

Moscheles, Ignaz, 219, 235

Mosengeil, Friedrich, 141–44

Möser, Karl, 40–41, 147–48; string quartets, 147

Mozart, Franz Xaver Wolfgang, 18

Mozart, W. A., 59, 64–65, 68, 85, 89, 96–97, 110–11, 117, 149, 159, 168, 170, 175, 189–94, 197–98, 204, 232, 245, 259; "Ch'io mi scordi di te . . . Non temer, amate bene," K. 505, 92; minuets, 162; operas, 176–77, 182, 188, 203, 205, 212, 219, 254, 257, 264; *La Clemenza di Tito*, 44; overture to *Cosí fan tutte*, 89, 191; *Die Entführung aus dem Serail*, 228–29; *Don Giovanni*, 44, 184, 188, 191, 227–30, 242, 245, 248, 250, 259, 261, 263–64, 267; *Le nozze di Figaro*, 44, 184, 188, 267; *La villanella rapita*, 38; overture to *Die Zauberflöte*, 60, 89, 184, 228–29, 239; piano music, 170; piano concertos, 18, 32, 130–31, 179; *Requiem*, 181; string quartets, 171; symphonies, 36, 66, 93, 95, 119, 145; Symphony, K. 504, 58, 118–19; Symphony, K. 543, 58, 97, 111, 118–19, 159–60, 232; Symphony, K. 550, 17–18, 36, 118–19; Symphony, K. 551, 17–18, 58, 118–19; Seven Variations on "Une fièvre brûlante," from Grétry's *Richard Coeur-de-Lion*, K. Anh. 287, 90–91

Müller, Adolph, 239

Müller, August Eberhard, 31–32, 35, 42–43, 50; capriccios, 92; fantasy for the pianoforte, 92; flute concerto, 50–51

Müller, Elisabeth Catherina, 43–44

Müller, Louise, 175, 180

Müllner, Amadeus Gottfried Adolf, 264, 267

Munich: Royal Court and National Theater, 248

Musikalische Eilpost, 3

Napoleon, 11, 88, 178–79, 228

Nasolini, 38

Neate, Charles, 218

Nestroy, Johann Nepomuk Eduard Ambrosius, 239–40

Neumann-Sessi. *See* Sessi, Anna Maria

Nicolai, 147

Novalis: *Die Lehrlinge zu Sais*, 170

Nürnberger Blätter für öffentliches Leben, Literatur und Kunst, 266

Oliveros, Pauline, 2

Paer, Ferdinando, 45, 84, 187–88, 192, *Camilla, ossia Il sotterraneo*, 182–84; *Leonore, ossia l'amore conjugale*, 45, 172, 178, 182, 202–03, 208, 211–12, 214–16, 219–22; *Sargino, ossia L'allievo dell'amore*, 229–31; *Sofonisba*, 44

Paganini, 86

Pär (clarinettist), 171

Pavarotti, 2

Pavesi, 120

Pestalozzi, 250

Peters (firm), 32

Pindar, 259, 267

Pleasants, Henry, 8, 12

Poissl: *Athalia*, 242

Pugni, Cesare: *Adelheit von Frankreich*, 239

Quarterly Musical Magazine and Review, 5

Queck, Miss (singer), 89

Radichi, Giulio, 181, 183, 228

Rasumovsky, Andreas, 52, 112–13

Rauscher, Jakob Wilhelm, 233–35, 237–38, 240

Rebenstein, Ludwig, 227–28

Reichardt, Johann Friedrich, 39, 87–88, 178; operas, 177

Reissiger, Karl Gottlieb, 266–67

Rellstab, Ludwig, 7, 11, 61–64, 246–47

Reuling, L. W.: *Das Küchenregiment*, 175

Richter, Jean Paul Friedrich, 34–35, 56–58, 62, 144, 201, 219, 250; *Titan*, 182

Ries, Ferdinand, 66, 81, 83–84, 132, 218

Righini, Vincenzo, 242
Risse, Carl, 265–67
Rochlitz, Friedrich, 51, 140, 185
Röckel, Joseph August, 175
Romberg, Andreas, 70
Romberg, Anton, 80, 225
Romberg, Berhard, 113; string quartets, 171; Variations for Cello on Russian Songs, 120
Rosenfelt (singer), 265, 267
Rossini, Gioacchino Antonio, 120; operas, 242, 259, 264; *The Barber of Seville,* 184, 245; *Diebscher Elster,* 120; *La gazza ladra,* 235; *Semiramis,* 89; *Siege of Corinth,* 255
Rothe (singer), 175
Rothstein, Edward, 1, 11
Rudolph, Archduke, 245

Saal (bass singer), 180–82
St. John. Rev., 141,144
Salieri, Anton, 68, 224–25; cantatas, 179; operas, 188; *Axur, re d'Ormus,* 222
Salis-Seewis, Johann Gaudenz von, 39
Schauberg, Gereon, 115–18
Schauberg, Katharina, 118
Schechner-Waagen, Anna, 249–50, 265
Schicht, Costanza (née Valdestrula), 92
Schicht, Gottfried, 92
Schicht, Miss (singer), 92
Schiller, Friedrich, 114, 191–92, 217–19, 254; "An die Freude," 222; "Music," 222
Schimon (singer), 249–50
Schindler, Anton, 140
Schlesinger (firm), 71
Schnabel, Artur, 48
Schneider, Friedrich, 36, 51, 81–83, 95, 112, 115, 230; *Das Weltgericht,* 81–83; *Der Zitterschläger [Der Zettelträger?],* 50–51; Symphonies, 35
Schmidt, J. P., 255
Schmitt (musician), 54
Schopenhauer, Arthur, 8, 12
Schott (firm), 68, 129, 132, 257
Schrieber (violist), 171
Schröder-Devrient, Wilhelmine, 233–36, 238, 240, 243–44, 254, 265

Schubart, Daniel, 140
Schubert, Franz, 39, 181; piano music, 170; *Schwanengesang,* 63, 111
Schulze, Josefine. *See* Killitzky, Josefine
Schuppanzigh, Ignaz, 112–13, 170–71
Sebastiani, Constanze, 227–28, 242
Seconda, Franz [or Joseph], 184, 203, 219
Seidl, H., 50–51
Seidler, Caroline, 84–86
Seidler, Karl, 84, 86, 120
Sessa, Karl Boromäus Alexander: *Unser Verkehr,* 225, 231
Sessi, Anna Maria, 44, 115
Seyfried, Ignaz Ritter von, 129–32
Shakespeare, William, 5, 72, 79, 97, 143, 189, 205–06, 218, 232
Siebert, Franz, 230–32, 244
Simrock (firm), 54, 59
Slonimsky, Nicolas: *Lexicon of Musical Invective,* 4–5, 12
Society of the Friends of Music (Cologne), 80, 82
Solie, Ruth, 9, 13
Sonnleitner, 89, 176, 179, 204
Spazier, Richard Otto, 257–67
Spohr, Louis, 67, 225; Overture to *Faust,* 147–48; string quartets, 147; symphonies, 66–67
Spontini, Gaspare Luigi Pacifico, 146–47; *La Vestale,* 250, 257, 266
Staudacher (singer), 249–50
Stegmann, C. D., 54
Steiner (firm), 89
Storace, Nancy, 92
Streicher/Stein (firm), 169
Stümer, Heinrich, 241–44

Taruskin, Richard, 1
Tchaikovsky, 2
Telle, Friedrich Wilhelm, 254–55
Thayer, A. W., 16–17
Tieck, Ludwig, 6, 79; *Herzensergeißungen einer kunstliebenden Klosterbruders,* 12; *Phantasien über die Kunst,* 12
Tietz, Ludwig, 93, 95
Tredici, David del, 2
Treitschke, Georg Friedrich, 226–27, 229

Index of Periodicals

Index of Subjects

Unless otherwise specified, when a music genre such as symphonies is listed it refers to symphonies by composers other than Beethoven or to the symphony as a genre, without reference to particular works. Discussions of the meanings of Beethoven's music as interpreted by the critics are listed under either affective descriptions or program music.

abstract music, 6–7

accompaniments, 174, 207–17, 219, 234, 240–41, 248, 253–54, 260

actors, 72, 113–14

advice to Beethoven about style and subjects, 5, 16–17, 23, 29, 33, 36, 47, 56, 69, 72, 87–88, 91, 201–02

Aeolian harp, 156, 169

aesthetics, 6–13, 20, 30, 35, 47, 97, 133, 145, 177, 179, 185, 187, 192, 219, 260, 264, 267

affective descriptions of Beethoven's music: agreeable or good-humored feelings, 134, 158; anger or wrath, 62–63, 204; anxiety or uneasiness, 74, 99, 106, 116, 209, 214–16; aristocratic, 159, 162; calm or restfulness, 109, 158; cheerfulness, 56, 146, 206; contemplation, 135; courageousness, 204, 211; delight, 189, 206; ecstasy, 151, 216–17; embarrassment, 209; enthusiasm or eagerness, 109, 189; expectation, 209, 239; foreboding, 57, 61, 108, 156; fright, horror, dread, or terror, 72, 102, 105–06, 114, 116, 122, 132, 138, 143, 206, 212, 214–15, 246, 261; gentleness, 135; gloominess, 70, 93, 114, 116, 206; gracefulness, 63; grand, 57, 70; gratitude or thankfulness, 143, 214–15; happiness, 139, 141, 146, 151; hope, 103, 211; joy, rejoicing, and jubilation, 5, 51, 63, 108–10, 112, 114, 117, 122, 132, 135, 139, 142–44, 146, 151, 174, 189, 206, 208, 212, 216–17, 246, 253–54; longing, 74, 99, 106, 110, 116–17, 122, 132, 211; love or ardor, 146, 162, 189, 239; melancholy or plaintiveness, 19, 24–25, 151, 154, 157, 218; mischievousness, 63; monstrousness, 114, 254; numbness, 210, oppression, 61, 100; pain, 110, 117, 122, 151, 189, 206, 253; peace, 146, 204, 216; pity, 215; rapturous, 116, 122; religious gratitude, 144; restlessness or agitation, 19, 99, 105, 117, 157, 210, 213, 215; restraint, 214; revenge, 210; self-avowal, 208; seriousness or solemnity, 70, 93, 116, 157–59, 189; struggle, 153, 189, 204, 209; sublime, 206; suffering, 212, 238; tenderness, 206; tender pleas, 62–63, 215; tragedy, 206; transcendence, 6, 9; transfiguration, 5; triumphant, 5, 107, 117; uncanniness, 106

amateurs (dilettantes), 15, 20, 38–39, 53, 55, 124, 127–28, 176, 192, 202, 205

arias, 89, 92, 113, 195

arrangements and arrangers, 20, 30–32, 35, 37, 41–42, 54, 59, 67–68, 95, 110–12, 128–31, 184–85, 207–12, 219–20, 233, 235, 255–57

art, 16, 185, 192, 194, 199–200, 224–25

art music, 193, 219

audience behavior, 33, 38, 41, 53, 57, 66, 68, 72, 84, 94, 114, 121–27, 172, 182–84, 203, 226–28, 230, 232–33, 236–38, 240, 243–44, 254–56, 258, 265 audience requirements, 24–25, 33, 37, 40, 53, 85–86, 95. *See also* listeners: and necessity of repeated hearings

bagpipe sounds in Beethoven's music, 142
bassoons and bassoonists, 80, 232
battle music, 5, 96
Beethoven: attendance at performances, 239; birthplace, 81, 84; birth year, 117–18; conducting, 16–17 (1805), 36 (1808), 49 (1808), 55 (1808); deafness, 61; fame of, 5, 15–16, 54, 56, 59, 66, 95, 112, 114, 117, 122, 128, 145, 147, 150, 181, 189, 204, 226, 233, 245, 251, 253, 256; friends, 15; genius and ingenuity of, 4–5, 17, 24, 27, 30, 33–34, 36, 39, 41–42, 56–58, 72, 79–80, 83, 96–98, 110, 112, 114–15, 135, 138, 140, 142, 146–47, 149, 154, 157, 159–60, 164, 176, 178, 180, 189–91, 196, 200–02, 222–23, 238, 245, 248, 253, 256, 259, 264; greatness of, 5, 15, 39, 41, 45, 59, 69, 98, 112, 114, 139, 144, 151, 180, 201, 205, 224, 233, 245, 248, 252; as hero, 5, 117; humor, 117, 189; illnesses, 118; isolation of, 224; lack of manners, 16, 49; mannerism, 201–02; nationalism, 169; new or original paths taken by, 4, 19, 21, 41, 43, 47, 64, 78, 96–99, 112, 114, 137, 171–72, 180, 189–90, 198, 200, 261–62, 264; opera plans, 36–37, portraits, 144; reputation as virtuoso or "very capable" pianist, 90, 117, 149, 198; views on Cherubini, 176; views on Clement, 16; weaknesses as a theater or vocal composer, 97, 149, 172–77, 179, 182, 202, 207–17, 241, 248, 260
bird songs, 94–95, 135, 137, 141, 145–46, 223, 225
Bocksfuß (goat's foot), 57–58

cantatas, 18, 179
choral music, 81, 83
church music, 197
clarinetists, 171
clarinets, 191, 218

Classical music (early period), 196
comedy in music, 3
comparisons of Beethoven: to Bachs (unspecified), 30; to Benda, 190; to Cantemire, 232; to Cherubini, 70, 74, 176–77, 190, 200, 203, 205, 219; to composers of program music, 96, 138, 141; to Dittersdorf, 96; to Eberl, 17–18, 53, 55; to German composers, 41; to Gluck, 261; to Goethe, 191, 259; to Gyrowetz, 35; to Handel, 254; to Haydn, 25–26, 32, 36, 57, 64, 94, 96–97, 103, 105, 110–11, 114, 119, 145, 149, 162, 169, 177–78, 190, 197–98, 245, 254; to Hiller, 190; to Icarus, 200, 219; to Jean-Paul, 34–35, 56–57, 201, 219; to Kant, 191; to Klopstock, 180–81, 191; to living composers, 69, 78, 144, 147, 189–90; to Mozart, 17–18, 36, 60, 64, 66, 85, 89–90, 96–97, 110–11, 117, 119, 145, 149, 159, 162, 176–77, 190–91, 197–98, 203–05, 211–12, 230, 245, 248, 250, 259, 261, 263–64; to older classical composers, 112; to other unnamed opera composers, 204, 211, 222, 233, 235, 244, 246, 249, 262; to other unnamed symphony and instrumental composers, 15–16, 19, 24, 35–36, 66, 72, 96; to Paer, 172, 182, 202, 208, 211–12, 215–16, 222; to Pegasus, 223, 225; to Phoebus, 260; to Reichardt, 177; to Schiller, 191; to Schneider, 35; to Shakespeare, 5, 97, 143, 189, 205–06, 218; to Spohr, 66; to symphony composers, 57, 64–67; to Vanhall, 190
composition, Beethoven's knowledge of, 19, 34, 45, 61, 70, 116, 149, 1–3
concertos, 15, 18, 50–51, 71, 80, 120, 130–31, 150, 179
concert performances of Fidelio, 228, 255–56
concert programs and programming, 3, 18, 25–26, 30, 32–33, 37, 39–40, 118
concerts, amateur: in Vienna, 55
concerts, benefit: in Berlin, 228; in Leipzig, 55; in Vienna, 15, 37, 179, 183, 251
concerts, private: in Bohemia, 16; in

Mannheim, 57; in Vienna, 52–53, 170–71, 178
concerts, public: in Berlin, 40–41, 66–67, 84, 88, 119–21, 146–47, 232; in Bonn, 64; in Cologne, 65–66, 80–83; in Düsseldorf, 60; in Kassel, 39, 59–60; in Leipzig, 32–35, 38, 43–44, 51, 70, 88–89, 92–93, 115; in Magdeburg, 118; in Mannheim, 19, 56; in Milan, 58; in Munich, 39, 71, 144–45; in Prague, 34; in unnamed city, 121–27; in Vienna, 15–18; 33–40, 48–50, 55, 61–63, 68–69, 71–72, 80, 112–13
conductors, concertmasters, and conducting, 31, 34, 40–41, 66, 81, 110, 112, 123, 147–48, 223–25, 227, 230, 242, 254–55, 258, 266
connoisseurs, 15, 33–35, 40, 52–53, 68–69, 71, 72, 80, 128, 153–54, 168, 176, 182, 188, 192, 202, 233, 235, 237, 252–53, 264
contrabassists, 113
counterpoint and textures (including fugue), 17, 19, 21, 24–29, 62, 103, 116–17, 151–54, 156–58, 160, 166–67, 174, 220
critics and criticism, 1–13, 63–65, 67, 79, 88, 111, 118–19, 140, 169, 179, 184–85, 217–18, 242, 266–67
csákány, 129, 132
cult of Isis, 170
currencies, xv–xviii

dance music, 130, 132, 143, 146, 192
dedications, 16, 52
doctrine of affects, 7–9, 145, 186, 189, 253
drinking games, 86
dynamics and dynamic markings in Beethoven's music, 7, 19

editions of Beethoven's music: arrangements, 20, 31, 35, 37, 41–42, 54, 59, 67–68, 95, 110–12, 130–31, 184–85, 207–12, 219–20, 233, 235, 255–57; first, 16–20, 31–32, 47, 49, 52–53, 59, 70–71, 88, 92–94, 131, 171; early, ; score, 34, 41, 52, 59, 131, 168

enharmonic system, 164
Enlightenment, 140
epigrams, 217, 222
extramusical ideas, 5. *See also* affective descriptions of Beethoven's music; program music in Beethoven's music

fantasy, fancy, and fantasies, 12, 35, 41, 45, 92, 110, 117, 145, 189, 198–201, 205, 231, 238, 253, 260
feminist criticism, 1–2, 9, 12–13
fermata, 15–16
festivals: in Cologne, 65–66, 80–84; in Düsseldorf, 60, 132
finales in Beethoven's music, 19, 44, 46, 51
flute music, 120, 123
flutists, 123
folk songs, 192, 197, 236–37
form and design, 61, 112, 128, 150, 162, 194, 197, 253

gendered criticism, 62, 256
genius (not applied to Beethoven), 15, 185–86
German idealism, 8
German literature, 258, 267
German music and nationalism, 41, 82–83, 144–45, 172, 190, 192–96, 198, 201–02, 208, 258–59, 265–66
Greek beauty, 260, 267
Greek drama and choruses, 261

harmonica, 156
harmonies in Beethoven's music, 3–4, 6–7, 19, 21–31, 46, 53, 55, 70, 94, 100–02, 104, 151, 160, 171, 195, 198–200, 209, 211, 215, 237–38, 253, 260, 262
harmony, 192–94, 197–98
horn players, 124–25, 148

idea(s) (content), 67, 97, 149–50, 160, 185, 187, 197–98; abundance and richness of, in Beethoven's music, 17, 19, 21–22, 24, 43, 73, 112, 132, 171, 178, 189, 199, 222, 235, 237; Beethoven's development of, 17, 19–30, 42, 46, 52, 55, 92–94, 98–109, 116, 139–40, 143, 165, 173, 199–200, 214, 216, 241, 248, 253

improvisation, 47
improvisations by Beethoven, 49–50
influences: Beethoven's on future, 4–6,
9, 16, 69; Beethoven's on other
composers, 198, 200–02, 261;
Haydn's on Beethoven, 91, 114,
189–90; Mozart's on Beethoven, 117,
189–90
instrumental music, 96, 145, 186, 190,
192–96
instrumentation and orchestration in
Beethoven's music, 6–7, 15–17, 19,
21–30, 37, 57, 59, 72–73, 76–78,
84, 87, 94, 98–109, 112, 116–17,
134–40, 143, 151–67, 190, 194–95,
198, 204–05, 207–17, 223, 233,
240–41, 244, 253–54, 261–62
introductions in Beethoven's music, 55
Italian music and German nationalism,
177, 190–96, 208, 212–14, 245, 251,
257–59, 263, 266

Janissary instruments, 93, 95, 256

key characteristics, 135, 140, 211, 221
key signatures, 17, 57

language of music, 145, 151, 185
learned music, 193
librettists and librettos, 172, 176,
179–80, 182, 186–88, 194–95,
203–04, 206–07, 211–13, 221–22,
251, 256, 264
listeners: Beethoven's music pleasing to,
15, 19, 21, 29, 33–41, 44–45, 47, 50–
51, 53, 55–58, 60, 66, 68–71, 83, 90,
93–94, 115, 118–19, 134, 140, 142,
145, 147, 162, 171, 177–84, 202–17,
223–24, 226–28, 233–34, 236–38,
240, 246–47, 253–54, 255, 258, 262;
Beethoven's music unpleasing to, 15,
17, 19, 58, 71, 83–84, 93, 136–38,
145, 147, 172–76, 177, 180–81, 202,
205, 211, 228, 249; difficulties of
Beethoven's music for, 15–17, 25, 30,
32, 39, 43, 51–52, 56, 60, 71, 261 (see
also style, descriptions of Beethoven's:
obscure or incomprehensible); and
necessity of repeated hearings, 33, 35,
49–50, 51–52, 58, 85, 92–93, 121,

145, 147, 205, 253; transformed,
deeply moved, or overwhelmed by
Beethoven's music, 5–7, 30, 35, 57,
63, 67, 73, 93, 96–98, 103, 105, 110,
114, 117, 132, 138, 180–81, 190,
204–05, 212–14, 224, 226, 234, 238,
249, 253–54, 262

manuscripts of Beethoven's music: score,
33–34, 94, 133, 140
marble, 41–42
masculinity, 5, 9
"masterworks" or "masterpieces" by
Beethoven, 15, 36, 71, 95, 110, 112,
118, 128, 130, 133, 140, 147, 177,
180, 182, 205, 234, 236, 240, 253,
256, 259, 265
melodies and themes in Beethoven's
music, 4, 7, 39–40, 42, 45–46, 53,
72, 87, 89, 98–110, 134–40, 150–67,
171, 176–77, 195, 199–200, 205,
209, 211, 214, 223, 237, 253, 260
melodramas, 213, 215–16, 222
melody, 192–94, 198
military themes in Beethoven's music,
116
minuets, 114–15
modulations in Beethoven's music, 15,
20–30, 78, 90–91, 104–05, 108,
116–17, 134–39, 146, 155, 161, 163,
166, 192, 198, 207, 209, 211, 213,
233
monument of Beethoven, 251
motives in Beethoven's music, 7, 57,
62–63, 65, 160, 262
movement order, 110, 117
musical life and status of music: in
Aachen, 251, 254–5; in Berlin,
40–41, 52, 60, 63, 66–67, 84–86, 88,
119–21, 146–48, 223–28, 231–32,
240, 254; in Bohemia, 16; in Bonn,
64; in Boston, 245–46; in Bremen,
255–56; in Cologne, 65–66, 80–83,
254; on the Danube, 126; in Dresden,
93, 172, 244, 257–59, 265–67; in
Düsseldorf, 60, 132; in Frankfurt
am Main, 53; in Hamburg, 254; in
Karlsruhe, 232; in Kassel, 39, 59–60;
in Leipzig, 18, 32–35, 38, 43–45,
50–51, 55–56, 69–70, 85–86, 88–89,

premieres (*cont.*)
44–45, 184; in Vienna, 15–16, 48–50, 171–78, 245
prices of music, 59
printers, 53, 88, 130
printer and publisher errors, 19, 31–32, 54, 100, 111, 129, 175, 215, 220, 257
printing successes, 19, 31, 37, 54, 59, 88, 110, 131, 255, 257
program music, 7, 133, 141, 146, 189, 218
program music in Beethoven's music: Arcadia, country life, or pastorale, 15, 94, 133, 141–42, 144, 146; battles, 189; dances, 143, 146, 151; evil spirits, 45; funeral procession, 38–39; hero and heroism, 11, 25; interaction between angry husband and soothing wife, 62–63; life in nature, 89, 94; peasant gathering, 142–43, 145; heroic tragedy, 73, 77; "Scene by the Brook," 94, 135–37, 142, 145–46; storms (including thunder), 7, 61, 73, 94, 103, 138–39, 141, 145–46; streams of fire, 57; struggle, 65, 153; thankfulness for nature, 89, 189; triumphal procession, 57

reception history: of "best" or "most admired" works, 67, 118, 191; of "great mistakes," 199–200, 208; of little-known or infrequently performed works, 51, 55–56, 64, 144, 223, 256–57; of misunderstood works, 149; of popular or well-known works, 37, 61, 69, 115, 141, 255; of "successful" works, 115, 178, 182, 202, 234, 241; of symphonies, 59; of unpopular works, 53, 83–84, 145, 147; of unsuccessful works, 146, 172–76, 181, 183, 202, 214, 217
rehearsals, 25, 31, 33, 79, 191, 223, 249, 258
relationship between music and poetry in vocal music, 186, 205
religious experiences, 144
rescue operas, 176, 182–84, 219
rhythm, meter, or time signatures, 3–4, 21, 65, 159

Romanticism, 6–9, 12, 72, 79, 96–98, 110, 115–17, 128, 149, 158, 189–90, 204, 240, 247, 253. *See also* style, descriptions of Beethoven's: romantic
rondo form, 216
rondo-variation form, 103–04, 162

scenas, 92, 120
scherzos and scherzandos: innovations of, 15–16, 26, 57, 60, 147; popularity of, 34, 56
score editions, 4
septets, 147
sexuality in music, 1–2, 9
shepherds' or cowherders' songs or calls in Beethoven's music, 139–43, 146, 189
shrikes, 223, 225
singers: female, 44–45, 49–50, 56, 84–86, 89, 92, 113–15, 122–23, 174–75, 180–83, 224–31, 233–44, 249–50, 254, 256, 265, 267; male, 92, 115, 174–75, 178–79, 181–83, 227–28, 230–45, 249–50, 255–56, 265–67
slow movements: innovations of, 17, 19, 24–25, 34, 89; popularity of, 52; problems of, 55
sonatas, 45, 47
songs and singing, 32, 39, 96, 190, 193–96, 226. *See also* singers
soul and "soul painter," 34, 46, 61, 87, 105, 108, 110, 114, 116–17, 135, 149, 151, 154, 156, 160, 186, 188–90, 195, 198–99, 205, 217, 245, 253, 258–59, 261
sound recordings, 18
spirit kingdom, 97–98, 105, 110, 114, 116–17, 122, 151
string quartets, 147, 170–71
string quartet series, 170–71
style, Beethoven's: earlier period, 66; early period, 15; and length, 15–20, 24–26, 30, 32–34, 37–39, 45, 49, 52–53, 87, 94, 117, 128, 147, 172–73, 183, 207, 211, 244, 248; music for the future, 15
style, descriptions of Beethoven's: artificial, affected, or contrived, 30, 180; artistic and artistically rich, 20,

24, 26, 36–37, 42, 45–46, 50, 62, 78, 100, 136, 152, 183, 233; baroque, 127; beautiful or lovely, 5, 15, 21, 23–25, 29, 36, 42–43, 45, 51, 55, 68, 87–88, 112, 116, 131–32, 135–36, 139, 142, 147–48, 167, 171, 174, 179, 183, 208–17, 223. 233–35, 241, 243, 248–49, 251, 253–54; bizarre, odd, peculiar, or strange, 15, 17, 19, 26, 29–30, 34, 39, 43, 45, 53, 56, 60, 71, 93–94, 116–17, 145, 155, 164, 173, 200–01, 207, 226, 260; bold or audacious, 166, 207; bombastic, 60, 223; brilliant, 30, 51, 55, 94, 117, 140, 149, 167, 248; capricious or arbitrary, 93, 207; characteristic or characterization in *Fidelio*, 46, 191, 211, 241 244, 253, 260; charming, 27, 42, 56, 135, 142, 209, 214; childlike, 142; chorale-like, 160; clarity and ease of comprehension, 19, 33, 41, 56–57, 142, 253; colossal, 19–20, 34, 37, 41; depth of conception or profound, 36, 41, 52, 63, 66, 110, 114, 117, 132, 143, 148, 180, 204, 207, 212, 226, 233, 237–38, 245, 248, 253; digressive, disjointed, or lacking unity, 11, 15, 17, 43, 69, 207; energetic, 57; excessive, exaggerated, or extravagant, 5, 15, 30, 36, 43, 260; expressive, 51; fiery, 33, 36, 55, 57, 93, 97, 109, 116, 132, 149, 205; forbidding, 60; frivolous, 177; gentle, 94; grand (as part of title or descriptor), 5, 32, 35–39, 42–45, 47, 49, 52–53, 56, 60, 70, 92–94, 112, 119, 176, 207, 238; harsh, 5, 36; humorous, 65, 94, 106, 137; imaginative, 36, 43, 59, 97, 112, 116, 145, 149, 180; inexpressive, 176; ingenious, 36, 38–40, 57, 94, 105, 110, 112, 117, 121, 127, 154, 223, 261–62 (*see also* Beethoven, genius and ingenuity of); ingratiating, 42; insipid, 212; inspired, 41; interesting, 21, 36, 42, 182, 200; ironic, 63; lacking artificiality, 209, 213, 262; lacking beauty, 15, 90, 127–28, 172; lacking bizarreness or caprice, 57, 67, 205; lacking brilliance, 73; lacking

characterization, 173, 176–77, 205; lacking clarity, 17, 199, 201; lacking coherence, 17; lacking content, 19; lacking distinctiveness, 87, 173; lacking flow of thoughts or fantasy, 15, 207, 217; lacking good taste, 128; lacking inventiveness or newness, 173, 177; lacking naturalness, 30, 217; lacking order, 199; lacking originality, 103, 116, 173, 182, 209, 213; lacking pathos, 73; lacking power, 15; lacking purity, 36, 87; lacking simplicity, 18, 30; lacking songfulness, 58; lacking sublimity, 15, 177; lacking substance, 60; learned, 31, 43, 45, 93; minced or forced, 46; monotonous or lacking variety, 94, 137, 217; natural or unaffected, 19, 61, 117, 139, 253, 261–62; noble, 45, 93, 116, 213, 223, 256; noisy, 128, 240; obscure or incomprehensible, 5, 83, 168, 199; original, 4, 15, 20–21, 24,-26, 34–36, 51, 55–57, 65, 68, 70, 93–94, 114, 127, 139, 156–57, 163, 180, 199–201, 208, 245, 264; ostentatious, 91; overburdened, 43; overly ornate, 174; overwhelming, 143; piquant, 26, 105, 117, 164; powerful, 19, 24, 30, 34, 36, 46, 51, 55, 57, 66, 70, 87, 89, 112, 134, 143, 161, 184, 210, 216, 231, 239, 244, 251, 260, 262; pretentious, 91, 180; pure, 19, 33, 253, 256; repetitive, 69, 128, 137–38, 172–73, 201; rhapsodic, 147; romantic, 64, 115–17, 147–48, 177, 198; shrill, 18, 30; simple or unpretentious, 45, 51–52, 65, 94, 134, 136, 142, 208–09, 213, 223, 260–62; songfulness, 204–05; spirited, 55, 184; spontaneous, 171; striving, 15; sublime, 15, 19, 36, 39, 57, 60, 80, 138, 143, 146, 158, 247; surprising, 42, 171; sweetness of, 42; tender, 143, 148; tiring, fatiguing, or exhausting, 87, 127, 134, 137, 147; too deep, 178; too learned, 176, 178; too transcendent, 178; trite, 91; unified or organic, 11, 19, 24, 33, 67, 103, 116, 143, 148, 150, 155, 160, 164, 195, 260, 263; unique or individual, style (*cont.*)

53, 55, 59, 65, 93, 147, 253; unusual, 50; use and effectiveness of choruses in *Fidelio*, 211–12, 217, 223, 238, 249–50, 261–62; use of extremes or heterogeneous, 5, 11, 21, 43, 87, 93, 116–18, 260; violent, 15, 112, 143; well-declaimed, 205, 208, 210, 212, 215, 230, 234, 262; wild, 127, 143; without vocal ornamentation, 209, 213, 216

sublime (aesthetic category), 189, 194, 201. *See also* style, descriptions of Beethoven's: sublime

swan song, 97, 111

symphonies, 17, 35, 52, 58, 64, 66–67, 70, 81, 83, 89, 93, 95–96, 118–19, 144–45, 162, 170, 179

tempos, 26, 34, 66, 87

tension and expectation, 57

theater music, 197, 212

thematic recall, 108–09, 161

time signatures, 57

timpani, 60–62

tonality in Beethoven's music, 19, 21–23, 27, 29, 57, 98–108, 116, 134–39, 152–67, 173

tragedies, 221, 264

transitions in Beethoven's music, 15, 42, 47

trombones and trombonists, 54, 190–91, 213, 249

tunings and intonation, 161, 237

variation form and variations, 19, 24, 26–29, 35, 45–46, 49, 91, 103, 112–13, 120, 162, 170

violence in music, 1–2, 5

violists, 171

violoncellists, 44, 53–54, 71, 113–14, 123–24, 171

violoncello writing in Beethoven's music, 78–79

violinists, 15–16, 18, 44, 53, 68, 71, 86, 89, 95, 112–13, 123, 170–71

virtuosity and virtuosos, 40, 131, 168, 190, 224–25, 229

vocal composition, 186–88

wind instruments, 29, 37, 61, 65, 78

writers, 111–13, 144, 182

Index of Beethoven's Works

For individual stylistic traits in Beethoven's works, see the subject index.

Twelve Variations on "Ein Mädchen
oder Weibchen" from Mozart's
Die *Zauberflöte* (Op. 66), 90–91
Sonata (Op. 69), 148
quintets
Quintet for Piano and Wind
Instruments (Op. 16), 17
trios, 150
Trio for Piano, Clarinet or Violin, and
Cello (Op. 38), 53
Two Trios for Piano and Strings
(Op. 70), 6, 65, 79, 111–12, 148,
149–51, 167–70; No. 1, 151–58,
No. 2, 53, 158–70

CHAMBER MUSIC WITHOUT PIANO
quartets, 113, 150, 170–71, 245
Three Quartets for Strings
("Razumovsky," Op. 59), 52–
53, 171; No. 2, 53, 54 (arr. for
piano four-hands)
String Quartet (Op. 131), 131–32
String Quartet (Op. 132), 147
quintets, 15, 69
String Quintet (Op. 4), 17
String Quintet (Op. 29), 17, 69
Quintet Fugue (Op. 137), 16
septet
Septet for Violin, Viola, Clarinet,
French Horn, Bassoon, Cello, and
Double Bass (Op. 20), 15–16, 69
sextet
Sextet for clarinets, horns, and
bassons (Op. 71), 170–71

MUSIC FOR KEYBOARD ALONE
sonatas and sonatinas, 47
Sonata (Op. 27, no. 2), 46, 48
Sonata (Op. 57), 45–48
Sonata (Op. 109), 4–5
Sonata (Op. 110), 4–5
Sonata (Op. 111), 4–5
variations
Fifteen Variations ("Prometheus,"
Op. 35), 26, 32, 35
on a Russian Dance from Wranitzky's
Das Waldmädchen (WoO 71),
113
on "Une fièvre brûlante" from
Grétry's *Richard Coeur de Lion*
(WoO 72), 90

VOCAL MUSIC
general, 241

MASSES AND ORATORIO
Christus am Ölberg (Op. 85), 115,
173, 177–78
Mass in C (Op. 86), 49–50, 79,
81–83, 111
Missa solemnis (Op. 123), 84,
131–32, 235, 245

WORKS FOR STAGE
incidental music
Music to Goethe's *Egmont* (Op. 84),
79, 144
Triumphal March for Tarpeja (WoO
2a), 113–14
opera
Fidelio (1805), 111, 172–78, 184
Duet, "O namenlose Freude,"
173–74
Quartet, "Mir ist so wunderbar,"
174
Chorus, "O welche Lust," 174–75
Aria, "O du, für den ich alles trug,"
174–75
Recitative, "Ach, brich noch nicht,
du mattes Herz!," 174
Aria, "Auf euch nur will ich
bauen," 175
Choral passage, "Zur Rache, zur
Rache!," 220
Fidelio (1806), 111, 172, 178–80,
184, 184–85 (vocal score), 248
Aria, "Komm Hoffnung," 174,
211, 220–21
Recitative, "Ach brich noch nicht,
du mattes Herz!," 184, 211,
220–21
Aria, "O wär' ich schon mit dir
vereint," 208, 220
Duet, "Jetzt, Schätzchen, jetzt sind
wir allein!," 208, 220
Trio, "Ein Mann ist bald
genommen," 208–09, 220, 248
Quartet, "Mir ist so wunderbar,"
209, 220
Aria, "Hat man nicht auch Gold
beineben," 209
Trio, "Gut Sönchen, gut!," 209,
220

Duet, "Um in der Ehe froh zu Leben," 209, 220

March, 211, 220–21

Aria, "Ha! welch ein Augenblick!," 210, 219–20

Duet, "Jetzt, Alter, jetzt hat es Eile," 210–11, 220

Duet, "Um in der Ehe froh zu leben," 220

Chorus, "O welche Lust," 211, 220

Act II finale (three-act version), 211–12, 220–21

Introduction, "Gott! Welch dunkel hier!," 212

Aria, "In des Lebens Frühlingstagen," 212–13

Duet, "Nur hurtig fort, nur frische gegraben!," 213

Trio, "Euch werde Lohn," 214–15

Quartet, "Er sterbe," 215

Duet, "O namenlose Freude," 216, 222,

Choral passage, "Zur Rache, zur Rache!," 216, 222

Act III finale (three-act version), 216–17

Fidelio (1814), 50, 172, 180–85, 191, 196, 219 (vocal score), 223–32, 233 (vocal score), 233–55, 255 (piano score without text), 255–56, 256–57 (arr. for keyboard and violin), 257–67

compared to 1806 version, 202–22, 230–31

Quartet, "Mir ist so wunderbar," 182–83, 227–28, 234, 237–38, 240, 253, 265

Aria, "Hat man nicht auch Gold beineben," 183

Trio, "Gut, Söhnchen, gut," 227, 238

Aria, "Komm, Hoffnung," 183–84, 211, 221, 238, 253–54

Duet, "Jetzt, Alter, hat es Eile," 227, 237, 260

Recitative, "Abscheulicher! wo eilst du hin!," 183–84, 211, 221, 227, 238, 253, 256

Aria, "Ha! welch' ein Augenblick," 195, 210, 219, 227, 238, 253

Duet, "Jetzt, Schätzchen, jetzt sind wir allein!," 208, 220

Aria, "O wär ich schon mit dir vereint," 227

Chorus, "O welche Lust," 212, 234, 237–38, 242, 249–50, 253–54, 261–62

Act I finale, 212, 227, 234, 253–54

Introduction, "Gott! Welche dunkel hier!," 213, 238, 253–54

Aria, "In des Lebens Frühlingstagen," 213, 234, 238, 253–54

Melodrama and duet, "Nur hurtig fort, nur frisch gegraben!," 213–14, 222, 230, 234, 246–47, 261

Trio, "Euch werde Lohn in bessern Welten," 227, 253–54

Quartet, "Er sterbe," 215, 222, 227, 229, 234, 236–38, 253–54, 261, 267

Duet, "O namenlose Freude," 216, 227–28, 234, 236, 239–40, 243, 246–47, 253–54, 260

Act II finale, 217, 227, 237, 239, 242, 244, 253–54, 265

WORKS WITH LARGER INSTRUMENTAL ENSEMBLES

for chorus and solos

Choral Fantasy (Op. 80), 49–50, 111, 114, 148

for solo voices

Ah! perfido (Op. 65), 49–50, 56, 87–89, 225, 256

WORKS WITH PIANO

songs

Adelaide (Op. 46), 218, 241

Ich denke dein (WoO 74), 218

MISCELLANEOUS

projected and unfinished works

Melusine, 245

Der Sieg des Kreuzes, 245